Neural Networks with Keras Cookbook

Over 70 recipes leveraging deep learning techniques across image, text, audio, and game bots

V Kishore Ayyadevara

BIRMINGHAM - MUMBAI

Neural Networks with Keras Cookbook

Copyright © 2019 Packt Publishing

All rights reserved. No part of this book may be reproduced, stored in a retrieval system, or transmitted in any form or by any means, without the prior written permission of the publisher, except in the case of brief quotations embedded in critical articles or reviews.

Every effort has been made in the preparation of this book to ensure the accuracy of the information presented. However, the information contained in this book is sold without warranty, either express or implied. Neither the author, nor Packt Publishing or its dealers and distributors, will be held liable for any damages caused or alleged to have been caused directly or indirectly by this book.

Packt Publishing has endeavored to provide trademark information about all of the companies and products mentioned in this book by the appropriate use of capitals. However, Packt Publishing cannot guarantee the accuracy of this information.

Commissioning Editor: Pravin Dhandre
Acquisition Editor: Karan Jain
Content Development Editor: Karan Thakkar
Technical Editor: Dinesh Pawar
Copy Editor: Safis Editing
Project Coordinator: Hardik Bhinde
Proofreader: Safis Editing
Indexer: Priyanka Dhadke
Graphics: Jisha Chirayil
Production Coordinator: Arvindkumar Gupta

First published: February 2019

Production reference: 1280219

Published by Packt Publishing Ltd.
Livery Place
35 Livery Street
Birmingham
B3 2PB, UK.

ISBN 978-1-78934-664-0

www.packtpub.com

I would like to dedicate this book to my dear parents, Hema and Subrahmanyeswara Rao, to my lovely wife, Sindhura, and my dearest daughter, Hemanvi. This work would not have been possible without their patience, support, and encouragement.

mapt.io

Mapt is an online digital library that gives you full access to over 5,000 books and videos, as well as industry leading tools to help you plan your personal development and advance your career. For more information, please visit our website.

Why subscribe?

- Spend less time learning and more time coding with practical eBooks and Videos from over 4,000 industry professionals

- Improve your learning with Skill Plans built especially for you

- Get a free eBook or video every month

- Mapt is fully searchable

- Copy and paste, print, and bookmark content

Packt.com

Did you know that Packt offers eBook versions of every book published, with PDF and ePub files available? You can upgrade to the eBook version at `www.packt.com` and as a print book customer, you are entitled to a discount on the eBook copy. Get in touch with us at `customercare@packtpub.com` for more details.

At `www.packt.com`, you can also read a collection of free technical articles, sign up for a range of free newsletters, and receive exclusive discounts and offers on Packt books and eBooks.

Contributors

About the author

V Kishore Ayyadevara leads a team focused on using AI to solve problems in the healthcare space. He has 10 years' experience in data science, solving problems to improve customer experience in leading technology companies. In his current role, he is responsible for developing a variety of cutting edge analytical solutions that have an impact at scale while building strong technical teams.

Prior to this, Kishore authored three books—*Pro Machine Learning Algorithms*, *Hands-on Machine Learning with Google Cloud Platform*, and *SciPy Recipes*.

Kishore is an active learner with keen interest in identifying problems that can be solved using data, simplifying the complexity and in transferring techniques across domains to achieve quantifiable results.

I am grateful to my wife, Sindhura, for her love, her constant support, and for being a source of inspiration all throughout.

Sincere thanks to the Packt team, Karan Thakkar, and Tushar Gupta, for their support and belief in me. Special thanks to Giuseppe Ciaburro for his review and helpful feedback. This book would not have been in this shape without the great support I received from Kartik Chaudhary, Kiran Kumar Meetakoti, and Yeshwanth Reddy Yerraguntla.

About the reviewer

Giuseppe Ciaburro holds a PhD in environmental technical physics, and two master's degrees. His research focuses on machine learning applications in the study of urban sound environments. He works at Built Environment Control Laboratory in the Università degli Studi della Campania Luigi Vanvitelli, Italy. He has over 15 years' work experience in programming (in Python, R, and MATLAB), first in the field of combustion and then in acoustics and noise control. He has several publications to his credit.

Packt is searching for authors like you

If you're interested in becoming an author for Packt, please visit `authors.packtpub.com` and apply today. We have worked with thousands of developers and tech professionals, just like you, to help them share their insight with the global tech community. You can make a general application, apply for a specific hot topic that we are recruiting an author for, or submit your own idea.

Table of Contents

Preface	1
Chapter 1: Building a Feedforward Neural Network	9
Introduction	9
Architecture of a simple neural network	10
Training a neural network	12
Applications of a neural network	12
Feed-forward propagation from scratch in Python	13
Getting ready	14
How to do it...	20
Building back-propagation from scratch in Python	23
Getting ready	23
How to do it...	25
There's more...	28
Building a neural network in Keras	30
How to do it...	30
Installing Keras	31
Building our first model in Keras	31
Chapter 2: Building a Deep Feedforward Neural Network	35
Training a vanilla neural network	35
Getting ready	36
How to do it...	37
How it works...	43
Scaling the input dataset	44
Getting ready	44
How to do it...	46
How it works...	48
There's more...	49
Impact on training when the majority of inputs are greater than zero	49
Getting ready	50
How to do it...	50
Impact of batch size on model accuracy	55
Getting ready	55
How to do it...	55
How it works...	57
Building a deep neural network to improve network accuracy	57
Getting ready	57
How to do it...	58
Varying the learning rate to improve network accuracy	60

Getting ready	61
How to do it...	64
Varying the loss optimizer to improve network accuracy	**66**
Getting ready	67
There's more...	68
Understanding the scenario of overfitting	**68**
Overcoming over-fitting using regularization	70
How to do it	71
Overcoming overfitting using dropout	72
Speeding up the training process using batch normalization	**74**
How to do it...	75

Chapter 3: Applications of Deep Feedforward Neural Networks — 79
Introduction	**79**
Predicting credit default	**80**
Getting ready	81
How to do it...	82
How it works...	86
Assigning weights for classes	**86**
Getting ready	86
How to do it...	87
Predicting house prices	**89**
Getting ready	89
How to do it...	90
Defining the custom loss function	91
Categorizing news articles into topics	**92**
Getting ready	92
How to do it...	93
Classifying common audio	**96**
How to do it...	97
Stock price prediction	**99**
Getting ready	99
How to do it...	99
Leveraging a functional API	**101**
How to do it...	101
Defining weights for rows	**106**
How to do it...	106

Chapter 4: Building a Deep Convolutional Neural Network — 109
Introduction	**109**
Inaccuracy of traditional neural networks when images are translated	**110**
How to do it...	110
Problems with traditional NN	112
Building a CNN from scratch using Python	**114**

Getting ready	115
Understanding convolution	115
Filter	115
Strides	117
Padding	117
From convolution to activation	117
From convolution activation to pooling	118
How do convolution and pooling help?	119
How to do it...	120
Validating the CNN output	123
CNNs to improve accuracy in the case of image translation	**125**
Getting ready	125
How to do it...	126
Gender classification using CNNs	**129**
Getting ready	129
How to do it...	130
There's more...	135
Data augmentation to improve network accuracy	**136**
Getting ready	136
How to do it...	137
Model accuracy without data augmentation	137
Model accuracy with data augmentation	140

Chapter 5: Transfer Learning — 143

Gender classification of the person in an image using CNNs	**143**
Getting ready	144
How to do it...	144
Scenario 1 – big images	145
Scenario 2 – smaller images	150
Scenario 3 – aggressive pooling on big images	152
Gender classification of the person in image using the VGG16 architecture-based model	**155**
Getting ready	155
How to do it...	157
Visualizing the output of the intermediate layers of a neural network	**161**
Getting ready	161
How to do it...	162
Gender classification of the person in image using the VGG19 architecture-based model	**169**
Getting ready	169
How to do it...	170
Gender classification using the Inception v3 architecture-based model	**173**
How to do it...	174
Gender classification of the person in image using the ResNet 50 architecture-based model	**177**

Table of Contents

How to do it...	178
Detecting the key points within image of a face	**181**
Getting ready	182
How to do it...	183

Chapter 6: Detecting and Localizing Objects in Images — 189
Introduction — 190
Creating the dataset for a bounding box — 190
    How to do it... — 191
        Windows — 191
        Ubuntu — 194
        MacOS — 194
Generating region proposals within an image, using selective search — 194
    Getting ready — 195
    How to do it... — 196
Calculating an intersection over a union between two images — 198
    How to do it... — 198
Detecting objects, using region proposal-based CNN — 202
    Getting ready — 202
    How to do it... — 203
Performing non-max suppression — 213
    Getting ready — 213
    How to do it... — 214
Detecting a person using an anchor box-based algorithm — 219
    Getting ready — 219
    How to do it... — 221
    There's more... — 232

Chapter 7: Image Analysis Applications in Self-Driving Cars — 233
Traffic sign identification — 233
    Getting ready — 233
    How to do it... — 234
Predicting the angle within which a car needs to be turned — 239
    Getting ready — 239
    How to do it... — 240
Instance segmentation using the U-net architecture — 245
    Getting ready — 245
    How to do it... — 247
Semantic segmentation of objects in an image — 252
    Getting ready — 252
    How to do it... — 253

Chapter 8: Image Generation — 259
Introduction — 259

Generating images that can fool a neural network using adversarial attack — 260
- Getting ready — 260
- How to do it... — 261

DeepDream algorithm to generate images — 266
- Getting ready — 267
- How to do it... — 267

Neural style transfer between images — 271
- Getting ready — 271
- How to do it... — 272

Generating images of digits using Generative Adversarial Networks — 277
- Getting ready — 277
- How to do it... — 279
- There's more... — 285

Generating images using a Deep Convolutional GAN — 286
- How to do it... — 286

Face generation using a Deep Convolutional GAN — 288
- Getting ready — 288
- How to do it... — 289

Face transition from one to another — 293
- Getting ready — 293
- How to do it... — 294

Performing vector arithmetic on generated images — 296
- Getting ready — 296
- How to do it... — 296
- There's more... — 298

Chapter 9: Encoding Inputs — 299
Introduction — 299
Need for encoding — 300
- Need for encoding in text analysis — 300
- Need for encoding in image analysis — 301
- Need for encoding in recommender systems — 302

Encoding an image — 302
- Getting ready — 302
- How to do it... — 303
  - Vanilla autoencoder — 304
  - Multilayer autoencoder — 307
  - Convolutional autoencoder — 309
  - Grouping similar images — 312

Encoding for recommender systems — 314
- Getting ready — 315
- How to do it... — 316

Chapter 10: Text Analysis Using Word Vectors — 321
Introduction — 321

Building a word vector from scratch in Python — 322
Getting ready — 323
How to do it... — 325
Measuring the similarity between word vectors — 329
Building a word vector using the skip-gram and CBOW models — 330
Getting ready — 330
How to do it — 331
Performing vector arithmetic using pre-trained word vectors — 336
How to do it... — 336
Creating a document vector — 338
Getting ready — 339
How to do it... — 340
Building word vectors using fastText — 342
Getting ready — 343
How to do it... — 343
Building word vectors using GloVe — 345
Getting ready — 345
How to do it... — 348
Building sentiment classification using word vectors — 351
How to do it... — 351
There's more... — 354

Chapter 11: Building a Recurrent Neural Network — 355
Introduction — 356
Intuition of RNN architecture — 356
Interpreting an RNN — 358
Why store memory? — 358
Building an RNN from scratch in Python — 359
Getting ready — 359
How to do it... — 360
Validating the output — 365
Implementing RNN for sentiment classification — 368
How to do it... — 368
There's more... — 373
Building a LSTM Network from scratch in Python — 374
Getting ready — 374
How to do it... — 377
Validating the output — 380
Implementing LSTM for sentiment classification — 383
How to do it... — 383
Implementing stacked LSTM for sentiment classification — 386
How to do it... — 386
There's more... — 388

Chapter 12: Applications of a Many-to-One Architecture RNN — 389
Generating text — 389

| Getting ready | 389 |
| How to do it... | 390 |

Movie recommendations — 395
- Getting ready — 395
- How to do it... — 396
  - Taking user history into consideration — 399

Topic-modeling, using embeddings — 400
- Getting ready — 401
- How to do it... — 402
- There's more... — 406

Forecasting the value of a stock's price — 406
- Getting ready — 407
- How to do it... — 408
  - The last five days' stock prices only — 409
  - The pitfalls — 411
  - Assigning different weights to different time periods — 413
  - The last five days' stock prices plus news data — 415
- There's more... — 421

Chapter 13: Sequence-to-Sequence Learning — 423
Introduction — 424
Returning sequences of outputs from a network — 427
Building a chatbot — 435
- Getting ready — 436
- How to do it... — 437
  - Intent extraction — 444
  - Putting it all together — 446

Machine translation — 448
- Getting ready — 448
- How to do it... — 449
  - Preprocessing the data — 449
  - Traditional many to many architecture — 453
  - Many to hidden to many architecture — 456

Encoder decoder architecture for machine translation — 459
- Getting ready — 459
- How to do it... — 460

Encoder decoder architecture with attention for machine translation — 464
- How to do it... — 464

Chapter 14: End-to-End Learning — 471
Introduction — 471
Connectionist temporal classification (CTC) — 472
- Decoding CTC — 472
- Calculating the CTC loss value — 473

Handwritten-text recognition — 475
- Getting ready — 476

How to do it...	477
Image caption generation	485
Getting ready	487
How to do it...	487
Generating captions, using beam search	493
Getting ready	494
How to do it...	495

Chapter 15: Audio Analysis — 497

Classifying a song by genre	497
Getting ready	497
How to do it...	498
Generating music using deep learning	502
Getting ready	503
How to do it...	503
Transcribing audio into text	508
Getting ready	508
How to do it...	510
There's more...	515

Chapter 16: Reinforcement Learning — 517

The optimal action to take in a simulated game with a non-negative reward	517
Getting ready	518
How to do it...	519
The optimal action to take in a state in a simulated game	520
Getting ready	520
How to do it...	522
There's more...	524
Q-learning to maximize rewards when playing Frozen Lake	524
Getting ready	525
How to do it...	526
Deep Q-learning to balance a cart pole	530
Getting ready	530
How to do it...	532
Deep Q-learning to play Space Invaders game	536
Getting ready	537
How to do it...	537

Other Books You May Enjoy — 545

Index — 549

Preface

Deep learning is advancing at a rapid pace, both in terms of its constituent neural network architectures, as well as their applications in real-world scenarios. This book takes you from the basics of building a neural network to the development of multiple advanced architectures that are used in various applications. You will find this book is divided into five parts.

In the first part, you will learn about how a neural network functions by building its components from scratch in Python before building them in Keras. Further, you will learn about the impact of various hyperparameters on a network's accuracy, in addition to learning about the flexibility of leveraging neural networks for multiple applications in various domains.

In the second part, you will learn about building a **Convolutional Neural Network** (**CNN**) from scratch in Python before leveraging it for image classification, where you will be learning about building a model to detect gender of persons in image and also to identify facial key points on the image of a face. Furthermore, you will be learning about the power of transfer learning in object detection and localization exercises to classify objects in image and also to identify the location of a person in image. Additionally, you will also be learning about the various applications of image analysis in self-driving car applications, leveraging semantic segmentation and more.

In the third part, we will pivot from image to text analysis by learning about encoding input both for image and text data, so that we can group similar images and similar bodies of text together using Autoencoders and Word vectors respectively. Additionally, you will learn about the various modeling aspects of building a recommender system so that you can recommend relevant movies to a user. You will also learn about leveraging **Generative Adversarial Networks** (**GANs**) for generating new images, as well as generating artistic images while learning about adversarial attacks to fool a network.

In the fourth part, you will dive deep into text analysis, where you will be learning about **Recurrent Neural Networks** (**RNNs**) and **long short-term memory** (**LSTM**) networks by building them from scratch in Python and then progressing toward building multiple use cases that leverage text analysis, such as stock price prediction, sentiment classification, machine translation, and building a chatbot, using advanced neural network architectures such as bi-directional LSTMs and attention mechanisms.

In the final part, you will be learning about end-to-end learning, where you will be transcribing images and audio along with generating captions. You will also be learning about Deep Q-learning, where you will build agents to play various Atari games.

By the end of this book, you will have developed the skills necessary for being able to apply various deep learning architectures to a majority of the deep learning problems that you might come across.

Who this book is for

This book caters to beginner-level and intermediate-level machine learning practitioners and data scientists who have just started their journey with neural networks and are looking for a resource that guides them through the various architectures of neural networks by helping them to build multiple architectures. The case studies of the book are ordered by the complexity of problem, with the simplest being first. A basic understanding of Python programming and familiarity with basic machine learning is all you need to get started with this book.

What this book covers

Chapter 1, *Building a Feedforward Neural Network*, will teach you about the basics of building a neural network by building a feedforward network from scratch and looking at backward propagation in Python. Additionally, you will be learning about the various components of building a neural network in Keras.

Chapter 2, *Building a Deep Feedforward Neural Network*, will teach you about the various hyperparameters that impact the accuracy of neural networks by having you implement multiple models on a handwritten digit dataset.

Chapter 3, *Applications of Deep Feedforward Neural Networks*, will see you appreciate the flexibility of neural networks by having you implement models to predict the likelihood of a customer defaulting on a loan, identify the sentiment of a text review, and classify audio signals. Additionally, you will learn about fine-tuning a neural network to assign higher weightage to certain rows and certain classes of output.

Chapter 4, *Building a Deep Convolutional Neural Network*, will explore how CNNs work by having you implement one from scratch in Python. You will also learn about how CNNs help in improving prediction accuracy when images are translated. Finally, you will learn about classifying gender of person in image along with improving network accuracy through data augmentation.

Chapter 5, *Transfer Learning*, will look at leveraging pre-trained models, such as VGG16, VGG19, ResNet50, Inception architectures that were built on millions of images, based on which we fine-tune the weights of our model to further improve its accuracy. Finally, you will learn about detecting the locations of key points in the image of a face.

Chapter 6, *Detecting and Localizing Objects in Images*, will teach you about the various components of building a model that detects the location of objects in an image. Additionally, you will build a region proposal-based algorithm and an anchor box-based algorithm from scratch to identify the location of objects in image.

Chapter 7, *Image Analysis Applications in Self-Driving Cars*, will teach you about building a U-Net architecture so that you can perform semantic segmentation on images to group similar objects in an image of a road together. Additionally, you will be performing analysis to identify the angle at which a car needs to be steered based on the image of a road.

Chapter 8, *Image Generation*, delves into the technique of adversarial attacks to fool a neural network. Additionally, you will also learn about different ways of generating new images while changing the input pixel values of image, as well as by leveraging GANs.

Chapter 9, *Encoding Inputs*, is where we will pivot from image analysis to text analysis, by converting high-dimensional input values to low-dimensional values and performing vector arithmetic to identify ways to encode an image, encode users, and recommend new movies to a user.

Chapter 10, *Text Analysis Using Word Vectors*, will dive deep into understanding the various ways of encoding text, such as word2vec, GloVe, and FastText. Additionally, we will be working on predicting the sentiment of text using generated word vectors.

Chapter 11, *Building a Recurrent Neural Network*, is where we will build an RNN from scratch using Python. Additionally, we'll be learning about the limitations of RNNs and will be building an LSTM-based architecture to overcome the RNN's limitations. Finally, we'll contrast the sentiment classification accuracy of word vector-based models with RNN-based models and LSTM-based models.

Chapter 12, *Applications of a Many-to-One Architecture RNN*, will dive deep into multiple applications leveraging the RNN architecture that we will have learned about. We'll build a model that is able to generate text, predict the next movie a user can be recommended, and forecast stock prices, and we'll look at the various pitfalls associated with the model.

Preface

Chapter 13, *Sequence-to-Sequence Learning*, explores returning sequences of output. We'll be leveraging bidirectional LSTMs and encoder-decoder architecture, along with attention mechanisms, to build machine translation models and a chatbot.

Chapter 14, *End-to-End Learning*, will teach you about using CNNs and RNNs together to solve case studies on handwritten text recognition and caption generation for images. We will also learn about a new loss function, **Connectionist Temporal Classification (CTC)**. Finally, you will also learn about beam search to generate plausible captions.

Chapter 15, *Audio Analysis*, will dive deep into multiple applications, including ones about the classification of songs by genre as well as the generation of music. Finally, you will learn about transcribing audio to text.

Chapter 16, *Reinforcement Learning*, will be about how to find the optimal action to take in a certain state of a game. You will also learn about using the OpenAI Gym environment, and you will leverage Q-learning and Deep Q-learning to navigate games of Frozen lake, Cart-pole and Space Invaders.

To get the most out of this book

- You should have prior knowledge of Keras and be comfortable with Python and have basic understanding of Machine Learning. Additionally, refer to the code files in GitHub while you are going through recipes. Due care is taken to ensure that all code is properly indented in book. However, it is highly recommended that you follow the code present in GitHub while implementing the code yourself

Download the example code files

You can download the example code files for this book from your account at `www.packt.com`. If you purchased this book elsewhere, you can visit `www.packt.com/support` and register to have the files emailed directly to you.

You can download the code files by following these steps:

1. Log in or register at `www.packt.com`.
2. Select the **SUPPORT** tab.
3. Click on **Code Downloads & Errata**.
4. Enter the name of the book in the **Search** box and follow the onscreen instructions.

Once the file is downloaded, please make sure that you unzip or extract the folder using the latest version of:

- WinRAR/7-Zip for Windows
- Zipeg/iZip/UnRarX for Mac
- 7-Zip/PeaZip for Linux

The code bundle for the book is also hosted on GitHub at https://github.com/PacktPublishing/Neural-Networks-with-Keras-Cookbook. In case there's an update to the code, it will be updated on the existing GitHub repository.

We also have other code bundles from our rich catalog of books and videos available at https://github.com/PacktPublishing/. Check them out!

Download the color images

We also provide a PDF file that has color images of the screenshots/diagrams used in this book. You can download it here: https://www.packtpub.com/sites/default/files/downloads/9781789346640_ColorImages.pdf.

Conventions used

There are a number of text conventions used throughout this book.

`CodeInText`: Indicates code words in text, database table names, folder names, filenames, file extensions, pathnames, dummy URLs, user input, and Twitter handles. Here is an example: "The variable named `Defaultin2yrs` is the output variable that we need to predict."

A block of code is set as follows:

```
data['DebtRatio_newoutlier']=np.where(data['DebtRatio']>1,1,0)
data['DebtRatio']=np.where(data['DebtRatio']>1,1,data['DebtRatio'])
```

Preface

Bold: Indicates a new term, an important word, or words that you see onscreen.

 Warnings or important notes appear like this.

 Tips and tricks appear like this.

Sections

In this book, you will find several headings that appear frequently (*Getting ready, How to do it..., How it works..., There's more...,* and *See also*).

To give clear instructions on how to complete a recipe, use these sections as follows:

Getting ready

This section tells you what to expect in the recipe and describes how to set up any software or any preliminary settings required for the recipe.

How to do it...

This section contains the steps required to follow the recipe.

How it works...

This section usually consists of a detailed explanation of what happened in the previous section.

There's more...

This section consists of additional information about the recipe in order to make you more knowledgeable about the recipe.

See also

This section provides helpful links to other useful information for the recipe.

Get in touch

Feedback from our readers is always welcome.

General feedback: If you have questions about any aspect of this book, mention the book title in the subject of your message and email us at `customercare@packtpub.com`.

Errata: Although we have taken every care to ensure the accuracy of our content, mistakes do happen. If you have found a mistake in this book, we would be grateful if you would report this to us. Please visit `www.packt.com/submit-errata`, selecting your book, clicking on the Errata Submission Form link, and entering the details.

Piracy: If you come across any illegal copies of our works in any form on the Internet, we would be grateful if you would provide us with the location address or website name. Please contact us at `copyright@packt.com` with a link to the material.

If you are interested in becoming an author: If there is a topic that you have expertise in and you are interested in either writing or contributing to a book, please visit `authors.packtpub.com`.

Reviews

Please leave a review. Once you have read and used this book, why not leave a review on the site that you purchased it from? Potential readers can then see and use your unbiased opinion to make purchase decisions, we at Packt can understand what you think about our products, and our authors can see your feedback on their book. Thank you!

For more information about Packt, please visit `packt.com`.

Building a Feedforward Neural Network

In this chapter we will cover the following recipes:

- Feed-forward propagation from scratch in Python
- Building back-propagation from scratch in Python
- Building a neural network in Keras

Introduction

A neural network is a supervised learning algorithm that is loosely inspired by the way the brain functions. Similar to the way neurons are connected to each other in the brain, a neural network takes input, passes it through a function, certain subsequent neurons get excited, and consequently the output is produced.

In this chapter, you will learn the following:

- Architecture of a neural network
- Applications of a neural network
- Setting up a feedforward neural network
- How forward-propagation works
- Calculating loss values
- How gradient descent works in back-propagation
- The concepts of epochs and batch size
- Various loss functions
- Various activation functions
- Building a neural network from scratch
- Building a neural network in Keras

Architecture of a simple neural network

An artificial neural network is loosely inspired by the way the human brain functions. Technically, it is an improvement over linear and logistic regression as neural networks introduce multiple non-linear measures in estimating the output. Additionally, neural networks provide a great flexibility in modifying the network architecture to solve the problems across multiple domains leveraging structured and unstructured data.

The more complex the function, the greater the chance that the network has to tune to the data that is given as input, hence the better the accuracy of the predictions.

The typical structure of a feed-forward neural network is as follows:

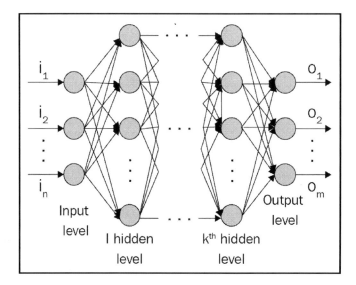

A layer is a collection of one or more nodes (computation units), where each node in a layer is connected to every other node in the next immediate layer. The input level/layer is constituted of the input variables that are required to predict the output values.

The number of nodes in the output layer depends on whether we are trying to predict a continuous variable or a categorical variable. If the output is a continuous variable, the output has one unit.

If the output is categorical with n possible classes, there will be n nodes in the output layer. The hidden level/layer is used to transform the input layer values into values in a higher-dimensional space, so that we can learn more features from the input. The hidden layer transforms the output as follows:

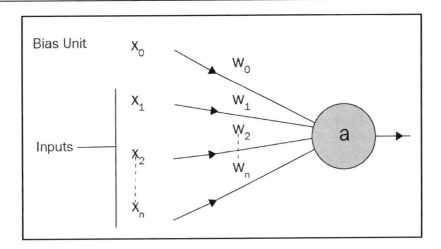

In the preceding diagram, $x_1, x_2, ..., x_n$ are the independent variables, and x_0 is the bias term (similar to the way we have bias in linear/logistic regression).

Note that $w_1, w_2, ..., w_n$ are the weights given to each of the input variables. If a is one of the units in the hidden layer, it will be equal to the following:

$$a = f\left(\sum_{i=0}^{N} w_i x_i\right)$$

The f function is the activation function that is used to apply non-linearity on top of the sum-product of the input and their corresponding weight values. Additionally, higher non-linearity can be achieved by having more than one hidden layer.

In sum, a neural network is a collection of weights assigned to nodes with layers connecting them. The collection is organized into three main parts: the input layer, the hidden layer, and the output layer. Note that you can have n hidden layers, with the term deep learning implying multiple hidden layers. Hidden layers are necessary when the neural network has to make sense of something really complicated, contextual, or not obvious, such as image recognition. The intermediate layers (layers that are not input or output) are known as hidden, since they are practically not visible (there's more on how to visualize the intermediate layers in Chapter 4, *Building a Deep Convolutional Neural Network*).

Training a neural network

Training a neural network basically means calibrating all of the weights in a neural network by repeating two key steps: forward-propagation and back-propagation.

In forward-propagation, we apply a set of weights to the input data, pass it through the hidden layer, perform the nonlinear activation on the hidden layer output, and then connect the hidden layer to the output layer by multiplying the hidden layer node values with another set of weights. For the first forward-propagation, the values of the weights are initialized randomly.

In back-propagation, we try to decrease the error by measuring the margin of error of output and then adjust weight accordingly. Neural networks repeat both forward- and back-propagation to predict an output until the weights are calibrated.

Applications of a neural network

Recently, we have seen a huge adoption of neural networks in a variety of applications. In this section, let's try to understand the reason why adoption might have increased considerably. Neural networks can be architected in multiple ways. Here are some of the possible ways:

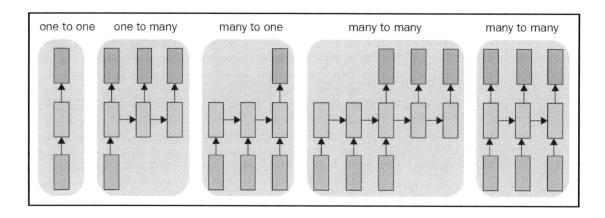

The box at the bottom is the input, followed by the hidden layer (the middle box), and the box at the top is the output layer. The one-to-one architecture is a typical neural network with a hidden layer between the input and output layer. Examples of different architectures are as follows:

Architecture	Example
One-to-many	The input is an image and the output is a caption for the image
Many-to-one	The input is a movie review (multiple words) and the output is the sentiment associated with the review
Many-to-many	Machine translation of a sentence in one language to a sentence in another language

Apart from the preceding points, neural networks are also in a position to understand the content in an image and detect the position where the content is located using an architecture named **Convolutional Neural Network (CNN)**, which looks as follows:

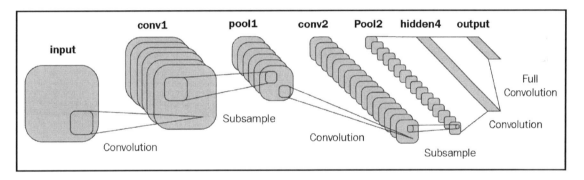

Here, we saw examples of recommender systems, image analysis, text analysis, and audio analysis, and we can see that neural networks give us the flexibility to solve a problem using multiple architectures, resulting in increased adoption as the number of applications increases.

Feed-forward propagation from scratch in Python

In order to build a strong foundation of how feed-forward propagation works, we'll go through a toy example of training a neural network where the input to the neural network is (1, 1) and the corresponding output is 0.

Building a Feedforward Neural Network

Getting ready

The strategy that we'll adopt is as follows: our neural network will have one hidden layer (with neurons) connecting the input layer to the output layer. Note that we have more neurons in the hidden layer than in the input layer, as we want to enable the input layer to be represented in more dimensions:

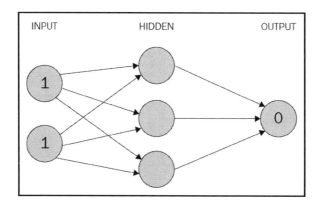

Calculating the hidden layer unit values

We now assign weights to all of the connections. Note that these weights are selected randomly (based on Gaussian distribution) since it is the first time we're forward-propagating. In this specific case, let's start with initial weights that are between 0 and 1, but note that the final weights after the training process of a neural network don't need to be between a specific set of values:

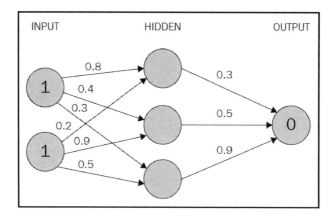

In the next step, we perform the multiplication of the input with weights to calculate the values of hidden units in the hidden layer.

The hidden layer's unit values are obtained as follows:

$$h_1 = 1 * 0.8 + 1 * 0.2 = 1$$

$$h_2 = 1 * 0.4 + 1 * 0.9 = 1.3$$

$$h_3 = 1 * 0.3 + 1 * 0.5 = 0.8$$

The hidden layer's unit values are also shown in the following diagram:

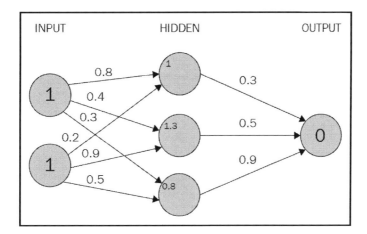

Note that in the preceding output we calculated the hidden values. For simplicity, we excluded the bias terms that need to be added at each unit of a hidden layer.

Now, we will pass the hidden layer values through an activation function so that we attain non-linearity in our output.

 If we do not apply the activation function in the hidden layer, the neural network becomes a giant linear connection from input to output.

Applying the activation function

Activation functions are applied at multiple layers of a network. They are used so that we achieve high non-linearity in input, which can be useful in modeling complex relations between the input and output.

The different activation functions are as follows:

Name	Plot	Equation
Identity		$f(x) = x$
Binary step		$f(x) = \begin{cases} 0 & \text{for } x < 0 \\ 1 & \text{for } x \geq 0 \end{cases}$
Logistic (a.k.a Soft step)		$f(x) = \dfrac{1}{1+e^{-x}}$
TanH		$f(x) = \tanh(x) = \dfrac{2}{1+e^{-2x}} - 1$
ArcTan		$f(x) = \tan^{-1}(x)$
Rectified Linear Unit (ReLU)		$f(x) = \begin{cases} 0 & \text{for } x < 0 \\ x & \text{for } x \geq 0 \end{cases}$
Parameteric Rectified Linear Unit (PReLU) [2]		$f(x) = \begin{cases} \alpha x & \text{for } x < 0 \\ x & \text{for } x \geq 0 \end{cases}$
Exponential Linear Unit (ELU) [3]		$f(x) = \begin{cases} \alpha(e^x - 1) & \text{for } x < 0 \\ x & \text{for } x \geq 0 \end{cases}$
SoftPlus		$f(x) = \log_e(1+e^x)$

For our example, let's use the sigmoid function for activation. The sigmoid function looks like this, graphically:

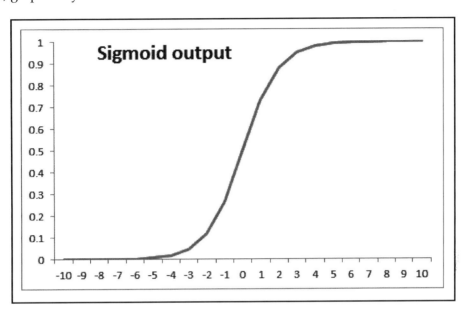

By applying sigmoid activation, $S(x)$, to the three hidden-layer *sums*, we get the following:

$$final\_h_1 = S(1.0) = 0.73$$

$$final\_h_2 = S(1.3) = 0.78$$

$$final\_h_3 = S(0.8) = 0.69$$

Calculating the output layered values

Now that we have calculated the hidden layer values, we will be calculating the output layer value. In the following diagram, we have the hidden layer values connected to the output through the randomly-initialized weight values. Using the hidden layer values and the weight values, we will calculate the output values for the following network:

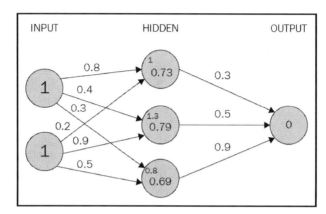

We perform the sum product of the hidden layer values and weight values to calculate the output value. For simplicity, we excluded the bias terms that need to be added at each unit of the hidden layer:

$$0.73 * 0.3 + 0.79 * 0.5 + 0.69 * 0.9 = 1.235$$

The values are shown in the following diagram:

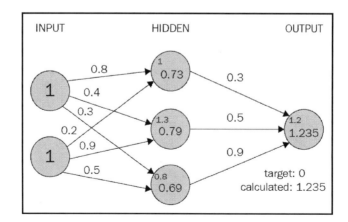

Because we started with a random set of weights, the value of the output neuron is very different from the target, in this case by +1.235 (since the target is 0).

Calculating the loss values

Loss values (alternatively called cost functions) are values that we optimize in a neural network. In order to understand how loss values get calculated, let's look at two scenarios:

- Continuous variable prediction
- Categorical variable prediction

Calculating loss during continuous variable prediction

Typically, when the variable is a continuous one, the loss value is calculated as the squared error, that is, we try to minimize the mean squared error by varying the weight values associated with the neural network:

$$J(\theta) = \frac{1}{m} \sum_{i=1}^{m} (h(\theta)(x^{(i)}) - y^{(i)})^2$$

In the preceding equation, *y(i)* is the actual value of output, *h(x)* is the transformation that we apply on the input (*x*) to obtain a predicted value of *y*, and *m* is the number of rows in the dataset.

Calculating loss during categorical variable prediction

When the variable to predict is a discrete one (that is, there are only a few categories in the variable), we typically use a categorical cross-entropy loss function. When the variable to predict has two distinct values within it, the loss function is binary cross-entropy, and when the variable to predict has multiple distinct values within it, the loss function is a categorical cross-entropy.

Here is binary cross-entropy:

(ylog(p)+(1−y)log(1−p))

Here is categorical cross-entropy:

$$-\sum_{n=1}^{M} y_n log(p_n)$$

Building a Feedforward Neural Network

y is the actual value of output p, is the predicted value of the output and n is the total number of data points. For now, let's assume that the outcome that we are predicting in our toy example is continuous. In that case, the loss function value is the mean squared error, which is calculated as follows:

$error = 1.235^2 = 1.52$

In the next step, we will try to minimize the loss function value using back-propagation (which we'll learn about in the next section), where we update the weight values (which were initialized randomly earlier) to minimize the loss (error).

How to do it...

In the previous section, we learned about performing the following steps on top of the input data to come up with error values in forward-propagation (the code file is available as Neural_network_working_details.ipynb in GitHub):

1. Initialize weights randomly
2. Calculate the hidden layer unit values by multiplying input values with weights
3. Perform activation on the hidden layer values
4. Connect the hidden layer values to the output layer
5. Calculate the squared error loss

A function to calculate the squared error loss values across all data points is as follows:

```
import numpy as np
def feed_forward(inputs, outputs, weights):
    pre_hidden = np.dot(inputs,weights[0])+ weights[1]
    hidden = 1/(1+np.exp(-pre_hidden))
    out = np.dot(hidden, weights[2]) + weights[3]
    squared_error = (np.square(pred_out - outputs))
    return squared_error
```

In the preceding function, we take the input variable values, weights (randomly initialized if this is the first iteration), and the actual output in the provided dataset as the input to the feed-forward function.

We calculate the hidden layer values by performing the matrix multiplication (dot product) of the input and weights. Additionally, we add the bias values in the hidden layer, as follows:

```
pre_hidden = np.dot(inputs,weights[0])+ weights[1]
```

The preceding scenario is valid when `weights[0]` is the weight value and `weights[1]` is the bias value, where the weight and bias are connecting the input layer to the hidden layer.

Once we calculate the hidden layer values, we perform activation on top of the hidden layer values, as follows:

```
hidden = 1/(1+np.exp(-pre_hidden))
```

We now calculate the output at the hidden layer by multiplying the output of the hidden layer with weights that connect the hidden layer to the output, and then adding the bias term at the output, as follows:

```
pred_out = np.dot(hidden, weights[2]) + weights[3]
```

Once the output is calculated, we calculate the squared error loss at each row, as follows:

```
squared_error = (np.square(pred_out - outputs))
```

In the preceding code, `pred_out` is the predicted output and `outputs` is the actual output.

We are then in a position to obtain the loss value as we forward-pass through the network.

While we considered the sigmoid activation on top of the hidden layer values in the preceding code, let's examine other activation functions that are commonly used.

Tanh

The tanh activation of a value (the hidden layer unit value) is calculated as follows:

```
def tanh(x):
    return (exp(x)-exp(-x))/(exp(x)+exp(-x))
```

ReLu

The **Rectified Linear Unit (ReLU)** of a value (the hidden layer unit value) is calculated as follows:

```
def relu(x):
    return np.where(x>0,x,0)
```

Linear

The linear activation of a value is the value itself.

Softmax

Typically, softmax is performed on top of a vector of values. This is generally done to determine the probability of an input belonging to one of the n number of the possible output classes in a given scenario. Let's say we are trying to classify an image of a digit into one of the possible 10 classes (numbers from 0 to 9). In this case, there are 10 output values, where each output value should represent the probability of an input image belonging to one of the 10 classes.

The softmax activation is used to provide a probability value for each class in the output and is calculated explained in the following sections:

```
def softmax(x):
    return np.exp(x)/np.sum(np.exp(x))
```

Apart from the preceding activation functions, the loss functions that are generally used while building a neural network are as follows.

Mean squared error

The error is the difference between the actual and predicted values of the output. We take a square of the error, as the error can be positive or negative (when the predicted value is greater than the actual value and vice versa). Squaring ensures that positive and negative errors do not offset each other. We calculate the mean squared error so that the error over two different datasets is comparable when the datasets are not the same size.

The mean squared error between predicted values (p) and actual values (y) is calculated as follows:

```
def mse(p, y):
    return np.mean(np.square(p - y))
```

The mean squared error is typically used when trying to predict a value that is continuous in nature.

Mean absolute error

The mean absolute error works in a manner that is very similar to the mean squared error. The mean absolute error ensures that positive and negative errors do not offset each other by taking an average of the absolute difference between the actual and predicted values across all data points.

The mean absolute error between the predicted values (p) and actual values (y) is implemented as follows:

```
def mae(p, y):
    return np.mean(np.abs(p-y))
```

Similar to the mean squared error, the mean absolute error is generally employed on continuous variables.

Categorical cross-entropy

Cross-entropy is a measure of the difference between two different distributions: actual and predicted. It is applied to categorical output data, unlike the previous two loss functions that we discussed.

Cross-entropy between two distributions is calculated as follows:

$$-(ylog_2 p + 1(1-y)log_2(1-p))$$

y is the actual outcome of the event and p is the predicted outcome of the event.

Categorical cross-entropy between the predicted values (p) and actual values (y) is implemented as follows:

```
def cat_cross_entropy(p, y):
    return -np.sum((y*np.log2(p)+(1-y)*np.log2(1-p)))
```

Note that categorical cross-entropy loss has a high value when the predicted value is far away from the actual value and a low value when the values are close.

Building back-propagation from scratch in Python

In forward-propagation, we connected the input layer to the hidden layer to the output layer. In back-propagation, we take the reverse approach.

Getting ready

We change each weight within the neural network by a small amount – one at a time. A change in the weight value will have an impact on the final loss value (either increasing or decreasing loss). We'll update the weight in the direction of decreasing loss.

Additionally, in some scenarios, for a small change in weight, the error increases/decreases considerably, while in some cases the error decreases by a small amount.

By updating the weights by a small amount and measuring the change in error that the update in weights leads to, we are able to do the following:

- Determine the direction of the weight update
- Determine the magnitude of the weight update

Before implementing back-propagation, let's understand one additional detail of neural networks: the learning rate.

Intuitively, the learning rate helps us to build trust in the algorithm. For example, when deciding on the magnitude of the weight update, we would potentially not change it by a huge amount in one go, but take a more careful approach in updating the weights more slowly.

This results in obtaining stability in our model; we will look at how the learning rate helps with stability in the next chapter.

The whole process by which we update weights to reduce error is called a gradient-descent technique.

Stochastic gradient descent is the means by which error is minimized in the preceding scenario. More intuitively, **gradient** stands for difference (which is the difference between actual and predicted) and **descent** means reduce. **Stochastic** stands for the selection of number of random samples based on which a decision is taken.

Apart from stochastic gradient descent, there are many other optimization techniques that help to optimize for the loss values; the different optimization techniques will be discussed in the next chapter.

Back-propagation works as follows:

- Calculates the overall cost function from the feedforward process.
- Varies all the weights (one at a time) by a small amount.
- Calculates the impact of the variation of weight on the cost function.
- Depending on whether the change has an increased or decreased the cost (loss) value, it updates the weight value in the direction of loss decrease. And then repeats this step across all the weights we have.

If the preceding steps are performed n number of times, it essentially results in n **epochs**.

In order to further cement our understanding of back-propagation in neural networks, let's start with a known function and see how the weights could be derived:

For now, we will have the known function as $y = 2x$, where we try to come up with the weight value and bias value, which are 2 and 0 in this specific case:

x	y
1	2
2	4
3	6
4	8

If we formulate the preceding dataset as a linear regression, $(y = a*x+b)$, where we are trying to calculate the values of *a* and *b* (which we already know are 2 and 0, but are checking how those values are obtained using gradient descent), let's randomly initialize the *a* and *b* parameters to values of 1.477 and 0 (the ideal values of which are 2 and 0).

How to do it...

In this section, we will build the back-propagation algorithm by hand so that we clearly understand how weights are calculated in a neural network. In this specific case, we will build a simple neural network where there is no hidden layer (thus we are solving a regression equation). The code file is available as Neural_network_working_details.ipynb in GitHub.

1. Initialize the dataset as follows:

    ```
    x = [[1],[2],[3],[4]]
    y = [[2],[4],[6],[8]]
    ```

2. Initialize the weight and bias values randomly (we have only one weight and one bias value as we are trying to identify the optimal values of *a* and *b* in the $y = a*x + b$ equation):

    ```
    w = [[[1.477867]], [0.]]
    ```

3. Define the feed-forward network and calculate the squared error loss value:

    ```
    import numpy as np
    def feed_forward(inputs, outputs, weights):
        out = np.dot(inputs,weights[0]) + weights[1]
        squared_error = (np.square(out - outputs))
        return squared_error
    ```

In the preceding code, we performed a matrix multiplication of the input with the randomly-initialized weight value and summed it up with the randomly-initialized bias value.

Once the value is calculated, we calculate the squared error value of the difference between the actual and predicted values.

4. Increase each weight and bias value by a very small amount (0.0001) and calculate the squared error loss value one at a time for each of the weight and bias updates.

If the squared error loss value decreases as the weight increases, the weight value should be increased. The magnitude by which the weight value should be increased is proportional to the amount of loss value the weight change decreases by.

Additionally, ensure that you do not increase the weight value as much as the loss decrease caused by the weight change, but weigh it down with a factor called the learning rate. This ensures that the loss decreases more smoothly (there's more on how the learning rate impacts the model accuracy in the next chapter).

In the following code, we are creating a function named `update_weights`, which performs the back-propagation process to update weights that were obtained in *step 3*. We are also mentioning that the function needs to be run for `epochs` number of times (where `epochs` is a parameter we are passing to `update_weights` function):

```
def update_weights(inputs, outputs, weights, epochs):
    for epoch in range(epochs):
```

5. Pass the input through a feed-forward network to calculate the loss with the initial set of weights:

```
org_loss = feed_forward(inputs, outputs, weights)
```

6. Ensure that you `deepcopy` the list of weights, as the weights will be manipulated in further steps, and hence `deepcopy` takes care of any issues resulting from the change in the child variable impacting the parent variable that it is pointing to:

```
wts_tmp = deepcopy(weights)
wts_tmp2 = deepcopy(weights)
```

7. Loop through all the weight values, one at a time, and change them by a small value (0.0001):

   ```
   for i in range(len(weights)):
       wts_tmp[-(i+1)] += 0.0001
   ```

8. Calculate the updated feed-forward loss when the weight is updated by a small amount. Calculate the change in loss due to the small change in input. Divide the change in loss by the number of input, as we want to calculate the mean squared error across all the input samples we have:

   ```
   loss = feed_forward(inputs, outputs, wts_tmp)
   delta_loss = np.sum(org_loss - loss)/(0.0001*len(inputs))
   ```

Updating the weight by a small value and then calculating its impact on loss value is equivalent to performing a derivative with respect to change in weight.

9. Update the weights by the change in loss that they are causing. Update the weights slowly by multiplying the change in loss by a very small number (0.01), which is the learning rate parameter (more about the learning rate parameter in the next chapter):

   ```
   wts_tmp2[-(i+1)] += delta_loss*0.01
   wts_tmp = deepcopy(weights)
   ```

10. The updated weights and bias value are returned:

    ```
    weights = deepcopy(wts_tmp2)
    return wts_tmp2
    ```

One of the other parameters in a neural network is the batch size considered in calculating the loss values.

In the preceding scenario, we considered all the data points in order to calculate the loss value. However, in practice, when we have thousands (or in some cases, millions) of data points, the incremental contribution of a greater number of data points while calculating loss value would follow the law of diminishing returns and hence we would be using a batch size that is much smaller compared to the total number of data points we have.

The typical batch size considered in building a model is anywhere between 32 and 1,024.

There's more...

In the previous section, we built a regression formula *(Y = a*x + b)* where we wrote a function to identify the optimal values of *a* and *b*. In this section, we will build a simple neural network with a hidden layer that connects the input to the output on the same toy dataset that we worked on in the previous section.

We define the model as follows (the code file is available as `Neural_networks_multiple_layers.ipynb` in GitHub):

- The input is connected to a hidden layer that has three units
- The hidden layer is connected to the output, which has one unit in output layer

Let us go ahead and code up the strategy discussed above, as follows:

1. Define the dataset and import the relevant packages:

    ```
    from copy import deepcopy
    import numpy as np

    x = [[1],[2],[3],[4]]
    y = [[2],[4],[6],[8]]
    ```

    We use `deepcopy` so that the value of the original variable does not change when the variable to which the original variable's values are copied has its values changed.

2. Initialize the weight and bias values randomly. The hidden layer has three units in it. Hence, there are a total of three weight values and three bias values – one corresponding to each of the hidden units.

    Additionally, the final layer has one unit that is connected to the three units of the hidden layer. Hence, a total of three weights and one bias dictate the value of the output layer.

    The randomly-initialized weights are as follows:

    ```
    w = [[[-0.82203424, -0.9185806 , 0.03494298]], [0., 0., 0.], [[ 1.0692896 ],[ 0.62761235],[-0.5426246 ]], [0]]
    ```

3. Implement the feed-forward network where the hidden layer has a ReLU activation in it:

```
def feed_forward(inputs, outputs, weights):
    pre_hidden = np.dot(inputs,weights[0])+ weights[1]
    hidden = np.where(pre_hidden<0, 0, pre_hidden)
    out = np.dot(hidden, weights[2]) + weights[3]
    squared_error = (np.square(out - outputs))
    return squared_error
```

4. Define the back-propagation function similarly to what we did in the previous section. The only difference is that we now have to update the weights in more layers.

In the following code, we are calculating the original loss at the start of an epoch:

```
def update_weights(inputs, outputs, weights, epochs):
    for epoch in range(epochs):
        org_loss = feed_forward(inputs, outputs, weights)
```

In the following code, we are copying weights into two sets of weight variables so that they can be reused in a later code:

```
wts_new = deepcopy(weights)
wts_new2 = deepcopy(weights)
```

In the following code, we are updating each weight value by a small amount and then calculating the loss value corresponding to the updated weight value (while every other weight is kept unchanged). Additionally, we are ensuring that the weight update happens across all weights and also across all layers in a network.

The change in the squared loss (`del_loss`) is attributed to the change in the weight value. We repeat the preceding step for all the weights that exist in the network:

```
for i, layer in enumerate(reversed(weights)):
    for index, weight in np.ndenumerate(layer):
        wts_tmp[-(i+1)][index] += 0.0001
        loss = feed_forward(inputs, outputs, wts_tmp)
        del_loss = np.sum(org_loss - loss)/(0.0001*len(inputs))
```

The weight value is updated by weighing down by the learning rate parameter – a greater decrease in loss will update weights by a lot, while a lower decrease in loss will update the weight by a small amount:

```
wts_tmp2[-(i+1)][index] += del_loss*0.01
wts_tmp = deepcopy(weights)
```

Building a Feedforward Neural Network

 Given that the weight values are updated one at a time in order to estimate their impact on the loss value, there is a potential to parallelize the process of weight updates. Hence, GPUs come in handy in such scenarios as they have more cores than a CPU and thus more weights can be updated using a GPU in a given amount of time compared to a CPU.

Finally, we return the updated weights:

```
        weights = deepcopy(wts_tmp2)
return wts_tmp2
```

5. Run the function an epoch number of times to update the weights an epoch number of times:

```
update_weights(x,y,w,1)
```

The output (updated weights) of preceding code is as follows:

```
[array([[-1.0281681 ,  0.11109705, -0.08701682]], dtype=float32),
 array([ 0.        ,  -0.10836656,  0.        ], dtype=float32),
 array([[ 0.5071335 ],
        [-0.74833566],
        [ 0.10594594]], dtype=float32),
 array([0.11973583], dtype=float32)]
```

In the preceding steps, we learned how to build a neural network from scratch in Python. In the next section, we will learn about building a neural network in Keras.

Building a neural network in Keras

In the previous section, we built a neural network from scratch, that is, we wrote functions that perform forward-propagation and back-propagation.

How to do it...

We will be building a neural network using the Keras library, which provides utilities that make the process of building a complex neural network much easier.

[30]

Installing Keras

Tensorflow and Keras are implemented in Ubuntu, using the following commands:

```
$pip install --no-cache-dir tensorflow-gpu==1.7
```

Note that it is preferable to install a GPU-compatible version, as neural networks work considerably faster when they are run on top of a GPU. Keras is a high-level neural network API, written in Python, and capable of running on top of TensorFlow, CNTK, or Theano.

It was developed with a focus on enabling fast experimentation, and it can be installed as follows:

```
$pip install keras
```

Building our first model in Keras

In this section, let's understand the process of building a model in Keras by using the same toy dataset that we worked on in the previous sections (the code file is available as Neural_networks_multiple_layers.ipynb in GitHub):

1. Instantiate a model that can be called sequentially to add further layers on top of it. The Sequential method enables us to perform the model initialization exercise:

```
from keras.models import Sequential
model = Sequential()
```

2. Add a dense layer to the model. A dense layer ensures the connection between various layers in a model. In the following code, we are connecting the input layer to the hidden layer:

```
model.add(Dense(3, activation='relu', input_shape=(1,)))
```

In the dense layer initialized with the preceding code, we ensured that we provide the input shape to the model (we need to specify the shape of data that the model has to expect as this is the first dense layer).

Additionally, we mentioned that there will be three connections made to each input (three units in the hidden layer) and also that the activation that needs to be performed in the hidden layer is the ReLu activation.

3. Connect the hidden layer to the output layer:

   ```
   model.add(Dense(1, activation='linear'))
   ```

   Note that in this dense layer, we don't need to specify the input shape, as the model would already infer the input shape from the previous layer.

   Also, given that each output is one-dimensional, our output layer has one unit and the activation that we are performing is the linear activation.

   The model summary can now be visualized as follows:

   ```
   model.summary()
   ```

   A summary of model is as follows:

   ```
   Layer (type)                 Output Shape              Param #
   =================================================================
   dense_1 (Dense)              (None, 3)                 6
   _____
   dense_2 (Dense)              (None, 1)                 4
   =================================================================
   Total params: 10
   Trainable params: 10
   Non-trainable params: 0
   ```

   The preceding output confirms our discussion in the previous section: that there will be a total of six parameters in the connection from the input layer to the hidden layer—three weights and three bias terms—we have a total of six parameters corresponding to the three hidden units. In addition, three weights and one bias term connect the hidden layer to the output layer.

4. Compile the model. This ensures that we define the loss function and the optimizer to reduce the loss function and the learning rate corresponding to the optimizer (we will look at different optimizers and loss functions in next chapter):

   ```
   from keras.optimizers import sgd
   sgd = sgd(lr = 0.01)
   ```

In the preceding step, we specified that the optimizer is the stochastic gradient descent that we learned about in the previous section and the learning rate is 0.01. Pass the predefined optimizer and its corresponding learning rate as a parameter and reduce the mean squared error value:

```
model.compile(optimizer=sgd,loss='mean_squared_error')
```

5. Fit the model. Update the weights so that the model is a better fit:

```
model.fit(np.array(x), np.array(y), epochs=1, batch_size = 4,
verbose=1)
```

The `fit` method expects that it receives two NumPy arrays: an input array and the corresponding output array. Note that `epochs` represents the number of times the total dataset is traversed through, and `batch_size` represents the number of data points that need to be considered in an iteration of updating the weights. Furthermore, `verbose` specifies that the output is more detailed, with information about losses in training and test datasets as well as the progress of the model training process.

6. Extract the weight values. The order in which the weight values are presented is obtained by calling the weights method on top of the model, as follows:

```
model.weights
```

The order in which weights are obtained is as follows:

```
[<tf.Variable 'dense_1/kernel:0' shape=(1, 3) dtype=float32_ref>,
 <tf.Variable 'dense_1/bias:0' shape=(3,) dtype=float32_ref>,
 <tf.Variable 'dense_2/kernel:0' shape=(3, 1) dtype=float32_ref>,
 <tf.Variable 'dense_2/bias:0' shape=(1,) dtype=float32_ref>]
```

From the preceding output, we see that the order of weights is the three weights (`kernel`) and three bias terms in the `dense_1` layer (which is the connection between the input to the hidden layer) and the three weights (`kernel`) and one bias term connecting the hidden layer to the `dense_2` layer (the output layer).

Now that we understand the order in which weight values are presented, let's extract the values of these weights:

```
model.get_weights()
```

Notice that the weights are presented as a list of arrays, where each array corresponds to the value that is specified in the `model.weights` output.

The output of above lines of code is as follows:

```
[array([[-1.0281681 ,  0.11109705, -0.08701682]], dtype=float32),
 array([ 0.        , -0.10836656,  0.        ], dtype=float32),
 array([[ 0.5071335 ],
        [-0.74833566],
        [ 0.10594594]], dtype=float32),
 array([0.11973583], dtype=float32)]
```

You should notice that the output we are observing here matches with the output we obtaining while hand-building the neural network

7. Predict the output for a new set of input using the `predict` method:

   ```
   x1 = [[5],[6]]
   model.predict(np.array(x1))
   ```

   Note that x1 is the variable that holds the values for the new set of examples for which we need to predict the value of the output. Similarly to the `fit` method, the `predict` method also expects an array as its input.

   The output of preceding code is as follows:

   ```
   array([[0.09999999],
          [0.09999999]], dtype=float32)
   ```

Notice that, while the preceding output is incorrect, the output when we run for 100 epochs is as follows:

```
array([[ 9.865341],
       [11.799512]], dtype=float32)
```

The preceding output will match the expected output (which are 10, 12) as we run for even higher number of epochs.

[34]

2
Building a Deep Feedforward Neural Network

In this chapter, we will cover the following recipes:

- Training a vanilla neural network
- Scaling the input dataset
- Impact of training when the majority of inputs are greater than zero
- Impact of batch size on model accuracy
- Building a deep neural network to improve network accuracy
- Varying the learning rate to improve network accuracy
- Varying the loss optimizer to improve network accuracy
- Understanding the scenario of overfitting
- Speeding up the training process using batch normalization

In the previous chapter, we looked at the basics of the function of a neural network. We also learned that there are various hyperparameters that impact the accuracy of a neural network. In this chapter, we will get into the details of the functions of the various hyperparameters within a neural network.

All the codes for this chapter are available at https://github.com/kishore-ayyadevara/Neural-Networks-with-Keras-Cookbook/blob/master/Neural_network_hyper_parameters.ipynb

Training a vanilla neural network

To understand how to train a vanilla neural network, we will go through the task of predicting the label of a digit in the MNIST dataset, which is a popular dataset of images of digits (one digit per image) and the corresponding label of the digit that is contained in the image.

Getting ready

Training a neural network is done in the following steps:

1. Import the relevant packages and datasets
2. Preprocess the targets (convert them into one-hot encoded vectors) so that we can perform optimization on top of them:
     - We shall be minimizing categorical cross entropy loss
3. Create train and test datasets:
     - We have the train dataset so that we create a model based on it
     - The test dataset is not seen by the model:
         - Hence, the accuracy on the test dataset is an indicator of how well the model is likely to work on data when the model is productionalized, as data in the production scenario (which might occur a few days/weeks after building the model) cannot be seen by the model
4. Initialize a model
5. Define the model architecture:
     - Specify the number of units in a hidden layer
     - Specify the activation function that is to be performed in a hidden layer
     - Specify the number of hidden layers
     - Specify the loss function that we want to minimize
     - Provide the optimizer that will minimize the loss function
6. Fit the model:
     - Mention the batch size to update weights
     - Mention the total number of epochs
7. Test the model:
     - Mention the validation data, otherwise, mention the validation split, which will consider the last x% of total data as test data
     - Calculate the accuracy and loss values on top of the test dataset
8. Check for anything interesting in the way in which loss value and accuracy values changed over an increasing number of epochs

Using this strategy, let's go ahead and build a neural network model in Keras, in the following section.

How to do it...

1. Import the relevant packages and dataset, and visualize the input dataset:

   ```
   from keras.datasets import mnist
   import numpy
   from keras.datasets import mnist
   from keras.models import Sequential
   from keras.layers import Dense
   from keras.layers import Dropout
   from keras.utils import np_utils
   (X_train, y_train), (X_test, y_test) = mnist.load_data()
   ```

   In the preceding code, we are importing the relevant Keras files and are also importing the MNIST dataset (which is provided as a built-in dataset in Keras).

2. The MNIST dataset contains images of digits where the images are of 28 x 28 in shape. Let's plot a few images to see what they will look like in the code here:

   ```
   import matplotlib.pyplot as plt
   %matplotlib inline
   plt.subplot(221)
   plt.imshow(X_train[0], cmap=plt.get_cmap('gray'))
   plt.grid('off')
   plt.subplot(222)
   plt.imshow(X_train[1], cmap=plt.get_cmap('gray'))
   plt.grid('off')
   plt.subplot(223)
   plt.imshow(X_train[2], cmap=plt.get_cmap('gray'))
   plt.grid('off')
   plt.subplot(224)
   plt.imshow(X_train[3], cmap=plt.get_cmap('gray'))
   plt.grid('off')
   plt.show()
   ```

The following screenshot shows the output of the previous code block:

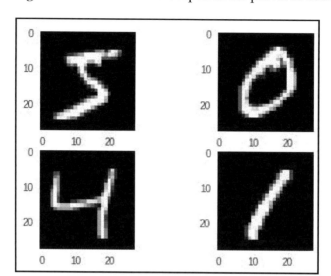

3. Flatten the 28 x 28 images so that the input is all the 784 pixel values. Additionally, one-hot encode the outputs. This step is key in the dataset preparation process:

```
# flatten 28*28 images to a 784 vector for each image
num_pixels = X_train.shape[1] * X_train.shape[2]
X_train = X_train.reshape(X_train.shape[0],
num_pixels).astype('float32')
X_test = X_test.reshape(X_test.shape[0],
num_pixels).astype('float32')
```

In the preceding step, we are reshaping the input dataset using the reshape method that converts an array of a given shape into a different shape. In this specific case, we are converting an array that has an X_train.shape[0] number of data points (images) where there are X_train.shape[1] rows and X_train.shape[2] columns in each image, into an array of an X_train.shape[0] number of data points (images) and X_train.shape[1] * X_train.shape[2] values per image. Similarly, we perform the same exercise on the test dataset:

```
# one hot encode outputs
y_train = np_utils.to_categorical(y_train)
y_test = np_utils.to_categorical(y_test)
num_classes = y_test.shape[1]
```

Let's try to understand how one-hot encoding works. If the unique possible labels are {0, 1, 2, 3}, they will be one-hot encoded, as follows:

Label	0	1	2	3
0	1	0	0	0
1	0	1	0	0
2	0	0	1	0
3	0	0	0	1

Essentially, each label will occupy a unique column in the dataset, and if the label is present, the column value will be one, and every other column value will be zero.

In Keras, the one-hot encoding approach on top of labels is performed using the to_categorical method, which figures out the number of unique labels in the target data, and then converts them into a one-hot encoded vector.

4. Build a neural network with a hidden layer with 1,000 units:

```
model = Sequential()
model.add(Dense(1000, input_dim=784, activation='relu'))
model.add(Dense(10, activation='softmax'))
```

In the preceding step, we mention that the input has 784 values that are connected to 1,000 values in a hidden layer. Additionally, we are also specifying that the activation, which is to be performed in the hidden layer after the matrix multiplication of the input and the weights connecting the input and hidden layer, is the ReLu activation.

Finally, the hidden layer is connected to an output that has 10 values (as there are 10 columns in the vector created by the to_categorical method), and we perform softmax on top of the output so that we obtain the probability of an image belonging to a certain class.

5. The preceding model architecture can be visualized as follows:

   ```
   model.summary()
   ```

   A summary of model is as follows:

   ```
   Layer (type)                   Output Shape              Param #
   =================================================================
   dense_1 (Dense)                (None, 1000)              785000
   _____
   dense_2 (Dense)                (None, 10)                10010
   =================================================================
   Total params: 795,010
   Trainable params: 795,010
   Non-trainable params: 0
   _____
   ```

   In the preceding architecture, the number of parameters in the first layer is 785,000, as the 784 input units are connected to 1,000 hidden units, resulting in 784 * 1,000 weight values, and 1,000 bias values, for the 1,000 hidden units, resulting in a total of 785,000 parameters.

   Similarly, the output layer has 10 outputs, which are connected to each of the 1,000 hidden layers, resulting in 1,000 * 10 parameters and 10 biases—a total of 10,010 parameters.

   The output layer has 10 units as there are 10 possible labels in the output. The output layer now gives us a probability value for each class for a given input image.

6. Compile the model as follows:

   ```
   model.compile(loss='categorical_crossentropy', optimizer='adam',
   metrics=['accuracy'])
   ```

   Note that because the target variable is a one-hot encoded vector with multiple classes in it, the loss function will be a categorical cross-entropy loss.

   Additionally, we are using the Adam optimizer to minimize the cost function (more on different optimizers in the *Varying the loss optimizer to improve network accuracy* recipe).

   We are also noting that we will need to look at the accuracy metric while the model is getting trained.

7. Fit the model as follows:

```
history = model.fit(X_train, y_train, validation_data=(X_test,
y_test), epochs=500, batch_size=32, verbose=1)
```

In the preceding code, we have specified the input (X_train) and the output (y_train) that the model will fit. Additionally, we also specify the input and output of the test dataset, which the model will not use to train weights; however it, will give us an idea of how different the loss value and accuracy values are between the training and the test datasets.

8. Extract the training and test loss and accuracy metrics over different epochs:

```
history_dict = history.history
loss_values = history_dict['loss']
val_loss_values = history_dict['val_loss']
acc_values = history_dict['acc']
val_acc_values = history_dict['val_acc']
epochs = range(1, len(val_loss_values) + 1)
```

While fitting a model, the history variable will have stored the accuracy and loss values corresponding to the model in each epoch for both the training and the test datasets. In the preceding steps, we are storing those values in a list so that we can plot the variation of accuracy and loss in both the training and test datasets over an increasing number of epochs.

9. Visualize the training and test loss and the accuracy over a different number of epochs:

```
import matplotlib.pyplot as plt
%matplotlib inline

plt.subplot(211)
plt.plot(epochs, history.history['loss'], 'rx', label='Training
loss')
plt.plot(epochs, val_loss_values, 'b', label='Test loss')
plt.title('Training and test loss')
plt.xlabel('Epochs')
plt.ylabel('Loss')
plt.legend()
plt.show()

plt.subplot(212)
plt.plot(epochs, history.history['acc'], 'rx', label='Training
accuracy')
plt.plot(epochs, val_acc_values, 'b', label='Test accuracy')
plt.title('Training and test accuracy')
```

Building a Deep Feedforward Neural Network

```
plt.xlabel('Epochs')
plt.ylabel('Accuracy')
plt.gca().set_yticklabels(['{:.0f}%'.format(x*100) for x in
plt.gca().get_yticks()])
plt.legend()
plt.show()
```

The preceding code produces the following diagram, where the first plot shows the training and test loss values over increasing epochs, and the second plot shows the training and test accuracy over increasing epochs:

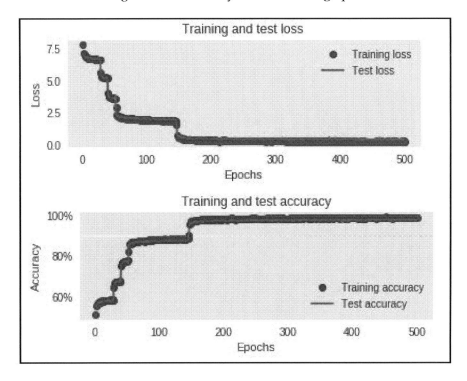

Note that the previous network resulted in an accuracy of 97%. Also, note that loss values (and thereby, accuracy) have a step change over a different number of epochs. We will contrast this change in loss with the scenario when the input dataset is scaled in the next section.

10. Let's calculate the accuracy of the model manually:

```
preds = model.predict(X_test)
```

[42]

In the preceding step, we are using the `predict` method to calculate the expected output values for a given input (`X_test` in this case) to the model. Note that we are specifying it as `model.predict`, as we have initialized a sequential model named `model`:

```
import numpy as np
correct = 0
for i in range(len(X_test)):
    pred = np.argmax(preds[i],axis=0)
    act = np.argmax(y_test[i],axis=0)
    if(pred==act):
        correct+=1
    else:
        continue

correct/len(X_test)
```

In the preceding code, we are looping all of the test predictions one at a time. For each test prediction, we are perming `argmax` to obtain the index that has the highest probability value.

Similarly, we perform the same exercise for the actual values of the test dataset. The prediction of the index of the highest value is the same in both the prediction and the actual values of the test dataset.

Finally, the number of correct predictions over the total number of data points in the test dataset is the accuracy of the model on the test dataset.

How it works...

The key steps that we have performed in the preceding code are as follows:

- We flattened the input dataset so that each pixel is considered a variable using the `reshape` method
- We performed one-hot encoding on the output values so that we can distinguish between different labels using the `to_categorical` method in the `np_utils` package
- We built a neural network with a hidden layer using the sequential addition of layers

- We compiled the neural network to minimize the categorical cross entropy loss (as the output has 10 different categories) using the `model.compile` method
- We fitted the model with training data using the `model.fit` method
- We extracted the training and test loss accuracies across all the epochs that were stored in the history
- We predicted the probability of each class in the test dataset using the `model.predict` method
- We looped through all the images in the test dataset and identified the class that has the highest probability
- Finally, we calculated the accuracy (the number of instances in which a predicted class matches the actual class of the image out of the total number of instances)

In the next section, we will look at the reasons for the step change in the loss and accuracy values, and move toward making the change more smooth.

Scaling the input dataset

Scaling a dataset is a process where we limit the variables within a dataset to ensure they do not have a very wide range of different values. One way to achieve this is to divide each variable in the dataset by the maximum value of the variable. Typically, neural networks perform well when we scale the input datasets.

In this section, let's understand the reason neural networks perform better when the dataset is scaled.

Getting ready

To understand the impact of the scaling input on the output, let's contrast the scenario where we check the output when the input dataset is not scaled, with the output when the input dataset is scaled.

Input data is not scaled:

Scenario	Input	Weight	bias	Sigmoid
1	255	0.01	0	0.93
2	255	0.1	0	1.00
3	255	0.2	0	1.00
4	255	0.3	0	1.00
5	255	0.4	0	1.00
6	255	0.5	0	1.00
7	255	0.6	0	1.00
8	255	0.7	0	1.00
9	255	0.8	0	1.00
10	255	0.9	0	1.00

In the preceding table, note that the output (sigmoid) did not vary a lot, even though the weight value varied from 0.01 to 0.9. The sigmoid function is calculated as the sigmoid value of the multiplication of the input with the weight, and then adding a bias to it:

```
output = 1/(1+np.exp(-(w*x + b))
```

Where `w` is the weight, `x` is the input, and `b` is the bias value.

The reason for no change in the sigmoid output is due to the fact that the multiplication of `w*x` is a large number (as x is a large number) resulting in the sigmoid value always falling in the saturated portion of the sigmoid curve (saturated value on the top-right or bottom-left of the sigmoid curve).

In this scenario, let's multiply different weight values by a small input number, as follows:

Scenario	Input	Weight	bias	Sigmoid
1	1	0.01	0	0.50
2	1	0.1	0	0.52
3	1	0.2	0	0.55
4	1	0.3	0	0.57
5	1	0.4	0	0.60
6	1	0.5	0	0.62
7	1	0.6	0	0.65
8	1	0.7	0	0.67
9	1	0.8	0	0.69
10	1	0.9	0	0.71

The sigmoid output in the preceding table varies, as the input and weight values are small, resulting in a smaller value when the input and the weight are multiplied, further resulting in the sigmoid value having variation in output.

From this exercise, we learned about the importance of scaling the input dataset so that it results in a smaller value when the weights (provided the weights do not have a high range) are multiplied by the input values. This phenomenon results in the weight value not getting updated quickly enough.

Thus, to achieve the optimal weight value, we should scale our input dataset while initializing the weights to not have a huge range (typically, weights have a random value between -1 and +1 during initialization).

These issues hold true when the weight value is also a very big number. Hence, we are better off initializing the weight values as a small value that is closer to zero.

How to do it...

Let's go through the set up of scaling the dataset that we have used in the previous section, and compare the results with and without scaling:

1. Import the relevant packages and datasets:

```
from keras.datasets import mnist
import numpy as np
from keras.datasets import mnist
from keras.models import Sequential
from keras.layers import Dense
from keras.layers import Dropout
from keras.utils import np_utils

(X_train, y_train), (X_test, y_test) = mnist.load_data()
```

2. There are multiple ways to scale a dataset. One way is to convert all the data points to a value between zero and one (by dividing each data point with the maximum value in the total dataset, which is what we are doing in the following code). Another popular method, among the multiple other ways, is to normalize the dataset so that the values are between -1 and +1 by subtracting each data point with the overall dataset mean, and then dividing each resulting data point by the standard deviation of values in the original dataset.

Now we will be flattening the input dataset and scaling it, as follows:

```
# flatten 28*28 images to a 784 vector for each image
num_pixels = X_train.shape[1] * X_train.shape[2]
X_train = X_train.reshape(X_train.shape[0],
num_pixels).astype('float32')
X_test = X_test.reshape(X_test.shape[0],
num_pixels).astype('float32')

X_train = X_train/255
X_test = X_test/255
```

In the preceding step, we have scaled the training and test inputs to a value between zero and one by dividing each value by the maximum possible value in the dataset, which is 255. Additionally, we convert the output dataset into a one-hot encoded format:

```
# one hot encode outputs
y_train = np_utils.to_categorical(y_train)
y_test = np_utils.to_categorical(y_test)
num_classes = y_test.shape[1]
```

3. Build the model and compile it using the following code:

```
model = Sequential()
model.add(Dense(1000, input_dim=784, activation='relu'))
model.add(Dense(10, activation='softmax'))
model.compile(loss='categorical_crossentropy', optimizer='adam',
metrics=['accuracy'])
```

Note that the preceding model is exactly the same as the one we built in the previous section. However, the only difference is that it will be executed on the training dataset that is scaled, whereas the previous one was not scaled.

4. Fit the model as follows:

```
history = model.fit(X_train, y_train, validation_data=(X_test,
y_test), epochs=500, batch_size=32, verbose=1)
```

You will notice that the accuracy of the preceding model is ~98.25%.

Building a Deep Feedforward Neural Network

5. Plot the training and test accuracy and the loss values over different epochs (the code to generate the following plots remains the same as the one we used in step 8 of the *Training a vanilla neural network* recipe):

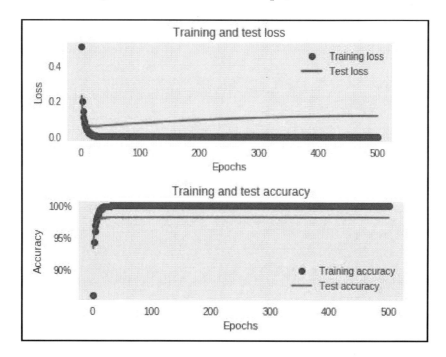

From the preceding diagram, you should notice that training and test losses decreased smoothly over increasing epochs when compared to the non-scaled dataset that we saw in the previous section.

While the preceding network gave us good results in terms of a smoothly decreasing loss value, we noticed that there is a gap between the training and test accuracy/loss values, indicating that there is potential overfitting on top of the training dataset. **Overfitting** is the phenomenon where the model specializes on the training data that it might not work as well on the test dataset.

How it works...

The key steps that we have performed in the preceding code are as follows:

- We flattened the input dataset so that each pixel is considered a variable using the reshape method

- Additionally, we scaled the dataset so that each variable now has a value between zero and one
  - We achieved the preceding by dividing the values of a variable with the maximum value of that variable
- We performed one-hot encoding on the output values so that we can distinguish between different labels using the `to_categorical` method in the `np_utils` package
- We built a neural network with a hidden layer using the sequential addition of layers
- We compiled the neural network to minimize categorical cross entropy loss (as the output has 10 different categories) using the `model.compile` method
- We fitted the model with training data using the `model.fit` method
- We extracted the training and test losses accuracies across all the epochs that were stored in the history
- We also identified a scenario that we consider overfitting

There's more...

In addition to scaling a variable's values by dividing the values by the maximum among the values in a variable, the other commonly used scaling methods are as follows:

- Min-max normalization
- Mean normalization
- Standardization

More information about these scaling methods can be found on Wikipedia here: https://en.wikipedia.org/wiki/Feature_scaling.

Impact on training when the majority of inputs are greater than zero

So far, in the dataset that we have considered, we have not looked at the distribution of values in the input dataset. Certain values of the input result in faster training. In this section, we will understand a scenario where weights are trained faster when the training time depends on the input values.

Building a Deep Feedforward Neural Network

Getting ready

In this section, we will follow the model-building process in exactly the same way as we did in the previous section.

However, we will adopt a small change to our strategy:

- We will invert the background color, and also the foreground color. Essentially, the background will be colored white in this scenario, and the label will be written in black.

The intuition for this change impacting the model accuracy is as follows.

The pixels in the corner of images do not contribute toward predicting the label of an image. Given that a black pixel (original scenario) has a pixel value of zero, it is automatically taken care of, as when this input is multiplied by any weight value, the output is zero. This will result in the network learning that any change in the weight value connecting this corner pixel to a hidden layer will not have an impact on changing the loss value.

However, if we have a white pixel in the corner (where we already know that the corner pixels do not contribute toward predicting the label of an image), it will contribute toward certain hidden unit values, and thus the weights need to be fine-tuned until the impact of the corner pixels on the predicted label is minimal.

How to do it...

1. Load and scale the input dataset:

```
(X_train, y_train), (X_test, y_test) = mnist.load_data()
num_pixels = X_train.shape[1] * X_train.shape[2]
X_train = X_train.reshape(X_train.shape[0],
num_pixels).astype('float32')
X_test = X_test.reshape(X_test.shape[0],
num_pixels).astype('float32')
X_train = X_train/255
X_test = X_test/255
y_train = np_utils.to_categorical(y_train)
y_test = np_utils.to_categorical(y_test)
num_classes = y_test.shape[1]
```

2. Let's look at the distribution of the input values:

   ```
   X_train.flatten()
   ```

   The preceding code flattens all the inputs into a single list, and hence, is of the shape (47,040,000), which is the same as the `28 x 28 x X_train.shape[0]`. Let's plot the distribution of all the input values:

   ```
   plt.hist(X_train.flatten())
   plt.grid('off')
   plt.title('Histogram of input values')
   plt.xlabel('Input values')
   plt.ylabel('Frequency of input values')
   ```

   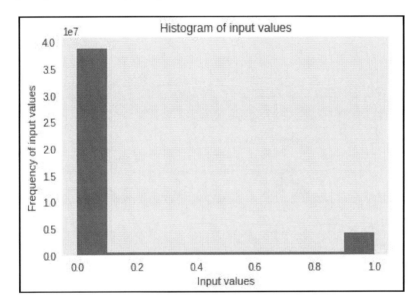

   We notice that the majority of the inputs are zero (you should note that all the input images have a background that is black hence, a majority of the values are zero, which is the pixel value of the color black).

3. In this section, let's explore a scenario where we invert the colors, in which the background is white and the letters are written in black, using the following code:

   ```
   X_train = 1-X_train
   X_test = 1-X_test
   ```

Let's plot the images:

```
import matplotlib.pyplot as plt
%matplotlib inline
plt.subplot(221)
plt.imshow(X_train[0].reshape(28,28), cmap=plt.get_cmap('gray'))
plt.grid('off')
plt.subplot(222)
plt.imshow(X_train[1].reshape(28,28), cmap=plt.get_cmap('gray'))
plt.grid('off')
plt.subplot(223)
plt.imshow(X_train[2].reshape(28,28), cmap=plt.get_cmap('gray'))
plt.grid('off')
plt.subplot(224)
plt.imshow(X_train[3].reshape(28,28), cmap=plt.get_cmap('gray'))
plt.grid('off')
plt.show()
```

They will look as follows:

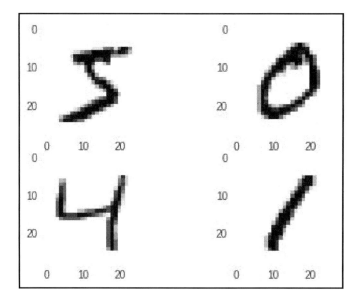

The histogram of the resulting images now looks as follows:

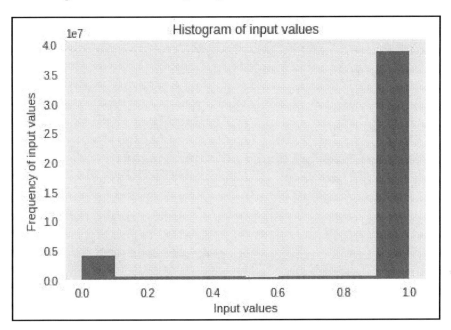

You should notice that the majority of the input values now have a value of one.

4. Let's go ahead and build our model using the same model architecture that we built in the *Scaling input dataset* section:

```
model = Sequential()
model.add(Dense(1000,input_dim=784,activation='relu'))
model.add(Dense(10, activation='softmax'))
model.compile(loss='categorical_crossentropy', optimizer='adam',
metrics=['accuracy'])
history = model.fit(X_train, y_train, validation_data=(X_test,
y_test), epochs=10, batch_size=32, verbose=1)
```

5. Plot the training and test accuracy and loss values over different epochs (the code to generate the following plots remains the same as the one we used in step 8 of the *Training a vanilla neural network* recipe):

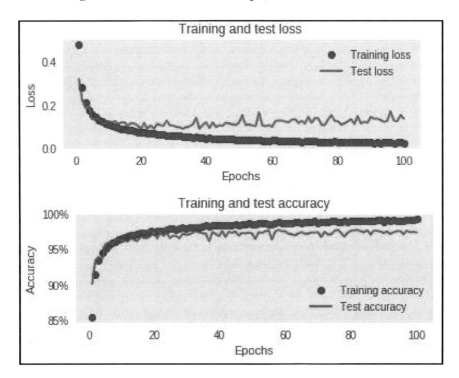

We should note that model accuracy has now fallen to ~97%, compared to ~98% when using the same model for the same number of epochs and batch size, but on a dataset that has a majority of zeros (and not a majority of ones). Additionally, the model achieved an accuracy of 97%, considerably more slowly than in the scenario where the majority of the input pixels are zero.

The intuition for the decrease in accuracy, when the majority of the data points are non-zero is that, when the majority of pixels are zero, the model's task was easier (less weights had to be fine-tuned), as it had to make predictions based on a few pixel values (the minority that had a pixel value greater than zero). However, a higher number of weights need to be fine-tuned to make predictions when a majority of the data points are non-zero.

Impact of batch size on model accuracy

In the previous sections, for all the models that we have built, we considered a batch size of 32. In this section, we will try to understand the impact of varying the batch size on accuracy.

Getting ready

To understand the reason batch size has an impact on model accuracy, let's contrast two scenarios where the total dataset size is 60,000:

- Batch size is 30,000
- Batch size is 32

When the batch size is large, the number of times of weight update per epoch is small, when compared to the scenario when the batch size is small.

The reason for a high number of weight updates per epoch when the batch size is small is that less data points are considered to calculate the loss value. This results in more batches per epoch, as, loosely, in an epoch, you would have to go through all the training data points in a dataset.

Thus, the lower the batch size, the better the accuracy for the same number of epochs. However, while deciding the number of data points to be considered for a batch size, you should also ensure that the batch size is not too small so that it might overfit on top of a small batch of data.

How to do it...

In the previous recipe, we built a model with a batch size of 32. In this recipe, we will go ahead and implement the model to contrast the scenario between a low batch size and a high batch size for the same number of epochs:

1. Preprocess the dataset and fit the model as follows:

```
(X_train, y_train), (X_test, y_test) = mnist.load_data()
num_pixels = X_train.shape[1] * X_train.shape[2]
X_train = X_train.reshape(X_train.shape[0],
num_pixels).astype('float32')
X_test = X_test.reshape(X_test.shape[0],
num_pixels).astype('float32')
X_train = X_train/255
```

```
X_test = X_test/255
y_train = np_utils.to_categorical(y_train)
y_test = np_utils.to_categorical(y_test)
num_classes = y_test.shape[1]
model = Sequential()
model.add(Dense(1000,input_dim=784,activation='relu'))
model.add(Dense(10, activation='softmax'))
model.compile(loss='categorical_crossentropy', optimizer='adam',
metrics=['accuracy'])
history = model.fit(X_train, y_train, validation_data=(X_test,
y_test), epochs=10, batch_size=30000, verbose=1)
```

Note that the only change in code is the `batch_size` parameter in the model fit process.

2. Plot the training and test accuracy and loss values over different epochs (the code to generate the following plots remains the same as the code we used in step 8 of the *Training a vanilla neural network* recipe):

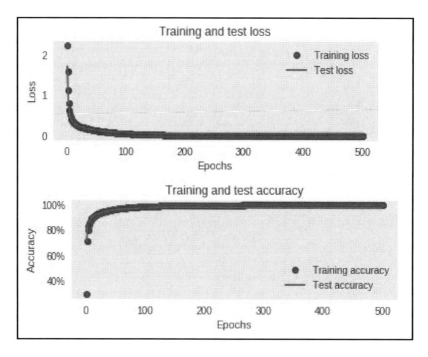

In the preceding scenario, you should notice that the model accuracy reached ~98% at a much later epoch, when compared to the model accuracy it reached when the batch size was smaller.

How it works...

You should notice that the accuracy is much lower initially and that it catches up only after a considerable number of epochs are run. The reason for a low accuracy during initial epochs is that the number of times of weight update is much lower in this scenario when compared to the previous scenario (where the batch size was smaller).

In this scenario, when the batch size is 30,000, and the total dataset size is 60,000, when we run the model for 500 epochs, the weight updates happens at epochs * (dataset size/ batch size) = 500 * (60,000/30,000) = 1,000 times.

In the previous scenario, the weight updates happens at 500 * (60,000/32) = 937,500 times.

Hence, the lower the batch size, the more times the weights get updated and, generally, the better the accuracy is for the same number of epochs.

At the same time, you should be careful not to have too few examples in the batch size, which might result in not only having a very long training time, but also a potential overfitting scenario.

Building a deep neural network to improve network accuracy

Until now, we have looked at model architectures where the neural network has only one hidden layer between the input and the output layers. In this section, we will look at the neural network where there are multiple hidden layers (and hence a deep neural network), while reusing the same MNIST training and test dataset that were scaled.

Getting ready

A deep neural network means that there are multiple hidden layers connecting the input to the output layer. Multiple hidden layers ensure that the neural network learns a complex non-linear relation between the input and output, which a simple neural network cannot learn (due to a limited number of hidden layers).

Building a Deep Feedforward Neural Network

A typical deep feedforward neural network looks as follows:

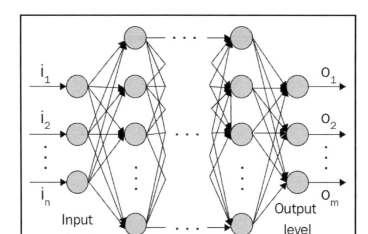

How to do it...

A deep neural network architecture is built by adding multiple hidden layers between input and output layers, as follows:

1. Load the dataset and scale it:

```
(X_train, y_train), (X_test, y_test) = mnist.load_data()
num_pixels = X_train.shape[1] * X_train.shape[2]
X_train = X_train.reshape(X_train.shape[0],
num_pixels).astype('float32')
X_test = X_test.reshape(X_test.shape[0],
num_pixels).astype('float32')
X_train = X_train/255
X_test = X_test/255
y_train = np_utils.to_categorical(y_train)
y_test = np_utils.to_categorical(y_test)
num_classes = y_test.shape[1]
```

2. Build a model with multiple hidden layers connecting the input and output layers:

```
model = Sequential()
model.add(Dense(1000, input dim=784, activation='relu'))
model.add(Dense(1000,activation='relu'))
model.add(Dense(1000,activation='relu'))
model.add(Dense(10,  activation='softmax'))
```

The preceding model architecture results in a model summary, as follows:

```
Layer (type)                 Output Shape              Param #
=================================================================
dense_3 (Dense)              (None, 1000)              785000
_____
dense_4 (Dense)              (None, 1000)              1001000
_____
dense_5 (Dense)              (None, 1000)              1001000
_____
dense_6 (Dense)              (None, 10)                10010
=================================================================
Total params: 2,797,010
Trainable params: 2,797,010
Non-trainable params: 0
```

Note that the preceding model results in a higher number of parameters, as a result of deep architectures (as there are multiple hidden layers in the model).

3. Now that the model is set up, let's compile and fit the model:

```
model.compile(loss='categorical_crossentropy', optimizer=adam, metrics=['accuracy'])
history = model.fit(X_train, y_train, validation_data=(X_test, y_test), epochs=250, batch_size=1024, verbose=1)
```

The preceding results in a model with an accuracy of 98.6%, which is slightly better than the accuracies we observed with the model architectures that we saw earlier. The training and test loss and accuracy are as follows (the code to generate the plots in the following diagram remains the same as the code we used in step 8 of the *Training a vanilla neural network* recipe):

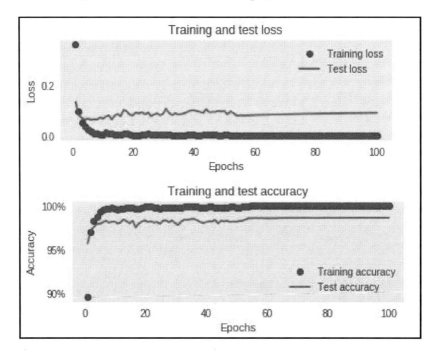

Note that, in this scenario, there is a considerable gap between training and test loss, indicating that the deep feedforward neural network specialized on training data. Again, in the sections on overfitting, we will learn about ways to avoid overfitting on training data.

Varying the learning rate to improve network accuracy

So far, in the previous recipes, we used the default learning rate of the Adam optimizer, which is 0.0001.

In this section, we will manually set the learning rate to a higher number and see the impact of changing the learning rate on model accuracy, while reusing the same MNIST training and test dataset that were scaled in the previous recipes.

Getting ready

In the previous chapter on building feedforward neural networks, we learned that the learning rate is used in updating weights and the change in weight is proportional to the amount of loss reduction.

Additionally, a change in a weight's value is equal to the decrease in loss multiplied by the learning rate. Hence, the lower the learning rate, the lower the change in the weight value, and vice versa.

You can essentially think of the weight values as a continuous spectrum where the weights are initialized randomly. When the change in the weight values is great, there is a good possibility that the various weight values in the spectrum are not considered. However, when the change in the weight value is slight, the weights might achieve a global minima, as more possible weight values could be considered.

To understand this further, let's consider the toy example of fitting the $y = 2x$ line where the initial weight value is 1.477 and the initial bias value is zero. The feedforward and back propagation functions will remain the same as we saw in the previous chapter:

```
def feed_forward(inputs, outputs, weights):
    hidden = np.dot(inputs,weights[0])
    out = hidden+weights[1]
    squared_error = (np.square(out - outputs))
    return squared_error

def update_weights(inputs, outputs, weights, epochs, lr):
    for epoch in range(epochs):
        org_loss = feed_forward(inputs, outputs, weights)
        wts_tmp = deepcopy(weights)
        wts_tmp2 = deepcopy(weights)
        for ix, wt in enumerate(weights):
            print(ix, wt)
            wts_tmp[-(ix+1)] += 0.0001
            loss = feed_forward(inputs, outputs, wts_tmp)
            del_loss = np.sum(org_loss - loss)/(0.0001*len(inputs))
            wts_tmp2[-(ix+1)] += del_loss*lr
            wts_tmp = deepcopy(weights)
        weights = deepcopy(wts_tmp2)
    return wts_tmp2
```

Building a Deep Feedforward Neural Network

Note that the only change from the backward propagation function that we saw in the previous chapter is that we are passing the learning rate as a parameter in the preceding function. The value of weight when the learning rate is 0.01 over a different number of epochs is as follows:

```
w_val = []
b_val = []
for k in range(1000):
    w_new, b_new = update_weights(x,y,w,(k+1),0.01)
    w_val.append(w_new)
    b_val.append(b_new)
```

The plot of the change in weight over different epochs can be obtained using the following code:

```
import matplotlib.pyplot as plt
%matplotlib inline
plt.plot(w_val)
plt.title('Weight value over different epochs when learning rate is 0.01')
plt.xlabel('epochs')
plt.ylabel('weight value')
plt.grid('off')
```

The output of the preceding code is as follows:

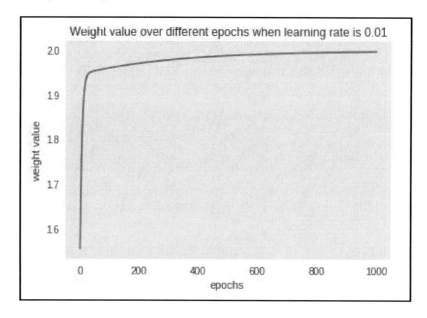

In a similar manner, the value of the weight over a different number of epochs when the learning rate is 0.1 is as follows:

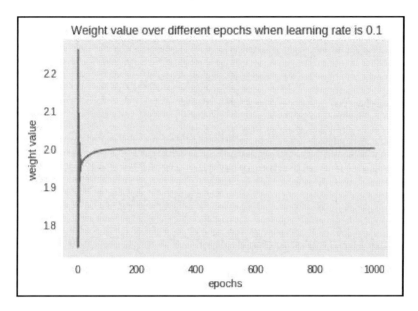

This screenshot shows the value of the weight over a different number of epochs when the learning rate is 0.5:

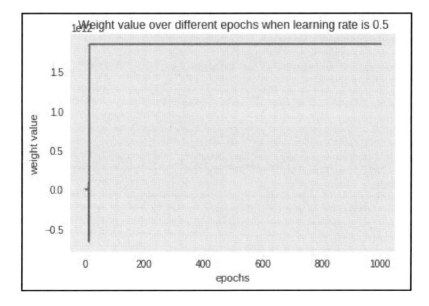

Note that, in the preceding scenario, there was a drastic change in the weight values initially, and the 0.1 learning rate converged, while the 0.5 learning rate did not converge to an optimal solution, and thus became stuck in a local minima.

In the case when the learning rate was 0.5, given the weight value was stuck in a local minima, it could not reach the optimal value of two.

How to do it...

Now that we understand how learning rate influences the output values, let's see the impact of the learning rate in action on the MNIST dataset we saw earlier, where we keep the same model architecture but will only be changing the learning rate parameter.

Note that we will be using the same data-preprocessing steps as those of step 1 and step 2 in the *Scaling input dataset* recipe.

Once we have the dataset preprocessed, we vary the learning rate of the model by specifying the optimizer in the next step:

1. We change the learning rate as follows:

```
from keras import optimizers
adam=optimizers.Adam(lr=0.01)
```

With the preceding code, we have initialized the Adam optimizer with a specified learning rate of 0.01.

2. We build, compile, and fit the model as follows:

```
model = Sequential()
model.add(Dense(1000, input_dim=784, activation='relu'))
model.add(Dense(10, activation='softmax'))
model.compile(loss='categorical_crossentropy', optimizer=adam,
metrics=['accuracy'])

history = model.fit(X_train, y_train, validation_data=(X_test,
y_test), epochs=500, batch_size=1024, verbose=1)
```

The accuracy of the preceding network is ~90% at the end of 500 epochs. Let's have a look at how loss function and accuracy vary over a different number of epochs (the code to generate the plots in the following diagram remains the same as the code we used in step 8 of the *Training a vanilla neural network* recipe):

Chapter 2

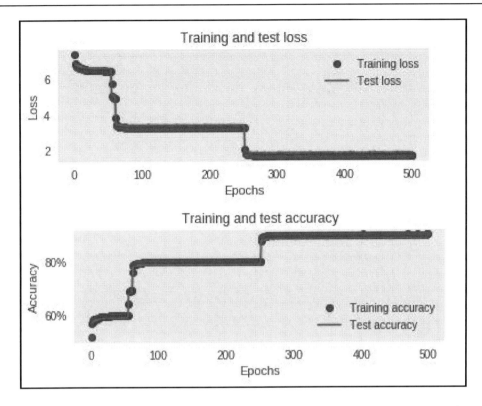

Note that when the learning rate was high (0.01 in the current scenario) compared to 0.0001 (in the scenario considered in the *Scaling input dataset* recipe), the loss decreased less smoothly when compared to the low-learning-rate model.

The low-learning-rate model updates the weights slowly, thereby resulting in a smoothly reducing loss function, as well as a high accuracy, which was achieved slowly over a higher number of epochs.

Alternatively, the step changes in loss values when the learning rate is higher are due to the loss values getting stuck in a local minima until the weight values change to optimal values. A lower learning rate gives a better possibility of arriving at the optimal weight values faster, as the weights are changed slowly, but steadily, in the right direction.

In a similar manner, let's explore the network accuracy when the learning rate is as high as 0.1:

```
from keras import optimizers
adam=optimizers.Adam(lr=0.1)

model = Sequential()
```

```
model.add(Dense(1000, input_dim=784, activation='relu'))
model.add(Dense(10,  activation='softmax'))
model.compile(loss='categorical_crossentropy', optimizer=adam,
metrics=['accuracy'])
history = model.fit(X_train, y_train, validation_data=(X_test, y_test),
epochs=500, batch_size=1024, verbose=1)
```

It is to be noted that the loss values could not decrease much further, as the learning rate was high; that is, potentially the weights got stuck in a local minima:

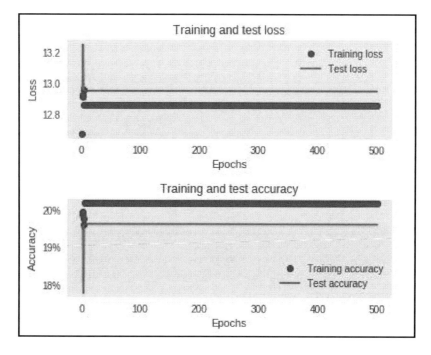

Thus, it is, in general, a good idea to set the learning rate to a low value and let the network learn over a high number of epochs.

Varying the loss optimizer to improve network accuracy

So far, in the previous recipes, we considered the loss optimizer to be the Adam optimizer. However, there are multiple other variants of optimizers, and a change in the optimizer is likely to impact the speed with which the model learns to fit the input and the output.

Chapter 2

In this recipe, we will understand the impact of changing the optimizer on model accuracy.

Getting ready

To understand the impact of varying the optimizer on network accuracy, let's contrast the scenario laid out in previous sections (which was the Adam optimizer) with using a **stochastic gradient descent optimizer** in this section, while reusing the same MNIST training and test datasets that were scaled (the same data-preprocessing steps as those of step 1 and step 2 in the *Scaling the dataset* recipe):

```
model = Sequential()
model.add(Dense(1000, input_dim=784, activation='relu'))
model.add(Dense(10, activation='softmax'))
model.compile(loss='categorical_crossentropy', optimizer='sgd',
metrics=['accuracy'])
history = model.fit(X_train, y_train, validation_data=(X_test, y_test),
epochs=100, batch_size=32, verbose=1)
```

Note that when we used the stochastic gradient descent optimizer in the preceding code, the final accuracy after 100 epochs is ~98% (the code to generate the plots in the following diagram remains the same as the code we used in step 8 of the *Training a vanilla neural network* recipe):

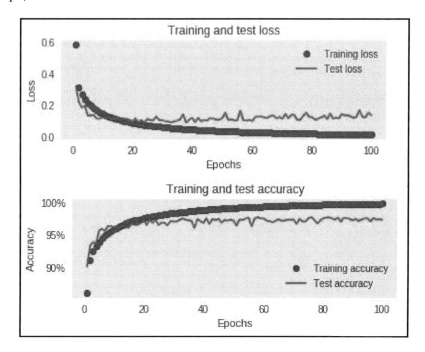

However, we should also note that the model achieved the high accuracy levels much more slowly when compared to the model that used Adam optimization.

There's more...

Some of the other loss optimizers available are as follows:

- RMSprop
- Adagrad
- Adadelta
- Adamax
- Nadam

You can learn more about the various optimizers here: `https://keras.io/optimizers/`.

Additionally, you can find the source code of each optimizer here: `https://github.com/keras-team/keras/blob/master/keras/optimizers.py`.

Understanding the scenario of overfitting

In some of the previous recipes, we have noticed that the training accuracy is ~100%, while test accuracy is ~98%, which is a case of overfitting on top of a training dataset. Let's gain an intuition of the delta between the training and the test accuracies.

To understand the phenomenon resulting in overfitting, let's contrast two scenarios where we compare the training and test accuracies along with a histogram of the weights:

- Model is run for five epochs
- Model is run for 100 epochs

The comparison-of-accuracy metric between training and test datasets between the two scenarios is as follows:

Scenario	Training dataset	Test dataset
5 epochs	97.59%	97.1%
100 epochs	100%	98.28%

Once we plot the histogram of weights that are connecting the hidden layer to the output layer, we will notice that the 100-epochs scenario has a higher spread of weights when compared to the five-epochs scenario:

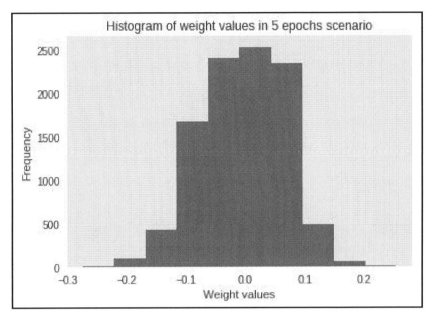

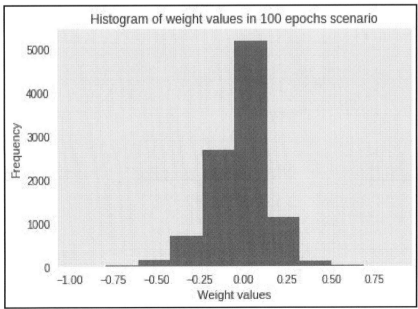

From the preceding pictures, you should note that the 100 epochs scenario had a higher dispersion of weight values when compared to the five-epochs scenario. This is because of the higher amount of opportunity that the model had to overfit on top of the training dataset when the model is run for 100-epochs, when compared to when the model is run for five epochs, as the number of weight updates in the 100-epochs scenario is higher than the number of weight updates in the five-epochs scenario.

A high value of weight (along with a difference in the training and test dataset) is a good indication of a potential over-fitting of the model and/or a potential opportunity to scale input/weights to increase the accuracy of the model.

Additionally, also note that a neural network can have hundreds of thousands of weights (and millions in certain architectures) that need to be adjusted, and thus, there is always a chance that one or the other weight can get updated to a very high number to fine-tune for one outlier row of the dataset.

Overcoming over-fitting using regularization

In the previous section, we established that a high weight magnitude is one of the reasons for over-fitting. In this section, we will look into ways to get around the problem of over-fitting, such as penalizing for high weight magnitude values.

Regularization gives a penalty for having a high magnitude of weights in model. L1 and L2 regularizations are among the most commonly used regularization techniques and work as follows:

L2 regularization minimizes the weighted sum of squares of weights at the specified layer of the neural network, in addition to minimizing the loss function (which is the sum of squared loss in the following formula):

$$Overall\ loss = \sum(y - \bar{y})^2 + \Lambda \sum w_i^2$$

Where Λ is the weightage associated with the regularization term and is a hyperparameter that needs to be tuned, y is the predicted value of $\bar{y}$, and w_i is the weight values across all the layers of the model.

L1 regularization minimizes the weighted sum of absolute values of weights at the specified layer of the neural network in addition to minimizing the loss function (which is the sum of the squared loss in the following formula):

$$Overall\ loss = \sum(y - \bar{y})^2 + \Lambda \sum |w_i|$$

This way, we ensure that weights do not get customized for extreme cases in the training dataset only (and thus, not generalizing on the test data).

How to do it

L1/L2 regularization is implemented in Keras, as follows:

```
model = Sequential()
model.add(Dense(1000,input_dim=784,activation='relu',kernel_regularizer=l2(0.1)))model.add(Dense(10,
activation='softmax',kernel_regularizer=l2(0.1)))
model.compile(loss='categorical_crossentropy', optimizer=adam,
metrics=['accuracy'])
history = model.fit(X_train, y_train, validation_data=(X_test, y_test),
epochs=500, batch_size=1024, verbose=1)
```

Note that the preceding involves invoking an additional hyperparameter—kernel_regularizer—and then specifying whether it is an L1/L2 regularization. Furthermore, we also specify the lambda value that gives the weight to regularization.

We notice that, post regularization, the training dataset accuracy does not happen to be at ~100%, while the test data accuracy is at 98%. The histogram of weights post-L2 regularization is visualized in the next graph.

The weights of connecting the hidden layer to the output layer are extracted as follows:

```
model.get_weights()[0].flatten()
```

Once the weights are extracted, they are plotted as follows:

```
plt.hist(model.get_weights()[0].flatten())
```

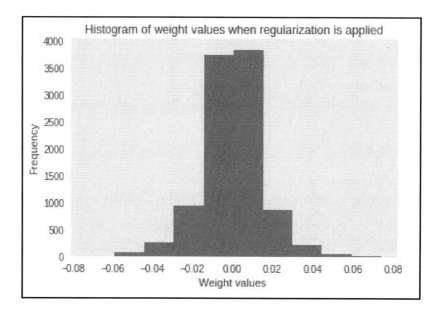

We notice that the majority of weights are now much closer to zero when compared to the previous scenario, thus presenting a case to avoid the overfitting issue. We would see a similar trend in the case of L1 regularization.

Notice that the weight values when regularization exists are much lower when compared to the weight values when regularization is performed.

Thus, the L1 and L2 regularizations help us to avoid the overfitting issue on top of the training dataset.

Overcoming overfitting using dropout

In the previous section of overcoming overfitting using regularization, we used L1/L2 regularization as a means to avoid overfitting. In this section, we will use another tool that is helpful to achieve the same—**dropout**.

Dropout can be considered a way in which only a certain percentage of weights get updated, while the others do not get updated in a given iteration of weight updates. This way, we are in a position where not all weights get updated in a weight update process, thus avoiding certain weights to achieve a very high magnitude when compared to others:

```
model = Sequential()
model.add(Dense(1000, input_dim=784, activation='relu'))
model.add(Dropout(0.75))
model.add(Dense(10, activation='softmax'))
model.compile(loss='categorical_crossentropy', optimizer=adam,
metrics=['accuracy'])
history = model.fit(X_train, y_train, validation_data=(X_test, y_test),
epochs=100, batch_size=1024, verbose=1)
```

In the preceding code, we have given a dropout of 0.75; that is, randomly, 75% of weights do not get updated in a certain weight update iteration.

The preceding would result in the gap between the training and test accuracy being not as high as it is when the model was built without dropout in the previous scenario, where the spread of weights was higher.

Note the histogram of weights of the first layer now:

```
plt.hist(model.get_weights()[-2].flatten())
```

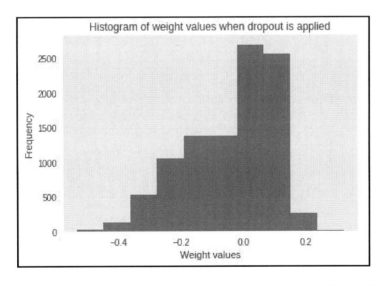

Note that in the preceding scenario, the frequency count of weights that are beyond 0.2 or -0.2 is less when compared to the 100-epochs scenario.

Speeding up the training process using batch normalization

In the previous section on the scaling dataset, we learned that optimization is slow when the input data is not scaled (that is, it is not between zero and one).

The hidden layer value could be high in the following scenarios:

- Input data values are high
- Weight values are high
- The multiplication of weight and input are high

Any of these scenarios can result in a large output value on the hidden layer.

Note that the hidden layer is the input layer to output layer. Hence, the phenomenon of high input values resulting in a slow optimization holds true when hidden layer values are large as well.

Batch normalization comes to the rescue in this scenario. We have already learned that, when input values are high, we perform scaling to reduce the input values. Additionally, we have learned that scaling can also be performed using a different method, which is to subtract the mean of the input and divide it by the standard deviation of the input. Batch normalization performs this method of scaling.

Typically, all values are scaled using the following formula:

$$\mu_B = \frac{1}{m} \sum_{i=1}^{m} x_i \quad \text{Batch mean}$$

$$\sigma_B^2 = \frac{1}{m} \sum_{i=1}^{m} (x_i - \mu_B)^2 \quad \text{Batch Variance}$$

$$\bar{x}_i = \frac{x_i - \mu_B}{\sqrt{\sigma_B^2 + \epsilon}}$$

$$y_i = \gamma \bar{x}_i + \beta$$

Notice that γ and β are learned during training, along with the original parameters of the network.

How to do it...

In code, batch normalization is applied as follows:

Note that we will be using the same data-preprocessing steps as those we used in step 1 and step 2 in the *Scaling the input dataset* recipe.

1. Import the `BatchNormalization` method as follows:

   ```
   from keras.layers.normalization import BatchNormalization
   ```

2. Instantiate a model and build the same architecture as we built when using the regularization technique. The only addition is that we perform batch normalization in a hidden layer:

   ```
   model = Sequential()
   model.add(Dense(1000, input_dim=784,activation='relu',
   kernel_regularizer = l2(0.01)))
   model.add(BatchNormalization())
   model.add(Dense(10, activation='softmax', kernel_regularizer =
   l2(0.01)))
   ```

3. Build, compile, and fit the model as follows:

   ```
   from keras.optimizers import Adam
   model.compile(loss='categorical_crossentropy', optimizer='adam',
   metrics=['accuracy'])
   history = model.fit(X_train, y_train, validation_data=(X_test,
   y_test), epochs=100, batch_size=1024, verbose=1)
   ```

The preceding results in training that is much faster than when there is no batch normalization, as follows:

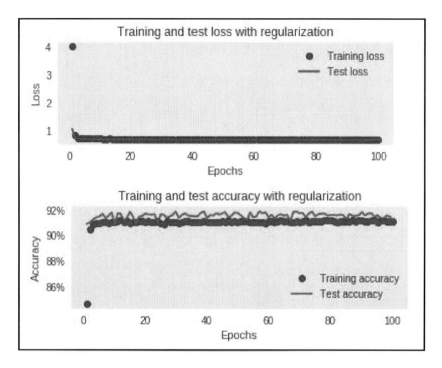

The previous graphs show the training and test loss and accuracy when there is no batch normalization, but only regularization. The following graphs show the training and test loss and accuracy with both regularization and batch normalization:

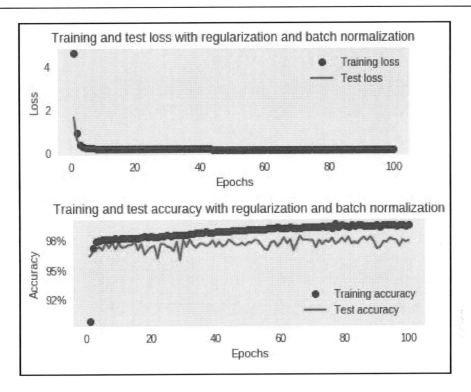

Note that, in the preceding two scenarios, we see much faster training when we perform batch normalization (test dataset accuracy of ~97%) than compared to when we don't (test dataset accuracy of ~91%).

Thus, batch normalization results in much quicker training.

3
Applications of Deep Feedforward Neural Networks

In this chapter, we will be covering the following recipes:

- Predicting credit default
- Predicting house prices
- Categorizing news articles into topics
- Classifying common audio
- Predicting stock prices

Introduction

In the previous chapters, we learned about building a neural network and the various parameters that need to be tweaked to ensure that the model built generalizes well. Additionally, we learned about how neural networks can be leveraged to perform image analysis using MNIST data.

In this chapter, we will learn how neural networks can be used for prediction on top of the following:

- Structured dataset
    - Categorical output prediction
    - Continuous output prediction

- Text analysis
- Audio analysis

Additionally, we will also be learning about the following:

- Implementing a custom loss function
- Assigning higher weights for certain classes of output over others
- Assigning higher weights for certain rows of a dataset over others
- Leveraging a functional API to integrate multiple sources of data

We will learn about all the preceding by going through the following recipes:

- Predicting a credit default
- Predicting house prices
- Categorizing news articles
- Predicting stock prices
- Classifying common audio

However, you should note that these applications are provided only for you to understand how neural networks can be leveraged to analyze a variety of input data. Advanced ways of analyzing text, audio, and time-series data will be provided in later chapters about the Convolutional Neural Network and the Recurrent Neural Network.

Predicting credit default

In the financial services industry, one of the major sources of losing out on revenues is the default of certain customers. However, a very small percentage of the total customers default. Hence, this becomes a problem of classification and, more importantly, identifying rare events.

In this case study, we will analyze a dataset that tracks certain key attributes of a customer at a given point in time and tries to predict whether the customer is likely to default.

Let's consider the way in which you might operationalize the predictions from the model we build. Businesses might want to have a special focus on the customers who are more likely to default—potentially giving them alternative payment options or a way to reduce the credit limit, and so on.

Getting ready

The strategy that we'll adopt to predict default of a customer is as follows:

- **Objective**: Assign a high probability to the customers who are more likely to default.
- **Measurement criterion**: Maximize the number of customers who have actually defaulted when we consider only the top 10% of members by decreasing the default probability.

The strategy we will be adopting to assign a probability of default for each member will be as follows:

- Consider the historic data of all members.
- Understand the variables that can help us to identify a customer who is likely to default:
    - Income-to-debt ratio is a very good indicator of whether a member is likely to default.
    - We will be extracting a few other variables similar to that.
- In the previous step, we created the input variables; now, let's go ahead and create the dependent variable:
    - We will extract the members who have actually defaulted in the next 2 years by first going back in history and then looking at whether members defaulted in the next 2 years
    - It is important to have a time lag, as it might not give us any levers to change the outcome if we do not have a time gap between when a member is likely to default and the date of prediction.
- Given that the outcome is binary, we will minimize the binary cross-entropy loss.
- The model shall have a hidden layer that connects the input layer and the output layer.
- We shall calculate the number of the top 10% probability members who have actually defaulted, in the test dataset.

Note that we assume that test data is representative here, as we are not in a position to assess the performance of a model on unseen dataset without productionalizing the model. We shall assume that the model's performance on an unseen dataset is a good indicator of how well the model will perform on future data.

How to do it...

We'll code up the strategy as follows (Please refer to the `Credit default prediction.ipynb` file in GitHub while implementing the code):

1. Import the relevant packages and the dataset:

   ```
   import pandas as pd
   data = pd.read_csv('...') # Please add path to the file you downloaded
   ```

   The first three rows of the dataset we downloaded are as follows:

Defaultin2yrs	Age	Debt_income_ratio	Income
0	23	0.4	40000
1	57	2	30000
0	35	0.6	100000

   The preceding screenshot is a subset of variables in the original dataset. The variable named `Defaultin2yrs` is the output variable that we need to predict, based on the rest of the variables present in the dataset.

2. Summarize the dataset to understand the variables better:

   ```
   data.describe()
   ```

   Once you look at the output you will notice the following:

- Certain variables have a small range (`age`), while others have a much bigger range (`Income`).
- Certain variables have missing values (`Income`).
- Certain variables have outlier values (`Debt_income_ratio`). In the next steps, we will go ahead and correct all the issues flagged previously.
- Impute missing values in a variable with the variable's median value:

   ```
   vars = data.columns[1:]
   import numpy as np
   for var in vars:
       data[var]= np.where(data[var].isnull(),data[var].median(),data[var])
   ```

In the preceding code, we excluded the first variable, as it is the variable that we are trying to predict, and then we imputed the missing values in the rest of the variables (provided the variable does have a missing value).

3. Cap each variable to its corresponding 95th percentile value so that we do not have outliers in our input variables:

```
for var in vars:
    x=data[var].quantile(0.95)
    data[var+"outlier_flag"]=np.where(data[var]>x,1,0)
    data[var]=np.where(data[var]>x,x,data[var])
```

In the preceding code, we have identified the 95th percentile value of each variable, created a new variable that has a value of one if the row contains an outlier in the given variable, and zero otherwise. Additionally, we have capped the variable values to the 95th percentile value of the original value.

4. Once we summarize the modified data, we notice that except for the Debt_income_ratio variable every other variable does not seem to have outliers anymore. Hence, let's constrain Debt_income_ratio further to have a limited range of output, by capping it at the 80th percentile value:

```
data['Debt_income_ratio_outlier']=np.where(data['Debt_incomerat
io']>1,1,0)
data['Debt_income_ratio']=np.where(data['Debt_income_ratio']>1,
1,data['Debt_income_ratio'])
```

5. Normalize all variables to the same scale for a value between zero and one:

```
for var in vars:
    data[var]= data[var]/data[var].max()
```

In the preceding code, we are limiting all the variables to a similar range of output, which is between zero and one, by dividing each input variable value with the input variable column's maximum value.

6. Create the input and the output dataset:

```
X = data.iloc[:,1:]
Y = data['Defaultin2yrs']
```

7. Split the datasets into train and test datasets:

```
from sklearn.model_selection import train_test_split
X_train, X_test, y_train, y_test = train_test_split(X, Y,
test_size = 0.3, random_state= 42)
```

[83]

In the preceding step, we use the `train_test_split` method to split the input and output arrays into train and test datasets where the test dataset has 30% of the total number of data points in the input and the corresponding output arrays.

8. Now that the datasets are created, let's define the neural network model, as follows:

```
from keras.models import Sequential
from keras.layers import Dense
from keras.layers import Dropout
from keras.utils import np_utils
model = Sequential()
model.add(Dense(1000, input_dim=X_train.shape[1],
activation='relu'))
model.add(Dense(1, activation='sigmoid'))
model.summary()
```

A summary of the model is as follows:

```
Layer (type)                 Output Shape              Param #
=================================================================
dense_5 (Dense)              (None, 1000)              22000
_____
dense_6 (Dense)              (None, 1)                 1001
=================================================================
Total params: 23,001
Trainable params: 23,001
Non-trainable params: 0
```

In the previous architecture, we connect the input variables to a hidden layer that has 1,000 hidden units.

9. Compile the model. We shall employ binary cross entropy, as the output variable has only two classes. Additionally, we will specify that `optimizer` is an `adam` optimization:

```
model.compile(loss='binary_crossentropy', optimizer='adam',
metrics=['accuracy'])
```

10. Fit the model:

```
history = model.fit(X_train, y_train, validation_data=(X_test,
y_test), epochs=20, batch_size=1024, verbose=1)
```

The variation of training and test loss, accuracy over increasing epochs is as follows:

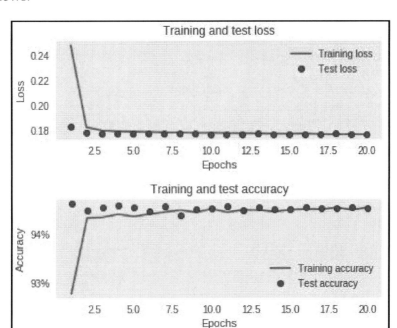

11. Make predictions on the test dataset:

    ```
    pred = model.predict(X_test)
    ```

12. Check for the number of actual defaulters that are captured in the top 10% of the test dataset when ranked in order of decreasing probability:

    ```
    test_data = pd.DataFrame([y_test]).T
    test_data['pred']=pred
    test_data = test_data.reset_index(drop='index')
    test_data = test_data.sort_values(by='pred',ascending=False)
    print(test_data[:4500]['Defaultin2yrs'].sum())
    ```

In the preceding code, we concatenated the predicted values with actual values and then sorted the dataset by probability. We checked the actual number of defaulters that are captured in the top 10% of the test dataset (which is the first 4,500 rows).

We should note that there are 1,580 actual defaulters that we have captured by going through the 4,500 high-probability customers. This is a good prediction, as on average only 6% of the total customers default. Hence, in this case, ~35% of customers who have a high probability of default actually defaulted.

How it works...

In this recipe, we have learned about the following concepts:

- **Imputing missing values**: We have learned that one of the ways to impute the missing values of a variable is by replacing the missing values with the median of the corresponding variable. Other ways to deal with the missing values is by replacing them with the mean value, and also by replacing the missing value with the mean of the variable's value in the rows that are most similar to the row that contains a missing value (this technique is called i**dentifying the K-Nearest Neighbours**).
- **Capping the outlier values**: We have also learned that one way to cap the outliers is by replacing values that are above the 95th percentile value with the 95th percentile value. The reason we performed this exercise is to ensure that the input variable does not have all the values clustered around a small value (when the variable is scaled by the maximum value, which is an outlier).
- **Scaling dataset**: Finally, we scaled the dataset so that it can then be passed to a neural network.

Assigning weights for classes

When we assign equal weightage to the rows that belong to a defaulter and the rows that belong to a non-defaulter, potentially the model can fine-tune for the non-defaulters. In this section, we will look into ways of assigning a higher weightage so that our model classifies defaulters better.

Getting ready

In the previous section, we assigned the same weightage for each class; that is, the categorical cross entropy loss is the same if the magnitude of difference between actual and predicted is the same, irrespective of whether it is for the prediction of a default or not a default.

To understand the scenario further, let's consider the following example:

Scenario	Probability of default	Actual value of default	Cross entropy loss
1	0.2	1	1*log(0.2)
2	0.8	0	(1-0)*log(1-0.8)

In the preceding scenario, the cross-entropy loss value is just the same, irrespective of the actual value of default.

However, we know that our objective is to capture as many actual defaulters as possible in the top 10% of predictions when ranked by probability.

Hence, let's go ahead and assign a higher weight of loss (a weight of *100*) when the actual value of default is *1* and a lower weightage (a weight of *1*) when the actual value of default is *0*.

The previous scenario now changes as follows:

Scenario	Probability of default	Actual value of default	Cross entropy loss
1	0.2	1	100*1*log(0.2)
2	0.8	0	1*(1-0)*log(1-0.8)

Now, if we notice the cross entropy loss, it is much higher when the predictions are wrong when the actual value of default is *1* compared to the predictions when the actual value of default is *0*.

Now that we have understood the intuition of assigning weightages to classes, let's go ahead and assign weights to output classes in the credit default dataset.

All the steps performed to build the dataset and model remain the same as in the previous section, except for the model-fitting process.

How to do it...

The model fitting process is done by following these steps (Please refer to `Credit default prediction.ipynb` file in GitHub while implementing the code):

```
history = model.fit(X_train, y_train, validation_data=(X_test, y_test), epochs=10, batch_size=1024, verbose=1, class_weight = {0:1,1:100})
```

Note that, in the preceding code snippet, we created a dictionary with the weights that correspond to the distinct classes in output that is then passed as an input to the `class_weight` parameter.

The preceding step ensures that we assign a weightage of `100` to calculating the loss value when the actual outcome is `1` and a weightage of `1` when calculating the loss value when the actual outcome is `0`.

The variation of accuracy and loss values over increasing epochs is as follows:

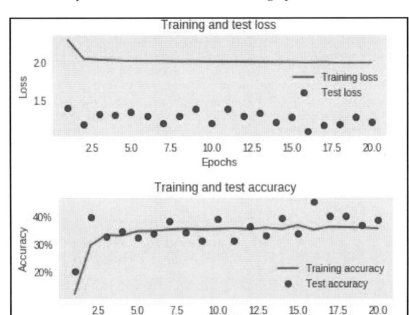

Note that the accuracy values are much lower in this iteration, as we are predicting more number of data points to have a value 1 than in the scenario of equal weightage to both classes.

Once the model is fitted, let's proceed and check for the number of actual defaulters that are captured in the top 10% of predictions, as follows:

```
pred = model.predict(X_test)
test_data = pd.DataFrame([y_test[:,1]]).T
test_data['pred']=pred[:,1]
test_data = test_data.reset_index(drop='index')
test_data = test_data.sort_values(by='pred',ascending=False)
test_data.columns = ['Defaultin2yrs','pred']
print(test_data[:4500]['Defaultin2yrs'].sum())
```

You notice that compared to the previous scenario of 1,580 customers being captured in the the top 10%, we have 1,640 customers captured in the top 10% in this scenario, and thus a better outcome for the objective we have set where we have captured 36% of all defaulters in top 10% of high probable customers in this scenario, when compared to 35% in the previous scenario.

It is not always necessary that accuracy improves as we increase class weights. Assigning class weights is a mechanism to give higher weightage to the prediction of our interest.

Predicting house prices

In the previous case study, we had an output that was categorical. In this case study, we shall look into an output that is continuous in nature, by trying to predict the price of a house where 13 variables that are likely to impact the house price are provided as input.

The objective is to minimize the error by which we predict the price of a house.

Getting ready

Given that the objective is to minimize error, let's define the error that we shall be minimizing—we should ensure that a positive error and a negative error do not cancel out each other. Hence, we shall minimize the absolute error. An alternative of this is to minimize the squared error.

Now that we have fine-tuned our objective, let's define our strategy of solving this problem:

- Normalize the input dataset so that all variables range between zero to one.
- Split the given data to train and test datasets.
- Initialize the hidden layer that connects the input of 13 variables to the output of one variable.
- Compile the model with the Adam optimizer, and define the loss function to minimize as the mean absolute error value.
- Fit the model.
- Make a prediction on the test dataset.
- Calculate the error in the prediction on the test dataset.

Now that we have defined our approach, let's go ahead and perform it in code in the next section.

How to do it...

1. Import the relevant dataset (Please refer to the `Predicting house price.ipynb` file in GitHub while implementing the code and for the recommended dataset):

   ```
   from keras.datasets import boston_housing
   (train_data, train_targets), (test_data, test_targets) = boston_housing.load_data()
   ```

2. Normalize the input and output dataset so that all variables have a range from zero to one:

   ```
   import numpy as np
   train_data2 = train_data/np.max(train_data,axis=0)
   test_data2 = test_data/np.max(train_data,axis=0)
   train_targets = train_targets/np.max(train_targets)
   test_targets = test_targets/np.max(train_targets)
   ```

   Note that we have normalized the test dataset with the maximum value in the train dataset itself, as we should not be using any of the values from the test dataset in the model-building process. Additionally, note that we have normalized both the input and the output values.

3. Now that the input and output datasets are prepared, let's proceed and define the model:

   ```
   from keras.models import Sequential
   from keras.layers import Dense, Dropout
   from keras.utils import np_utils
   from keras.regularizers import l1
   model = Sequential()
   model.add(Dense(64, input_dim=13, activation='relu', kernel_regularizer = l1(0.1)))
   model.add(Dense(1, activation='relu', kernel_regularizer = l1(0.1)))
   model.summary()
   ```

A summary of the model is as follows:

```
Layer (type)                  Output Shape              Param #
=================================================================
dense_7 (Dense)               (None, 64)                896
_____
dense_8 (Dense)               (None, 1)                 65
=================================================================
Total params: 961
Trainable params: 961
Non-trainable params: 0
```

Note that we performed `L1` regularization in the model-building process so that the model does not overfit on the training data (as the number of data points in the training data is small).

4. Compile the model to minimize the mean absolute error value:

   ```
   model.compile(loss='mean_absolute_error', optimizer='adam')
   ```

5. Fit the model:

   ```
   history = model.fit(train_data2, train_targets,
   validation_data=(test_data2, test_targets), epochs=100,
   batch_size=32, verbose=1)
   ```

6. Calculate the mean absolute error on the test dataset:

   ```
   np.mean(np.abs(model.predict(test_data2) - test_targets))*50
   ```

We should note that the mean absolute error is ~6.7 units.

In the next section, we will vary the loss function and add custom weights to see whether we can improve upon the mean absolute error values.

Defining the custom loss function

In the previous section, we used the predefined mean absolute error `loss` function to perform the optimization. In this section, we will learn about defining a custom loss function to perform optimization.

The custom loss function that we shall build is a modified mean squared error value, where the error is the difference between the square root of the actual value and the square root of the predicted value.

The custom loss function is defined as follows:

```
import keras.backend as K
def loss_function(y_true, y_pred):
    return K.square(K.sqrt(y_pred)-K.sqrt(y_true))
```

Now that we have defined the `loss` function, we will be reusing the same input and output datasets that we prepared in previous section, and we will also be using the same model that we defined earlier.

Now, let's compile the model:

```
model.compile(loss=loss_function, optimizer='adam')
```

In the preceding code, note that we defined the `loss` value as the custom loss function that we defined earlier—`loss_function`.

```
history = model.fit(train_data2, train_targets,
validation_data=(test_data2, test_targets), epochs=100, batch_size=32,
verbose=1)
```

Once we fit the model, we will note that the mean absolute error is ~6.5 units, which is slightly less than the previous iteration where we used the `mean_absolute_error` loss function.

Categorizing news articles into topics

In the previous case studies, we analyzed datasets that were structured, that is, contained variables and their corresponding values. In this case study, we will be working on a dataset that has text as input, and the expected output is one of the 46 possible topics that the text is related to.

Getting ready

To understand the intuition of performing text analysis, let's consider the Reuters dataset, where each news article is classified into one of the 46 possible topics.

We will adopt the following strategy to perform our analysis:

- Given that a dataset could contain thousands of unique words, we will shortlist the words that we shall consider.
- For this specific exercise, we shall consider the top 10,000 most frequent words.

- An alternative approach would be to consider the words that cumulatively constitute 80% of all words within a dataset. This ensures that all the rare words are excluded.
- Once the words are shortlisted, we shall one-hot-encode the article based on the constituent frequent words.
- Similarly, we shall one-hot-encode the output label.
- Each input now is a 10,000-dimensional vector, and the output is a 46-dimensional vector:
- We will divide the dataset into train and test datasets. However, in code, you will notice that we will be using the in-built dataset of `reuters` in Keras that has built-in function to identify the top n frequent words and split the dataset into train and test datasets.
- Map the input and output with a hidden layer in between.
- We will perform softmax at the output layer to obtain the probability of the input belonging to one of the 46 classes.
- Given that we have multiple possible outputs, we shall employ a categorical cross entropy loss function.
- We shall compile and fit the model to measure its accuracy on a test dataset.

How to do it...

We'll code up the strategy defined previously as follows (please refer to the `Categorizing news articles into topics.ipynb` file in GitHub while implementing the code):

1. Import the dataset :

    ```
    from keras.datasets import reuters
    (train_data, train_labels), (test_data, test_labels) = reuters.load_data(num_words=10000)
    ```

    In the preceding code snippet, we loaded data from the `reuters` dataset that is available in Keras. Additionally, we consider only the `10000` most frequent words in the dataset.

2. Inspect the dataset:

    ```
    train_data[0]
    ```

A sample of the loaded training dataset is as follows:

```
[1,
2,
2,
8,
43,
10,
447,
```

Note that the numbers in the preceding output represent the index of words that are present in the output.

3. We can extract the index of values as follows:

   ```
   word_index = reuters.get_word_index()
   ```

4. Vectorize the input. We will convert the text into a vector in the following way:
   - One-hot-encode the input words—resulting in a total of 10000 columns in the input dataset.
   - If a word is present in the given text, the column corresponding to the word index shall have a value of one and every other column shall have a value of zero.
   - Repeat the preceding step for all the unique words in a text. If a text has two unique words, there will be a total of two columns that have a value of one, and every other column will have a value of zero:

   ```
   import numpy as np
   def vectorize_sequences(sequences, dimension=10000):
       results = np.zeros((len(sequences), dimension))
       for i, sequence in enumerate(sequences):
           results[i, sequence] = 1.
       return results
   ```

In the preceding function, we initialized a variable that is a zero matrix and imputed it with a value of one, based on the index values present in the input sequence.

In the following code, we are converting the words into IDs.

```
x_train = vectorize_sequences(train_data)
x_test = vectorize_sequences(test_data)
```

5. One-hot-encode the output:

   ```
   from keras.utils.np_utils import to_categorical
   one_hot_train_labels = to_categorical(train_labels)
   one_hot_test_labels = to_categorical(test_labels)
   ```

   The preceding code converts each output label into a vector that is 46 in length, where one of the 46 values is one and the rest are zero, depending on the label's index value.

6. Define the model and compile it:

   ```
   from keras.models import Sequential
   from keras.layers import Dense
   model = Sequential()
   model.add(Dense(64, activation='relu', input_shape=(10000,)))
   model.add(Dense(64, activation='relu'))
   model.add(Dense(46, activation='softmax'))
   model.summary()
   model.compile(optimizer='adam',loss='categorical_crossentropy',metrics=['accuracy'])
   ```

Layer (type)	Output Shape	Param #
dense_1 (Dense)	(None, 64)	640064
dense_2 (Dense)	(None, 64)	4160
dense_3 (Dense)	(None, 46)	2990

   Total params: 647,214
   Trainable params: 647,214
   Non-trainable params: 0

   Note that while compiling, we defined `loss` as `categorical_crossentropy` as the output in this case is categorical (multiple classes in output).

7. Fit the model:

   ```
   history = model.fit(X_train,
   y_train,epochs=20,batch_size=512,validation_data=(X_test, y_test))
   ```

The preceding code results in a model that has 80% accuracy in classifying the input text into the right topic, as follows:

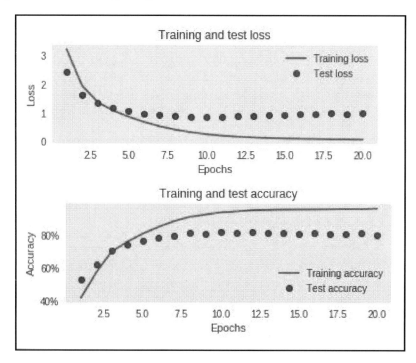

Classifying common audio

In the previous sections, we have understood the strategy to perform modeling on a structured dataset and also on unstructured text data.

In this section, we will be learning about performing a classification exercise where the input is raw audio.

The strategy we will be adopting is that we will be extracting features from the input audio, where each audio signal is represented as a vector of a fixed number of features.

There are multiple ways of extracting features from an audio—however, for this exercise, we will be extracting the **Mel Frequency Cepstral Coefficients** (**MFCC**) corresponding to the audio file.

Once we extract the features, we shall perform the classification exercise in a way that is very similar to how we built a model for MNIST dataset classification—where we had hidden layers connecting the input and output layers.

In the following section, we will be performing classification on top of an audio dataset where there are ten possible classes of output.

How to do it...

The strategy that we defined previously is coded as follows (Please refer to the `Audio classification.ipynb` file in GitHub while implementing the code):

1. Import the dataset:

    ```
    import pandas as pd
    data = pd.read_csv('/content/train.csv')
    ```

2. Extract features for each audio input:

    ```
    ids = data['ID'].values
    def extract_feature(file_name):
        X, sample_rate = librosa.load(file_name)
        stft = np.abs(librosa.stft(X))
        mfccs = np.mean(librosa.feature.mfcc(y=X,sr=sample_rate,
    n_mfcc=40).T,axis=0)
        return mfccs
    ```

    In the preceding code, we defined a function that takes `file_name` as input, extracts the 40 MFCC corresponding to the audio file, and returns the same.

3. Create the input and the output dataset:

    ```
    x = []
    y = []
    for i in range(len(ids)):
        try:
            filename = '/content/Train/'+str(ids[i])+'.wav'
            y.append(data[data['ID']==ids[i]]['Class'].values)
            x.append(extract_feature(filename))
        except:
            continue
    x = np.array(x)
    ```

Applications of Deep Feedforward Neural Networks

In the preceding code, we loop through one audio file at a time, extracting its features and storing it in the input list. Similarly, we will be storing the output class in the output list. Additionally, we will convert the output list into a categorical value that is one-hot-encoded:

```
y2 = []
for i in range(len(y)):
    y2.append(y[i][0])
y3 = np.array(pd.get_dummies(y2))
```

The `pd.get_dummies` method works very similar to the `to_categorical` method we used earlier; however, `to_categorical` does not work on text classes (it works on numeric values only, which get converted to one-hot-encoded values).

4. Build the model and compile it:

```
model = Sequential()
model.add(Dense(1000, input_shape = (40,), activation = 'relu'))
model.add(Dense(10,activation='sigmoid'))
from keras.optimizers import Adam
adam = Adam(lr=0.0001)
model.compile(optimizer=adam, loss='categorical_crossentropy', metrics=['acc'])
```

The summary of the preceding model is as follows:

```
Layer (type)                  Output Shape              Param #
=================================================================
dense_1 (Dense)               (None, 1000)              41000
_____
dense_2 (Dense)               (None, 10)                10010
=================================================================
Total params: 51,010
Trainable params: 51,010
Non-trainable params: 0
```

5. Create the train and test datasets and then fit the model:

```
from sklearn.model_selection import train_test_split
X_train, X_test, y_train, y_test = train_test_split(x, y3, test_size=0.30, random_state=10)
model.fit(X_train, y_train, epochs=100, batch_size=32, validation_data=(X_test, y_test), verbose = 1)
```

Chapter 3

Once the model is fitted, you will notice that the model has 91% accuracy in classifying audio in the right class.

Stock price prediction

In the previous sections, we learned about performing audio, text, and structured data analysis using neural networks. In this section, we will learn about performing a time-series analysis using a case study of predicting a stock price.

Getting ready

To predict a stock price, we will perform the following steps:

1. Order the dataset from the oldest to the newest date.
2. Take the first five stock prices as input and the sixth stock price as output.
3. Slide it across so that in the next data point the second to the sixth data points are input and the seventh data point is the output, and so on, till we reach the final data point.
4. Given that it is a continuous number that we are predicting, the `loss` function this time shall be the mean squared error value.

Additionally, we will also try out the scenario where we integrate the text data into the historic numeric data to predict the next day's stock price.

How to do it...

The above strategy is coded as follows (please refer to `Chapter 3 - stock price prediction.ipynb` file in GitHub while implementing the code and for the recommended dataset):

1. Import the relevant packages and the dataset:

    ```
    import pandas as pd
    data2 = pd.read_csv('/content/stock_data.csv')
    ```

2. Prepare the dataset where the input is the previous five days' stock price value and the output is the stock price value on the sixth day:

    ```
    x= []
    ```

Applications of Deep Feedforward Neural Networks

```
y = []
for i in range(data2.shape[0]-5):
 x.append(data2.loc[i:(i+4)]['Close'].values)
 y.append(data2.loc[i+5]['Close'])
import numpy as np
x = np.array(x)
y = np.array(y)
```

3. Prepare the train and test datasets, build the model, compile it, and fit it:

```
from sklearn.model_selection import train_test_split
X_train, X_test, y_train, y_test = train_test_split(x, y,
test_size=0.30,random_state=10)
```

Build the model and compile it:

```
from keras.layers import Dense
from keras.models import Sequential, Model
model = Sequential()
model.add(Dense(100, input_dim = 5, activation = 'relu'))
model.add(Dense(1,activation='linear'))
model.compile(optimizer='adam', loss='mean_squared_error')
```

The previous code results in a summary of model as follows:

```
Layer (type)                 Output Shape              Param #
=================================================================
dense_1 (Dense)              (None, 100)               600
_____
dense_2 (Dense)              (None, 1)                 101
=================================================================
Total params: 701
Trainable params: 701
Non-trainable params: 0
```

```
model.fit(X_train, y_train, epochs=100, batch_size=64,
validation_data=(X_test, y_test), verbose = 1)
```

Once we fit the model, we should note that the mean squared error value ~$360 in predicting the stock price or ~$18 in predicting the stock price.

Note that there is a pitfall in predicting a stock price this way. However, that will be dealt with in the chapter on RNN applications.

For now, we will focus on learning how neural networks can be useful in a variety of different scenarios.

In the next section, we will understand the ways in which we can integrate the numeric data with the text data of news headlines in a single model.

Leveraging a functional API

In this section, we will continue to improve the accuracy of the stock price prediction by integrating historical price points data with the most-recent headlines of the company for which we are predicting the stock price.

The strategy that we will adopt to integrate data from multiple sources—structured (historical price) data and unstructured (headline) data is as follows:

- We will convert the unstructured text into a structured format in a manner that is similar to the way we categorized news articles into topics.
- We will pass the structured format of text through a neural network and extract the hidden layer output.
- Finally, we pass the hidden layer output to the output layer, where the output layer has one node.
- In a similar manner, we pass the input historical price data through the neural network to extract the hidden layer values, which then get passed to the output layer that has one unit in output.
- We multiply the output of each of the individual neural network operations to extract the final output.
- The squared error value of the final output shall now be minimized.

How to do it...

The previous strategy is coded as follows:

1. Let's fetch the headline data from the API provided by the Guardian, as follows:

```
from bs4 import BeautifulSoup
import urllib, json

dates = []
titles = []
for i in range(100):
    try:
        url =
'https://content.guardianapis.com/search?from-date=2010-01-01&s
```

```
ection=business&page-size=200&order-
by=newest&page='+str(i+1)+'&q=amazon&api-key=207b6047-
a2a6-4dd2-813b-5cd006b780d7'
        response = urllib.request.urlopen(url)
        encoding = response.info().get_content_charset('utf8')
        data = json.loads(response.read().decode(encoding))
    for j in range(len(data['response']['results'])):
dates.append(data['response']['results'][j]['webPublicationDate
'])
titles.append(data['response']['results'][j]['webTitle'])
    except:
        break
```

2. Once `titles` and `dates` are extracted, we shall preprocess the data to convert the `date` values to a `date` format, as follows:

```
import pandas as pd
data = pd.DataFrame(dates, titles)
data['date']=data['date'].str[:10]
data['date']=pd.to_datetime(data['date'], format = '%Y-%m-%d')
data = data.sort_values(by='date')
data_final = data.groupby('date').first().reset_index()
```

3. Now that we have the most recent headline for every date on which we are trying to predict the stock price, we will integrate the two data sources, as follows:

```
data2['Date'] = pd.to_datetime(data2['Date'],format='%Y-%m-%d')
data3 = pd.merge(data2,data_final, left_on = 'Date', right_on =
'date', how='left')
```

4. Once the datasets are merged, we will go ahead and normalize the text data so that we remove the following:
    - Convert all words in a text into lowercase so that the words like `Text` and `text` are treated the same.
    - Remove punctuation so that words such as `text.` and `text` are treated the same.
    - Remove stop words such as `a`, `and`, `the`, which do not add much context to the text:

```
import nltk
import re
nltk.download('stopwords')
stop = nltk.corpus.stopwords.words('english')
def preprocess(text):
    text = str(text)
```

```
            text=text.lower()
            text=re.sub('[^0-9a-zA-Z]+',' ',text)
            words = text.split()
            words2=[w for w in words if (w not in stop)]
            words4=' '.join(words2)
            return(words4)
      data3['title'] = data3['title'].apply(preprocess)
```

5. Replace all the null values in the `title` column with a hyphen -:

   ```
   data3['title']=np.where(data3['title'].isnull(),'-','-
   '+data3['title'])
   ```

   Now that we have preprocessed the text data, let's assign an ID to each word. Once we have finished this assignment, we can perform text analysis in a way that is very similar to what we did in the *Categorizing news articles into topics* section, as follows:

   ```
   docs = data3['title'].values

   from collections import Counter
   counts = Counter()
   for i,review in enumerate(docs):
         counts.update(review.split())
   words = sorted(counts, key=counts.get, reverse=True)
   vocab_size=len(words)
   word_to_int = {word: i for i, word in enumerate(words, 1)}
   ```

6. Given that we have encoded all the words, let's replace them with their corresponding text in the original text:

   ```
   encoded_docs = []
   for doc in docs:
         encoded_docs.append([word_to_int[word] for word in
   doc.split()])

   def vectorize_sequences(sequences, dimension=vocab_size):
         results = np.zeros((len(sequences), dimension+1))
         for i, sequence in enumerate(sequences):
               results[i, sequence] = 1.
         return results
   vectorized_docs = vectorize_sequences(encoded_docs)
   ```

   Now that we have encoded the texts, we understand the way in which we will integrate the two data sources.

Applications of Deep Feedforward Neural Networks

7. First, we shall prepare the training and test datasets, as follows:

```
x1 = np.array(x)
x2 = np.array(vectorized_docs[5:])
y = np.array(y)

X1_train = x1[:2100,:]
X2_train = x2[:2100, :]
y_train = y[:2100]
X1_test = x1[2100:,:]
X2_test = x2[2100:,:]
y_test = y[2100:]
```

Typically, we would use a functional API when there are multiple inputs or multiple outputs expected. In this case, given that there are multiple inputs, we will be leveraging a functional API.

8. Essentially, a functional API takes out the sequential process of building the model and is performed as follows. Take the input of the vectorized documents and extract the output from it:

```
input1 = Input(shape=(2406,))
input1_hidden = (Dense(100, activation='relu'))(input1)
input1_output = (Dense(1, activation='tanh'))(input1_hidden)
```

In the preceding code, note that we have not used the sequential modeling process but defined the various connections using the Dense layer.

Note that the input has a shape of 2406, as there are 2406 unique words that remain after the filtering process.

9. Take the input of the previous 5 stock prices and build the model:

```
input2 = Input(shape=(5,))
input2_hidden = (Dense(100, activation='relu'))(input2)
input2_output = (Dense(1, activation='linear'))(input2_hidden)
```

10. We will multiply the output of the two inputs:

```
from keras.layers import multiply
out = multiply([model, model2])
```

Chapter 3

11. Now that we have defined the output, we will build the model as follows:

    ```
    model = Model([input1, input2], out)
    model.summary()
    ```

    Note that, in the preceding step, we used the `Model` layer to define the input (passed as a list) and the output:

    ```
    Layer (type)                    Output Shape         Param #     Connected to
    ================================================================================
    input_1 (InputLayer)            (None, 2406)         0
    _____
    input_2 (InputLayer)            (None, 5)            0
    _____
    dense_1 (Dense)                 (None, 100)          240700      input_1[0][0]
    _____
    dense_3 (Dense)                 (None, 100)          600         input_2[0][0]
    _____
    dense_2 (Dense)                 (None, 1)            101         dense_1[0][0]
    _____
    dense_4 (Dense)                 (None, 1)            101         dense_3[0][0]
    _____
    multiply_1 (Multiply)           (None, 1)            0           dense_2[0][0]
                                                                     dense_4[0][0]
    ================================================================================
    Total params: 241,502
    Trainable params: 241,502
    Non-trainable params: 0
    ```

    A visualization of the preceding output is as follows:

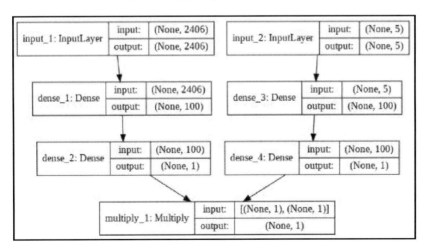

12. Compile and fit the model:

```
model.compile(optimizer='adam', loss='mean_squared_error')
model.fit(x=[X2_train, X1_train], y=y_train,
epochs=100,batch_size = 32, validation_data = ([X2_test,
X1_test], y_test))
```

The preceding code results in a mean squared error of ~5000 and clearly shows that the model overfits, as the training dataset loss is much lower than the test dataset loss.

Potentially, the overfitting is a result of a very high number of dimensions in the vectorized text data. We will look at how we can improve upon this in Chapter 11, *Building a Recurrent Neural Network*.

Defining weights for rows

In the *Predicting house prices* recipe, we learned about defining a custom loss function. However, we are not in a position yet to assign a higher weightage for certain rows over others. (We did a similar exercise for a credit default prediction case study where we assigned higher weightage to one class over the other; however, that was a classification problem, and the current problem that we are solving is a continuous variable-prediction problem.)

In this section, we will define weights for each row and then pass them to the custom_loss function that we will define.

We will continue working on the same dataset that we analyzed in the *Stock price prediction* recipe.

How to do it...

1. To perform specifying weightages at a row level, we will modify our train and test datasets in such a way that the first 2100 data points after ordering the dataset are in the train dataset and the rest are in the test dataset:

```
X_train = x[:2100,:,:]
y_train = y[:2100]
X_test = x[2100:,:,:]
y_test = y[2100:]
```

2. A row in input shall have a higher weight if it occurred more recently and less weightage otherwise:

   ```
   weights =
   np.arange(X_train.shape[0]).reshape((X_train.shape[0]),1)/2100
   ```

   The preceding code block assigns lower weightage to initial data points and a higher weightage to data points that occurred more recently.

   Now that we have defined the weights for each row, we will include them in the custom loss function. Note that in this case our custom loss function shall include both the predicted and actual values of output as well as the weight that needs to be assigned to each row.

3. The partial method enables us to pass more variables than just the actual and predicted values to the custom loss function:

   ```
   import keras.backend as K
   from functools import partial
   ```

4. To pass `weights` to the `custom_loss` function, we shall be using the partial function to pass both `custom_loss` and `weights` as a parameter in step 7. In the code that follows, we are defining the `custom_loss` function:

   ```
   def custom_loss_4(y_true, y_pred, weights):
       return K.square(K.abs(y_true - y_pred) * weights)
   ```

5. Given that the model we are building has two inputs, input variables and weights corresponding to each row, we will first define the shape input of the two as follows:

   ```
   input_layer = Input(shape=(5,1))
   weights_tensor = Input(shape=(1,))
   ```

6. Now that we have defined the inputs, let's initialize `model` that accepts the two inputs as follows:

   ```
   inp1 = Dense(1000, activation='relu')(input_layer)
   out = Dense(1, activation='linear')(i3)
   model = Model([input_layer, weights_tensor], out)
   ```

7. Now that we have initialized `model`, we will define the optimization function as follows:

   ```
   cl4 = partial(custom_loss_4, weights=weights_tensor)
   ```

In the preceding scenario, we specify that we need to minimize the `custom_loss_4` function and also that we provide an additional variable (`weights_tensor`) to the custom loss function.

8. Finally, before fitting the model, we will also provide `weights` for each row corresponding to the test dataset. Given that we are predicting these values, it is of no use to provide a low weightage to certain rows over others, as the test dataset is not provided to model. However, we will only specify this to make a prediction using the model we defined (which accepts two inputs):

```
test_weights = np.ones((156,1))
```

9. Once we specify the `weights` of test data, we will go ahead and fit the model as follows:

```
model = Model([input_layer, weights_tensor], out)
model.compile(adam, cl4)
model.fit(x=[X_train, weights], y=y_train,
epochs=300,batch_size = 32, validation_data = ([X_test,
test_weights], y_test))
```

The preceding results in a test dataset loss that is very different to what we saw in the previous section. We will look at the reason for this in more detail in the `Chapter 11`, *Building a Recurrent Neural Network* chapter.

You need to be extremely careful while implementing the preceding model, as it has a few pitfalls. However, in general, it is advised to implement models to predict stock price movements only after sufficient due diligence.

4
Building a Deep Convolutional Neural Network

In this chapter, we will cover the following recipes:

- Inaccuracy of traditional neural network when images are translated
- Building a CNN from scratch using Python
- CNNs to improve accuracy in case of image translation
- Gender classification using CNN
- Data augmentation to improve network accuracy

Introduction

In the previous chapter, we looked at a traditional deep feedforward neural network. One of the limitations of a traditional deep feedforward neural network is that it is not translation-invariant, that is, a cat image in the upper-right corner of an image would be considered different from an image that has a cat in the center of the image. Additionally, traditional neural networks are affected by the scale of an object. If the object is big in the majority of the images and a new image has the same object in it but with a smaller scale (occupies a smaller portion of the image), traditional neural networks are likely to fail in classifying the image.

Convolutional Neural Networks (CNNs) are used to deal with such issues. Given that a CNN is able to deal with translation in images and also the scale of images, it is considered a lot more useful in object classification/ detection.

In this chapter, you will learn about the following:

- Inaccuracy of traditional neural network when images are translated
- Building a CNN from scratch using Python
- Using CNNs to improve image classification on a MNIST dataset
- Implementing data augmentation to improve network accuracy
- Gender classification using CNNs

Inaccuracy of traditional neural networks when images are translated

To understand the need of CNNs further, we will first understand why a feed forward **Neural Network** (**NN**) does not work when an image is translated and then see how the CNN improves upon traditional feed forward NN.

Let's go through the following scenario:

- We will build a NN model to predict labels from the MNIST dataset
- We will consider all images that have a label of 1 and take an average of all of them (generating an average of 1 image)
- We will predict the label of the average 1 image that we have generated in the previous step using traditional NN
- We will translate the average 1 image by 1 pixel to the left or right
- We will make a prediction of the translated image using our traditional NN model

How to do it...

The strategy defined above is coded as follows (please refer to `Issue_with_image translation.ipynb` file in GitHub while implementing the code)

1. Download the dataset and extract the train and test MNIST datasets:

```
from keras.datasets import mnist
from keras.layers import Flatten, Dense
from keras.models import Sequential
import matplotlib.pyplot as plt
%matplotlib inline
(X_train, y_train), (X_test, y_test) = mnist.load_data()
```

2. Fetch the training set corresponding to label 1 only:

   ```
   X_train1 = X_train[y_train==1]
   ```

3. Reshape and normalize the original training dataset:

   ```
   num_pixels = X_train.shape[1] * X_train.shape[2]
   X_train = X_train.reshape(X_train.shape[0],num_pixels).astype('float32')
   X_test = X_test.reshape(X_test.shape[0],num_pixels).astype('float32')
   X_train = X_train / 255
   X_test = X_test / 255
   ```

4. One-hot-encode the output labels:

   ```
   y_train = np_utils.to_categorical(y_train)
   y_test = np_utils.to_categorical(y_test)
   num_classes = y_train.shape[1]
   ```

5. Build a model and fit it:

   ```
   model = Sequential()
   model.add(Dense(1000, input_dim=num_pixels, activation='relu'))
   model.add(Dense(num_classes, activation='softmax'))
   model.compile(loss='categorical_crossentropy', optimizer='adam',metrics=['accuracy'])
   model.fit(X_train, y_train, validation_data=(X_test, y_test),epochs=5, batch_size=1024, verbose=1)
   ```

6. Let's plot the average 1 image that we obtained in step 2:

   ```
   pic=np.zeros((28,28))
   pic2=np.copy(pic)
   for i in range(X_train1.shape[0]):
       pic2=X_train1[i,:,:]
       pic=pic+pic2
   pic=(pic/X_train1.shape[0])
   plt.imshow(pic)
   ```

In the preceding code, we initialized an empty picture that is 28 x 28 in dimension and took an average pixel value at the various pixel locations of images that have a label of 1 (the X_train1 object) by looping through all the values in the X_train1 object.

The plot of the average 1 image appears as follows:

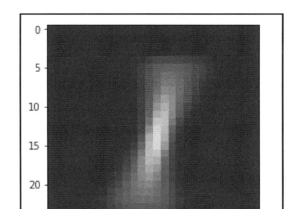

It is to be noted that the more yellow (thick) the pixel is, the more often people have written on top of the pixel, and the less yellow (more blue/less thick) the pixel, the less often people have written on top of the pixel. Also, it is to be noted that the pixel in the middle is the yellowest/thickest (this is because most people would be writing over the middle pixels, irrespective of whether the whole digit is written in a vertical line or is slanted toward the left or right).

Problems with traditional NN

Scenario 1: Let's create a new image where the original image is translated by 1 pixel toward the left. In the following code, we are looping through the columns of the image and copying the pixel values of the next column to the current column:

```
for i in range(pic.shape[0]):
    if i<20:
        pic[:,i]=pic[:,i+1]
    plt.imshow(pic)
```

The left translated average 1 image looks as follows:

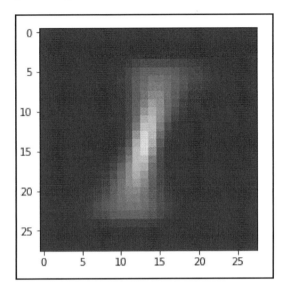

Let's go ahead and predict the label of the image using the built model:

```
model.predict(pic.reshape(1,784)/255)
```

The model's prediction on the translated image is as follows:

```
array([[2.3734521e-03, 6.3357157e-01, 9.0679098e-03, 2.4509018e-03,
        7.1080279e-04, 1.9571159e-02, 2.2253724e-02, 1.4216139e-03,
        3.0820316e-01, 3.7569081e-04]], dtype=float32)
```

We can see a prediction of 1, though with a lower probability than when pixels were not translated.

Scenario 2: A new image is created in which the pixels of the original average 1 image are shifted by 2 pixels to the right:

```
pic=np.zeros((28,28))
pic2=np.copy(pic)
for i in range(X_train1.shape[0]):
    pic2=X_train1[i,:,:]
    pic=pic+pic2
pic=(pic/X_train1.shape[0])
pic2=np.copy(pic)
for i in range(pic.shape[0]):
```

```
    if ((i>6) and (i<26)):
        pic[:,i]=pic2[:,(i-1)]
plt.imshow(pic)
```

The right translated average 1 image looks as follows:

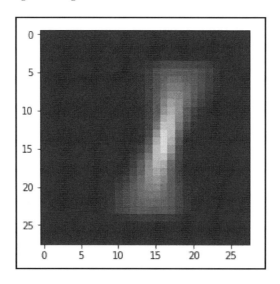

The prediction of this image is as follows:

```
model.predict(pic.reshape(1,784)/255)
```

The model's prediction on the translated image is as follows:

```
array([[0.00117591, 0.18717803, 0.03738188, 0.22529456, 0.07703815,
        0.00091598, 0.00041914, 0.40253484, 0.03939882, 0.02866266]],
      dtype=float32)
```

We can see that the prediction is incorrect with an output of 3. This is the problem that we will be addressing by using a CNN.

Building a CNN from scratch using Python

In this section, we will learn about how a CNN works by building a feedforward network from scratch using NumPy.

Getting ready

A typical CNN has multiple components. In this section, we will go through the various components of a CNN before we understand how the CNN improves prediction accuracy when an image is translated.

Understanding convolution

We are already aware of how a typical NN works. In this section, let's understand the working details of the convolution process in CNN.

Filter

A convolution is a multiplication between two matrices—one matrix being big and the other being small. To understand convolution, consider the following example:

Matrix *A* is as follows:

1	2	3	4
5	6	7	8
9	10	11	12
13	14	15	16

Matrix *B* is as follows:

1	2
3	4

When performing convolutions, think of it as we are sliding the smaller matrix over the larger matrix, that is, we can potentially come up with nine such multiplications as the smaller matrix is slid over the entire area of the bigger matrix. Note that it is not matrix multiplication.

The various multiplications that happen between the bigger and smaller matrix are as follows:

1. {1, 2, 5, 6} of the bigger matrix is multiplied with {1, 2, 3, 4} of the smaller matrix:

$$1*1 + 2*2 + 5*3 + 6*4 = 44$$

2. {2, 3, 6, 7} of the bigger matrix is multiplied with {1, 2, 3, 4} of the smaller matrix:

   $2*1 + 3*2 + 6*3 + 7*4 = 54$

3. {3, 4, 7, 8} of the bigger matrix is multiplied with {1, 2, 3, 4} of the smaller matrix:

   $3*1 + 4*2 + 7*3 + 8*4 = 64$

4. {5, 6, 9, 10} of the bigger matrix is multiplied with {1, 2, 3, 4} of the smaller matrix:

   $5*1 + 6*2 + 9*3 + 10*4 = 84$

5. {6, 7, 10, 11} of the bigger matrix is multiplied with {1, 2, 3, 4} of the smaller matrix:

   $6*1 + 7*2 + 10*3 + 11*4 = 94$

6. {7, 8, 11, 12} of the bigger matrix is multiplied with {1, 2, 3, 4} of the smaller matrix:

   $7*1 + 8*2 + 11*3 + 12*4 = 104$

7. {9,10,13,14} of the bigger matrix is multiplied with {1, 2, 3, 4} of the smaller matrix:

   $9*1 + 10*2 + 13*3 + 14*4 = 124$

8. {10, 11, 14, 15} of the bigger matrix is multiplied with {1, 2, 3 ,4} of the smaller matrix:

   $10*1 + 11*2 + 14*3 + 15*4 = 134$

9. {11, 12, 15, 16} of the bigger matrix is multiplied with {1, 2, 3, 4} of the smaller matrix:

   $11*1 + 12*2 + 15*3 + 16*4 = 144$

The result of the preceding steps would be the following matrix:

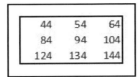

Conventionally, the smaller matrix is called a filter or kernel and the smaller matrix values are arrived at statistically through gradient descent. The values within the filter are the constituent weights.

Practically, when the image input shape is 224 x 224 x 3, where there are 3 channels, a filter that has a shape of 3 x 3 would also have 3 channels so that performing the matrix multiplication (sum product) is enabled.

> A filter will have as many channels as the number of channels in the matrix it multiplies with.

Strides

In the preceding steps, given that the filter moved one step at a time both horizontally and vertically, the strides for the filter are (1, 1). The higher the number of strides, the higher the number of values that are skipped from the matrix multiplication.

Padding

In the preceding steps, we missed out on multiplying the leftmost values of the filter with the rightmost values of the original matrix. If we were to perform such an operation, we would have ensure that there is zero padding around the edges (the edges of the image padded with zeros) of the original matrix. This form of padding is called **valid** padding. The matrix multiplication we performed in the *Filter* section of the *Understanding convolution* recipe was a result of the **same** padding.

From convolution to activation

In a traditional NN, a hidden layer not only multiplies the input values by the weights, but also applies a non-linearity to the data, that is, it passes the values through an activation function.

A similar activity happens in a typical CNN too, where the convolution is passed through an activation function. CNN supports the traditional activations functions we have seen so far: sigmoid, ReLU, tanh, and leaky ReLU.

For the preceding output, we can see that the output remains the same when passed through a ReLU activation function, as all the numbers are positive.

From convolution activation to pooling

In the previous section, we looked at how convolutions work. In this section, we will understand the typical next step after a convolution: pooling.

Let's say the output of the convolution step is as follows (we are not considering the preceding example, and this is a new example to only illustrate how pooling works):

In the preceding case, the output of a convolution step is a 2 x 2 matrix. Max pooling considers the 2 x 2 block and gives the maximum value as output. Similarly, imagine that the output of the convolution step is a bigger matrix, as follows:

11	22	1	2
32	65	3	4
11	12	25	63
13	14	45	32

Max pooling divides the big matrix into non-overlapping blocks of 2 x 2 (when the stride value is 2), as follows:

11	22	1	2
32	65	3	4
11	12	25	63
13	14	45	32

From each block, only the element that has the highest value is chosen. So, the output of the max pooling operation on the preceding matrix would be the following:

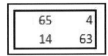

In practice, it is not necessary to have a 2 x 2 window in all cases, but it is used more often than not.

The other types of pooling involved are sum and average—again, in practice, we see a lot of max pooling when compared to other types of pooling.

How do convolution and pooling help?

One of the drawbacks of traditional NN in the MNIST example is that each pixel is associated with a distinct weight.

Thus, if an adjacent pixel, other than the original pixel, were to be highlighted, instead of the original pixel, the output would not be very accurate (the example of *scenario 1*, where the average one was slightly to the left of the middle).

This scenario is now addressed, as the pixels share weights that are constituted within each filter.

All the pixels get multiplied by all the weights that constitute a filter. In the pooling layer, only the values post convolution that have a high value are chosen.

This way, irrespective of whether the highlighted pixel is at the center or is slightly away from the center, the output would more often than not be the expected value.

 However, the issue still remains the same when the highlighted pixels are very far away from the center.

How to do it...

To gain a solid understanding, we'll build a CNN-based architecture using Keras and validate our understanding of how CNN works by matching the output obtained by building the feedforward propagation part of CNN from scratch with the output obtained from Keras.

Let's implement CNN with a toy example where the input and expected output data is defined (the code file is available as `CNN_working_details.ipynb` in GitHub):

1. Create the input and output dataset:

    ```
    import numpy as np
    X_train=np.array([[[1,2,3,4],[2,3,4,5],[5,6,7,8],[1,3,4,5]],
    [[-1,2,3,-4],[2,-3,4,5],[-5,6,-7,8],[-1,-3,-4,-5]]])
    y_train=np.array([0,1])
    ```

    In the preceding code, we created data where positive input gives an output of 0 and negative input gives an output of 1.

2. Scale the input dataset:

    ```
    X_train = X_train / 8
    ```

3. Reshape the input dataset so that each input image is represented in the format of width x height x number of channels:

    ```
    X_train =
    X_train.reshape(X_train.shape[0],X_train.shape[1],X_train.shape[1],
    1 ).astype('float32')
    ```

4. Build the model architecture:

    Instantiate the model after importing the relevant methods:

    ```
    from keras.layers import Conv2D, MaxPooling2D, Flatten, Dense
    from keras.models import Sequential
    model = Sequential()
    ```

    In the next step, we are performing the convolution operation:

    ```
    model.add(Conv2D(1, (3,3), input_shape=(4,4,1),activation='relu'))
    ```

    In the preceding step, we are performing a 2D convolution (the matrix multiplication that we saw in the section on *Understanding convolution*) on input data where we have 1 filter of size 3 x 3.

Additionally, given that this is the first layer since instantiating a model, we specify the input shape, which is (4 , 4, 1)

Finally, we perform ReLu activation on top of the output of the convolution.

The output of the convolution operation in this scenario is 2 x 2 x 1 in shape, as the matrix multiplication of weights with input would yield a 2 x 2 matrix (given that the default strides is 1 x 1).

Additionally, the size of output would shrink, as we have not padded the input (put zeros around the input image).

In the following step, we are adding a layer that performs a max pooling operation, as follows:

```
model.add(MaxPooling2D(pool_size=(2, 2)))
```

We are performing max pooling on top of the output obtained from the previous layer, where the pool size is 2 x 2. This means that the maximum value in a subset of the 2 x 2 portion of the image is calculated.

Note that a stride of 2 x 2 in the pooling layer would not affect the output in this case as the output of the previous step was 2 x 2. However, in general, a stride that is of a greater size than 1 x 1 would affect the output shape.

Let's flatten the output from the pooling layer:

```
model.add(Flatten())
```

Once we perform flattening, the process becomes very similar to what we performed in standard feedforward neural networks where the input is connected to the hidden layer and then to the output layer (we can connect the input to more hidden layers, too!).

We are directly connecting the output of the flatten layer to the output layer using the sigmoid activation:

```
model.add(Dense(1, activation='sigmoid'))
```

A summary of the model can be obtained and looks as follows:

```
model.summary()
```

A summary of the output is as follows:

```
Layer (type)                  Output Shape         Param #
=================================================================
Convolution_layer (Conv2D)    (None, 2, 2, 1)      10

Pooling_layer (MaxPooling2D)  (None, 1, 1, 1)      0

Flatten_layer (Flatten)       (None, 1)            0

Output_layer (Dense)          (None, 1)            2
=================================================================
Total params: 12
Trainable params: 12
Non-trainable params: 0
```

Note that there are 10 parameters in the convolution layer as the one 3 x 3 filter would have 9 weights and 1 bias term. The pooling layer and flatten layer do not have any parameters as they are either extracting maximum values in certain regioned (max pooling) or are flattening the output from the previous layer (flatten) and thus no operation where weights need to be modified in either of these layers.

The output layer has two parameters since the flatten layer has one output, which is connected to the output layer that has one value—hence we will have one weight and one bias term connecting the flatten layer and output layer.

5. Compile and fit the model:

    ```
    model.compile(loss='binary_crossentropy',
    optimizer='adam',metrics=['accuracy'])
    ```

    In the preceding code, we are specifying the loss as binary cross-entropy because the outcome is either a 1 or a 0.

6. Fit the model:

    ```
    model.fit(X_train, y_train, epochs = 500)
    ```

We are fitting the model to have optimal weights that connect the input layer with the output layer.

Validating the CNN output

Now that we have fit the model, let's validate the output we obtain from the model by implementing the feedforward portion of the CNN:

1. Let's extract the order in which weights and biases are presented:

    ```
    model.weights
    ```

    ```
    [<tf.Variable 'Convolution_layer_2/kernel:0' shape=(3, 3, 1, 1) dtype=float32_ref>,
     <tf.Variable 'Convolution_layer_2/bias:0' shape=(1,) dtype=float32_ref>,
     <tf.Variable 'Output_layer_1/kernel:0' shape=(1, 1) dtype=float32_ref>,
     <tf.Variable 'Output_layer_1/bias:0' shape=(1,) dtype=float32_ref>]
    ```

    You can see that the weights of the convolution layer are presented first, then the bias, and finally the weight and bias in the output layer.

    Also note that the shape of weights in the convolution layer is (3, 3, 1, 1) as the filter is 3 x 3 x 1 in shape (because the image is three-dimensional: 28 x 28 x 1 in shape) and the final 1 (the fourth value in shape) is for the number of filters that are specified in the convolution layer.

    If we had specified 64 as the number of filters in the convolution, the shape of weights would have been 3 x 3 x 1 x 64.

    Similarly, had the convolution operation been performed on an image with 3 channels, each filter's shape would have been 3 x 3 x 3.

2. Extract the weight values at various layers:

    ```
    model.get_weights()
    ```

3. Let's extract the output of the first input so that we can validate it with feedforward propagation:

    ```
    model.predict(X_train[0].reshape(1,4,4,1))
    ```

    ```
    array([[0.04289691]], dtype=float32)
    ```

    The output from the iteration we ran is 0.0428 (this could be different when you run the model, as the random initialization of weights could be different), which we will validate by performing matrix multiplication.

Building a Deep Convolutional Neural Network

 We are reshaping the input while passing it to the predict method as it expects the input to have a shape of (None, 4, 4, 1), where None specifies that the batch size could be any number.

4. Perform the convolution of the filter with the input image. Note that the input image is 4 x 4 in shape while the filter is 3 x 3 in shape. We will be performing the matrix multiplication (convolution) along the rows as well as columns in the code here:

```
sumprod = []
for i in range(X_train[0].shape[0]-
model.get_weights()[0].shape[0]+1):
    for j in range(X_train[0].shape[0]-
model.get_weights()[0].shape[0]+1):
        img_subset = np.array(X_train[0,i:(i+3),j:(j+3),0])
        filter = model.get_weights()[0].reshape(3,3)
        val = np.sum(img_subset*filter) + model.get_weights()[1]
        sumprod.append(val)
```

In the preceding code, we are initializing an empty list named `sumprod` that stores the output of each matrix multiplication of the filter with the image's subset (the subset of the image is of the size of filter).

5. Reshape the output of `sumprod` so that it can then be passed to the pooling layer:

```
sumprod= np.array(sumprod).reshape(2,2,1)
```

6. Perform activation on top of the convolution's output before it is passed to the pooling layer:

```
sumprod = np.where(sumprod>0,sumprod,0)
```

7. Pass the convolution output to the pooling layer. However, in the current case, given that the output of the convolution is 2 x 2, we will keep it simple and just take the maximum value in the output we obtained in *step 6*:

```
pooling_layer_output = np.max(sumprod)
```

8. Connect the output of the pooling layer to the output layer:

```
intermediate_output_value =
pooling_layer_output*model.get_weights()[2]+model.get_weights()[3]
```

We multiplied by the pooling layer's output with the weight in the output layer and added the bias in the output layer.

9. Calculate the sigmoid output:

   ```
   1/(1+np.exp(-intermediate_output_value))
   ```

   The output of preceding operation is as follows:

   ```
   array([[0.04289691]], dtype=float32)
   ```

The output that you see here will be the same as the one that we obtained using the `model.predict` method, thus validating our understanding of how a CNN works.

CNNs to improve accuracy in the case of image translation

In the previous sections, we learned about the issue of translation in images and how a CNN works. In this section, we will leverage that knowledge to learn how a CNN works toward improving prediction accuracy when an image is translated.

Getting ready

The strategy that we will be adopting to build a CNN model is as follows:

- Given that the input shape is 28 x 28 x 1, the filters shall be 3 x 3 x 1 in size:
    - Note that the size of filter can change, however the number of channels cannot change
- Let's initialize 10 filters
- We will perform pooling on top of the output obtained in the previous step of convolving 10 filters over the input image:
    - This would result in halving the image's dimension
- We will flatten the output obtained while pooling
- The flattened layer will be connected to another hidden layer that has 1,000 units
- Finally, we connect the hidden layer to the output layer where there are 10 possible classes (as there are 10 digits, from 0 to 9)

Once we build the model, we will translate the average 1 image by 1 pixel and then test the CNN model's prediction on the translated image. Note that the feedforward NN architecture was not able to predict the right class in this scenario.

How to do it...

Let's understand using a CNN on MNIST data in code (The code file is available as `CNN_image_translation.ipynb` in GitHub):

1. Load and preprocess the data:

```
(X_train, y_train), (X_test, y_test) = mnist.load_data()
X_train = X_train.reshape(X_train.shape[0],X_train.shape[1],X_train.shape[1], 1 ).astype('float32')
X_test = X_test.reshape(X_test.shape[0],X_test.shape[1],X_test.shape[1],1).astype('float32')

X_train = X_train / 255
X_test = X_test / 255

y_train = np_utils.to_categorical(y_train)
y_test = np_utils.to_categorical(y_test)

num_classes = y_test.shape[1]
```

Note that all the steps that we performed in this step are the same as what we performed in `Chapter 2`, *Building a Deep Feedforward Neural Network*.

2. Build and compile the model:

```
from keras.layers import Conv2D, MaxPooling2D, Flatten, Dense
from keras.models import Sequential
model = Sequential()
model.add(Conv2D(10, (3,3), input_shape=(28, 28,1),activation='relu'))
model.add(MaxPooling2D(pool_size=(2, 2)))
model.add(Flatten())
model.add(Dense(1000, activation='relu'))
model.add(Dense(num_classes, activation='softmax'))
```

A summary of the model that we initialized in the preceding code can be obtained and is as follows:

```
model.summary()
```

The summary of the model is as follows:

```
Layer (type)                 Output Shape              Param #
=================================================================
conv2d_1 (Conv2D)            (None, 26, 26, 10)        100
_____
max_pooling2d_1 (MaxPooling2 (None, 13, 13, 10)        0
_____
flatten_1 (Flatten)          (None, 1690)              0
_____
dense_1 (Dense)              (None, 1000)              1691000
_____
dense_2 (Dense)              (None, 10)                10010
=================================================================
Total params: 1,701,110
Trainable params: 1,701,110
Non-trainable params: 0
```

We have a total of 100 parameters in the convolution layer as there are 10 of the 3 x 3 x 1 filters, resulting in a total of 90 weight parameters. Additionally, 10 bias terms (1 for each filter) add up to form a total of 100 parameters in the convolution layer.

Note that max pooling does not have any parameters, as it is about extracting the maximum value within a patch that is 2 x 2 in size.

3. Fit the model:

```
model.fit(X_train, y_train, validation_data=(X_test,
y_test),epochs=5, batch_size=1024, verbose=1)
```

The preceding model gives an accuracy of 98% in 5 epochs:

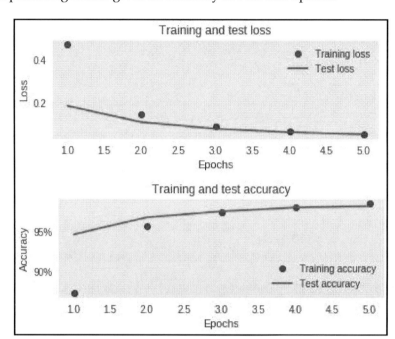

4. Let's identify the average 1 image and then translate it by 1 unit:

   ```
   X_test1 = X_test[y_test[:,1]==1]
   ```

   In the preceding code, we filtered all the image inputs that have a label of 1:

   ```
   import numpy as np
   pic=np.zeros((28,28))
   pic2=np.copy(pic)
   for i in range(X_test1.shape[0]):
        pic2=X_test1[i,:,:,0]
        pic=pic+pic2
   pic=(pic/X_test1.shape[0])
   ```

   In the preceding code, we took the average 1 image:

   ```
   for i in range(pic.shape[0]):
       if i<20:
           pic[:,i]=pic[:,i+1]
   ```

   In the preceding code, we translated each pixel in the average 1 image by 1 unit to the left.

5. Predict on the translated 1 image:

```
model.predict(pic.reshape(1,28,28,1))
```

The output of preceding step is as follows:

```
array([[5.3325198e-03, 9.5413315e-01, 1.1513928e-02, 2.7472648e-04,
        1.3497858e-03, 1.1531125e-03, 7.3857987e-03, 1.9941789e-03,
        1.6599722e-02, 2.6304892e-04]], dtype=float32)
```

Note that the prediction now (when we use a CNN) has more probability (0.9541) for 1 when compared to the scenario where the deep feed forward NN model, which is predicted as (0.6335) in the label of the translated image in the *Inaccuracy of traditional neural network when images are translated* section.

Gender classification using CNNs

In the previous sections, we learned about how a CNN works and how CNNs solve the image-translation problem.

In this section, we will further our understanding of how a CNN works by building a model that works toward detecting the gender of person present in image.

Getting ready

In this section, let's formulate our strategy of how we will solve this problem:

- We will collect a dataset of images and label each image based on the gender of person present in image
- We'll work on only 2,000 images, as the data fetching process takes a considerably long time for our dataset (as we are manually downloading images from a website in this case study)
- Additionally, we'll ensure that there is equal representation of male and female images in the dataset
- Once the dataset is in place, we will reshape the images into the same size so that they can be fed into a CNN model

Building a Deep Convolutional Neural Network

- We will build the CNN model where the output layer has as many classes as the number of labels two
- Given that this is a case of predicting one out of the two possible labels in the dataset, we will minimize the binary cross-entropy loss

How to do it...

In this section, we will code the strategy that we defined prior (the code file is available as `Gender classification.ipynb` in GitHub):

1. Download the dataset:

   ```
   $ wget
   https://d1p17r2m4rzlbo.cloudfront.net/wp-content/uploads/2017/04/a9
   43287.csv
   ```

2. Load the dataset and inspect its content:

   ```
   import pandas as pd, numpy as np
   from skimage import io
   # Location of file is /content/a943287.csv
   # be sure to change to location of downloaded file on your machine
   data = pd.read_csv('/content/a943287.csv')
   data.head()
   ```

   A sample of some of the key fields in the dataset is as follows:

	_unit_id	image_url	please_select_the_gender_of_the_person_in_the_picture
0	1023132475	https://d1qb2nb5cznatu.cloudfront.net/users/40...	male
1	1023132476	https://d1qb2nb5cznatu.cloudfront.net/users/42...	male
2	1023132477	https://d1qb2nb5cznatu.cloudfront.net/users/44...	male
3	1023132478	https://d1qb2nb5cznatu.cloudfront.net/users/47...	male
4	1023132479	https://d1qb2nb5cznatu.cloudfront.net/users/50...	male

3. Fetch 1,000 male images and 1,000 female images from the URL links provided in the dataset:

   ```
   data_male =
   data[data['please_select_the_gender_of_the_person_in_the_picture']=
   ="male"].reset_index(drop='index')
   data_female =
   data[data['please_select_the_gender_of_the_person_in_the_picture']=
   ```

```
="female"].reset_index(drop='index')
final_data =
pd.concat([data_male[:1000],data_female[:1000]],axis=0).reset_index
(drop='index')
```

In the preceding code, `final_data` contains URL links for 1,000 male images and 1,000 female images. Read the URL links and fetch the images corresponding to the URL links. Ensure that all images are 300 × 300 × 3 in shape (as the majority of the images in his dataset have that shape) and also that we take care of any forbidden to access issues:

```
x = []
y = []
for i in range(final_data.shape[0]):
    try:
        image = io.imread(final_data.loc[i]['image_url'])
        if(image.shape==(300,300,3)):
            x.append(image)
y.append(final_data.loc[i]['please_select_the_gender_of_the_person_
in_the_picture'])
    except:
        continue
```

A sample of the input and their corresponding emotion labels looks as follows:

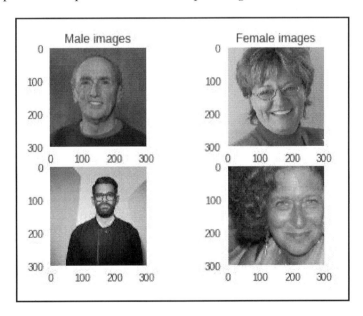

4. Create the input and output arrays:

```
x2 = []
y2 = []
for i in range(len(x)):
    img = cv2.cvtColor(x[i], cv2.COLOR_BGR2GRAY)
    img2 = cv2.resize(img, (50,50))
    x2.append(img2)
    img_label = np.where(y[i]=="male",1,0)
    y2.append(img_label)
```

In the preceding step, we have converted the color image into a grayscale image as the color of the image is likely to add additional information (we'll validate this hypothesis in Chapter 5, *Transfer Learning*).

Additionally, we have resized our images to a lower size (50 x 50 x 1) in shape. The result of this is as follows:

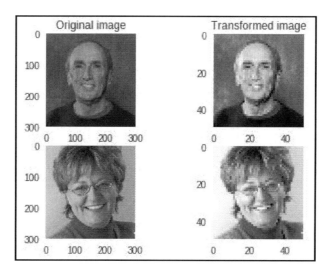

Finally, we converted the output into a one-hot-encoded version.

5. Create train and test datasets. First, we convert the input and output lists into arrays and then shape the input so that it is in a shape that can be be provided as input to the CNN:

```
x2 = np.array(x2)
x2 = x2.reshape(x2.shape[0],x2.shape[1],x2.shape[2],1)
Y = np.array(y2)
```

The output of the first value of x2 is as follows:

```
[[82, 87, 80, ..., 76, 77, 77],
 [79, 80, 86, ..., 75, 77, 74],
 [84, 79, 73, ..., 73, 75, 75],
 ...,
 [28, 26, 19, ..., 16, 16, 15],
 [14, 24, 15, ..., 12, 14, 13],
 [12, 20, 13, ..., 12, 13, 13]]
```

Note that the input has values between 0 to 255 and thus we have to scale it:

```
X = np.array(x2)/255
Y = np.array(y2)
```

Finally, we split the input and output arrays into train and test datasets:

```
from sklearn.model_selection import train_test_split
X_train, X_test, y_train, y_test = train_test_split(X,Y,
test_size=0.1, random_state=42)
print(X_train.shape, X_test.shape, y_train.shape, y_test.shape)
```

The shapes of the train and test input, output arrays are as follows:

```
(1591, 50, 50, 1) (177, 50, 50, 1) (1591,) (177,)
```

6. Build and compile the model:

```
from keras.layers import Conv2D, MaxPooling2D, Flatten, Dense
from keras.models import Sequential
model = Sequential()
model.add(Conv2D(64, kernel_size=(3, 3),
activation='relu',input_shape=(50,50,1)))
model.add(MaxPooling2D(pool_size=(5, 5)))
model.add(Conv2D(128, kernel_size=(3, 3),
activation='relu',padding='same'))
model.add(MaxPooling2D(pool_size=(2, 2)))
model.add(Conv2D(256, kernel_size=(3, 3),
activation='relu',padding='same'))
model.add(MaxPooling2D(pool_size=(2, 2)))
model.add(Conv2D(512, kernel_size=(3, 3),
activation='relu',padding='same'))
model.add(Flatten())
model.add(Dense(100, activation='relu'))
```

```
model.add(Dense(1, activation='sigmoid'))
model.summary()
```

A summary of the model is as follows:

```
Layer (type)                   Output Shape              Param #
=================================================================
conv2d_38 (Conv2D)             (None, 48, 48, 64)        640
_____
max_pooling2d_28 (MaxPooling   (None, 9, 9, 64)          0
_____
conv2d_39 (Conv2D)             (None, 9, 9, 128)         73856
_____
max_pooling2d_29 (MaxPooling   (None, 4, 4, 128)         0
_____
conv2d_40 (Conv2D)             (None, 4, 4, 256)         295168
_____
max_pooling2d_30 (MaxPooling   (None, 2, 2, 256)         0
_____
conv2d_41 (Conv2D)             (None, 2, 2, 512)         1180160
_____
flatten_10 (Flatten)           (None, 2048)              0
_____
dense_19 (Dense)               (None, 100)               204900
_____
dense_20 (Dense)               (None, 1)                 101
=================================================================
Total params: 1,754,825
Trainable params: 1,754,825
Non-trainable params: 0
```

Note that the number of channels in the output of the convolution layer would be equal to the number of filters specified in that layer. Additionally, we have performed a slightly more aggressive pooling on the first convolution layer's output.

Now, we'll compile the model to minimize binary cross entropy loss (as the output has only two classes) as follows:

```
model.compile(loss='binary_crossentropy',optimizer='adam',metrics=['accuracy'])
```

7. Fit the model:

```
history = model.fit(X_train, y_train, batch_size=32,
epochs=50,verbose=1,validation_data = (X_test, y_test))
```

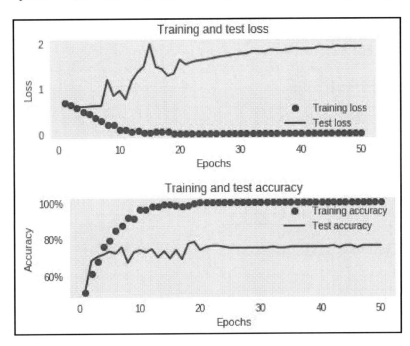

Once we fit the model, we can see that the preceding code results in an accuracy of ~80% in predicting the right gender in an image.

There's more...

The accuracy of classification can be further improved by:

- Working on more images
- Working on bigger images (rather than 50 x 50 images) that are used to train a larger network
- Leveraging transfer learning (which will be discussed in Chapter 5, *Transfer Learning*)
- Avoiding overfitting using regularization and dropout

Data augmentation to improve network accuracy

It is difficult to classify images accurately if they are translated from their original location. However, given an image, the label of the image will remain the same, even if we translate, rotate, or scale the image. Data augmentation is a way to create more images from the given set of images, that is, by rotating, translating, or scaling them and mapping them to the label of the original image.

An intuition for this is as follows: an image of a person will still be corresponding to the person, even if the image is rotated slightly or the person in the image is moved from the middle of the image to far right of the image.

Hence, we should be in a position to create more training data by rotating and translating the original images, where we already know the labels that correspond to each image.

Getting ready

In this recipe, we will be working on the CIFAR-10 dataset, which contains images of objects of 10 different classes.

The strategy that we'll use is as follows:

- Download the CIFAR-10 dataset
- Preprocess the dataset
    - Scale the input values
    - One-hot-encode the output classes
- Build a deep CNN with multiple convolution and pooling layers
- Compile and fit the model to test its accuracy on the test dataset
- Generate random translations of the original set of images in the training dataset
- Fit the same model architecture that was built in the previous step on the total images (generated images, plus the original images)
- Check the accuracy of the model on the test dataset

We will be implementing data augmentation using the `ImageDataGenerator` method in the `keras.preprocessing.image` package.

How to do it...

To understand the benefits of data augmentation, let's go through an example of calculating the accuracy on the CIFAR-10 dataset with data augmentation and without data augmentation (the code file is available as `Data_augmentation_to_improve_network_accuracy.ipynb` in GitHub).

Model accuracy without data augmentation

Let's calculate the accuracy without data augmentation in the following steps:

1. Import the packages and data:

   ```
   from matplotlib import pyplot as plt
   %matplotlib inline
   import numpy as np
   from keras.utils import np_utils
   from keras.models import Sequential
   from keras.layers.core import Dense, Dropout, Activation, Flatten
   from keras.layers import Conv2D, MaxPooling2D
   from keras.layers.normalization import BatchNormalization
   from keras import regularizers

   from keras.datasets import cifar10
   (X_train, y_train), (X_val, y_val) = cifar10.load_data()
   ```

2. Preprocess the data:

   ```
   X_train = X_train.astype('float32')/255.
   X_val = X_val.astype('float32')/255.

   n_classes = 10
   y_train = np_utils.to_categorical(y_train, n_classes)
   y_val = np_utils.to_categorical(y_val, n_classes)
   ```

Building a Deep Convolutional Neural Network

A sample of images, along with their corresponding labels, is as follows:

3. Build and compile the model:

```
input_shape = X_train[0].shape

model = Sequential()
model.add(Conv2D(32, (3,3), padding='same',
kernel_regularizer=regularizers.l2(weight_decay),
input_shape=X_train.shape[1:]))
model.add(Activation('relu'))
model.add(BatchNormalization())
model.add(Conv2D(32, (3,3), padding='same',
kernel_regularizer=regularizers.l2(weight_decay)))
model.add(Activation('relu'))
model.add(BatchNormalization())
model.add(MaxPooling2D(pool_size=(2,2)))
model.add(Dropout(0.2))
model.add(Conv2D(64, (3,3), padding='same',
kernel_regularizer=regularizers.l2(weight_decay)))
model.add(Activation('relu'))
model.add(BatchNormalization())
model.add(Conv2D(64, (3,3), padding='same',
kernel_regularizer=regularizers.l2(weight_decay)))
model.add(Activation('relu'))
model.add(BatchNormalization())
model.add(MaxPooling2D(pool_size=(2,2)))
model.add(Dropout(0.3))
model.add(Conv2D(128, (3,3), padding='same',
kernel_regularizer=regularizers.l2(weight_decay)))
model.add(Activation('relu'))
```

Chapter 4

```
model.add(BatchNormalization())
model.add(Conv2D(128, (3,3), padding='same',
kernel_regularizer=regularizers.l2(weight_decay)))
model.add(Activation('relu'))
model.add(BatchNormalization())
model.add(MaxPooling2D(pool_size=(2,2)))
model.add(Dropout(0.4))
model.add(Flatten())
model.add(Dense(10, activation='softmax'))

from keras.optimizers import Adam
adam = Adam(lr = 0.01)
model.compile(loss='categorical_crossentropy',
optimizer=adam,metrics=['accuracy'])
```

We have a higher learning rate only so that the model converges faster in fewer epochs. This enables a faster comparison of the non-data augmentation scenario with the data augmentation scenario. Ideally, we would let the model run for a greater number of epochs with a lesser learning rate.

4. Fit the model:

```
model.fit(X_train, y_train, batch_size=32,epochs=10, verbose=1,
validation_data=(X_val, y_val))
```

The accuracy of this network is ~66%:

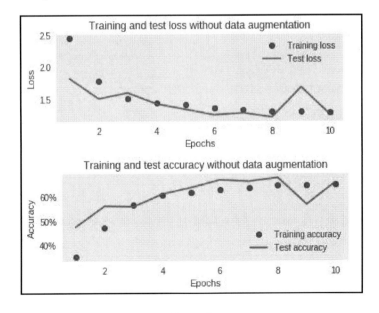

[139]

Model accuracy with data augmentation

In the following code, we will implement data augmentation:

1. Use the `ImageDataGenerator` method in the `keras.preprocessing.image` package:

    ```
    from keras.preprocessing.image import ImageDataGenerator
    datagen = ImageDataGenerator(
        rotation_range=20,
        width_shift_range=0,
        height_shift_range=0,
        fill_mode = 'nearest')

    datagen.fit(X_train)
    ```

    In the preceding code, we are generating new images where the images are randomly rotated between 0 to 20 degrees. A sample of images after being passed through the data generator is as follows:

    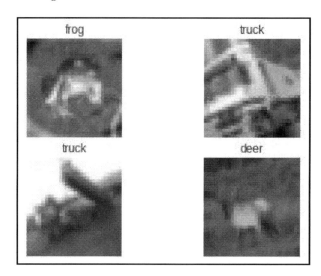

    Note that the images are tilted slightly when compared to the previous set of images.

2. Now, we will pass our total data through the data generator, as follows:

    ```
    batch_size = 32
    model = Sequential()
    model.add(Conv2D(32, (3,3), padding='same',
    kernel_regularizer=regularizers.l2(weight_decay),
    ```

```
            input_shape=X_train.shape[1:]))
model.add(Activation('relu'))
model.add(BatchNormalization())
model.add(Conv2D(32, (3,3), padding='same',
    kernel_regularizer=regularizers.l2(weight_decay)))
model.add(Activation('relu'))
model.add(BatchNormalization())
model.add(MaxPooling2D(pool_size=(2,2)))
model.add(Dropout(0.2))
model.add(Conv2D(64, (3,3), padding='same',
    kernel_regularizer=regularizers.l2(weight_decay)))
model.add(Activation('relu'))
model.add(BatchNormalization())
model.add(Conv2D(64, (3,3), padding='same',
    kernel_regularizer=regularizers.l2(weight_decay)))
model.add(Activation('relu'))
model.add(BatchNormalization())
model.add(MaxPooling2D(pool_size=(2,2)))
model.add(Dropout(0.3))
model.add(Conv2D(128, (3,3), padding='same',
    kernel_regularizer=regularizers.l2(weight_decay)))
model.add(Activation('relu'))
model.add(BatchNormalization())
model.add(Conv2D(128, (3,3), padding='same',
    kernel_regularizer=regularizers.l2(weight_decay)))
model.add(Activation('relu'))
model.add(BatchNormalization())
model.add(MaxPooling2D(pool_size=(2,2)))
model.add(Dropout(0.4))
model.add(Flatten())
model.add(Dense(10, activation='softmax'))
from keras.optimizers import Adam
adam = Adam(lr = 0.01)
model.compile(loss='categorical_crossentropy', optimizer=adam,
    metrics=['accuracy'])
```

3. Note that we are rebuilding the model so that the weights are initialized one more time as we are comparing between a data augmentation and non-data augmentation scenario:

```
model.fit_generator(datagen.flow(X_train, y_train,
batch_size=batch_size),steps_per_epoch=X_train.shape[0] //
batch_size, epochs=10,validation_data=(X_val,y_val))
```

Note that the `fit_generator` method fits the model while generating new images.

4. Additionally, `datagen.flow` specifies that new training data points need to be generated per the datagen strategy we initialized in step *1*. Along with this, we also specify the number of steps per epoch as the ratio of the total number of data points over the batch size:

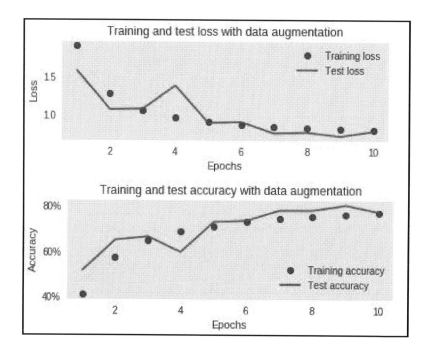

The accuracy of this code is ~80%, which is better than the accuracy of 66% using just the given dataset (without data augmentation).

5
Transfer Learning

In the previous chapter, we learned about recognizing the class that an image belongs to in a given image. In this chapter, we will learn about one of the drawbacks of CNN and also about how we can overcome it using certain pre-trained models.

In this chapter, we will cover the following recipes:

- Gender classification of a person in an image using CNNs
- Gender classification of a person in image using the VGG16 architecture-based model
- Visualizing the output of the intermediate layers of a neural network
- Gender classification of a person in image using the VGG19 architecture-based model
- Gender classification of a using the ResNet architecture-based model
- Gender classification of a using the inception architecture-based model
- Detecting the key points within image of a face

Gender classification of the person in an image using CNNs

To understand some of the limitations of CNNs, let's go through an example where we try to identify whether the given image contains the image of a cat or a dog.

Getting ready

We will gain an intuition of how a CNN predicts the class of object present in the image through the following steps:

- A convolution filter is activated by certain parts of the image:
    - For example, certain filters might activate if the image has a certain pattern—it contains a circular structure, for example
- A pooling layer ensures that image translation is taken care of:
    - This ensures that even if an image is big, over an increased number of pooling operations, the size of the image becomes small and the object can then be detected as the object is now expected to be in the smaller portion of the image (as it is pooled multiple times)
- The final flatten layer flattens all the patterns that are extracted by various convolution and pooling operations

Let's impose a scenario where the number of images in a training dataset is small. In such a case, the model does not have enough data points for it to generalize on a test dataset.

Additionally, given that the convolutions are learning various features from scratch, it could potentially take many epochs before the model starts to fit on top of the training dataset if the training dataset contains images that have a large shape (width and height).

Hence, in the next section, we will code the following scenario of building a CNN, where there are a few images (~1,700 images) and test the accuracy on different shapes of images:

- Accuracy in 10 epochs where the image size is 300 X 300
- Accuracy in 10 epochs where the image size is 50 X 50

How to do it...

In this section, we will fetch a dataset and perform classification analysis where the image size in one scenario is 300 x 300, while in the other scenario, it is 50 x 50. (Please refer to `Transfer_learning.ipynb` file in GitHub while implementing the code.)

Scenario 1 – big images

1. Fetch the dataset. For this analysis, we will continue with the male versus female classification dataset that we have downloaded in the Gender classification case study in Chapter 4, *Building a Deep Convolutional Neural Network*:

```
$ wget
https://d1p17r2m4rzlbo.cloudfront.net/wp-content/uploads/2017/04/a9
43287.csv
```

```
import pandas as pd, numpy as np
from skimage import io
# Location of file is /content/a943287.csv
# be sure to change to location of downloaded file on your machine
data = pd.read_csv('/content/a943287.csv')

 data_male =
data[data['please_select_the_gender_of_the_person_in_the_picture']=
="male"].reset_index(drop='index')
data_female =
data[data['please_select_the_gender_of_the_person_in_the_picture']=
="female"].reset_index(drop='index')
final_data =
pd.concat([data_male[:1000],data_female[:1000]],axis=0).reset_index
(drop='index')
```

2. Extract the image paths and then prepare the input and output data:

```
x = []
y = []
for i in range(final_data.shape[0]):
    try:
        image = io.imread(final_data.loc[i]['image_url'])
        if(image.shape==(300,300,3)):
            x.append(image)
y.append(final_data.loc[i]['please_select_the_gender_of_the_person_
in_the_picture'])
    except:
        continue
```

[145]

3. A sample of the images is as follows:

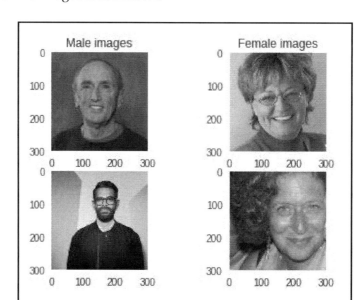

Note that all the images are 300 x 300 x 3 in size.

4. Create the input and output dataset arrays:

```
x2 = []
y2 = []
for i in range(len(x)):
    x2.append(x[i])
    img_label = np.where(y[i]=="male",1,0)
    y2.append(img_label)
```

In the preceding step, we are looping through all the images (one at a time), reading the image into an array (we could have gotten away without this step in this iteration. However, in the next scenario of resizing the image, we will resize images in this step). Additionally, we are storing the labels of each image.

5. Prepare the input array so that it can be passed to a CNN. Additionally, prepare the output array:

```
x2 = np.array(x2)
x2 = x2.reshape(x2.shape[0],x2.shape[1],x2.shape[2],3)
```

Here, we are converting the list of arrays into a numpy array so that it can then be passed to the neural network.

Scale the input array and create input and output arrays:

```
X = np.array(x2)/255
Y = np.array(y2)
```

6. Create train and test datasets:

```
from sklearn.model_selection import train_test_split
X_train, X_test, y_train, y_test = train_test_split(X,Y, test_size=0.1, random_state=42)
```

7. Define the model and compile it:

```
from keras.models import Sequential
from keras.layers.core import Dense, Dropout, Activation, Flatten
from keras.layers.convolutional import Conv2D
from keras.layers.pooling import MaxPooling2D
from keras.optimizers import SGD
from keras import backend as K

model = Sequential()
model.add(Conv2D(64, kernel_size=(3, 3), activation='relu',input_shape=(300,300,3)))
model.add(MaxPooling2D(pool_size=(2, 2)))
model.add(Conv2D(128, kernel_size=(3, 3), activation='relu',padding='same'))
model.add(MaxPooling2D(pool_size=(2, 2)))
model.add(Conv2D(256, kernel_size=(3, 3), activation='relu',padding='same'))
model.add(MaxPooling2D(pool_size=(2, 2)))
model.add(Conv2D(512, kernel_size=(3, 3), activation='relu',padding='same'))
model.add(Flatten())
model.add(Dense(100, activation='relu'))
model.add(Dense(1, activation='sigmoid'))
model.summary()
```

In the preceding code, we are building a model that has multiple layers of convolution, pooling, and dropout. Furthermore, we are passing the output of final dropout through a flattening layer and then connecting the flattened output to a 512 node hidden layer before connecting the hidden layer to the output layer.

A summary of the model is as follows:

```
Layer (type)                 Output Shape              Param #
=================================================================
conv2d_1 (Conv2D)            (None, 298, 298, 64)      1792
_____
max_pooling2d_1 (MaxPooling2 (None, 149, 149, 64)      0
_____
conv2d_2 (Conv2D)            (None, 149, 149, 128)     73856
_____
max_pooling2d_2 (MaxPooling2 (None, 74, 74, 128)       0
_____
conv2d_3 (Conv2D)            (None, 74, 74, 256)       295168
_____
max_pooling2d_3 (MaxPooling2 (None, 37, 37, 256)       0
_____
conv2d_4 (Conv2D)            (None, 37, 37, 512)       1180160
_____
flatten_1 (Flatten)          (None, 700928)            0
_____
dense_1 (Dense)              (None, 100)               70092900
_____
dense_2 (Dense)              (None, 1)                 101
=================================================================
Total params: 71,643,977
Trainable params: 71,643,977
Non-trainable params: 0
```

In the following code, we are compiling the model to reduce binary cross entropy loss, as follows:

```
model.compile(loss='binary_crossentropy',optimizer='adam',metrics=['accuracy'])
```

8. Fit the model:

```
history = model.fit(X_train, y_train,
batch_size=32, epochs=10, verbose=1, validation_data = (X_test,
y_test))
```

In the preceding step, you can see that the model does not train over increasing epochs, as shown in the following graph (the code for this diagram is the same as we saw in the *Scaling input data* section in Chapter 2, *Building a Deep Feedforward Neural Network*, and it can be found in the GitHub repository of this chapter):

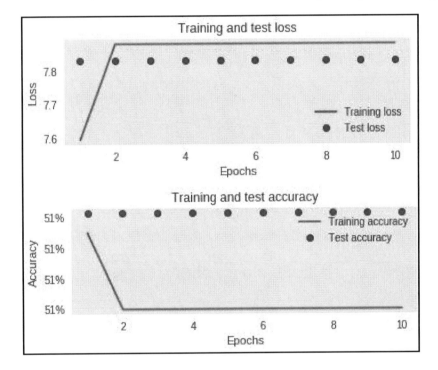

In the preceding graph, you can see that the model hardly learned anything, as the loss did not vary much. Also, the accuracy was stuck near the 51% mark (which is roughly the distribution of male versus female images in the original dataset).

Scenario 2 – smaller images

In this scenario, we will modify the following in the model:

- Input image size:
    - We will reduce the size from 300 X 300 to 50 X 50
- Model architecture:
    - The structure of the architecture remains the same as what we saw in *Scenario 1 – big images*

1. Create a dataset with the input of the reduced image size (50 X 50 X 3) and output labels. For this, we will continue from *step 4* of Scenario 1:

    ```
    import cv2
    x2 = []
    y2 = []
    for i in range(len(x)):
      img = cv2.resize(x[i],(50,50))
      x2.append(img)
      img_label = np.where(y[i]=="male",1,0)
      y2.append(img_label)
    ```

2. Create the input and output arrays for the train, test datasets:

    ```
    x2 = np.array(x2)
    x2 = x2.reshape(x2.shape[0],x2.shape[1],x2.shape[2],3)
    X = np.array(x2)/255
    Y = np.array(y2)
    from sklearn.model_selection import train_test_split
    X_train, X_test, y_train, y_test = train_test_split(X,Y,
    test_size=0.1, random_state=42)
    ```

3. Build and compile the model:

    ```
    model = Sequential()
    model.add(Conv2D(64, kernel_size=(3, 3),
    activation='relu',input_shape=(50,50,3)))
    model.add(MaxPooling2D(pool_size=(2, 2)))
    model.add(Conv2D(128, kernel_size=(3, 3),
    activation='relu',padding='same'))
    model.add(MaxPooling2D(pool_size=(2, 2)))
    model.add(Conv2D(256, kernel_size=(3, 3),
    activation='relu',padding='same'))
    model.add(MaxPooling2D(pool_size=(2, 2)))
    model.add(Conv2D(512, kernel_size=(3, 3),
    activation='relu',padding='same'))
    model.add(Flatten())
    ```

```
model.add(Dense(100, activation='relu'))
model.add(Dense(1, activation='sigmoid'))
model.summary()

model.compile(loss='binary_crossentropy',optimizer='adam',metrics=[
'accuracy'])
```

A summary of the model is as follows:

Layer (type)	Output Shape	Param #
conv2d_5 (Conv2D)	(None, 48, 48, 64)	1792
max_pooling2d_4 (MaxPooling2	(None, 24, 24, 64)	0
conv2d_6 (Conv2D)	(None, 24, 24, 128)	73856
max_pooling2d_5 (MaxPooling2	(None, 12, 12, 128)	0
conv2d_7 (Conv2D)	(None, 12, 12, 256)	295168
max_pooling2d_6 (MaxPooling2	(None, 6, 6, 256)	0
conv2d_8 (Conv2D)	(None, 6, 6, 512)	1180160
flatten_2 (Flatten)	(None, 18432)	0
dense_3 (Dense)	(None, 100)	1843300
dense_4 (Dense)	(None, 1)	101

Total params: 3,394,377
Trainable params: 3,394,377
Non-trainable params: 0

4. Fit the model:

```
history = model.fit(X_train, y_train,
batch_size=32,epochs=10,verbose=1,validation_data = (X_test,
y_test))
```

The accuracy and loss of the model training across train and test datasets over increasing epochs is as follows:

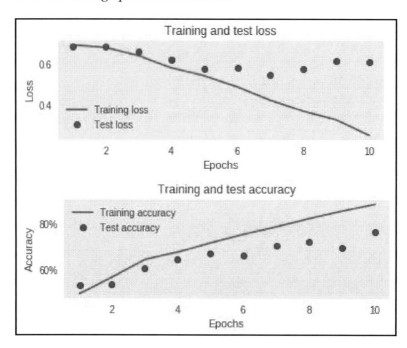

Note that, while the accuracy increased and the loss decreased steadily in both the training and test datasets initially, over increasing epochs, the model started to overfit (specialize) on training data and had an accuracy of ~76% on the test dataset.

From this, we can see that the CNN works when the input size is small and thus the filters had to learn from a smaller portion of the image. However, as, the image size increased, the CNN had a tough time learning.

 Given that we have discovered that the image size has an impact on model accuracy, in the new scenario, let's use aggressive pooling to ensure that the bigger image (300 x 300 shape) reduces to a smaller one quickly.

Scenario 3 – aggressive pooling on big images

In the following code, we will retain the analysis we have done until step 6 in Scenario 1. However, the only change will be the model architecture; in the following model architecture, we have more aggressive pooling than what we used in Scenario 1.

In the following architecture, having a bigger window of pooling in each layer ensures that we capture the activations in a larger area compared to the scenario of having lower pool sizes. The architecture of the model is as follows:

```
model = Sequential()
model.add(Conv2D(64, kernel_size=(3, 3),
activation='relu',input_shape=(300,300,3)))
model.add(MaxPooling2D(pool_size=(3, 3)))
model.add(Conv2D(128, kernel_size=(3, 3),
activation='relu',padding='same'))
model.add(MaxPooling2D(pool_size=(3, 3)))
model.add(Conv2D(256, kernel_size=(3, 3),
activation='relu',padding='same'))
model.add(MaxPooling2D(pool_size=(3, 3)))
model.add(Conv2D(512, kernel_size=(3, 3),
activation='relu',padding='same'))
model.add(Flatten())
model.add(Dense(100, activation='relu'))
model.add(Dense(1, activation='sigmoid'))
model.summary()
```

Note that in this architecture, the pool size is 3 x 3 and not 2 x 2, as we had in the previous scenario:

Layer (type)	Output Shape	Param #
conv2d_9 (Conv2D)	(None, 298, 298, 64)	1792
max_pooling2d_7 (MaxPooling2	(None, 99, 99, 64)	0
conv2d_10 (Conv2D)	(None, 99, 99, 128)	73856
max_pooling2d_8 (MaxPooling2	(None, 33, 33, 128)	0
conv2d_11 (Conv2D)	(None, 33, 33, 256)	295168
max_pooling2d_9 (MaxPooling2	(None, 11, 11, 256)	0
conv2d_12 (Conv2D)	(None, 11, 11, 512)	1180160
flatten_3 (Flatten)	(None, 61952)	0
dense_5 (Dense)	(None, 100)	6195300
dense_6 (Dense)	(None, 1)	101

```
Total params: 7,746,377
Trainable params: 7,746,377
Non-trainable params: 0
```

Once we fit a model on the input and output arrays, the variation of accuracy and loss on the train and test datasets is as follows:

```
model.compile(loss='binary_crossentropy',optimizer='adam',metrics=['accuracy'])
history = model.fit(X_train, y_train,
batch_size=32,epochs=10,verbose=1,validation_data = (X_test, y_test))
```

The following is the output of the preceding code:

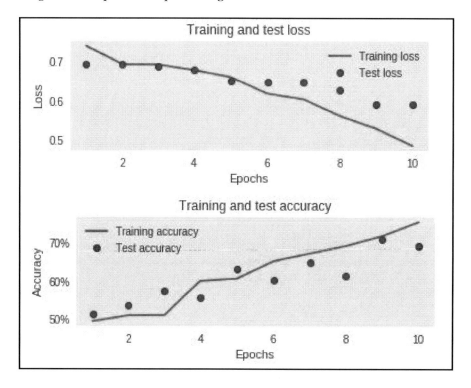

We can see that the test data has ~70% accuracy in correctly classifying gender in images.

However, you can see that there is a considerable amount of overfitting on top of the training dataset (as the loss decreases steadily on the training dataset, while not on the test dataset).

Gender classification of the person in image using the VGG16 architecture-based model

In the previous section on gender classification using CNN, we saw that when we build a CNN model from scratch, we could encounter some of the following scenarios:

- The number of images that were passed is not sufficient for the model to learn
- Convolutions might not be learning all the features in our images when the images are big in size

The first problem could be tackled by performing our analysis on a large dataset. The second one could be tackled by training a larger network on the larger dataset for a longer number of epochs.

However, while we are able to perform all of this, more often than not, we do not have the amount of data that is needed to perform such an analysis. Transfer learning using pre-trained models comes to the rescue in such scenarios.

ImageNet is a popular competition where participants are asked to predict the various classes of an image, where the images are of various sizes and also contain multiple classes of objects.

There were multiple research teams that competed in this competition to come up with a model that is able to predict images of multiple classes where there are millions of images in a dataset. Given that there were millions of images, the first problem of a limited dataset is resolved. Additionally, given the huge networks the research teams have built, the problem of coming up with convolutions that learn a variety of features is also resolved.

Hence, we are in a position to reuse the convolutions that were built on a different dataset, where the convolutions are learning to predict the various features in an image and then pass them through a hidden layer so that we can predict the class of an image for our specific dataset. There are multiple pre-trained models that were developed by different groups. We will go through VGG16 here.

Getting ready

In this section, let's try to understand how we can leverage the VGG16 pre-trained network for our gender classification exercise.

The VGG16 model's architecture is as follows:

```
Layer (type)                 Output Shape              Param #
=================================================================
input_1 (InputLayer)         (None, 300, 300, 3)       0
_____
block1_conv1 (Conv2D)        (None, 300, 300, 64)      1792
_____
block1_conv2 (Conv2D)        (None, 300, 300, 64)      36928
_____
block1_pool (MaxPooling2D)   (None, 150, 150, 64)      0
_____
block2_conv1 (Conv2D)        (None, 150, 150, 128)     73856
_____
block2_conv2 (Conv2D)        (None, 150, 150, 128)     147584
_____
block2_pool (MaxPooling2D)   (None, 75, 75, 128)       0
_____
block3_conv1 (Conv2D)        (None, 75, 75, 256)       295168
_____
block3_conv2 (Conv2D)        (None, 75, 75, 256)       590080
_____
block3_conv3 (Conv2D)        (None, 75, 75, 256)       590080
_____
block3_pool (MaxPooling2D)   (None, 37, 37, 256)       0
_____
block4_conv1 (Conv2D)        (None, 37, 37, 512)       1180160
_____
block4_conv2 (Conv2D)        (None, 37, 37, 512)       2359808
_____
block4_conv3 (Conv2D)        (None, 37, 37, 512)       2359808
_____
block4_pool (MaxPooling2D)   (None, 18, 18, 512)       0
_____
block5_conv1 (Conv2D)        (None, 18, 18, 512)       2359808
_____
block5_conv2 (Conv2D)        (None, 18, 18, 512)       2359808
_____
block5_conv3 (Conv2D)        (None, 18, 18, 512)       2359808
_____
block5_pool (MaxPooling2D)   (None, 9, 9, 512)         0
=================================================================
Total params: 14,714,688
Trainable params: 14,714,688
Non-trainable params: 0
```

Notice that the model's architecture is very similar to the model that we trained in the Gender classification using CNNs section. The major difference is that this model is deeper (more hidden layers). Additionally, the weights of the VGG16 network are obtained by training on millions of images.

We'll ensure that the VGG16 weights are frozen from updating while training our model to classify gender in an image. The output of passing an image in the gender classification exercise (which is of 300 x 300 x 3 in shape) is 9 x 9 x 512 in shape.

We shall keep the weights as they were in the original network, extract the 9 x 9 x 512 output, pass it through another convolution pooling operation, flatten it, connect it to a hidden layer, and then pass it through the sigmoid activation to determine whether the image is of a male or a female.

Essentially, by using the convolution and pooling layers of the VGG16 model, we are using the filters that were trained on a much bigger dataset. Ultimately, we will be fine-tuning the output of these convolution and pooling layers for the objects that we are trying to predict.

How to do it...

With this strategy in place, let's code up our solution as follows (Please refer to `Transfer_learning.ipynb` file in GitHub while implementing the code):

1. Import the pre-trained model:

```
from keras.applications import vgg16
from keras.utils.vis_utils import plot_model
from keras.applications.vgg16 import preprocess_input
vgg16_model = vgg16.VGG16(include_top=False,
weights='imagenet',input_shape=(300,300,3))
```

Note that we are excluding the last layer in the VGG16 model. This is to ensure that we fine-tune the VGG16 model for the problem that we are trying solve. Additionally, given that our input image shape is 300 X 300 X 3, we are specifying the same while downloading the VGG16 model.

2. Preprocess the set of images. This preprocessing step ensures that the images are processed in a manner that the pre-trained model can take as input. For example, in the following code, we are performing preprocessing for one of the images, named `img`:

```
from keras.applications.vgg16 import preprocess_input
img = preprocess_input(img.reshape(1,224,224,3))
```

We are preprocessing the image as per the preprocessing requirement in VGG16 using the `preprocess_input` method.

3. Create the input and output datasets. For this exercise, we will continue from the end of step 3 in Scenario 1 of Gender classification using CNN. Here, the process of creating input and output datasets remains the same as what we have already done, with a minor modification of extracting features using the VGG16 model.

We will pass each image through `vgg16_model` so that we take the output of `vgg16_model` as the processed input. Additionally, we will be performing the preprocessing on top of the input as follows:

```
import cv2
x2_vgg16 = []
for i in range(len(x)):
    img = x[i]
    img = preprocess_input(img.reshape(1,300,300,3))
```

Now, we pass the pre-processed input to the VGG16 model to extract features, as follows:

```
img_new = vgg16_model.predict(img.reshape(1,300,300,3))
x2_vgg16.append(img_new)
```

In the preceding code, in addition to passing the image through VGG16 model, we have also stored the input values in a list.

4. Convert the input and output to NumPy arrays and create training and test datasets:

```
x2_vgg16 = np.array(x2_vgg16)
x2_vgg16=
x2_vgg16.reshape(x2_vgg16.shape[0],x2_vgg16.shape[2],x2_vgg16.shape[3],x2_vgg16.shape[4])
Y = np.array(y2)
from sklearn.model_selection import train_test_split
X_train, X_test, y_train, y_test = train_test_split(x2_vgg16,Y, test_size=0.1, random_state=42)
```

5. Build and compile the model:

```
model_vgg16 = Sequential()
model_vgg16.add(Conv2D(512, kernel_size=(3, 3),
activation='relu',input_shape=(X_train.shape[1],X_train.shape[2],X_
train.shape[3])))
model_vgg16.add(MaxPooling2D(pool_size=(2, 2)))
model_vgg16.add(Flatten())
model_vgg16.add(Dense(512, activation='relu'))
model_vgg16.add(Dropout(0.5))
model_vgg16.add(Dense(1, activation='sigmoid'))
model_vgg16.summary()
```

The summary of the model is as follows:

```
Layer (type)                 Output Shape              Param #
=================================================================
conv2d_14 (Conv2D)           (None, 7, 7, 512)         2359808
_____
max_pooling2d_11 (MaxPooling (None, 3, 3, 512)         0
_____
flatten_5 (Flatten)          (None, 4608)              0
_____
dense_9 (Dense)              (None, 512)               2359808
_____
dropout_2 (Dropout)          (None, 512)               0
_____
dense_10 (Dense)             (None, 1)                 513
=================================================================
Total params: 4,720,129
Trainable params: 4,720,129
Non-trainable params: 0
```

Compile the model:

```
model_vgg16.compile(loss='binary_crossentropy',optimizer='adam',met
rics=['accuracy'])
```

6. Fit the model while scaling the input data:

```
history_vgg16 = model_vgg16.fit(X_train/np.max(X_train), y_train,
batch_size=16,epochs=10,verbose=1,validation_data =
(X_test/np.max(X_train), y_test))
```

Transfer Learning

Once we fit the model, we should see that we are able to attain an accuracy of ~89% on the test dataset in the first few epochs:

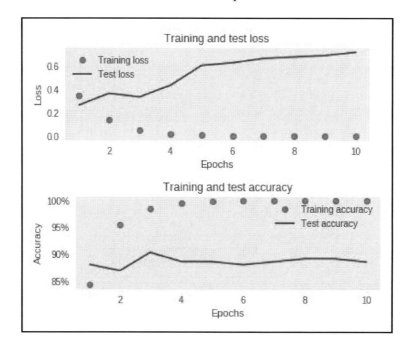

Contrast this with the models we built in the Gender classification using CNN section, where in any of the scenarios, we were not able to reach 80% accuracy in classification in 10 epochs.

A sample of some of the images where the model mis-classified is as follows:

Note that, in the preceding picture, the model potentially mis-classified when the input image is either a part of a face or if the object in the image occupies a much smaller portion of the total image or potentially, if the label was provided incorrectly.

Visualizing the output of the intermediate layers of a neural network

In the previous section, we built a model that learns to classify gender from images with an accuracy of 89%. However, as of now, it is a black box for us in terms of what the filters are learning.

In this section, we will learn how to extract what the various filters in a model are learning. Additionally, we will contrast the scenario of what the filters in the initial layers are learning with what the features in the last few layers are learning.

Getting ready

To understand how to extract what the various filters are learning, let's adopt the following strategy:

- We will select an image on which to perform analysis.
- We will select the first convolution to understand what the various filters in the first convolution are learning.
- Calculate the output of the convolution of weights in the first layer and the input image:
    - In this step, we will extract the intermediate output of our model:
        - We will be extracting the output of the first layer of the model.
- To extract the output of first layer, we will use the functional API:
    - The input to the functional API is the input image, and the output will be the output of the first layer.
- This returns the output of the intermediate layer across all the channels (filters).

- We will perform these steps on both the first layer and the last layer of the convolution.
- Finally, we will visualize the output of the convolution operations across all channels.
- We will also visualize the output of a given channel across all images.

How to do it...

In this section, we will code up the process of visualizing what the filters are learning across the convolution filters of the initial layers as well as the final layers.

We'll reuse the data that we prepared in the *Gender classification using CNN* recipe's Scenario 1 from *step 1* to *step 4* (please refer to `Transfer_learning.ipynb` file in GitHub while implementing the code):

1. Identify an image for which you want to visualize the intermediate output:

    ```
    plt.imshow(x[3])
    plt.grid('off')
    ```

2. Define the functional API that takes the image as an input, and the first convolution layer's output as output:

```
from keras.applications.vgg16 import preprocess_input
model_vgg16.predict(vgg16_model.predict(preprocess_input(x[3].resha
pe(1,300,300,3)))/np.max(X_train))
from keras import models
activation_model =
models.Model(inputs=vgg16_model.input,outputs=vgg16_model.layers[1]
.output)
activations =
activation_model.predict(preprocess_input(x[3].reshape(1,300,300,3)
))
```

We have defined an intermediate model named `activation_model`, where we are passing the image of interest as input and extracting the first layer's output as the model's output.

Once we have defined the model, we will extract the activations of the first layer by passing the input image through the model. Note that we will have to reshape the input image so that it is the shape the model expects.

3. Let's visualize the first 36 filters in the output, as follows:

```
fig, axs = plt.subplots(6, 6, figsize=(10, 10))
fig.subplots_adjust(hspace = .5, wspace=.5)
first_layer_activation = activations[0]
for i in range(6):
  for j in range(6):
    try:
      axs[i,j].set_ylim((224, 0))
axs[i,j].contourf(first_layer_activation[:,:,((6*i)+j)],6,cmap='vir
idis')
      axs[i,j].set_title('filter: '+str((6*i)+j))
      axs[i,j].axis('off')
    except:
      continue
```

4. In the preceding code, we created a 6 x 6 frame on which we can plot 36 images. Furthermore, we are looping through all the channels in `first_layer_activation` and plotting the output of the first layer, as follows:

Here, we can see that certain filters extract the contours of the original image (filter 0, 4, 7, 10, for example). Additionally, certain filters have learned to recognize only a few aspects, such as ears, eyes, and nose (filter 30, for example).

5. Let's validate our understanding that certain filters are able to extract contours of the original image by going through the output of filter 7 for 36 images, as follows:

```
activation_model = models.Model(inputs=vgg16_model.input,outputs=vgg16_model.layers[1].output)
activations = activation_model.predict(preprocess_input(np.array(x[:36]).reshape(36,300,300,3)))
fig, axs = plt.subplots(6, 6, figsize=(10, 10))
fig.subplots_adjust(hspace = .5, wspace=.5)
first_layer_activation = activations
for i in range(6):
  for j in range(6):
    try:
      axs[i,j].set_ylim((224, 0))
axs[i,j].contourf(first_layer_activation[((6*i)+j),:,:,7],6,cmap='viridis')
      axs[i,j].set_title('filter: '+str((6*i)+j))
      axs[i,j].axis('off')
    except:
      continue
```

[165]

In the preceding code, we are looping through the first 36 images and plotting the output of the first convolution layer for all 36 images:

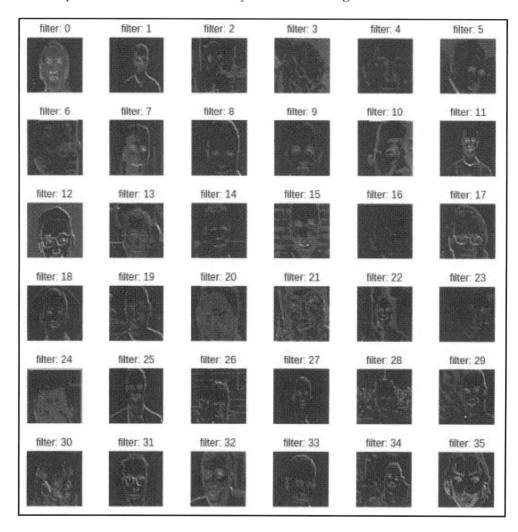

Note that, across all the images, the seventh filter is learning the contours within an image.

6. Let's try to understand what the filters in the last convolution layer are learning. To understand where the last convolution layer is located in our model, let's extract the various layers in our model:

```
for i, layer in enumerate(model.layers):
    print(i, layer.name)
```

The following layers name will be displayed by executing the preceding code:

```
0  conv2d_1
1  conv2d_2
2  max_pooling2d_1
3  dropout_1
4  conv2d_3
5  conv2d_4
6  max_pooling2d_2
7  dropout_2
8  conv2d_5
9  conv2d_6
10 dropout_3
11 flatten_1
12 dense_1
13 dropout_4
14 dense_2
```

7. Note that the last convolution layer is the ninth output of our model and can be extracted as follows:

```
activation_model = models.Model(inputs=vgg16_model.input,outputs=vgg16_model.layers[-1].output)
activations = activation_model.predict(preprocess_input(x[3].reshape(1,300,300,3)))
```

Transfer Learning

The size of the image has now shrunk considerably (to 1, 9,9,512), due to the multiple pooling operations that were performed on top of the image. A visualization of what the various filters in the last convolution layer are learning is as follows:

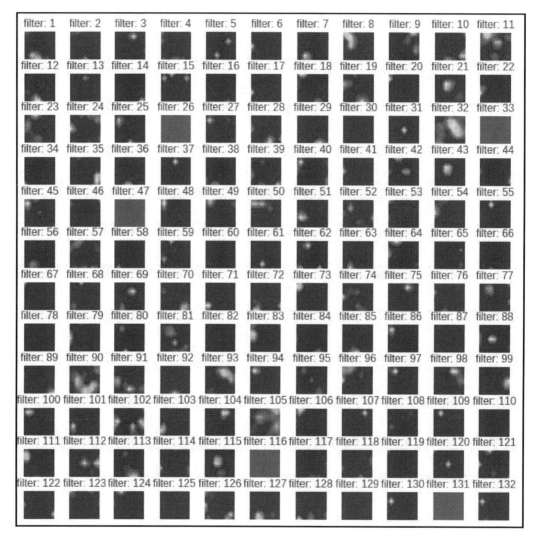

Note that, in this iteration, it is not as clear to understand what the last convolution layer's filters are learning (as the contours are not easy to attribute to one of the parts of original image), as these are more granular than the contours that were learned in the first convolution layer.

Gender classification of the person in image using the VGG19 architecture-based model

In the previous section, we learned about how VGG16 works. VGG19 is an improved version of VGG16, with a greater number of convolution and pooling operations.

Getting ready

The architecture of the VGG19 model is as follows:

```
Layer (type)                 Output Shape              Param #
=================================================================
input_1 (InputLayer)         (None, 300, 300, 3)       0
block1_conv1 (Conv2D)        (None, 300, 300, 64)      1792
block1_conv2 (Conv2D)        (None, 300, 300, 64)      36928
block1_pool (MaxPooling2D)   (None, 150, 150, 64)      0
block2_conv1 (Conv2D)        (None, 150, 150, 128)     73856
block2_conv2 (Conv2D)        (None, 150, 150, 128)     147584
block2_pool (MaxPooling2D)   (None, 75, 75, 128)       0
block3_conv1 (Conv2D)        (None, 75, 75, 256)       295168
block3_conv2 (Conv2D)        (None, 75, 75, 256)       590080
block3_conv3 (Conv2D)        (None, 75, 75, 256)       590080
block3_pool (MaxPooling2D)   (None, 37, 37, 256)       0
block4_conv1 (Conv2D)        (None, 37, 37, 512)       1180160
block4_conv2 (Conv2D)        (None, 37, 37, 512)       2359808
block4_conv3 (Conv2D)        (None, 37, 37, 512)       2359808
block4_pool (MaxPooling2D)   (None, 18, 18, 512)       0
block5_conv1 (Conv2D)        (None, 18, 18, 512)       2359808
block5_conv2 (Conv2D)        (None, 18, 18, 512)       2359808
block5_conv3 (Conv2D)        (None, 18, 18, 512)       2359808
block5_pool (MaxPooling2D)   (None, 9, 9, 512)         0
=================================================================
Total params: 14,714,688
Trainable params: 14,714,688
Non-trainable params: 0
```

Transfer Learning

Note that the preceding architecture has more layers, as well as more parameters.

Note that the 16 and 19 in the VGG16 and VGG19 architectures stand for the number of layers in each of these networks. Once we extract the 9 x 9 x 512 output after we pass each image through the VGG19 network, that output will be the input for our model.

Additionally, the process of creating input and output datasets and then building, compiling, and fitting a model will remain the same as what we saw in the Gender classification using a VGG16 model-based architecture recipe.

How to do it...

In this section, we will code up the VGG19 pre-trained model, as follows (Please refer to `Transfer_learning.ipynb` file in GitHub while implementing the code):

1. Prepare the input and output data (we'll continue from *step 3* in Scenario 1 of the *Gender classification using CNN* recipe):

    ```
    import cv2
    x2 = []
    for i in range(len(x)):
        img = x[i]
        img = preprocess_input(img.reshape(1,300,300,3))
        img_new = vgg19_model.predict(img.reshape(1,300,300,3))
        x2.append(img_new)
    ```

2. Convert the input and output into their corresponding arrays and create the training and test datasets:

    ```
    x2 = np.array(x2)
    x2= x2.reshape(x2.shape[0],x2.shape[2],x2.shape[3],x2.shape[4])
    from sklearn.model_selection import train_test_split
    X_train, X_test, y_train, y_test = train_test_split(x2,Y, test_size=0.1, random_state=42)
    ```

3. Build and compile the model:

   ```
   model_vgg19 = Sequential()
   model_vgg19.add(Conv2D(512, kernel_size=(3, 3),
   activation='relu',input_shape=(X_train.shape[1],X_train.shape[2],X_
   train.shape[3])))
   model_vgg19.add(MaxPooling2D(pool_size=(2, 2)))
   model_vgg19.add(Flatten())
   model_vgg19.add(Dense(512, activation='relu'))
   model_vgg19.add(Dropout(0.5))
   model_vgg19.add(Dense(1, activation='sigmoid'))
   model_vgg19.summary()
   ```

   A visualization of the model is as follows:

   ```
   Layer (type)                 Output Shape              Param #
   =================================================================
   conv2d_6 (Conv2D)            (None, 7, 7, 512)         2359808
   _____
   max_pooling2d_5 (MaxPooling2 (None, 3, 3, 512)         0
   _____
   flatten_3 (Flatten)          (None, 4608)              0
   _____
   dense_5 (Dense)              (None, 512)               2359808
   _____
   dropout_2 (Dropout)          (None, 512)               0
   _____
   dense_6 (Dense)              (None, 1)                 513
   =================================================================
   Total params: 4,720,129
   Trainable params: 4,720,129
   Non-trainable params: 0
   ```

   ```
   model_vgg19.compile(loss='binary_crossentropy',optimizer='adam',met
   rics=['accuracy'])
   ```

4. Fit the model while scaling the input data:

   ```
   history_vgg19 = model_vgg19.fit(X_train/np.max(X_train), y_train,
   batch_size=16,epochs=10,verbose=1,validation_data =
   (X_test/np.max(X_train), y_test))
   ```

Let's plot the training and test datasets' loss and accuracy measures:

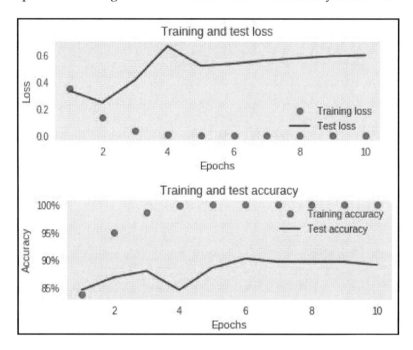

We should note that we were able to achieve ~89% accuracy on the test dataset when we used the VGG19 architecture, which is very similar to that of the VGG16 architecture.

A sample of mis-classified images is as follows:

Note that, VGG19 seems to mis-classify based on the space occupied by a person in an image. Additionally, it seems to give higher weightage to predict that a male with long hair is a female.

Gender classification using the Inception v3 architecture-based model

In the previous recipes, we implemented gender classification based on the VGG16 and VGG19 architectures. In this section, we'll implement the classification using the Inception architecture.

An intuition of how inception model comes in handy, is as follows.

There will be images where the object occupies the majority of the image. Similarly, there will be images where the object occupies a small portion of the total image. If we have the same size of kernels in both scenario, we are making it difficult for the model to learn – some images might have objects that are small and others might have objects that are larger.

To address this problem, we will have filters of multiple sizes that operate at the same layer.

In such a scenario, the network essentially gets wide rather than getting deep, as follows:

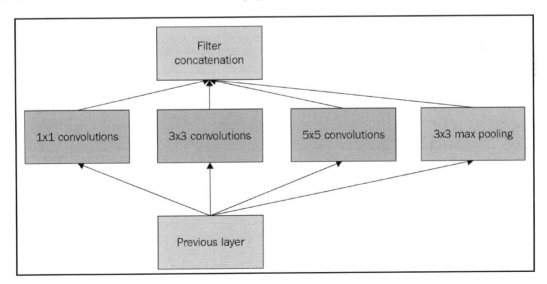

In the preceding diagram, note that we are performing convolutions of multiple filters in a given layer. The inception v1 module has nine such modules stacked linearly, as follows:

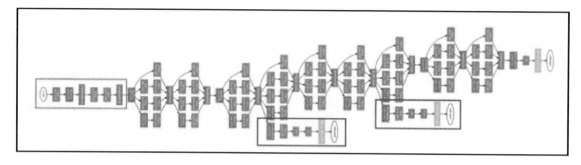

Source: http://joelouismarino.github.io/images/blog_images/blog_googlenet_keras/googlenet_diagram.png

Note that this architecture is fairly deep as well as wide. This is likely to result in a vanishing gradient problem (as we saw in the case for batch normalization in Chapter 2, *Building a Deep Feedforward Neural Network*).

To get around the problem of a vanishing gradient, inception v1 has two auxiliary classifiers that stem out of the inception modules. The overall loss of inception based network tries to minimize is as follows:

```
total_loss = real_loss + 0.3 * aux_loss_1 + 0.3 * aux_loss_2
```

Note that auxiliary losses are used only during training and are ignored during the prediction process.

Inception v2 and v3 are improvements on top of the inception v1 architecture where in v2, the authors have performed optimizations on top of convolution operations to process images faster and in v3, the authors have added 7 x 7 convolutions on top of the existing convolutions so that they can be concatenated together.

How to do it...

The process in which we code up inception v3 is very similar to the way in which we built the VGG19 model-based classifier (Please refer to Transfer_learning.ipynb file in GitHub while implementing the code):

1. Download the pre-trained Inception model:

    ```
    from keras.applications import inception_v3
    from keras.applications.inception_v3 import preprocess_input
    ```

```
from keras.utils.vis_utils import plot_model
inception_model = inception_v3.InceptionV3(include_top=False,
weights='imagenet',input_shape=(300,300,3))
```

Note that we would need an input image that is at least 300 x 300 in shape for the inception v3 pre-trained model to work.

2. Create the input and output datasets (we'll continue from step 3 in Scenario 1 of the *Gender classification using CNNs* recipe):

```
import cv2
x2 = []
for i in range(len(x)):
    img = x[i]
    img = preprocess_input(img.reshape(1,300,300,3))
    img_new = inception_model.predict(img.reshape(1,300,300,3))
    x2.append(img_new)
```

3. Create the input and output arrays, along with the training and test datasets:

```
x2 = np.array(x2)
x2= x2.reshape(x2.shape[0],x2.shape[2],x2.shape[3],x2.shape[4])
from sklearn.model_selection import train_test_split
X_train, X_test, y_train, y_test = train_test_split(x2,Y,
test_size=0.1, random_state=42)
```

4. Build and compile the model:

```
model_inception_v3 = Sequential()
model_inception_v3.add(Conv2D(512, kernel_size=(3, 3),
activation='relu',input_shape=(X_train.shape[1],X_train.shape[2],X_
train.shape[3])))
model_inception_v3.add(MaxPooling2D(pool_size=(2, 2)))
model_inception_v3.add(Flatten())
model_inception_v3.add(Dense(512, activation='relu'))
model_inception_v3.add(Dropout(0.5))
model_inception_v3.add(Dense(1, activation='sigmoid'))
model_inception_v3.summary()

model.compile(loss='binary_crossentropy',optimizer='adam',metrics=[
'accuracy'])
```

The preceding model can be visualized as follows:

```
Layer (type)                 Output Shape              Param #
=================================================================
conv2d_101 (Conv2D)          (None, 6, 6, 512)         9437696
_____
max_pooling2d_10 (MaxPooling (None, 3, 3, 512)         0
_____
flatten_4 (Flatten)          (None, 4608)              0
_____
dense_7 (Dense)              (None, 512)               2359808
_____
dropout_3 (Dropout)          (None, 512)               0
_____
dense_8 (Dense)              (None, 1)                 513
=================================================================
Total params: 11,798,017
Trainable params: 11,798,017
Non-trainable params: 0
```

5. Fit the model while scaling the input data:

   ```
   history_inception_v3 =
   model_inception_v3.fit(X_train/np.max(X_train), y_train,
   batch_size=16,epochs=10,verbose=1,validation_data =
   (X_test/np.max(X_train), y_test))
   ```

   The variation of accuracy and loss values is as follows:

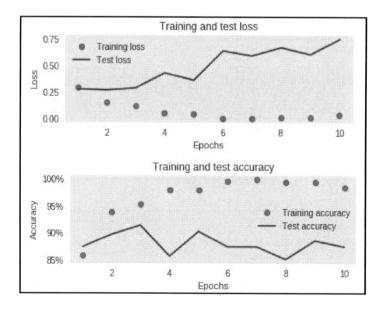

You should notice that the accuracy in this scenario too is also ~90%.

Gender classification of the person in image using the ResNet 50 architecture-based model

From VGG16 to VGG19, we have increased the number of layers and generally, the deeper the neural network, the better its accuracy. However, if merely increasing the number of layers is the trick, then we could keep on adding more layers (while taking care to avoid over-fitting) to the model to get a more accurate results.

Unfortunately, that does not turn out to be true and the issue of the vanishing gradient comes into the picture. As the number of layers increases, the gradient becomes so small as it traverses the network that it becomes hard to adjust the weights, and the network performance deteriorates.

ResNet comes into the picture to address this specific scenario.

Imagine a scenario where a convolution layer does nothing but pass the output of the previous layer to the next layer if the model has nothing to learn. However, if the model has to learn a few other features, the convolution layer takes the previous layer's output as input and learns the additional features that need to be learnt to perform classification.

The term residual is the additional feature that the model is expected to learn from one layer to the next layers.

A typical ResNet architecture looks as follows:

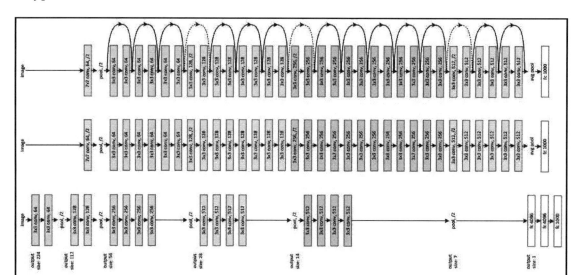

Source: https://arxiv.org/pdf/1512.03385.pdf

Note that we have skip connections that are connecting a previous layer to a layer down the line, along with the traditional convolution layers in this network.

Furthermore, the 50 in ResNet50 comes from the fact that we have a total of 50 layers in the network.

How to do it...

The ResNet50 architecture is built as follows (please refer to `Transfer_learning.ipynb` file in GitHub while implementing the code):

1. Download the pre-trained inception model:

   ```
   from keras.applications import resnet50
   from keras.applications.resnet50 import preprocess_input
   resnet50_model = resnet50.ResNet50(include_top=False,
   weights='imagenet',input_shape=(300,300,3))
   ```

   Note that we need an input image that is at least 224 x 224 in shape for the ResNet50 pre-trained model to work.

Chapter 5

2. Create the input and output datasets (we'll continue from *step 3* in Scenario 1 of the *Gender classification using CNNs* recipe):

```
import cv2
x2 = []
for i in range(len(x)):
    img = x[i]
    img = preprocess_input(img.reshape(1,300,300,3))
    img_new = resnet50_model.predict(img.reshape(1,300,300,3))
    x2.append(img_new)
```

3. Create the input and output arrays, along with the training and test datasets:

```
x2 = np.array(x2)
x2= x2.reshape(x2.shape[0],x2.shape[2],x2.shape[3],x2.shape[4])
from sklearn.model_selection import train_test_split
X_train, X_test, y_train, y_test = train_test_split(x2,Y,
test_size=0.1, random_state=42)
```

4. Build and compile the model:

```
model_resnet50 = Sequential()
model_resnet50.add(Conv2D(512, kernel_size=(3, 3),
activation='relu',input_shape=(X_train.shape[1],X_train.shape[2],X_train.shape[3])))
model_resnet50.add(MaxPooling2D(pool_size=(2, 2)))
model_resnet50.add(Conv2D(512, kernel_size=(3, 3),
activation='relu'))
model_resnet50.add(MaxPooling2D(pool_size=(2, 2)))
model_resnet50.add(Flatten())
model_resnet50.add(Dense(512, activation='relu'))
model_resnet50.add(Dropout(0.5))
model_resnet50.add(Dense(1, activation='sigmoid'))
model_resnet50.summary()

model_resnet50.compile(loss='binary_crossentropy',optimizer='adam',
metrics=['accuracy'])
```

A summary of the model is as follows:

```
Layer (type)                 Output Shape              Param #
=================================================================
conv2d_102 (Conv2D)          (None, 8, 8, 512)         9437696
_____
max_pooling2d_12 (MaxPooling (None, 4, 4, 512)         0
_____
conv2d_103 (Conv2D)          (None, 2, 2, 512)         2359808
_____
max_pooling2d_13 (MaxPooling (None, 1, 1, 512)         0
_____
flatten_5 (Flatten)          (None, 512)               0
_____
dense_9 (Dense)              (None, 512)               262656
_____
dropout_4 (Dropout)          (None, 512)               0
_____
dense_10 (Dense)             (None, 1)                 513
=================================================================
Total params: 12,060,673
Trainable params: 12,060,673
Non-trainable params: 0
```

5. Fit the model while scaling the input data:

```
history_resnet50 = model_resnet50.fit(X_train/np.max(X_train),
y_train, batch_size=32,epochs=10,verbose=1,validation_data =
(X_test/np.max(X_train), y_test))
```

The variation of the accuracy and loss values is as follows:

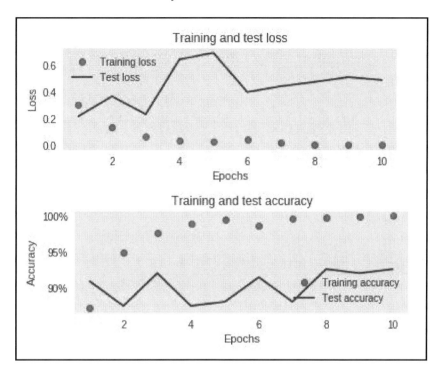

Note that the preceding model gives an accuracy of 92%.

 There is no considerable difference in the accuracy levels of multiple pre-trained models on gender classification, as potentially they were trained to extract the general features, but not necessarily the features to classify gender.

Detecting the key points within image of a face

In this recipe, we will learn about detecting the key points of a human face, which are the boundaries of the left and right eyes, the nose, and the four coordinates of the mouth.

Here are two sample pictures with the key points:

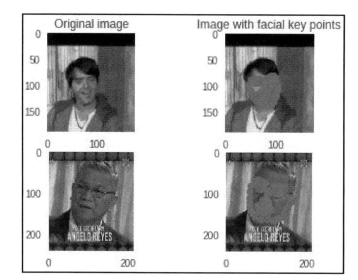

Note that the key points that we are expected to detect are plotted as dots in this picture. A total of 68 key points are detected on the image of face, where the key points of the face include - Mouth, right eyebrow, left eyebrow, right eye, left eye, nose, jaw.

In this case study, we will leverage the VGG16 transfer learning technique that we learned in the *Gender classification in image using the VGG16 architecture-based model* section to detect the key points on the face.

Getting ready

For the key-point detection task, we will work on a dataset where we annotate the points that we want to detect. For this exercise, the input will be the image on which we want to detect the key points and the output will be the *x* and *y* coordinates of the key points. The dataset can be downloaded from here: `https://github.com/udacity/P1_Facial_Keypoints`.

The steps we'll follow are as follows:

1. Download the dataset
2. Resize the images to a standard shape
    1. While resizing the images, ensure that the key points are modified so that they represent the modified (resized) image

3. Pass the resized images through VGG16 model
4. Create input and output arrays, where the input array is the output of passing image through VGG16 model and the output array is the modified facial key point locations
5. Fit a model that minimizes the absolute error value of the difference between predicted and actual facial key points

How to do it...

The strategy that we discussed is coded as follows (Please refer to `Facial_keypoints.ipynb` file in GitHub while implementing the code):

1. Download and import the dataset:

   ```
   $ git clone https://github.com/udacity/P1_Facial_Keypoints.git
   import pandas as pd
   data =
   pd.read_csv('/content/P1_Facial_Keypoints/data/training_frames_keyp
   oints.csv')
   ```

   Inspect this dataset.

	Unnamed: 0	0	1	2	3	4	5	6	7	8	...	126
0	Luis_Fonsi_21.jpg	45.0	98.0	47.0	106.0	49.0	110.0	53.0	119.0	56.0	...	83.0
1	Lincoln_Chafee_52.jpg	41.0	83.0	43.0	91.0	45.0	100.0	47.0	108.0	51.0	...	85.0
2	Valerie_Harper_30.jpg	56.0	69.0	56.0	77.0	56.0	86.0	56.0	94.0	58.0	...	79.0
3	Angelo_Reyes_22.jpg	61.0	80.0	58.0	95.0	58.0	108.0	58.0	120.0	58.0	...	98.0
4	Kristen_Breitweiser_11.jpg	58.0	94.0	58.0	104.0	60.0	113.0	62.0	121.0	67.0	...	92.0

5 rows × 137 columns

There are a total of 137 columns of which the first column is the name of image and the rest of 136 columns represent the x and y co-ordinate values of the 68 key points of face of the corresponding image.

Transfer Learning

2. Preprocess the dataset to extract the image, resized image, VGG16 features of image, modified key point locations as the output:

   Initialize lists that will be appended to create input and output arrays:

```
import cv2, numpy as np
from copy import deepcopy
x=[]
x_img = []
y=[]
```

   Loop through the images and read them:

```
for i in range(data.shape[0]):
    img_path = '/content/P1_Facial_Keypoints/data/training/' + data.iloc[i,0]
    img = cv2.imread(img_path)
```

   Capture the key point values and store them

```
kp = deepcopy(data.iloc[i,1:].tolist())
kp_x = (np.array(kp[0::2])/img.shape[1]).tolist()
kp_y = (np.array(kp[1::2])/img.shape[0]).tolist()
kp2 = kp_x + kp_y
```

   Resize the images

```
img = cv2.resize(img, (224,224))
```

   Preprocess the image so that it can be passed through VGG16 model and extract features:

```
preprocess_img = preprocess_input(img.reshape(1,224,224,3))
vgg16_img = vgg16_model.predict(preprocess_img)
```

   Append the input and output values to corresponding lists:

```
x_img.append(img)
x.append(vgg16_img)
y.append(kp2)
```

   Create input and output arrays:

```
x = np.array(x)
x = x.reshape(x.shape[0],7,7,512)
y = np.array(y)
```

3. Build and compile a model

```
from keras.models import Sequential
from keras.layers import Conv2D, MaxPooling2D, Flatten, Dense,
Dropout
model_vgg16 = Sequential()
model_vgg16.add(Conv2D(512, kernel_size=(3, 3),
activation='relu',input_shape=(x.shape[1],x.shape[2],x.shape[3])))
model_vgg16.add(MaxPooling2D(pool_size=(2, 2)))
model_vgg16.add(Flatten())
model_vgg16.add(Dense(512, activation='relu'))
model_vgg16.add(Dropout(0.5))
model_vgg16.add(Dense(y.shape[1], activation='sigmoid'))
model_vgg16.summary()
```

```
Layer (type)                   Output Shape              Param #
=================================================================
conv2d_11 (Conv2D)             (None, 5, 5, 512)         2359808
_____
max_pooling2d_11 (MaxPooling   (None, 2, 2, 512)         0
_____
flatten_11 (Flatten)           (None, 2048)              0
_____
dense_21 (Dense)               (None, 512)               1049088
_____
dropout_11 (Dropout)           (None, 512)               0
_____
dense_22 (Dense)               (None, 136)               69768
=================================================================
Total params: 3,478,664
Trainable params: 3,478,664
Non-trainable params: 0
```

Compile the model:

```
model_vgg16.compile(loss='mean_absolute_error',optimizer='adam')
```

4. Fit the model

```
history = model_vgg16.fit(x/np.max(x), y, epochs=10, batch_size=32,
verbose=1, validation_split = 0.1)
```

Note that, we are dividing the input array with maximum value of input array so that we scale the input dataset. The variation of training and test loss over increasing epochs is as follows:

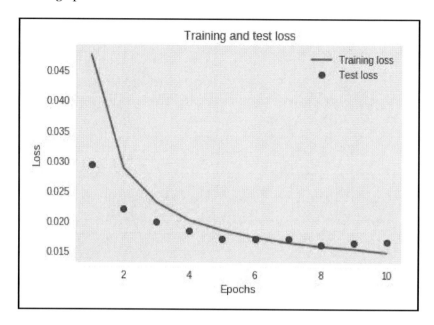

5. Predict on a test image. In the following code, we are predicting on the second image from last in input array (note that, as `validation_split` is `0.1`, second image from last was not supplied to model while training). We are ensuring that we are passing our image through `preprocess_input` method and then through `VGG16_model` and finally, the scaled version of `VGG16_model` output to the `model_vgg16` that we built:

```
pred =
model_vgg16.predict(vgg16_model.predict(preprocess_input(x_img[-2].
reshape(1,224,224,3)))/np.max(x))
```

The preceding prediction on test image can be visualized as follows:

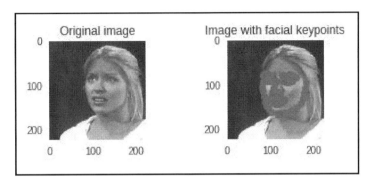

We can see that the key points are detected very accurately on the test image.

6
Detecting and Localizing Objects in Images

In the chapters on building a deep convolutional neural network and transfer learning, we have learned about detecting the class that an image belongs to using deep CNN and also by leveraging transfer learning.

While object classification works, in the real world, we will also be encountering a scenario where we would have to locate the object within an image.

For example, in the case of a self-driving car, we would not only have to detect that a pedestrian is in the view point of a car, but also be able to detect how far the pedestrian is located away from the car so that an appropriate action can then be taken.

In this chapter, we will be discussing the various techniques of detecting objects in an image. The case studies we will be covering in this chapter are as follows:

- Creating the training dataset of bounding box
- Generating region proposals within an image using selective search
- Calculating an intersection over a union between two images
- Detecting objects using region proposal-based CNN
- Performing non-max suppression
- Detecting a person using the anchor box-based algorithm

Introduction

With the rise of autonomous cars, facial detection, smart video surveillance, and people counting solutions, fast and accurate object detection systems are in great demand. These systems include not only object recognition and classification in an image, but can also locate each one of them by drawing appropriate boxes around them. This makes object detection a harder task than its traditional computer vision predecessor, image classification.

To understand how the output of object detection looks like, let's go through the following picture:

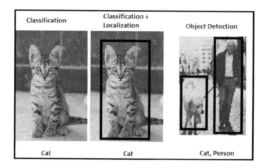

So far, in the previous chapters, we have learned about classification.

In this chapter, we will learn about having a tight bounding box around the object in the picture, which is the localization task.

Additionally, we will also learn about detecting the multiple objects in the picture, which is the object detection task.

Creating the dataset for a bounding box

We have learned that object detection gives us the output where a bounding box surrounds the object of interest in an image. For us to build an algorithm that detects the bounding box surrounding the object in an image, we would have to create the input–output mapping, where the input is the image and the output is the bounding boxes surrounding the objects in the given image.

Note that when we detect the bounding box, we are detecting the pixel locations of the top-left corner of the bounding box surrounding the image, and the corresponding width and height of the bounding box.

Chapter 6

To train a model that provides the bounding box, we need the image, and also the corresponding bounding-box coordinates of all the objects in an image.

In this section, we will highlight one of the ways to create the training dataset where the image shall be given as input and the corresponding bounding boxes are stored in an XML file.

We shall be using the `labelImg` package to annotate the bounding boxes and the corresponding classes.

How to do it...

Bounding boxes around objects in image can be prepared as follows:

Windows

1. Download the executable file of `labelImg` from the link here: https://github.com/tzutalin/labelImg/files/2638199/windows_v1.8.1.zip.
2. Extract and open the `labelImg.exe` GUI, shown in the following screenshot:

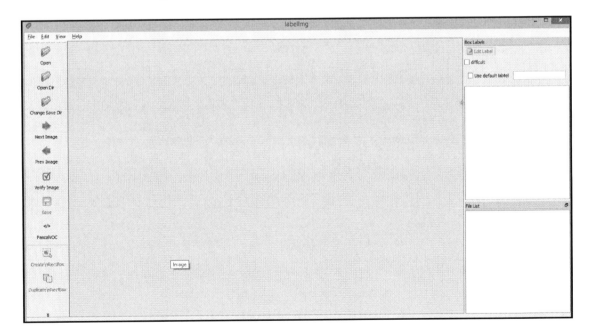

Detecting and Localizing Objects in Images

3. Specify all the possible labels in an image in the `predefined_classes.txt` file in the `data` folder. We need to ensure that all the classes are listed in a separate line, as follows:

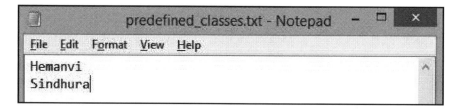

4. Open an image by clicking **Open** in the GUI and annotate the image by clicking on **Create RectBox**, which will pop up the classes that will be selected as follows:

5. Click on **Save** and save the XML file.
6. Inspect the XML file. A snapshot of the XML file after drawing the rectangular bounding box looks as follows:

```xml
<annotation>
    <folder>07-02-2018</folder>
    <filename>DSC_4740.JPG</filename>
    <path>F:/07-02-2018/DSC_4740.JPG</path>
    <source>
        <database>Unknown</database>
    </source>
    <size>
        <width>4928</width>
        <height>3264</height>
        <depth>3</depth>
    </size>
    <segmented>0</segmented>
    <object>
        <name>Hemanvi</name>
        <pose>Unspecified</pose>
        <truncated>0</truncated>
        <difficult>0</difficult>
        <bndbox>
            <xmin>2639</xmin>
            <ymin>136</ymin>
            <xmax>3881</xmax>
            <ymax>1857</ymax>
        </bndbox>
    </object>
    <object>
        <name>Sindhura</name>
        <pose>Unspecified</pose>
        <truncated>0</truncated>
        <difficult>0</difficult>
        <bndbox>
            <xmin>381</xmin>
            <ymin>615</ymin>
            <xmax>2129</xmax>
            <ymax>2494</ymax>
        </bndbox>
    </object>
</annotation>
```

From the preceding screenshot, you should note that the bndbox contains the coordinates of the minimum and maximum values of the *x* and *y* coordinates corresponding to the objects of interest in the image. Additionally, we should also be in a position to extract the classes corresponding to the objects in image.

Ubuntu

In Ubuntu, the same steps as preceding ones can be executed by keying in the following commands:

```
$sudo apt-get install pyqt5-dev-tools
$sudo pip3 install -r requirements/requirements-linux-python3.txt
$make qt5py3
$python3 labelImg.py
```

The script `labelImg.py` can be found in the GitHub link here: https://github.com/tzutalin/labelImg.

Once we execute the preceding code, we should be in a position to perform the same analysis as we have seen in the *Windows* section.

MacOS

In macOS, the same preceding steps can be executed by keying in the following commands:

```
$brew install qt    # will install qt-5.x.x
$brew install libxml2
$make qt5py3
$python3 labelImg.py
```

The script `labelImg.py` can be found in the GitHub link here: https://github.com/tzutalin/labelImg.

Once we execute the preceding script, we should be in a position to perform the same analysis as we have seen in the *Windows* section.

Generating region proposals within an image, using selective search

To understand what a region proposal is, let's break the term into its constituents—region and proposal.

A **region** is a portion of the total image where the pixels in that portion have very similar values.

A **region proposal** is the smaller portion of the total image, where there is a higher chance of the portion belonging to a particular object.

A region proposal is useful, as we generate candidates from the image where the chances of an object being located in one of those regions is high. This comes in handy in the object localization tasks, where we need to have a bounding box around the object that is similar to what we have in the picture in the previous section.

Getting ready

In this section, we will look into a way of generating a bounding box within an image of a person.

Selective search is a region proposal algorithm used in object detection. It is designed to be fast with a very high recall. It is based on computing a hierarchical grouping of similar regions based on color, texture, size, and shape compatibility.

Region proposals can be generated using a Python package named `selectivesearch` as follows.

The selective search starts by over-segmenting the image (generating thousands of region proposals) based on intensity of the pixels using a graph-based segmentation method by Felzenszwalb and Huttenlocher.

Selective search algorithm takes these over-segments as the initial input and performs the following steps:

1. Add all bounding boxes corresponding to segmented parts to the list of regional proposals
2. Group adjacent segments based on similarity
3. Go to step one

At each iteration, larger segments are formed and added to the list of region proposals. Hence, we create region proposals from smaller segments to larger segments in a bottom-up approach.

Selective search uses four similarity measures based on color, texture, size, and shape compatibility to come up with the region proposals.

> Region proposals help identify the possible objects of interest in an image. Thus, we could potentially convert the exercise of localization into a classification exercise where we shall classify each region as whether it contains the object of interest.

How to do it...

In this section, we will demonstrate the extracting of region proposals, as follows (The code file is available as Selective_search.ipynb in GitHub):

1. Install selectivesearch as follows:

   ```
   $pip install selectivesearch
   ```

2. Import the relevant packages, shown in the following code:

   ```
   import matplotlib.pyplot as plt
   %matplotlib inline
   import selectivesearch
   import cv2
   ```

3. Load the image, as follows:

   ```
   img = cv2.imread('/content/Hemanvi.jpeg')
   ```

4. Extract the region proposals:

   ```
   img_lbl, regions = selectivesearch.selective_search(img, scale=100, min_size=2000)
   ```

   The parameter min_size provides a constraint that the region proposal should be at least 2,000 pixels in size, and the parameter scale effectively sets a scale of observation, in that a larger scale causes a preference for larger components.

5. Check the resulting number of regions and store them in a list:

   ```
   print(len(regions))
   candidates = set()
   for r in regions:
       if r['rect'] in candidates:
           continue
   # excluding regions smaller than 2000 pixels
       if r['size'] < 2000:
           continue
       x, y, w, h = r['rect']
   candidates.add(r['rect'])
   ```

   In the preceding step, we have stored all the regions that are more than 2,000 pixels in size (area) into a set of candidates.

6. Plot the resulting image with candidates:

```
import matplotlib.patches as mpatches
fig, ax = plt.subplots(ncols=1, nrows=1, figsize=(6, 6))
ax.imshow(img)
for x, y, w, h in candidates:
    rect = mpatches.Rectangle(
        (x, y), w, h, fill=False, edgecolor='red', linewidth=1)
    ax.add_patch(rect)
plt.axis('off')
plt.show()
```

From the preceding screenshot, we see that there are multiple regions that are extracted from the image.

Calculating an intersection over a union between two images

To understand how accurate the proposed regions are, we use a metric named **Intersection over Union (IoU)**. IoU can be visualized as follows:

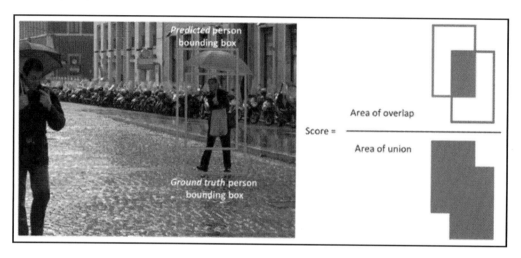

Note that, in the preceding picture, the blue box (lower one) is the ground truth and the red box (the upper rectangle) is the region proposal.

The intersection over the union of the region proposal is calculated as the ratio of the intersection of the proposal and the ground truth over the union of the region proposal and the ground truth.

How to do it...

IoU is calculated as follows (the code file is available as `Selective_search.ipynb` in GitHub):

1. Define the IoU extraction function, demonstrated in the following code:

    ```
    from copy import deepcopy
    import numpy as np
    def extract_iou(candidate, current_y,img_shape):
        boxA = deepcopy(candidate)
        boxB = deepcopy(current_y)
    ```

```
        img1 = np.zeros(img_shape)
        img1[boxA[1]:boxA[3],boxA[0]:boxA[2]]=1

        img2 = np.zeros(img_shape)
        img2[int(boxB[1]):int(boxB[3]),int(boxB[0]):int(boxB[2])]=1

        iou = np.sum(img1*img2)/(np.sum(img1)+np.sum(img2)-
np.sum(img1*img2))
        return iou
```

In the preceding function, we take the candidate, actual object region, and image shape as input.

Further, we initialized two zero-value arrays of the same shape for the candidate image and the actual object location image.

We have over-written the candidate image and the actual object location images with one, wherever the image and object are located.

Finally, we calculated the intersection over the union of the candidate image with the actual object location image.

2. Import the image of interest:

    ```
    img = cv2.imread('/content/Hemanvi.jpeg')
    ```

3. Plot the image and verify the actual location of the object of interest:

    ```
    plt.imshow(img)
    plt.grid('off')
    ```

Detecting and Localizing Objects in Images

Note that the region of interest is ~50 pixels from bottom left extending to ~290th pixel of the image. Additionally, on the *y* axis, it starts from ~50th pixel too till the end of the image.

So, the actual location of object is (50, 50, 290, 500), which is in the format of (xmin, ymin, xmax, ymax).

4. Extract the region proposals:

```
img_lbl, regions = selectivesearch.selective_search(img, scale=100,
min_size=2000)
```

The regions extracted from the selectivesearch method are in the format of (xmin, ymin, width, height). Hence, before extracting the IoU of the regions, we should ensure that the candidate and the actual location of image are in the same format that is, (xmin, ymin, xmax, ymax)

5. Apply the IoU extraction function to the image of interest. Note that the function takes the actual object's location and the candidate image shape as input:

```
regions =list(candidates)
actual_bb = [50,50,290,500]
iou = []
for i in range(len(regions)):
    candidate = list(regions[i])
    candidate[2] += candidate[0]
    iou.append(extract_iou(candidate, actual_bb, img.shape))
```

6. Identify the region that has the highest overlap with the actual object of interest (ground truth bounding box):

```
np.argmax(iou)
```

The preceding output for this specific image is the tenth candidate where the coordinates are 0, 0, 299, 515.

7. Let's print the actual bounding box and the candidate bounding box. For this, we have to convert the (xmin, ymin, xmax, ymax) format of output into (xmin, ymin, width, height):

```
max_region = list(regions[np.argmax(iou)])
max_region[2] -= max_region[0]
max_region[3] -= max_region[1]

actual_bb[2] -= actual_bb[0]
actual_bb[3] -= actual_bb[1]
```

[200]

Let's append the actual and the bounding box with the highest IoU:

```
maxcandidate_actual = [max_region,actual_bb]
```

Now, we will loop through the preceding list and assign a bigger line width for actual location of object in image, so that we are able to distinguish between candidate and the actual object's location:

```
import matplotlib.patches as mpatches
fig, ax = plt.subplots(ncols=1, nrows=1, figsize=(6, 6))
ax.imshow(img)
for i,(x, y, w, h) in enumerate(maxcandidate_actual):
 if(i==0):
 rect = mpatches.Rectangle(
 (x, y), w, h, fill=False, edgecolor='blue', linewidth=2)
 ax.add_patch(rect)
 else:
 rect = mpatches.Rectangle(
 (x, y), w, h, fill=False, edgecolor='red', linewidth=5)
 ax.add_patch(rect)
plt.axis('off')
plt.show()
```

In this way, we are in a position to identify each candidate's IoU with the actual location of an object in the image. Additionally, we are also in a position to identify the candidate that has the highest IoU with the actual location of an object in the image.

Detecting objects, using region proposal-based CNN

In the previous section, we have learned about generating region proposals from an image. In this section, we will leverage the region proposals to come up with object detection and localization within an image.

Getting ready

The strategy we shall be adopting to perform region proposal-based object detection and localization is as follows:

1. For the current exercise, we'll build the model based on images that contain only one object
2. We'll extract the various region proposals (candidates) within the image
3. We will calculate how close the candidate is to the actual object location:
    - Essentially, we calculate the intersection over the union of the candidate with the actual location of the object
4. If the intersection over the union is greater than a certain threshold—the candidate is considered to contain the object of interest—or else, it doesn't:
    - This creates the label for each candidate where the candidate's image is input and the intersection over the union threshold provides the output
5. We'll resize and pass each candidate image through the VGG16 model (which we have learned in the previous chapter) to extract features of the candidates
6. Additionally, we will create the training data of the bounding-box correction by comparing the location of the candidate and the actual location of an object
7. Build a classification model that maps the features of the candidate to the output of whether the region contains an object
8. For the regions that contain an image (as per the model), build a regression model that maps the input features of candidate to the correction required to extract the accurate bounding box of an object

9. Perform non-max suppression on top of the resulting bounding boxes:
    - Non-max suppression ensures that the candidates that overlap a lot are reduced to 1, where only the candidate that has the highest probability of containing an object is left
10. By performing a non-max suppression, we would be in a position to replicate the model that we built for images that contain multiple objects within the image too

A schematic of the preceding is shown as follows:

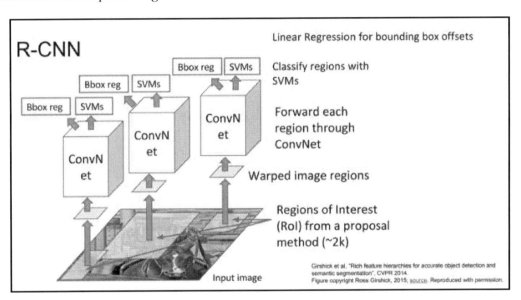

How to do it...

In this section, we will code up the algorithm that we have discussed in the previous section (the code file and corresponding recommended dataset link is available as `Region_proposal_based_object_detection.ipynb` in GitHub along with the recommended dataset):

1. Download the dataset that contains a set of images, the objects contained in them, and the corresponding bounding boxes of objects in the image. The dataset and the corresponding code files that you can work on are provided in GitHub.

A sample image and the corresponding bounding box co-ordinates and class of object in image are available as follows:

The class of object and bounding box co-ordinates would be available in an XML file (Details of how to obtain the XML file are available in code file in GitHub) and can be extracted from the XML file as follows:

If `xml["annotation"]["object"]` is a list, it indicates that there multiple objects present in the same image.

`xml["annotation"]["object"]["bndbox"]` extracts the bounding box of object present in image where the bounding box is available as "xmin","ymin","xmax" and "ymax" co-ordinates of object in image.

`xml["annotation"]["object"]["name"]` extracts the class of object present in image.

2. Import the relevant packages as follows:

```
import matplotlib.pyplot as plt
%matplotlib inline
import tensorflow as tf, selectivesearch
import json, scipy, os, numpy as np,argparse,time, sys, gc, cv2, xmltodict
from copy import deepcopy
```

3. Define the IoU extraction function, shown in the following code:

```
def extract_iou2(candidate, current_y,img_shape):
    boxA = deepcopy(candidate)
    boxB = deepcopy(current_y)
    boxA[2] += boxA[0]
    boxA[3] += boxA[1]
    iou_img1 = np.zeros(img_shape)
    iou_img1[boxA[1]:boxA[3],boxA[0]:boxA[2]]=1
    iou_img2 = np.zeros(img_shape)
    iou_img2[int(boxB[1]):int(boxB[3]),int(boxB[0]):int(boxB[2])]=1
    iou =
np.sum(iou_img1*iou_img2)/(np.sum(iou_img1)+np.sum(iou_img2)-
np.sum(iou_img1*iou_img2))
    return iou
```

4. Define the candidate extraction function, shown as follows:

```
def extract_candidates(img):
    img_lbl, regions = selectivesearch.selective_search(img,
scale=100, min_size=100)
    img_area = img.shape[0]*img.shape[1]
    candidates = []
    for r in regions:
        if r['rect'] in candidates:
            continue
        if r['size'] < (0.05*img_area):
            continue
        x, y, w, h = r['rect']
        candidates.append(list(r['rect']))
    return candidates
```

Note that, in the preceding function, we are excluding all candidates which occupy less than 5% of the area of image.

5. Import the pre-trained VGG16 model as follows:

```
from keras.applications import vgg16
from keras.utils.vis_utils import plot_model
vgg16_model = vgg16.VGG16(include_top=False, weights='imagenet')
```

6. Create the input and output mapping for the images that contain only one object within them. Initialize multiple lists that will be populated as we go through the images:

```
training_data_size = N = 1000

final_cls = []
```

Detecting and Localizing Objects in Images

```
final_delta = []
iou_list = []
imgs = []
```

We'll loop through the images and shall work on only those that contain a single object:

```
for ix, xml in enumerate(XMLs[:N]):
    print('Extracted data from {} xmls...'.format(ix), end='\r')
    xml_file = annotations + xml
    fname = xml.split('.')[0]
    with open(xml_file, "rb") as f: # notice the "rb" mode
        xml = xmltodict.parse(f, xml_attribs=True)
    l = []
    if isinstance(xml["annotation"]["object"], list):
        #'let us ignore cases with multiple objects...'
        continue
```

In the preceding code, we are extracting the `xml` attributes of an image and checking whether the image contains multiple objects (if the output of `xml["annotation"]["object"]` is a list, then the image contains multiple objects).

Normalize the object location coordinates so that we can work on the normalized bounding box. This is done so that the normalized bounding box does not change, even if the image shape is changed for further processing. For example, if the object's `xmin` is at 20% of *x* axis and 50% of *y* axis, it would be the same, even when the image is reshaped (however, had we been dealing with pixel values, the `xmin` value would be changed):

```
bndbox = xml['annotation']['object']['bndbox']
for key in bndbox:
    bndbox[key] = float(bndbox[key])
x1, x2, y1, y2 = [bndbox[key] for key in ['xmin', 'xmax', 'ymin', 'ymax']]

img_size = xml['annotation']['size']
for key in img_size:
    img_size[key] = float(img_size[key])
w, h = img_size['width'], img_size['height']

#'converting pixel values from bndbox to fractions...'
x1 /= w; x2 /= w; y1 /= h; y2 /= h
label = xml['annotation']['object']['name']

y = [x1, y1, x2-x1, y2-y1, label]   # top-left x & y, width and height
```

Chapter 6

In the preceding code, we have normalized the bounding-box coordinates.

Extract candidates of the image:

```
            filename = jpegs+fname+'.jpg' # Path to jpg files here
            img = cv2.resize(cv2.imread(filename), (224,224)) # since
VGG's input shape is 224x224
            candidates = extract_candidates(img)
```

In the preceding code, we are using the extract_candidates function to extract the region proposals of the resized image.

Loop through the candidates to calculate the intersection over union of each candidate with the actual bounding box of the object in the image and also the corresponding delta between the actual bounding box and the candidate:

```
            for jx, candidate in enumerate(candidates):
                    current_y2 = [int(i*224) for i in [x1,y1,x2,y2]] #
[int(x1*224), int(y1*224), int(x2*224), int(y2*224)]
                    iou = extract_iou2(candidate, current_y2, (224,
224))
                    candidate_region_coordinates = c_x1, c_y1, c_w, c_h
= np.array(candidate)/224

                    dx = c_x1 - x1
                    dy = c_y1 - y1
                    dw = c_w - (x2-x1)
                    dh = c_h - (y2-y1)

                    final_delta.append([dx,dy,dw,dh])
```

Calculate the VGG16 features of each region proposal and assign the target based on the IoU of the region proposal with the actual bounding box:

```
                    if(iou>0.3):
                            final_cls.append(label)
                    else:
                            final_cls.append('background')

                    #"We'll predict our candidate crop using VGG"
                    l = int(c_x1 * 224)
                    r = int((c_x1 + c_w) * 224)
                    t = int(c_y1 * 224)
                    b = int((c_y1 + c_h) * 224)

                    img2 = img[t:b,l:r,:3]
                    img3 = cv2.resize(img2,(224,224))/255
                    img4 =
```

[207]

Detecting and Localizing Objects in Images

```
vgg16_model.predict(img3.reshape(1,224,224,3))
        imgs.append(img4)
```

7. Create input and output arrays:

```
targets = pd.DataFrame(final_cls, columns=['label'])
labels = pd.get_dummies(targets['label']).columns
y_train = pd.get_dummies(targets['label']).values.astype(float)
```

We utilize the `get_dummies` method as the classes are categorical text values:

```
x_train = np.array(imgs)
x_train =
x_train.reshape(x_train.shape[0],x_train.shape[2],x_train.shape[3],
x_train.shape[4])
```

8. Build and compile the model:

```
model = Sequential()
model.add(Flatten(input_shape=((7,7,512))))
model.add(Dense(512, activation='relu'))
model.add(Dense(all_classes.shape[1],activation='softmax'))

model.compile(loss='binary_crossentropy',optimizer='adam',
metrics=['accuracy'])
```

9. Fit the model, shown as follows:

```
model.fit(xtrain3/x_train.max(),y_train,validation_split = 0.1,
epochs=5, batch_size=32, verbose=1)
```

The preceding results in a classification accuracy of 97% on a test dataset.

We are dividing the input array by `x_train.max()`, as the maximum value in an input array is ~11. Typically, it is a good idea to have input values between zero and one, and given that the VGG16 prediction on the scaled input has a maximum value of ~11, we divide the input array by `x_train.max()`—which is equal to ~11.

10. Make a prediction of the class from the dataset (ensure that we do not consider an image that was used for training).
11. Pick an image that was not used for testing:

```
import matplotlib.patches as mpatches
ix = np.random.randint(N, len(XMLs))
filename = jpegs + XMLs[ix].replace('xml', 'jpg')
```

Chapter 6

12. Build a function that performs image preprocessing to extract candidates, performs model prediction on resized candidates, filters out the predicted background class regions, and, finally, plots the region (candidate) that has the highest probability of containing a class that is other than the background class:

```
def test_predictions(filename):
    img = cv2.resize(cv2.imread(filename), (224,224))
    candidates = extract_candidates(img)
```

In the preceding code, we are resizing an input image and are extracting candidates from it:

```
_, ax = plt.subplots(1, 2)
ax[0].imshow(img)
ax[0].grid('off')
ax[0].set_title(filename.split('/')[-1])
pred = []
pred_class = []
```

In the preceding code, are plotting an image and are initializing the predicted probability and predicted class lists that will be populated in subsequent steps:

```
for ix, candidate in enumerate(candidates):
    l, t, w, h = np.array(candidate).astype(int)
    img2 = img[t:t+h,l:l+w,:3]
    img3 = cv2.resize(img2,(224,224))/255
    img4 = vgg16_model.predict(img3.reshape(1,224,224,3))
    final_pred = model.predict(img4/x_train.max())
    pred.append(np.max(final_pred))
    pred_class.append(np.argmax(final_pred))
```

In the preceding code, we are looping through the candidates, resizing them, and passing them through the VGG16 model. Furthermore, we are passing the VGG16 output through our model, which provides the probability of the image belonging to various classes:

```
pred = np.array(pred)
pred_class = np.array(pred_class)
pred2 = pred[pred_class!=1]
pred_class2 = pred_class[pred_class!=1]
candidates2 = np.array(candidates)[pred_class!=1]
x, y, w, h = candidates2[np.argmax(pred2)]
```

[209]

Detecting and Localizing Objects in Images

In the preceding code, we are extracting the candidate that has the highest probability of containing an object that is non-background (the predicted class of one corresponds to the background):

```
ax[1].set_title(labels[pred_class2[np.argmax(pred2)]])
ax[1].imshow(img)
ax[1].grid('off')
rect = mpatches.Rectangle((x, y), w, h, fill=False, edgecolor='red', linewidth=1)
ax[1].add_patch(rect)
```

In the preceding code, we are plotting the image along with rectangular patch of the bounding box.

13. Call the function defined with a new image:

```
filename = '...' #Path to new image
test_predictions(filename)
```

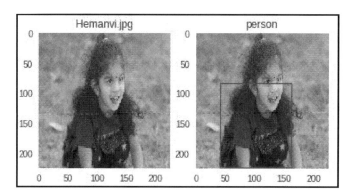

Note that the model accurately figured the class of the object in the image. Additionally, the bounding box (candidate) that has the highest probability of containing a person needs a little bit of correction.

In the next step, we will correct the bounding box further.

14. Build and compile a model that takes the VGG16 features of image as input and predicts the bounding-box corrections:

```
model2 = Sequential()
model2.add(Flatten(input_shape=((7,7,512))))
model2.add(Dense(512, activation='relu'))
model2.add(Dense(4,activation='linear'))

model2.compile(loss='mean_absolute_error',optimizer='adam')
```

[210]

15. Build the model to predict bounding-box corrections. However, we need to ensure that we predict bounding-box corrections only for those regions that are likely to contain an image:

```
for i in range(1000):
    samp=random.sample(range(len(x_train)),500)
    x_train2=[x_train[i] for i in samp if pred_class[i]!=1]
    x_train2 = np.array(x_train2)
    final_delta2 = [final_delta[i] for i in samp if pred_class[i]!=1]
    model2.fit(x_train2/x_train.max(), np.array(final_delta2), validation_split = 0.1, epochs=1, batch_size=32, verbose=0)
```

In the preceding code, we are looping through the input array dataset and creating a new dataset that is only for those regions that are likely to contain a non-background.

Additionally, we are repeating the preceding step 1,000 different times to fine tune the model.

16. Build a function that takes an image path as input and predicts the class of an image, along with correcting the bounding box:

```
'TESTING'
import matplotlib.patches as mpatches
def test_predictions2(filename):
    img = cv2.resize(cv2.imread(filename), (224,224))
    candidates = extract_candidates(img)
    _, ax = plt.subplots(1, 2)
    ax[0].imshow(img)
    ax[0].grid('off')
    ax[0].set_title(filename.split('/')[-1])
    pred = []
    pred_class = []
    del_new = []
    for ix, candidate in enumerate(candidates):
        l, t, w, h = np.array(candidate).astype(int)
        img2 = img[t:t+h,l:l+w,:3]
        img3 = cv2.resize(img2, (224,224))/255
        img4 = vgg16_model.predict(img3.reshape(1,224,224,3))
        final_pred = model.predict(img4/x_train.max())
        delta_new = model2.predict(img4/x_train.max())[0]
        pred.append(np.max(final_pred))
        pred_class.append(np.argmax(final_pred))
        del_new.append(delta_new)
    pred = np.array(pred)
    pred_class = np.array(pred_class)
```

Detecting and Localizing Objects in Images

```
        non_bgs = (pred_class!=1)
        pred = pred[non_bgs]
        pred_class = pred_class[non_bgs]
        del_new = np.array(del_new)
        del_new = del_new[non_bgs]
        del_pred = del_new*224
        candidates = C = np.array(candidates)[non_bgs]
        C = np.clip(C, 0, 224)
        C[:,2] += C[:,0]
        C[:,3] += C[:,1]
        bbs_pred = candidates - del_pred
        bbs_pred = np.clip(bbs_pred, 0, 224)
        bbs_pred[:,2] -= bbs_pred[:,0]
        bbs_pred[:,3] -= bbs_pred[:,1]
        final_bbs_pred = bbs_pred[np.argmax(pred)]
        x, y, w, h = final_bbs_pred
    ax[1].imshow(img)
    ax[1].grid('off')
    rect = mpatches.Rectangle((x, y), w, h, fill=False,
edgecolor='red', linewidth=1)
    ax[1].add_patch(rect)
    ax[1].set_title(labels[pred_class[np.argmax(pred)]])
```

17. Extract the test images that contain only one object (as we have built the model on images that contain a single object):

```
single_object_images = []
for ix, xml in enumerate(XMLs[N:]):
    xml_file = annotations + xml
    fname = xml.split('.')[0]
    with open(xml_file, "rb") as f: # notice the "rb" mode
        xml = xmltodict.parse(f, xml_attribs=True)
        l = []
        if isinstance(xml["annotation"]["object"], list):
            continue
        single_object_images.append(xml["annotation"]['filename'])
        if(ix>100):
            break
```

In the preceding code, we are looping through the image annotations and identifying the images that contain a single object.

18. Predict on the single object image:

    ```
    test_predictions2(filename)
    ```

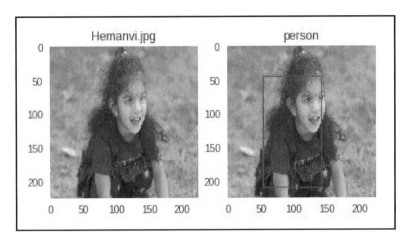

Note that the second model was able to correct the bounding box to fit the person; however, the bounding box still needs to be corrected a little more. This could potentially be achieved when trained on more data points.

Performing non-max suppression

So far, in the previous section, we have only considered the candidates that do not have a background, and further considered the candidate that has the highest probability of the object of interest. However, this fails in the scenario where there are multiple objects present in an image.

In this section, we will discuss the ways to shortlist the candidate region proposals so that we are in a position to extract as many objects as possible within the image.

Getting ready

The strategy we adopt to perform NMS is as follows:

- Extract the region proposals from an image
- Reshape the region proposals and predict the object that is contained in the image

Detecting and Localizing Objects in Images

- If the object is non-background, we shall keep the candidate
- For all the non-background class candidates, we'll order them by the probability that they contain an object
- The first candidate (post-rank ordering by decreasing probability of any class) will be compared with all the rest of candidates in terms of the IoU
- If there is considerable overlap between any other region with the first candidate, they shall be discarded
- Among the candidates that remain, we'll again consider the candidate that has the highest probability of containing an object
- We'll repeat the comparison of first candidate (among the filtered list that has limited overlap with the first candidate in the previous step) with the rest of the candidates
- This process continues until there are no candidates left for comparison
- We'll plot the candidates for the candidates that remain after the preceding steps as the final bounding boxes

How to do it...

Non-max suppression is coded in Python as follows. We'll continue from step 14 in the previous recipe (The code file and corresponding recommended dataset link is available as Region_proposal_based_object_detectionn.ipynb in GitHub).

1. Extract all the regions from an image where there is a high confidence of containing an object that is of a non-background class:

```
filename = jpegs + single_object_images[ix]
img = cv2.imread(filename)
img = cv2.resize(img, (224,224))
img_area = img.shape[0]*img.shape[1]
candidates = extract_candidates(img)
plt.imshow(img)
plt.grid('off')
```

The image that we are considering is as follows:

2. Pre-process the candidates—pass them through VGG16 model, and then predict the class of each region proposal, as well as the bounding boxes of the regions:

```
pred = []
pred_class = []
del_new = []

for ix, candidate in enumerate(candidates):
    l, t, w, h = np.array(candidate).astype(int)
    img2 = img[t:t+h,l:l+w,:3]
    img3 = cv2.resize(img2,(224,224))/255
    img4 = vgg16_model.predict(img3.reshape(1,224,224,3))
    final_pred = model.predict(img4/x_train.max())
    delta_new = model2.predict(img4/x_train.max())[0]
    pred.append(np.max(final_pred))
    pred_class.append(np.argmax(final_pred))
    del_new.append(delta_new)
pred = np.array(pred)
pred_class = np.array(pred_class)
```

3. Extract the non-background class predictions and their corresponding bounding-box corrections:

```
non_bgs = ((pred_class!=1))
pred = pred[non_bgs]
pred_class = pred_class[non_bgs]
```

Detecting and Localizing Objects in Images

```
del_new = np.array(del_new)
del_new = del_new[non_bgs]
del_pred = del_new*224
```

In the preceding step, we have filtered all the probabilities, classes, and bounding-box corrections for the regions that are non-background (predicted class 1 belongs to background class in our data preparation process).

4. Correct the candidates using the bounding-box correction values:

```
candidates = C = np.array(candidates)[non_bgs]
C = np.clip(C, 0, 224)
C[:,2] += C[:,0]
C[:,3] += C[:,1]

bbs_pred = candidates - del_pred
bbs_pred = np.clip(bbs_pred, 0, 224)
```

Additionally, we have also ensured that the xmax and ymax coordinates cannot be greater than 224.

Furthermore, we need to ensure that the width and height of bounding boxes cannot be negative:

```
bbs_pred[:,2] -= bbs_pred[:,0]
bbs_pred[:,3] -= bbs_pred[:,1]
bbs_pred = np.clip(bbs_pred, 0, 224)

bbs_pred2 = bbs_pred[(bbs_pred[:,2]>0) & (bbs_pred[:,3]>0)]
pred = pred[(bbs_pred[:,2]>0) & (bbs_pred[:,3]>0)]
pred_class = pred_class[(bbs_pred[:,2]>0) & (bbs_pred[:,3]>0)]
```

5. Plot the image along with the bounding boxes:

```
import matplotlib.patches as mpatches
fig, ax = plt.subplots(ncols=1, nrows=1, figsize=(6, 6))
ax.imshow(img)
for ix, (x, y, w, h) in enumerate(bbs_pred2):
    rect = mpatches.Rectangle(
        (x, y), w, h, fill=False, edgecolor='red', linewidth=1)
    ax.add_patch(rect)

plt.axis('off')
plt.show()
```

6. Perform non-max suppression on top of the bounding boxes. For this, we'll define a function that performs NMS by taking the minimum possible intersection that two bounding boxes can have (threshold), bounding-box coordinates, and the probability score associated with each bounding box in the following steps:

   1. Calculate the x, y, w, and h values of each bounding box, their corresponding areas, and, also, their probability order:

   ```
   def nms_boxes(threshold, boxes, scores):
       x = boxes[:, 0]
       y = boxes[:, 1]
       w = boxes[:, 2]
       h = boxes[:, 3]
       areas = w * h
       order = scores.argsort()[::-1]
   ```

   2. Calculate the intersection over union of the candidate with highest probability with the rest of the candidates:

   ```
   keep = []
   while order.size > 0:
       i = order[0]
       keep.append(i)
       xx1 = np.maximum(x[i], x[order[1:]])
       yy1 = np.maximum(y[i], y[order[1:]])
   ```

```
xx2 = np.minimum(x[i] + w[i], x[order[1:]] + w[order[1:]])
yy2 = np.minimum(y[i] + h[i], y[order[1:]] + h[order[1:]])
w1 = np.maximum(0.0, xx2 - xx1 + 1)
h1 = np.maximum(0.0, yy2 - yy1 + 1)
inter = w1 * h1
iou = inter / (areas[i] + areas[order[1:]] - inter)
```

3. Identify the candidates that have an IoU that is less than the threshold:

```
inds = np.where(ovr <= threshold)[0]
order = order[inds + 1]
```

In the preceding step, we are ensuring that we have the next set of candidates (other than the first candidate) that are to be looped through the same steps (notice the `while` loop at the start of the function).

4. Return the index of candidates that need to be kept:

```
keep = np.array(keep)
return keep
```

7. Execute the preceding function:

```
keep_box_ixs = nms_boxes(0.3, bbs_pred2, pred)
```

8. Plot those bounding boxes that were left from the previous step:

```
import matplotlib.patches as mpatches
fig, ax = plt.subplots(ncols=1, nrows=1, figsize=(6, 6))
ax.imshow(img)
for ix, (x, y, w, h) in enumerate(bbs_pred2):
    if ix not in keep_box_ixs:
        continue
    rect = mpatches.Rectangle((x, y), w, h, fill=False, edgecolor='red', linewidth=1)
    ax.add_patch(rect)
    centerx = x + w/2
    centery = y + h - 10
    plt.text(centerx, centery,labels[pred_class[ix]]+" "+str(round(pred[ix],2)),fontsize = 20,color='red')
plt.axis('off')
plt.show()
```

From the preceding screenshot, we see that we removed all the other bounding boxes that were generated as region proposals.

Detecting a person using an anchor box-based algorithm

One of the drawbacks of region proposal based CNN is that it does not enable a real-time object recognition, as selective search takes considerable time to propose regions. This results in region proposal-based object detection algorithms not being useful in cases like self-driving car, where real-time detection is very important.

In order to achieve real-time detection, we will build a model that is inspired by the **You Only Look Once** (**YOLO**) algorithm from scratch that looks at the images that contain a person in image and draws a bounding box around the person in image.

Getting ready

To understand how YOLO overcomes the drawback of consuming considerable time in generating region proposals, let us break the term YOLO into its constituent terms—we shall make all the predictions (class of image and also the bounding box) from a single forward pass of the neural network. Compare this with what we did with region proposal based CNN, where a selective search algorithm gave us the region proposals, and then we built a classification algorithm on top of it.

To figure out the working details of YOLO, let's go through a toy example. Let's say the input image looks as follows—where the image is divided into a 3 x 3 grid:

The output of our neural network model shall be of 3 x 3 x 5 in size, where the first 3 x 3 correspond to the number of grids we have in the image, and the first output of the five channels corresponds to the probability of the grid containing an object, and the other four constituents are the *delta of x, y, w, h* coordinates corresponding to the grid in the image.

One other lever that we use is the anchor boxes. Essentially, we already know that there are certain shapes within the set of images we have. For example, a car will have a shape where the width is greater than the height and a standing person would generally have a higher height when compared to the width.

Hence, we shall cluster all the height and width values we have in our image set into five clusters and that shall result in the five anchor boxes' height and width that we shall use to identify bounding boxes around the objects in our image.

If there are five anchor boxes working on an image, the output then shall be 3 x 3 x 5 x 5, where the 5 x 5 corresponds to the five constituents (one probability of the object and the four delta along *x, y, w,* and *h*) of each of the five anchor boxes.

From the preceding, we can see that the 3 x 3 x 5 x 5 output can be generated from a single forward pass through the neural network model.

In the following section, the pseudo code to understand the ways to generate the size of anchors:

- Extract the width and height of all images in a dataset
- Run a k-means clustering with five clusters to identify the clusters of width and height present in the image
- The five cluster centers correspond to the width and height of the five anchor boxes to build the model

Furthermore, in the following section, we will understand how the YOLO algorithm works:

- Divide the image into a fixed number of grid cells
- The grid that corresponds to the center of the ground truth of the bounding box of the image shall be the grid that is responsible in predicting the bounding box
- The center of anchor boxes shall be the same as the center of the grid
- Create the training dataset:
    - For the grid that contains the center of object, the dependent variable is one and the delta of x, y, w, and h need to be calculated for each anchor box
    - For the grids that do not contain the center of object, the dependent variable is zero and the delta of x, y, w, and h do not matter
- In the first model, we shall predict the anchor box and grid cell combination that contain the center of the image
- In the second model, we predict the bounding box corrections of the anchor box

How to do it...

We will build the code to perform person detection (The code file and corresponding recommended dataset link is available as Anchor_box_based_person_detection.ipynb in GitHub along with the recommended dataset):

1. Download the dataset that contains a set of images, the objects contained in them, and the corresponding bounding boxes of the objects in the images. The recommended dataset and the corresponding code files that you can work on are provided in GitHub.

Detecting and Localizing Objects in Images

A sample image and its corresponding bounding box location output would look similar to the one that we saw in step 1 of *"Object detection using region proposal based CNN"* recipe.

2. Import the relevant packages, as follows:

```
import matplotlib.pyplot as plt
%matplotlib inline
import tensorflow as tf, selectivesearch
import json, scipy, os, numpy as np,argparse,time, sys, gc, cv2, xmltodict
from copy import deepcopy
```

3. Define the IoU extraction function, shown in the following code:

```
def extract_iou2(candidate, current_y,img_shape):
    boxA = deepcopy(candidate)
    boxB = deepcopy(current_y)
    boxA[2] += boxA[0]
    boxA[3] += boxA[1]
    iou_img1 = np.zeros(img_shape)
    iou_img1[boxA[1]:boxA[3],boxA[0]:boxA[2]]=1
    iou_img2 = np.zeros(img_shape)
    iou_img2[int(boxB[1]):int(boxB[3]),int(boxB[0]):int(boxB[2])]=1
    iou =
np.sum(iou_img1*iou_img2)/(np.sum(iou_img1)+np.sum(iou_img2)-
np.sum(iou_img1*iou_img2))
    return iou
```

4. Define the anchor boxes' width and height as a percentage of total image's width and height:

   1. Identify all the possible widths and heights of the person in the bounding boxes:

```
y_train = []

for i in mylist[:10000]:
    xml_file = xml_filepath +i
    arg1=i.split('.')[0]
    with open(xml_file, "rb") as f: # notice the "rb" mode
        d = xmltodict.parse(f, xml_attribs=True)
        l=[]
        if type(d["annotation"]["object"]) == type(l):
            discard=1
        else:
            x1=((float(d['annotation']['object']
```

```
                        ['bndbox']['xmin'])))/(float(d['annotation']['size']['width
'])))
                        x2=((float(d['annotation']['object']
['bndbox']['xmax'])))/(float(d['annotation']['size']['width
'])))
                        y1=((float(d['annotation']['object']
['bndbox']['ymin'])))/(float(d['annotation']['size']['heigh
t'])))
                        y2=((float(d['annotation']['object']
['bndbox']['ymax'])))/(float(d['annotation']['size']['heigh
t'])))
                    cls=d['annotation']['object']['name']
                    if(cls == 'person'):
                        y_train.append([x2-x1, y2-y1])
```

In the preceding code, we are looping through all the images that have only one object within them, and are then calculating the width and height of bounding box, if the image contains a person.

2. Fit k-means clustering with five centers:

```
y_train = np.array(y_train)
from sklearn.cluster import KMeans
km = KMeans(n_clusters=5)
km.fit(y_train)
km.cluster_centers_
```

The preceding results in cluster centers, shown as follows:

```
anchors = [[[0.84638352, 0.90412013],
           [0.28036872, 0.58073186],
           [0.45700897, 0.87035502],
           [0.15685545, 0.29256264],
           [0.59814951, 0.64789503]]]
```

5. Create the training dataset:
   1. Initialize empty lists so that they can be appended with data in further processing:

```
k=-1
pre_xtrain = []
y_train = []
cls = []
xtrain=[]
final_cls = []
dx = []
dy = []
```

[223]

Detecting and Localizing Objects in Images

```
dw= []
dh = []
final_delta = []
av = 0
x_train = []
img_paths = []
label_coords = []
y_delta = []
anc = []
```

2. Loop through the dataset so that we work on images that contain only one object in it, and also the object is a person:

```
for i in mylist[:10000]:
    xml_file = xml_filepath +i
    arg1=i.split('.')[0]
    discard=0
    with open(xml_file, "rb") as f: # notice the "rb" mode
        d = xmltodict.parse(f, xml_attribs=True)
        l=[]
        if type(d["annotation"]["object"]) == type(l):
            discard=1
        else:
            coords={arg1:[]}
            pre_xtrain.append(arg1)
            m=pre_xtrain[(k+1)]
            k = k+1
            if(discard==0):
x1=((float(d['annotation']['object']['bndbox']['xmin'])))/(
float(d['annotation']['size']['width']))
x2=((float(d['annotation']['object']['bndbox']['xmax'])))/(
float(d['annotation']['size']['width']))
y1=((float(d['annotation']['object']['bndbox']['ymin'])))/(
float(d['annotation']['size']['height']))
y2=((float(d['annotation']['object']['bndbox']['ymax'])))/(
float(d['annotation']['size']['height']))
                cls=d['annotation']['object']['name']
                if(cls == 'person'):
                    coords[arg1].append(x1)
                    coords[arg1].append(y1)
                    coords[arg1].append(x2)
                    coords[arg1].append(y2)
                    coords[arg1].append(cls)
```

The preceding code appends the location of the object (post-normalized for the width and height of the image).

3. Resize the image of person so that all images are of the same shape. Additionally, scale the image so that the values are between zero and one:

```
filename = base_dir+m+'.jpg'
# reference to jpg files here
img = filename
img_size=224
img = cv2.imread(filename)
img2 = cv2.resize(img, (img_size,img_size))
img2 = img2/255
```

4. Extract the object bounding box location, and also the normalized bounding-box coordinates:

```
current_y = [int(x1*224), int(y1*224), int(x2*224), int(y2*224)]
current_y2 = [float(d['annotation']['object']['bndbox']['xmin']),
float(d['annotation']['object']['bndbox']['ymin']),
float(d['annotation']['object']['bndbox']['xmax'])-
float(d['annotation']['object']['bndbox']['xmin']),
float(d['annotation']['object']['bndbox']['ymax'])-
float(d['annotation']['object']['bndbox']['ymin'])]

label_center = [(current_y[0]+current_y[2])/2, (current_y[1]+current_y[3])/2]
label = current_y
```

5. Extract the VGG16 features of the input image:

```
vgg_predict =vgg16_model.predict(img2.reshape(1,img_size,img_size,3))
x_train.append(vgg_predict)
```

By this step, we have created the input features.

6. Let's create the output features—in this case, we shall have 5 x 5 x 5 outputs for class label and 5 x 5 x 20 labels for the bounding-box correction labels:

```
target_class = np.zeros((num_grids,num_grids,5))
target_delta = np.zeros((num_grids,num_grids,20))
```

Detecting and Localizing Objects in Images

In the preceding step, we have initialized zero arrays for the target class and bounding-box corrections:

```
def positive_grid_cell(label,img_width = 224, img_height = 224):
    label_center = [(label[0]+label[2])/(2),(label[1]+label[3])/(2)]
    a = int(label_center[0]/(img_width/num_grids))
    b = int(label_center[1]/(img_height/num_grids))
    return a, b
```

In the preceding step, we have defined a function that contains the center of the object:

```
a,b = positive_grid_cell(label)
```

The preceding code helps us assign a class of 1 to the grid that contains the center of object and every other grid shall have a label of zero.

Additionally, let's define a function that finds the anchor that is closest to the shape of the object of interest:

```
def find_closest_anchor(label,img_width, img_height):
    label_width = (label[2]-label[0])/img_width
    label_height = (label[3]-label[1])/img_height
    label_width_height_array = np.array([label_width, label_height])
    distance = np.sum(np.square(np.array(anchors) - label_width_height_array), axis=1)
    closest_anchor = anchors[np.argmin(distance)]
    return closest_anchor
```

The preceding code compares the width and height of the object of interest in an image, with all the possible anchors, and identifies the anchor that is closest to the width and height of the actual object in the image.

Finally, we shall also define a function that calculates the bounding-box corrections of anchor, as follows:

```
def closest_anchor_corrections(a, b, anchor, label, img_width, img_height):
    label_center = [(label[0]+label[2])/(2),(label[1]+label[3])/(2)]
    anchor_center = [a*img_width/num_grids , b*img_height/num_grids ]
    dx = (label_center[0] - anchor_center[0])/img_width
```

```
            dy = (label_center[1] - anchor_center[1])/img_height
            dw = ((label[2] - label[0])/img_width) / (anchor[0])
            dh = ((label[3] - label[1])/img_height) / (anchor[1])
            return dx, dy, dw, dh
```

We are all set to create the target data now:

```
         for a2 in range(num_grids):
             for b2 in range(num_grids):
                 for m in range(len(anchors)):
                     dx, dy, dw, dh =
closest_anchor_corrections(a2, b2, anchors[m], label,
224, 224)
                     target_class[a2,b2,m] = 0
                     target_delta[a2,b2,((4*m)):((4*m)+4)] =
[dx, dy, dw, dh]
                     anc.append(anchors[m])
                     if((anchors[m] ==
find_closest_anchor(label,224, 224)) & (a2 == a) & (b2
== b)):
                         target_class[a2,b2,m] = 1
```

In the preceding code, we have assigned a target class of 1 when the anchor considered is the closest anchor that matches the shape of the object in an image.

We have also stored the bounding-box corrections in another list:

```
y_train.append(target_class.flatten())
y_delta.append(target_delta)
```

6. Build a model to identify the grid cell and anchor that is most likely to contain an object:

```
from keras.optimizers import Adam
optimizer = Adam(lr=0.001)
from keras.layers import BatchNormalization
from keras import regularizers
model = Sequential()
model.add(BatchNormalization(input_shape=(7,7,512)))
model.add(Conv2D(1024, (3,3), activation='relu',padding='valid'))
model.add(BatchNormalization())
model.add(Conv2D(5, (1,1), activation='relu',padding='same'))
model.add(Flatten())
model.add(Dense(125, activation='sigmoid'))
model.summary()
```

7. Create the input and output array for classification:

   ```
   y_train = np.array(y_train)
   x_train = np.array(x_train)
   x_train = x_train.reshape(x_train.shape[0],7,7,512)
   ```

8. Compile and fit the model for classification:

   ```
   model.compile(loss='binary_crossentropy', optimizer=optimizer)

   model.fit(x_train/np.max(x_train), y_train, epochs=5, batch_size =
   32, validation_split = 0.1, verbose = 1)
   ```

9. From the preceding model, we are in a position to identify the grid cell and anchor box combination that is most likely to have a person. In this step, we shall build a dataset where we correct the bounding box for the predictions that are most likely to contain an object:

   ```
   delta_x = []
   delta_y = []
   for i in range(len(x_train)):
       delta_x.append(x_train[i])
       delta = y_delta[i].flatten()
       coord =
   np.argmax(model.predict(x_train[i].reshape(1,7,7,512)/12))
       delta_y.append(delta[(coord*4):((coord*4)+4)])
   ```

   In the preceding step, we have prepared the input (which is the VGG16 features of original image) and the output bounding-box corrections for the predictions that are most likely to contain an object.

   Note that we are multiplying `coord` by a factor of four, as for each grid cell and anchor box combination, there are four possible values of corrections for x, y, w, and h.

10. Build a model that predicts the correction in x, y, w, and h coordinates:
    1. Create input and output arrays, and normalize the four bounding-box correction values so that all four values have a similar range:

       ```
       delta_x = np.array(delta_x)
       delta_y = np.array(delta_y)

       max_y = np.max(delta_y, axis=0)
       delta_y2 = deltay/max_y
       ```

2. Build a model that predicts the bounding-box corrections, given the VGG16 features:

```
model2 = Sequential()
model2.add(BatchNormalization(input_shape=(7,7,512)))
model2.add(Conv2D(1024, (3,3),
activation='relu',padding='valid'))
model2.add(BatchNormalization())
model2.add(Conv2D(5, (1,1),
activation='relu',padding='same'))
model2.add(Flatten())
model2.add(Dense(2, activation='linear'))
```

11. Compile and fit the model:

```
model2.compile(loss = 'mean_absolute_error', optimizer = optimizer)
model2.fit(delta_x/np.max(x_train), delta_y2, epochs = 10,
batch_size = 32, verbose = 1, validation_split = 0.1)
```

12. Predict the bounding box on a new image:
    1. Extract the position that is most likely to contain the object:

    ```
    img = cv2.imread('/content/Hemanvi.jpg')
    img = cv2.resize(img, (224,224))
    img = img/255
    img2 = vgg16_model.predict(img.reshape(1,224,224,3))
    arg = np.argmax(model.predict(img2/np.max(x_train)))
    ```

    In the preceding step, we are picking an image that contains a person within it, and resizing it, so that it can be further processed to extract the VGG16 features. Finally, we are identifying the anchor that is most likely to contain the location of a person.

    2. Extract the grid cell and anchor box combination that is most likely to contain an image.

[229]

The preceding predicts the grid cell and anchor box combination that is most likely to contain the object of interest, which is done as follows:

```
count = 0
for a in range(num_grids):
    for b in range(num_grids):
        for c in range(len(anchors)):
            if(count == arg):
                a2 = a
                b2 = b
                c2 = c
            count+=1
```

In the preceding code, a2 and b2 would be the grid cell (the x axis and y axis combination) that is most likely to contain an object, and c2 is the anchor box that is possibly of the same shape as the object.

3. Predict the corrections in x, y, w, and h coordinates:

```
pred = model2.predict(img2/np.max(delta_x))[0]
```

4. De-normalize the predicted bounding-box corrections:

```
pred1 = pred*max_y
```

5. Extract the final corrected x, y, w, and h coordinates:

```
xmin = pred1[0]*224+a2*224/num_grids -
(anchors[c2][0]*pred1[2] * 224)/2
ymin = pred1[1]*224+b2*224/num_grids -
(anchors[c2][1]*pred1[3] * 224)/2

w = anchors[c2][0]*pred1[2] * 224
h = anchors[c2][1]*pred1[3] * 224
```

6. Plot the image along with the bounding box:

```
import matplotlib.patches as mpatches
cand = [xmin, ymin, w, h]
cand = np.clip(cand, 1, 223)
fig, ax = plt.subplots(ncols=1, nrows=1, figsize=(6, 6))
ax.imshow(img)
rect = mpatches.Rectangle(
(cand[0], cand[1]), cand[2], cand[3], fill=False,
edgecolor='red', linewidth=1)
ax.add_patch(rect)
plt.grid('off')
plt.show()
```

One of the drawbacks with this approach is that it gets difficult when we are detecting objects that are very small when compared to the image size.

There's more...

Let's consider a scenario where the object to be detected is small in size. If we passed this image through a pre-trained network, this object would be detected in earlier layers, as, in the last few layers, the image would be passed through multiple pooling layers, resulting in the object to be detected shrinking to a very small space.

Similarly, if the object to be detected is large in size, that object will be detected in the last layers of the pre-trained network.

A single shot detector uses a pre-trained network where different layers of the network work toward detecting different types of images:

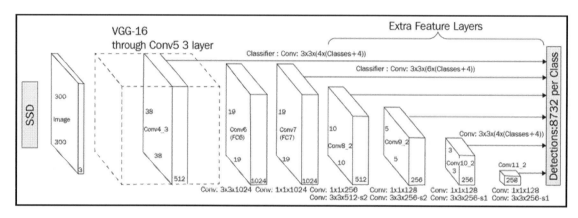

Source: https://arxiv.org/pdf/1512.02325.pdf

In the preceding diagram, you should note that features from different layers are passed through a dense layer, and, finally, concatenated together so that a model can be built and fine-tuned.

Additionally, YOLO can also be implemented based on the tutorial available here: `https://pjreddie.com/darknet/yolo/`.

7
Image Analysis Applications in Self-Driving Cars

In the previous chapters, we learned about object classification and also object localization. In this chapter, we will go through multiple case studies that are relevant to self-driving cars.

You will be learning about the following:

- Traffic sign identification
- Predicting the angle within which a car needs to be turned
- Identifying cars on the road using the U-net architecture
- Semantic segmentation of objects on the road

Traffic sign identification

In this case study, we will understand the way in which we can classify a signal into one of the 43 possible classes.

Getting ready

For this exercise, we will adopt the following strategy:

1. Download the dataset that contains all possible traffic signs
2. Perform histogram normalization on top of input images:
    - Certain images are taken in broad day light, while others might be taken in twilight
    - Different lighting conditions result in a variation in pixel values, depending on the lighting condition at which the picture is taken

- Histogram normalization performs normalization on pixel values so that they all have a similar distribution
2. Scale the input images
3. Build, compile, and fit a model to reduce the categorical cross entropy loss value

How to do it...

1. Download the dataset, as follows (the code file is available as `Traffic_signal_detection.ipynb` in GitHub). The dataset is available through the paper: J. Stallkamp, M. Schlipsing, J. Salmen, C. Igel, Man vs. computer: Benchmarking machine learning algorithms for traffic sign recognition:

```
$ wget http://benchmark.ini.rub.de/Dataset/GTSRB_Final_Training_Images.zip
$ unzip GTSRB_Final_Training_Images.zip
```

2. Read the image paths into a list, as follows:

```
from skimage import io
import os
import glob

root_dir = '/content/GTSRB/Final_Training/Images/'
all_img_paths = glob.glob(os.path.join(root_dir, '*/*.ppm'))
```

A sample of the images looks as follows:

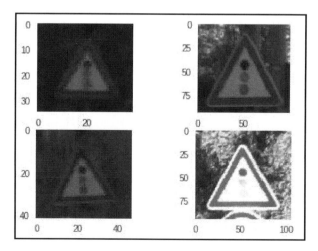

Note that certain images have a smaller shape when compared to others and also that certain images have more lighting when compared to others. Thus, we'll have to preprocess the images so that all images are normalized per exposure to lighting as well as shape.

3. Perform histogram normalization on top of the input dataset, as follows:

```
import numpy as np
from skimage import color, exposure, transform

NUM_CLASSES = 43
IMG_SIZE = 48

def preprocess_img(img):
    hsv = color.rgb2hsv(img)
    hsv[:, :, 2] = exposure.equalize_hist(hsv[:, :, 2])
    img = color.hsv2rgb(hsv)
    img = transform.resize(img, (IMG_SIZE, IMG_SIZE))
    return img
```

In the preceding code, we are first converting an image that is in RGB format into a **Hue Saturation Value (HSV)** format. By transforming the image from RGB to HSV format, we are essentially converting the combined RGB values into an array that can then be transformed into an array of single dimension.

Post that, we are normalizing the values obtained in HSV format so that they belong to the same scale by using the `equalize_hist` method.

Once the images are normalized in the last channel of the HSV format, we convert them back in to RGB format.

Finally, we resize the images to a standard size.

4. Check the image prior to passing it through histogram normalization and contrast that with post histogram normalization (post passing the image through the preprocess_img function), as follows:

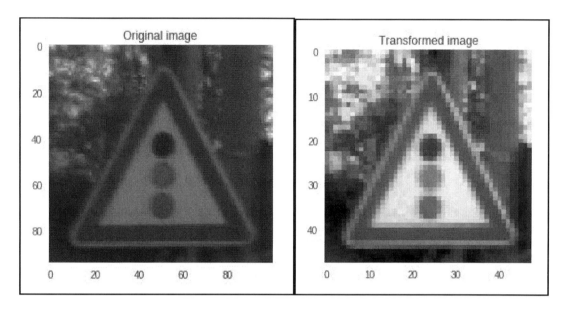

From the preceding pictures, we can see that there is a considerable change in the visibility of the image (the image on the left) post histogram normalization (the image on the right).

5. Prepare the input and output arrays, as follows:

```
count = 0
imgs = []
labels = []
for img_path in all_img_paths:
    img = preprocess_img(io.imread(img_path))
    label = img_path.split('/')[-2]
    imgs.append(img)
    labels.append(label)

X = np.array(imgs)
Y = to_categorical(labels, num_classes = NUM_CLASSES)
```

6. Build the training and test datasets, as follows:

```
from sklearn.model_selection import train_test_split
X_train, X_test, y_train, y_test = train_test_split(X, Y, test_size
= 0.2, random_state= 42)
```

7. Build and compile the model, as follows:

```
model = Sequential()
model.add(Conv2D(32, (3, 3), padding='same',input_shape=(IMG_SIZE,
IMG_SIZE, 3), activation='relu'))
model.add(Conv2D(32, (3, 3), activation='relu'))
model.add(MaxPooling2D(pool_size=(2, 2)))
model.add(Dropout(0.2))
model.add(Conv2D(64, (3, 3), padding='same',activation='relu'))
model.add(Conv2D(64, (3, 3), activation='relu'))
model.add(MaxPooling2D(pool_size=(2, 2)))
model.add(Dropout(0.2))
model.add(Conv2D(128, (3, 3), padding='same',activation='relu'))
model.add(Conv2D(128, (3, 3), activation='relu'))
model.add(MaxPooling2D(pool_size=(2, 2)))
model.add(Dropout(0.2))
model.add(Flatten())
model.add(Dense(512, activation='relu'))
model.add(Dropout(0.5))
model.add(Dense(NUM_CLASSES, activation='softmax'))
model.summary()

model.compile(loss='categorical_crossentropy',optimizer='adam',metr
ics=['accuracy']
```

A summary of the model is as follows:

```
Layer (type)                 Output Shape              Param #
=================================================================
conv2d_1 (Conv2D)            (None, 48, 48, 32)        896
_____
conv2d_2 (Conv2D)            (None, 46, 46, 32)        9248
_____
max_pooling2d_1 (MaxPooling2 (None, 23, 23, 32)        0
_____
dropout_1 (Dropout)          (None, 23, 23, 32)        0
_____
conv2d_3 (Conv2D)            (None, 23, 23, 64)        18496
_____
conv2d_4 (Conv2D)            (None, 21, 21, 64)        36928
_____
max_pooling2d_2 (MaxPooling2 (None, 10, 10, 64)        0
_____
dropout_2 (Dropout)          (None, 10, 10, 64)        0
_____
conv2d_5 (Conv2D)            (None, 10, 10, 128)       73856
_____
conv2d_6 (Conv2D)            (None, 8, 8, 128)         147584
_____
max_pooling2d_3 (MaxPooling2 (None, 4, 4, 128)         0
_____
dropout_3 (Dropout)          (None, 4, 4, 128)         0
_____
flatten_1 (Flatten)          (None, 2048)              0
_____
dense_1 (Dense)              (None, 512)               1049088
_____
dropout_4 (Dropout)          (None, 512)               0
_____
dense_2 (Dense)              (None, 43)                22059
=================================================================
Total params: 1,358,155
Trainable params: 1,358,155
Non-trainable params: 0
```

8. Fit the model, as follows:

   ```
   model.fit(X_train, y_train,batch_size=32,epochs=5,validation_data = (X_test, y_test))
   ```

The preceding code, results in a model that has an accuracy of ~99%:

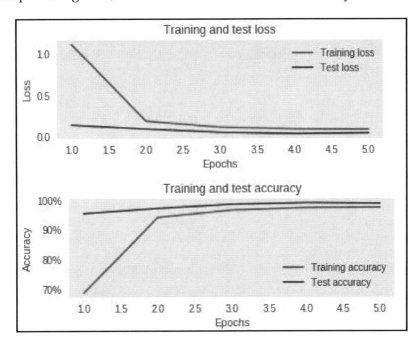

Additionally, if you perform the exact same analysis like we did, but without histogram normalization (correcting for exposure), the accuracy of the model is ~97%.

Predicting the angle within which a car needs to be turned

In this case study, we will understand the angle within which a car needs to be turned based on the image provided.

Getting ready

The strategy we adopt to build a steering angle prediction is as follows:

1. Gather a dataset that has the images of the road and the corresponding angle within which the steering needs to be turned
2. Preprocess the image

3. Pass the image through the VGG16 model to extract features
4. Build a neural network that performs regression to predict the steering angle, which is a continuous value to be predicted

How to do it...

1. Download the following dataset. This dataset is available from the following link: https://github.com/SullyChen/driving-datasets: (the code file is available as Car_steering_angle_detection.ipynb in GitHub):

    ```
    $ pip install PyDrive
    ```

    ```
    from pydrive.auth import GoogleAuth
    from pydrive.drive import GoogleDrive
    from google.colab import auth
    from oauth2client.client import GoogleCredentials

    auth.authenticate_user()
    gauth = GoogleAuth()
    gauth.credentials = GoogleCredentials.get_application_default()
    drive = GoogleDrive(gauth)

    file_id = '0B-KJCaaF7elleG1RbzVPZWV4Tlk' # URL id.
    downloaded = drive.CreateFile({'id': filc_id})
    downloaded.GetContentFile('steering_angle.zip')
    ```

    ```
    $ unzip steering_angle.zip
    ```

2. Import the relevant packages, as follows:

    ```
    import os
    import numpy as np
    import pandas as pd
    import matplotlib.pyplot as plt
    from scipy import pi
    import cv2
    import scipy.misc
    import tensorflow as tf
    ```

3. Read the images and their corresponding angles in radians into separate lists, as follows:

```
DATA_FOLDER = "/content/driving_dataset/"
DATA_FILE = os.path.join(DATA_FOLDER, "data.txt")
x = []
y = []

train_batch_pointer = 0
test_batch_pointer = 0

with open(DATA_FILE) as f:
    for line in f:
        image_name, angle = line.split()
        image_path = os.path.join(DATA_FOLDER, image_name)
        x.append(image_path)
        angle_radians = float(angle) * (pi / 180) #converting angle into radians
        y.append(angle_radians)
y = np.array(y)
```

4. Create the train and test datasets, as follows:

```
split_ratio = int(len(x) * 0.8)
train_x = x[:split_ratio]
train_y = y[:split_ratio]
test_x = x[split_ratio:]
test_y = y[split_ratio:]
```

5. Check the output label values in the train and test datasets, as follows:

```
fig = plt.figure(figsize = (10, 7))
plt.hist(train_y, bins = 50, histtype = "step",color='r')
plt.hist(test_y, bins = 50, histtype = "step",color='b')
plt.title("Steering Wheel angle in train and test")
plt.xlabel("Angle")
plt.ylabel("Bin count")
plt.grid('off')
plt.show()
```

[241]

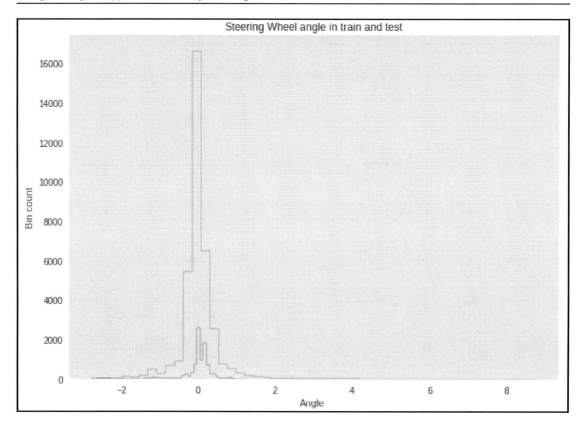

6. Remove the pixels in the first 100 rows, as they do not correspond to the image of a road, and then pass the resulting image through the VGG16 model. Additionally, for this exercise, we will work on only the first 10,000 images in the dataset so that we are able to build a model faster. Remove the pixels in the first 100 rows, as follows:

```
x = []
y = []
for i in range(10000):
    im = cv2.imread(train_x[i])
    im = im[100:,:,:]/255
    vgg_im = vgg16_model.predict(im.reshape(1,im.shape[0],im.shape[1],3))
    x.append(vgg_im)
    y.append(train_y[i])
x1 = np.array(x)
x1 = x1.reshape(x1.shape[0],4,14,512)
y1 = np.array(y)
```

7. Build and compile the model, as follows:

```
model = Sequential()
model.add(Flatten(input_shape=(4,14,512)))
model.add(Dense(512, activation='relu'))
model.add(Dropout(.5))
model.add(Dense(100, activation='linear'))
model.add(Dropout(.2))
model.add(Dense(50, activation='linear'))
model.add(Dropout(.1))
model.add(Dense(10, activation='linear'))
model.add(Dense(1, activation='linear'))
model.summary()
```

Note that the output layer has linear activation as the output is a continuous value that ranges from -9 to +9. A summary of the model is as follows:

Layer (type)	Output Shape	Param #
flatten_1 (Flatten)	(None, 28672)	0
dense_1 (Dense)	(None, 512)	14680576
dropout_1 (Dropout)	(None, 512)	0
dense_2 (Dense)	(None, 100)	51300
dropout_2 (Dropout)	(None, 100)	0
dense_3 (Dense)	(None, 50)	5050
dropout_3 (Dropout)	(None, 50)	0
dense_4 (Dense)	(None, 10)	510
dense_5 (Dense)	(None, 1)	11

Total params: 14,737,447
Trainable params: 14,737,447
Non-trainable params: 0

Now, we'll compile the model we've defined as follows:

```
model.compile(loss='mean_squared_error',optimizer='adam')
```

8. Fit the model, as follows:

```
model.fit(x1/11, y1,batch_size=32,epochs=10, validation_split = 0.1, verbose = 1)
```

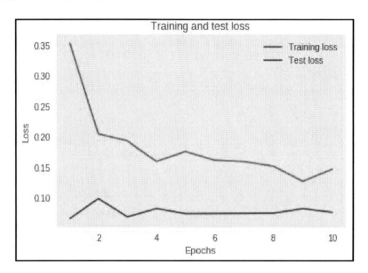

Test loss is the line that has the lower loss in the preceding diagram.

Note that we have divided the input dataset by 11 so that we can scale it to have a values between 0 to 1. Now, we should be in a position to simulate the movement of the car based on the angle that it is predicted.

The steering angle predictions obtained by the model for a sample of images are as follows:

 Note that you should be very careful while taking a model like the preceding one and implementing it. It should be first tested on multiple daylight conditions before finally going to production.

Instance segmentation using the U-net architecture

So far, in the previous two chapters, we have learned about detecting objects and also about identifying the bounding boxes within which the objects within an image are located. In this section, we will learn about performing instance segmentation, where all the pixels belonging to a certain object are highlighted while every other pixel isn't (this is similar to masking all the other pixels that do not belong to an object with zeros and masking the pixels that belong to the object with pixel values of one).

Getting ready

To perform instance segmentation, we will perform the following:

1. Work on a dataset that has the input image and the corresponding masked image of the pixels where the object is located in the image:
    - The image and its masked image

2. We'll pass the image through the pre-trained VGG16 model to extract features out of each convolution layer
3. We'll gradually up sample the convolution layers so that we get an output image that is of 224 x 224 x 3 in shape
4. We'll freeze the layers where VGG16 weights are used
5. Concatenate the up sampled convolution layers with the down sampled convolution layers:
    - This forms the U-shaped connection
    - The U-shaped connection helps in model having the context in a way similar to ResNet (previously down sampled layer provides context in addition to the up sampled layer)
    - Reconstructing an image is much easier if we take the first layer's output, as much of the image is intact in the first layer (earlier layers learn the contours). If we try to reconstruct an image from the last few layers by up sampling them, there is a good chance that the majority of the information about the image is lost
6. Fit a model that maps the input image to masked image:
    - Note that the masked image is binary in nature—where the black values correspond to a pixel value of 0 and the white pixels have a value of 1
7. Minimize the binary cross entropy loss function across all the 224 x 224 x 1 pixels

The reason this model is called a **U-net architecture** is because the visualization of the model looks as follows—a rotated U-like structure:

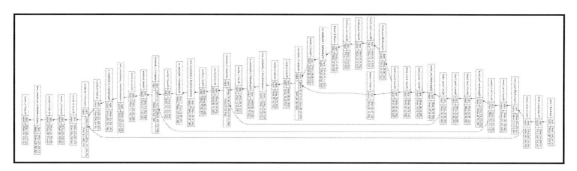

The U-like structure of the model is due to the early layers connecting to up sampled versions of the down sampled layers.

How to do it...

In the following code, we will perform instance segmentation to detect a car within an image:

1. Download and import files from `https://github.com/divamgupta/image-segmentation-keras`, as follows:

   ```
   $ wget https://www.dropbox.com/s/0pigmmmynbf9xwq/dataset1.zip
   $ unzip dataset1.zip
   dir_data = "/content/dataset1"
   dir_seg = dir_data + "/annotations_prepped_train/"
   dir_img = dir_data + "/images_prepped_train/"
   import glob, os
   all_img_paths = glob.glob(os.path.join(dir_img, '*.png'))
   all_mask_paths = glob.glob(os.path.join(dir_seg, '*.png'))
   ```

2. Read the images and their corresponding masks into arrays, as follows:

   ```
   import cv2
   from scipy import ndimage
   x = []
   y = []
   for i in range(len(all_img_paths)):
     img = cv2.imread(all_img_paths[i])
     img = cv2.resize(img,(224,224))
     mask_path = dir_seg+all_img_paths[i].split('/')[4]
     img_mask = ndimage.imread(mask_path)
     img_mask = cv2.resize(img_mask,(224,224))
     x.append(img)
     y.append(img_mask)

   x = np.array(x)/255
   y = np.array(y)/255
   y2 = np.where(y==8,1,0)
   ```

   In the preceding step, we have created the input and output arrays and also normalized the input array. Finally, we separated the mask of a car from everything else, as this dataset has 12 unique classes of which cars are masked with a pixel value of 8.

Image Analysis Applications in Self-Driving Cars

A sample of input and masked images are as follows:

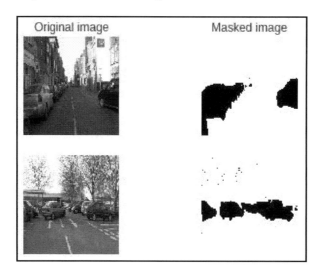

Furthermore, we create input and output arrays where we scale the input array and reshape the output array (so that it can be passed to network), as follows:

```
x = np.array(x)
x = x/255
y2 = np.array(y2)
y2 = y2.reshape(y2.shape[0],y2.shape[1],y2.shape[2],1)
```

4. Build the model where the image is first passed through the VGG16 model layers and the convolution features are extracted, as follows:

In the following code, we are importing the pre-trained VGG16 model:

```
from keras.applications.vgg16 import VGG16 as PTModel
from keras.layers import Input, Conv2D, concatenate, UpSampling2D, BatchNormalization, Activation, Cropping2D, ZeroPadding2D
from keras.layers import Input, merge, Conv2D, MaxPooling2D,UpSampling2D, Dropout, Cropping2D, merge, concatenate
from keras.optimizers import Adam
from keras.callbacks import ModelCheckpoint, LearningRateScheduler
from keras import backend as K
from keras.models import Model

base_pretrained_model = PTModel(input_shape = (224,224,3), include_top = False, weights = 'imagenet')
base_pretrained_model.trainable = False
```

In the following code, the features of various convolution layers when passed through the VGG16 model are extracted:

```
conv1 =
Model(inputs=base_pretrained_model.input,outputs=base_pretrained_mo
del.get_layer('block1_conv2').output).output
conv2 =
Model(inputs=base_pretrained_model.input,outputs=base_pretrained_mo
del.get_layer('block2_conv2').output).output
conv3 =
Model(inputs=base_pretrained_model.input,outputs=base_pretrained_mo
del.get_layer('block3_conv3').output).output
conv4 =
Model(inputs=base_pretrained_model.input,outputs=base_pretrained_mo
del.get_layer('block4_conv3').output).output
drop4 = Dropout(0.5)(conv4)
conv5 =
Model(inputs=base_pretrained_model.input,outputs=base_pretrained_mo
del.get_layer('block5_conv3').output).output
drop5 = Dropout(0.5)(conv5)
```

In the following code, we are up scaling the features using the `UpSampling` method and then concatenating with the down scaled VGG16 convolution features at each layer:

```
up6 = Conv2D(512, 2, activation = 'relu', padding =
'same',kernel_initializer = 'he_normal')(UpSampling2D(size
=(2,2))(drop5))
merge6 = concatenate([drop4,up6], axis = 3)

conv6 = Conv2D(512, 3, activation = 'relu', padding =
'same',kernel_initializer = 'he_normal')(merge6)
conv6 = Conv2D(512, 3, activation = 'relu', padding =
'same',kernel_initializer = 'he_normal')(conv6)
conv6 = BatchNormalization()(conv6)
up7 = Conv2D(256, 2, activation = 'relu', padding =
'same',kernel_initializer = 'he_normal')(UpSampling2D(size
=(2,2))(conv6))
merge7 = concatenate([conv3,up7], axis = 3)
conv7 = Conv2D(256, 3, activation = 'relu', padding =
'same',kernel_initializer = 'he_normal')(merge7)
conv7 = Conv2D(256, 3, activation = 'relu', padding =
'same',kernel_initializer = 'he_normal')(conv7)
conv7 = BatchNormalization()(conv7)
up8 = Conv2D(128, 2, activation = 'relu', padding =
'same',kernel_initializer = 'he_normal')(UpSampling2D(size
=(2,2))(conv7))
merge8 = concatenate([conv2,up8],axis = 3)
```

```
conv8 = Conv2D(128, 3, activation = 'relu', padding =
'same',kernel_initializer = 'he_normal')(merge8)
conv8 = Conv2D(128, 3, activation = 'relu', padding =
'same',kernel_initializer = 'he_normal')(conv8)
conv8 = BatchNormalization()(conv8)
up9 = Conv2D(64, 2, activation = 'relu', padding =
'same',kernel_initializer = 'he_normal')(UpSampling2D(size
=(2,2))(conv8))
merge9 = concatenate([conv1,up9], axis = 3)
conv9 = Conv2D(64, 3, activation = 'relu', padding =
'same',kernel_initializer = 'he_normal')(merge9)
conv9 = Conv2D(64, 3, activation = 'relu', padding =
'same',kernel_initializer = 'he_normal')(conv9)
conv9 = Conv2D(2, 3, activation = 'relu', padding =
'same',kernel_initializer = 'he_normal')(conv9)
conv9 = BatchNormalization()(conv9)
conv10 = Conv2D(1, 1, activation = 'sigmoid')(conv9)
```

In the following code, we are defining the input and output to the model, where the input is passed to the `base_pretrained_model` first and the output is `conv10` (which has the shape of 224 x 224 x 1—the intended shape of our output):

```
model = Model(input = base_pretrained_model.input, output = conv10)
```

5. Freeze the convolution layers obtained from the multiplication of the VGG16 model from training, as follows:

```
for layer in model.layers[:18]:
    layer.trainable = False
```

6. Compile and fit the model for the first 1,000 images in our dataset, as follows:

```
from keras import optimizers
adam = optimizers.Adam(1e-3, decay = 1e-6)
model.compile(loss='binary_crossentropy',optimizer=adam,metrics=['a
ccuracy'])
history = model.fit(x,y,validation_split =
0.1,batch_size=1,epochs=5,verbose=1)
```

Chapter 7

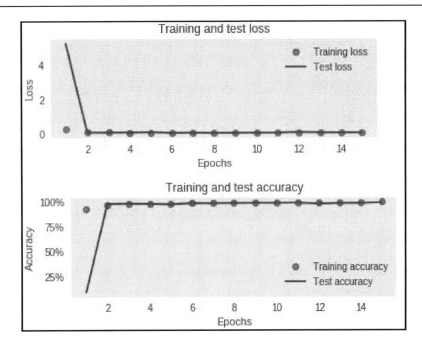

7. Test the preceding model on a test image (the last 2 images of our dataset—they are test images that have `validtion_split = 0.1`), as follows:

```
y_pred = model.predict(x[-2:].reshape(2,224,224,3))
```

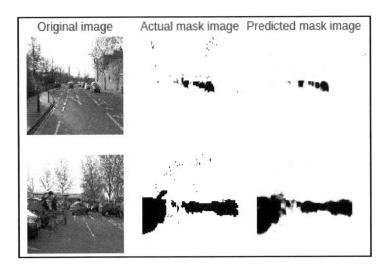

[251]

We can see that the generated mask is realistic for the given input of road and also in a way that's better than what we were doing prior as the noisy dots are not present in the predicted mask image.

Semantic segmentation of objects in an image

In the previous section, we learned about performing segmentation on top of an image where the image contained only one object. In this segmentation, we will learn about performing segmentation so that we are able to distinguish between multiple objects that are present in an image of a road.

Getting ready

The strategy that we'll adopt to perform semantic segmentation on top of images of a road is as follows:

1. Gather a dataset that has the annotation of where the multiple objects within an image are located:
   - A sample of the semantic image looks as follows:

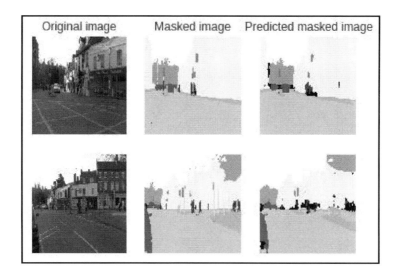

2. Convert the output mask into a multi dimensional array where there are as many columns as the number of all possible unique objects
3. If there are 12 possible unique values (12 unique objects), convert the output image into an image that is 224 x 224 x 12 in shape:
   - A value of a channel represents that the object corresponding to that channel is present in that location of image
4. Leverage the model architecture that we have seen in previous sections to train a model that has 12 possible output values
5. Reshape the prediction into three channels by assigning all three channels to have the same output:
   - The output is the argmax of prediction of the probabilities of the 12 possible classes

How to do it...

Semantic segmentation in code is performed as follows (The code file is available as Semantic_segmentation.ipynb in GitHub):

1. Download the dataset, as follows:

```
!wget https://www.dropbox.com/s/0pigmmmynbf9xwq/dataset1.zip
!unzip dataset1.zip
dir_data = "/content/dataset1"
dir_seg = dir_data + "/annotations_prepped_train/"
dir_img = dir_data + "/images_prepped_train/"
import glob, os
all_img_paths = glob.glob(os.path.join(dir_img, '*.png'))
all_mask_paths = glob.glob(os.path.join(dir_seg, '*.png'))
```

2. Read the images and their corresponding labels into separate lists, as follows:

```
import cv2
from scipy import ndimage
for i in range(len(all_img_paths)):
    img = cv2.imread(all_img_paths[i])
    img = cv2.resize(img, (224,224))
    mask_path = dir_seg+all_img_paths[i].split('/')[4]
    img_mask = ndimage.imread(mask_path)
    img_mask = cv2.resize(img_mask, (224,224))
    x.append(img)
    y.append(img_mask)
```

3. Define a function that converts the three channel output images into 12 channels where there are 12 unique values of output:
    1. Extract the number of unique values (objects) that are present in the output, as follows:

        ```
        n_classes = len(set(np.array(y).flatten()))
        ```

    2. Convert the masked image into a one-hot encoded version with as many channels as the number of objects in the total dataset, as follows:

        ```
        def getSegmentationArr(img):
            seg_labels = np.zeros(( 224, 224, n_classes ))
            for c in range(n_classes):
                seg_labels[: , : , c ] = (img == c
        ).astype(int)
            return seg_labels

        y2 = []
        for i in range(len(y)):
            y2.append(getSegmentationArr(y[i]))

        y2 = np.array(y2)
        x = x/255
        ```

4. Build the model:
    1. Pass the images through the pre-trained VGG16 model, as follows:

        ```
        from keras.applications.vgg16 import VGG16 as PTModel
        base_pretrained_model = PTModel(input_shape = (224,224,3),
        include_top = False, weights = 'imagenet')
        base_pretrained_model.trainable = False
        ```

    2. Extract the VGG16 features of the image, as follows:

        ```
        conv1 = Model(inputs=base_pretrained_model.input,outputs=base_pretrained_model.get_layer('block1_conv2').output).output
        conv2 = Model(inputs=base_pretrained_model.input,outputs=base_pretrained_model.get_layer('block2_conv2').output).output
        conv3 = Model(inputs=base_pretrained_model.input,outputs=base_pretrained_model.get_layer('block3_conv3').output).output
        conv4 = Model(inputs=base_pretrained_model.input,outputs=base_pretrained_model.get_layer('block4_conv3').output).output
        drop4 = Dropout(0.5)(conv4)
        ```

```
conv5 =
Model(inputs=base_pretrained_model.input,outputs=base_pretrained_mo
del.get_layer('block5_conv3').output).output
drop5 = Dropout(0.5)(conv5)
```

3. Pass the convolution features through up sampling layers and concatenate them to form a U-net architecture in a sim, as follows:

```
conv6 = Conv2D(512, 3, activation = 'relu', padding =
'same',kernel_initializer = 'he_normal')(merge6)
conv6 = Conv2D(512, 3, activation = 'relu', padding =
'same',kernel_initializer = 'he_normal')(conv6)
conv6 = BatchNormalization()(conv6)
up7 = Conv2D(256, 2, activation = 'relu', padding =
'same',kernel_initializer = 'he_normal')(UpSampling2D(size
=(2,2))(conv6))
merge7 = concatenate([conv3,up7], axis = 3)
conv7 = Conv2D(256, 3, activation = 'relu', padding =
'same',kernel_initializer = 'he_normal')(merge7)
conv7 = Conv2D(256, 3, activation = 'relu', padding =
'same',kernel_initializer = 'he_normal')(conv7)
conv7 = BatchNormalization()(conv7)
up8 = Conv2D(128, 2, activation = 'relu', padding =
'same',kernel_initializer = 'he_normal')(UpSampling2D(size
=(2,2))(conv7))
merge8 = concatenate([conv2,up8],axis = 3)
conv8 = Conv2D(128, 3, activation = 'relu', padding =
'same',kernel_initializer = 'he_normal')(merge8)
conv8 = Conv2D(128, 3, activation = 'relu', padding =
'same',kernel_initializer = 'he_normal')(conv8)
conv8 = BatchNormalization()(conv8)
up9 = Conv2D(64, 2, activation = 'relu', padding =
'same',kernel_initializer = 'he_normal')(UpSampling2D(size
=(2,2))(conv8))
merge9 = concatenate([conv1,up9], axis = 3)
conv9 = Conv2D(64, 3, activation = 'relu', padding =
'same',kernel_initializer = 'he_normal')(merge9)
conv9 = Conv2D(64, 3, activation = 'relu', padding =
'same',kernel_initializer = 'he_normal')(conv9)
conv9 = Conv2D(2, 3, activation = 'relu', padding =
'same',kernel_initializer = 'he_normal')(conv9)
conv9 = BatchNormalization()(conv9)
conv10 = Conv2D(1, 1, activation = 'sigmoid')(conv9)

model = Model(input = base_pretrained_model.input, output =
conv10)
```

Image Analysis Applications in Self-Driving Cars

5. Freeze the VGG16 layers, as follows:

```
for layer in model.layers[:18]:
    layer.trainable = False
```

6. Compile and fit the model, as follows:

```
model.compile(optimizer=Adam(1e-3, decay = 1e-6),
  loss='categorical_crossentropy', metrics = ['accuracy'])

history =
model.fit(x,y2,epochs=15,batch_size=1,validation_split=0.1)
```

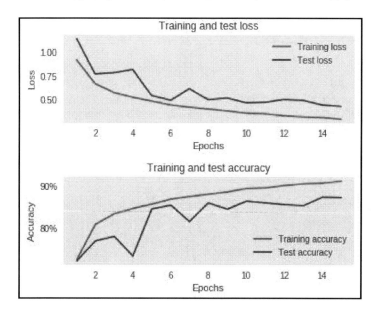

7. Predict on a test image, as follows:

```
y_pred = model.predict(x[-2:].reshape(2,224,224,3))
y_predi = np.argmax(y_pred, axis=3)
y_testi = np.argmax(y2[-2:].reshape(2,224,224,12), axis=3)

import matplotlib.pyplot as plt
%matplotlib inline
plt.subplot(231)
plt.imshow(x[-1])
plt.axis('off')
plt.title('Original image')
plt.grid('off')
plt.subplot(232)
```

Chapter 7

```
plt.imshow(y[-1])
plt.axis('off')
plt.title('Masked image')
plt.grid('off')
plt.subplot(233)
plt.imshow(y_predi[-1])
plt.axis('off')
plt.title('Predicted masked image')
plt.grid('off')
plt.subplot(234)
plt.imshow(x[-2])
plt.axis('off')
plt.grid('off')
plt.subplot(235)
plt.imshow(y[-2])
plt.axis('off')
plt.grid('off')
plt.subplot(236)
plt.imshow(y_predi[-2])
plt.axis('off')
plt.grid('off')
plt.show()
```

The preceding code results in an image where the predicted and actual semantic images are as follows:

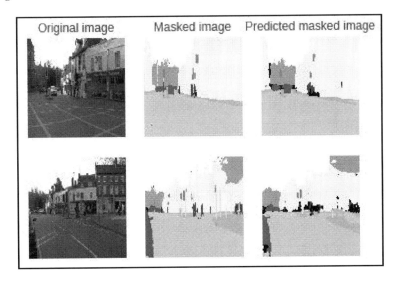

From the preceding images, we can see that we are able to accurately identify the semantic structures within an image with a high degree of accuracy (~90% for the model we trained).

8
Image Generation

In the previous chapters, we learned about predicting the class of an image and detecting where the object is located in the whole image. If we work backwards, we should be in a position to generate an image if we are given a class. Generative networks come in handy in this scenario, where we try to create new images that look very similar to the original image.

In this chapter, we will cover the following recipes:

- Generating images that can fool a neural network using an adversarial attack
- DeepDream algorithm to generate images
- Neural style transfer between images
- Generating images of digits using Generative Adversarial Networks
- Generating images of digits using a Deep Convolutional GAN
- Face generation using a Deep Convolutional GAN
- Face transition from one to another
- Performing vector arithmetic on generated images

Introduction

In the previous chapters, we identified the optimal weights that result in classifying an image into the right class. The output class of an image can be changed by varying the following:

- The weights connecting the input to the output layer, while the input pixels remain constant
- The input pixel values, while the weights remain constant

In this chapter, we will employ these two techniques to generate images.

In the case studies of an adversarial attack, the neural style transfer and DeepDream will leverage the technique of changing the input pixel values. In the techniques involving a **Generative Adversarial Network (GAN)**, we will leverage the technique of changing certain weights that connect input pixel values to the output.

The first three case studies in this chapter will leverage the technique of changing the input pixel values, while the rest leverage a change in weights that connect the input to the output.

Generating images that can fool a neural network using adversarial attack

To understand how to perform an adversarial attack on an image, let's understand how regular predictions are made using transfer learning first and then we will figure out how to tweak the input image so that the image's class is completely different, even though we barely changed the input image.

Getting ready

Let's go through an example where we will try to identify the class of the object within the image:

1. Read the image of a cat
2. Preprocess the image so that it can then be passed to an inception network
3. Import the pre-trained Inception v3 model
4. Predict the class of the object present in the image
5. The image will be predicted as a persian cat as Inception v3 works well in predicting objects that belong to one of the ImageNet classes

The task at hand is to change the image in such a way that it meets the following two criteria:

- The prediction of the new image using the same network should be an African elephant with a very high probability
- The new image should be visually indistinguishable from the original image by a human

To achieve this, we will follow this strategy:

1. Define a loss function:
   - The loss is the probability of the image (of the persian cat) belonging to the African elephant class
   - The higher the loss, the closer are we to our objective
   - Hence, in this case, we would be maximizing our loss function
2. Calculate the gradient of change in the loss with respect to the change in the input:
   - This step helps in understanding the input pixels that move the output toward our objective
3. Update the input image based on the calculated gradients:
   - Ensure that the pixel values in the original image is not translated by more than 3 pixels in the final image
   - This ensures that the resulting image is humanly indistinguishable from the original image
4. Repeat steps 2 and step 3 until the prediction of the updated image is an African elephant with a confidence of at least 0.8

How to do it...

Let's go ahead and implement this strategy in code (The code file is available as `Adversarial_attack.ipynb` in GitHub):

1. Read the image of a cat:

```
import matplotlib.pyplot as plt
%matplotlib inline
img = cv2.imread('/content/cat.JPG')
img = cv2.cvtColor(img, cv2.COLOR_BGR2RGB)
img = cv2.resize(img, (299,299))
plt.imshow(img)
plt.axis('off')
```

The plot of the image looks as follows:

2. Preprocess the image so that it can then be passed to an inception network:

   ```
   original_image = cv2.resize(img, (299,299)).astype(float)
   original_image /= 255.
   original_image -= 0.5
   original_image *= 2.
   original_image = np.expand_dims(original_image, axis=0)
   ```

3. Import the pre-trained model:

   ```
   import numpy as np
   from keras.preprocessing import image
   from keras.applications import inception_v3
   model = inception_v3.InceptionV3()
   ```

4. Predict the class of the object present in the image:

   ```
   predictions = model.predict(original_image)
   predicted_classes = inception_v3.decode_predictions(predictions, top=1)
   imagenet_id, name, confidence = predicted_classes[0][0]
   print("This is a {} with {:.4}% confidence".format(name, confidence * 100))
   ```

The preceding code results in the following:

```
" This is a Persian_cat with 95.45% confidence"
```

5. Define the input and output:

```
model = inception_v3.InceptionV3()
model_input_layer = model.layers[0].input
model_output_layer = model.layers[-1].output
```

`model_input_layer` is the input to the model and `model_output_layer` is the probability of various classes for the input image (the last layer with softmax activation).

6. Set the limits of change for the original image:

```
max_change_above = np.copy(original_image) + 0.01
max_change_below = np.copy(original_image) - 0.01
hacked_image = np.copy(original_image)
```

In the preceding code, we are specifying the limits to which the original image can be changed.

7. Initialize the cost function so that the object type to fake is an African elephant (386th index value in the prediction vector):

```
learning_rate = 0.1
object_type_to_fake = 386
cost_function = model_output_layer[0, object_type_to_fake]
```

The output of `model_output_layer` is the probability of various classes for the image of interest. In this instance, we are specifying that the cost function will be dictated by the index location of the object we are trying to fake our object into.

8. Initialize the gradient function of the cost with respect to the input:

```
gradient_function = K.gradients(cost_function,
model_input_layer)[0]
```

This code calculates the gradient of `cost_function` with respect to the change in `model_input_layer` (which is the input image).

9. Map the cost and gradient functions with respect to the input:

```
grab_cost_and_gradients_from_model =
K.function([model_input_layer], [cost_function, gradient_function])
cost = 0.0
```

In the preceding code, we are calculating the values of `cost_function` (the probability of the image belonging to the African elephant class) and the gradients with respect to the input image.

10. Keep updating the input image with respect to gradients until the probability of the resulting image being an African elephant is at least 80%:

```
while cost < 0.80:
    cost, gradients = grab_cost_and_gradients_from_model([hacked_image, 0])
    hacked_image += gradients * learning_rate
    hacked_image = np.clip(hacked_image, max_change_below, max_change_above)
    print("Model's predicted likelihood that the image is an African elephant: {:.8}%".format(cost * 100))
```

In the preceding code, we are obtaining the cost and gradients that correspond to the input image (`hacked_image`). Additionally, we are updating the input image by the gradient (which is multiplied by the learning rate). Finally, if the hacked image crosses the threshold of the maximum changes of the input image, we'll clip it.

Keep looping through these steps until you achieve a probability that the input image is at least 0.8.

The variation of the probability of the image of persian cat being detected as the image of an African elephant over increasing epochs is as follows:

```
epochs = range(1, len(prob_elephant) + 1)
plt.plot(epochs, prob_elephant, 'b')
plt.title('Probability of African elephant class')
plt.xlabel('Epochs')
plt.ylabel('Probability')
plt.grid('off')
```

The variation of probability of the modified image belonging to the African elephant class is as follows:

Chapter 8

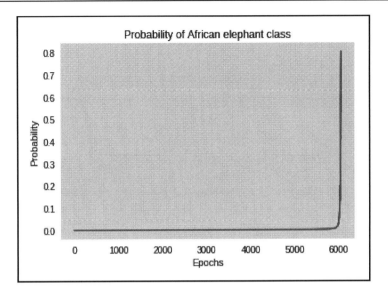

11. Predict the class of the updated image:

   ```
   model.predict(hacked_image)[0][386]
   ```

   The output of the `predict` method, which provides the probability of the modified image belonging to African elephant class, is 0.804.

12. De-process the updated input image (as it was pre-processed to scale it) so that it can be visualized:

   ```
   hacked_image = hacked_image/2
   hacked_image = hacked_image + 0.5
   hacked_image = hacked_image*255
   hacked_image = np.clip(hacked_image, 0, 255).astype('uint8')

   plt.subplot(131)
   plt.imshow(img)
   plt.title('Original image')
   plt.axis('off')
   plt.subplot(132)
   plt.imshow(hacked_image[0,:,:,:])
   plt.title('Hacked image')
   plt.axis('off')
   plt.subplot(133)
   plt.imshow(img - hacked_image[0,:,:,:])
   plt.title('Difference')
   plt.axis('off')
   ```

Image Generation

The combination of the original image, the modified (hacked) images and the difference between the two images is printed as follows:

Note that the output is now visually indistinguishable from the original image.

It is interesting to note that with hardly any change in pixel values from the original image, we have fooled the neural network (the inception v3 model) so that it now predicts a different class. This is a great example of some of the security flaws that you could encounter if the algorithm that was used to come up with a prediction is exposed to users who could build images that can fool the system.

DeepDream algorithm to generate images

In the previous section, we tweaked the input image's pixels slightly. In this section, we will tweak the input image a little more so that we can come up with an image that is still of the same object, however a little more artistic than the original one. This algorithm forms the backbone of style-transfer techniques using neural networks.

Let's go through the intuition of how DeepDream works.

We will pass our image through a pre-trained model (VGG19, in this example). We already learned that, depending on the input image, certain filters in the pre-trained model activate the most and certain filters activate the least.

We will supply the layers of neural network that we want to activate the most.

The neural network adjusts the input pixel values until we obtain the maximum value of the chosen layers.

However, we will also ensure that the maximum possible activation does not exceed a certain value as the resultant image in that case could be very different from the original image.

Getting ready

With this intuition in place, let's go through the steps of implementing the DeepDream algorithm:

1. Choose the layers of neural network that you want to activate the most and assign weightage to the amount of contribution the layers can make towards overall loss calculation.
2. Extract the output of the given layer when an image is passed through the layer and calculate the loss value at each layer:
    - An image activates the layer the most when the sum of squares of the output of the image in that layer is the highest
3. Extract the gradient of change in the input pixel values with respect to the loss.
4. Update the input pixel values based on the gradient extracted in the previous step.
5. Extract the loss value (the sum of the squares of the activation) across all chosen layers for the updated input pixel values.
6. If the loss value (the weighted sum of the squared activation) is greater than a predefined threshold, stop updating the image.

How to do it...

Let's implement these steps in code (The code file is available as `Deepdream.ipynb` in GitHub):

1. Import the relevant packages and import the image:

```
import keras.backend as K
import multiprocessing
import tensorflow as tf
import warnings
from keras.applications.vgg19 import VGG19
from keras.applications.imagenet_utils import preprocess_input
from scipy.optimize import minimize
from skimage import img_as_float, img_as_ubyte
from skimage.io import imread, imsave
from skimage.transform import pyramid_gaussian, rescale
import scipy
from keras.preprocessing import image
from keras.applications.vgg19 import preprocess_input
import matplotlib.pyplot as plt
%matplotlib inline
```

Image Generation

Preprocess the image so that it can then be passed to the VGG19 model:

```
def preprocess_image(image_path):
    img = image.load_img(image_path, target_size=(img_nrows, img_ncols))
    img = image.img_to_array(img)
    img = np.expand_dims(img, axis=0)
    img[:, :, :, 0] -= 103.939
    img[:, :, :, 1] -= 116.779
    img[:, :, :, 2] -= 123.68
    img = img[:, :, :, ::-1]/255
    return img
```

Build a function that de-processes the processed image:

```
def deprocess_image(x):
    x = x[:,:,:,::-1]*255
    x[:, :, :, 0] += 103.939
    x[:, :, :, 1] += 116.779
    x[:, :, :, 2] += 123.68
    x = np.clip(x, 0, 255).astype('uint8')
    return x
```

Preprocess the image:

```
img = preprocess_image('/content/cat.png')
```

2. Define the layers that contribute to the overall loss-value calculation:

```
layer_contributions = {
    'block2_pool':0.3,
    'block5_pool': 1.5}
```

In the preceding code, we are showing you that we will use the second and fifth pooling layers, and also assign the weights that these two layers will contribute to the overall loss value.

3. Initialize the loss function:

```
layer_dict = dict([(layer.name, layer) for layer in model.layers])
loss = K.variable(0.)
```

In the preceding step, we are initializing the loss value and a dictionary of the various layers in the model.

Calculate the overall loss value of the activations:

```
for layer_name in layer_contributions:
    coeff = layer_contributions[layer_name]
    activation = layer_dict[layer_name].output
    scaling = K.prod(K.cast(K.shape(activation), 'float32'))
    loss += coeff * K.sum(K.square(activation)) / scaling
    print(loss)
```

In the preceding code, we are looping through the layers that we are interested in (`layer_contributions`) and noting down the weights (`coeff`) that we have assigned to each layer. Additionally, we are calculating the output of the layers of interest (`activation`), and updating the loss value using the sum of squares of the activation values post scaling them.

4. Initialize the gradient value:

```
dream = model.input
grads = K.gradients(loss, dream)[0]
```

The `K.gradients` method gives us the gradient of the loss with respect to the change in the input, `dream`.

5. Normalize the gradient values so that the change in the gradients is slow:

```
grads /= K.maximum(K.mean(K.abs(grads)), 1e-7)
```

6. Create a function that maps the input image to the loss value and the gradient of the loss value with respect to the change in input pixel values (where the input image is `dream`):

```
outputs = [loss, grads]
fetch_loss_and_grads = K.function([dream], outputs)
```

7. Define a function that provides the loss and gradient values for a given input image:

```
def eval_loss_and_grads(img):
    outs = fetch_loss_and_grads([img])
    loss_value = outs[0]
    grad_values = outs[1]
    return loss_value, grad_values
```

8. Update the original image based on the obtained loss and gradient values over multiple iterations.

   In the following code, we are looping through the image 100 times. We are defining the learning rate of changing the image and the maximum possible loss (change in the image) that can happen:

   ```
   for i in range(100):
       learning_rate=0.01
       max_loss=20
   ```

   In the following code, we are extracting the loss and gradient values of the image and then stopping the change in the image if the loss value is more than the defined threshold:

   ```
   loss_value, grad_values = eval_loss_and_grads(img)
   if max_loss is not None and loss_value > max_loss:
       print(loss_value)
       break
   print('...Loss value at', i, ':', loss_value)
   ```

   In the following code, we are updating the image based on the gradient values and are de-processing the image and printing the image:

   ```
   img += learning_rate * grad_values
   img2 = deprocess_image(img.copy())
   plt.imshow(img2[0,:,:,:])
   plt.axis('off')
   plt.show()
   ```

The preceding code results in an image that looks as follows:

Note that the wavy patterns in the preceding image are obtained potentially because these are the patterns that maximize the various network layers' activations.

Here, we have seen another application of perturbing input pixels, which in this case resulted in a slightly more artistic image.

Neural style transfer between images

In the previous recipe, the modified pixel values were trying to maximize the filter activations. However, it does not give us the flexibility of specifying the style of the image; neural style transfer comes in handy in this scenario.

In neural style transfer, we have a content image and a style image, and we try to combine these two images in such a way that the content in the content image is preserved while maintaining the style of the style image.

Getting ready

The intuition of neural style transfer is as follows.

We try to modify the original image in a similar way to the DeepDream algorithm. However, the additional step is that the loss value is split into content loss and style loss.

Content loss refers to how different the generated image is from the content image. Style loss refers to how correlated the style image is to the generated image.

While we mentioned that the loss is calculated based on the difference in images, in practice, we modify it slightly by ensuring that the loss is calculated using the activations from images and not the original images. For example, the content loss at layer 2 will be the squared difference between activations of the content image and the generated image when passed through the second layer.

While calculating the content loss seems straightforward, let's try to understand how to calculate the similarity between the generated image and the style image.

A technique called gram matrix comes into the picture. Gram matrix calculates the similarity between a generated image and a style image, and is calculated as follows:

$$L_{GM}(S, G, l) = \frac{1}{4N_l^2 M_l^2} \sum_{ij}(GM[l](S)_{ij} - GM[l](G)_{ij})^2$$

Where *GM(l)* is the gram matrix value at layer *l* for the style image, S, and the generated image, G.

A gram matrix results from multiplying a matrix with the transpose of itself.

Now that we are in a position to calculate the style loss and content loss, the final modified input image is the image that minimizes the overall loss, that is, a weighted average of style and content loss.

Neural style transfer is implemented in the following steps:

1. Pass the image through a pre-trained model.
2. Extract the layer values at a predefined layer.
3. Initialize the generated image as the same as the content image.
4. Pass the generated image through the model and extract its values at the exact same layer.
5. Calculate the content loss.
6. Pass the style image through multiple layers of the model and calculate the gram matrix values of the style image.
7. Pass the generated image through the same layers that the style image passed through and calculate its corresponding gram matrix values.
8. Extract the squared difference of the gram matrix values of the two images. This will be the style loss.
9. The overall loss will be the weighted average of the style loss and content loss.
10. The input image that minimizes the overall loss will be the final image of interest.

How to do it...

1. Import the relevant packages and content, style images, that need to be combined to form an artistic image, as follows (The code file is available as `Neural_style_transfer.ipynb` in GitHub):

```
from keras.preprocessing.image import load_img, save_img, img_to_array
import numpy as np
import time
from keras.applications import vgg19
from keras.applications.imagenet_utils import preprocess_input
from keras import backend as K
import tensorflow as tf
import keras
```

```
style_img = cv2.imread('/content/style image.png')
style_img = cv2.cvtColor(style_img, cv2.COLOR_BGR2RGB)
style_img = cv2.resize(style_img,(224,224))

base_img = cv2.imread('/content/cat.png')
basc_img = cv2.cvtColor(base_img, cv2.COLOR_BGR2RGB)
base_img = cv2.resize(base_img,(224,224))
```

The style and base images look as follows:

2. Initialize the vgg19 model so that the images can be passed through its network:

   ```
   from keras.applications import vgg19
   model = vgg19.VGG19(include_top=False, weights='imagenet')
   ```

3. Reshape the base image and extract the feature values at the block3_conv4 layer of the VGG19 model:

   ```
   base_img = base_img.reshape(1,224,224,3)/255
   from keras import backend as K
   get_3rd_layer_output = K.function([model.layers[0].input],
   [model.get_layer('block3_conv4').output])
   layer_output_base = get_3rd_layer_output([base_img])[0]
   ```

In the preceding code, we are defining a function that takes the input image and extracts the output at the predefined layer.

Image Generation

4. Define the layers from which extractions need to be made to calculate the content and style losses as well as the corresponding weights that need to be assigned to each layer:

   ```
   layer_contributions_content = {'block3_conv4': 0.1}
   layer_contributions_style =  { 'block1_pool':1,
                                  'block2_pool':1,
                                  'block3_conv4':1}
   ```

   In the preceding code, we are defining the layers from which the content and style loss are calculated, as well as assigning the weights associated with the loss arising from each of these layers.

5. Define the gram matrix and style loss functions:

   In the following code, we are defining a function that calculates the gram matrix output output as the dot product of features obtained by flattening the image:

   ```
   def gram_matrix(x):
       features = K.batch_flatten(K.permute_dimensions(x, (2, 0, 1)))
       gram = K.dot(features, K.transpose(features))
       return gram
   ```

   In the following code, we are calculating the style loss as defined in the style loss equation specified in *Getting ready* section:

   ```
   def style_loss(style, combination):
       S = gram_matrix(style)
       C = gram_matrix(combination)
       channels = 3
       size = img_nrows * img_ncols
       return K.sum(K.square(S - C)) / (4. * (pow(channels,2)) * (pow(size,2)))
   ```

6. Initialize the loss value function:

   Calculating the content loss:

   ```
   layer_dict = dict([(layer.name, layer) for layer in model.layers])
   loss = K.variable(0.)
   for layer_name in layer_contributions_content:
       coeff = layer_contributions_content[layer_name]
       activation = layer_dict[layer_name].output
       scaling = K.prod(K.cast(K.shape(activation), 'float32'))
       loss += coeff * K.sum(K.square(activation - layer_output_base)) / scaling
   ```

In the preceding code, we are updating the loss value based on the loss at the layers that calculate the content loss. Note that `layer_output_base` is the output when we pass the original base image through the content layer (as defined in step 3).

The greater the difference between the activation (which is based on the modified image) and `layer_output_base` (which is based on the original image), the greater the content loss associated with the image.

Calculating the style loss:

```
for layer_name in layer_contributions_style:
    coeff = layer_contributions_style[layer_name]
    activation = layer_dict[layer_name].output
    scaling = K.prod(K.cast(K.shape(activation), 'float32'))
    style_layer_output = K.function([model.layers[0].input], 
model.get_layer(layer_name).output])
    layer_output_style = style_layer_output([style_img.reshape(1,224,224,3)/255])[0][0]
    loss += style_loss(layer_output_style, activation[0])
```

In the preceding code, we are calculating style loss in the same manner as we calculated the content loss but on different layers and using a different custom function we built: `style_loss`.

7. Build a function that maps the input image to the loss values and the corresponding gradient values:

```
dream = model.input
grads = K.gradients(loss, dream)[0]
grads /= K.maximum(K.mean(K.abs(grads)), 1e-7)
outputs = [loss, grads]
fetch_loss_and_grads = K.function([dream], outputs)

def eval_loss_and_grads(img):
    outs = fetch_loss_and_grads([img])
    loss_value = outs[0]
    grad_values = outs[1]
    return loss_value, grad_values
```

The preceding code fetches the loss and gradient values in a manner that is very similar to the *DeepDream algorithm to generate images* recipe.

Image Generation

8. Run the model for multiple epochs:

```
for i in range(2000):
    step=0.001
    loss_value, grad_values = eval_loss_and_grads(img)
    print('...Loss value at', i, ':', loss_value)
    img -= step * grad_values
    if(i%100 ==0):
        img2 = img.copy().reshape(224,224,3)
        img2 = np.clip(img2*255, 0, 255).astype('uint8')
        plt.imshow(img2)
        plt.axis('off')
        plt.show()
```

The preceding code results in an image that is a combination of the content and style images:

With differing layers that are selected to calculate the content and style loss, and differing weights assigned to coefficients of layers in their respective style or content contributions, the resulting generated image could be different.

In the previous three case studies, we saw how we can generate new images by changing the input pixel values. In the rest of this chapter, we will take a different approach to generating new images: using GANs.

Generating images of digits using Generative Adversarial Networks

A GAN uses a stack of neural networks to come up with a new image that looks very similar to the original set of images. It has a variety of applications in image generation, and the field of GAN research is progressing very quickly to come up with images that are very hard to distinguish from real ones. In this section, we will understand the basics of a GAN – how it works and the difference in the variations of GANs.

A GAN comprises two networks: a generator and a discriminator. The generator tries to generate an image and the discriminator tries to determine whether the image it is given as an input is a real image or a generated (fake) image.

To gain further intuition, let's assume that a discriminator model tries to classify a picture into a human face image, or not a human face from a dataset that contains thousands of human face images and non-human face images.

Once we train the model to classify human and non-human faces, if we show a new human face to the model, it would still classify it as a human face, while it learns to classify a non-human face as a non-human face.

The task of the generator network is to generate images that look so similar to the original set of images that a discriminator can get fooled into thinking that the generated image actually came from the original dataset.

Getting ready

The strategy we'll adopt to generate images is as follows:

1. Generate a synthetic image using the generator network, which in the initial step is a noisy image that is generated by reshaping a set of noise values to the shape of our images.

2. Concatenate the generated image with the original set of images where the discriminator predicts whether each of the images is a generated image or an original image—this ensures that the discriminator is trained:
    - Note that the weights of a discriminator network are trained in this iteration
    - The loss of a discriminator network is the binary cross-entropy of the prediction and actual values of an image
    - The output value of the generated image will be fake (0) and the values of the original images will be real (1)
3. Now that the discriminator has been trained for one iteration, train a generator network that modifies the input noise such that it looks more like a real image than a synthetic one – one that has the potential to fool the discriminator. This process goes through the following steps:
    1. The input noise is passed through a generator network, which reshapes the input into an image.
    2. The image generated from the generator network is then passed through a discriminator network – however, note that the weights in the discriminator network are frozen in this iteration so that they are not trained in this iteration (because they were already trained in step 2).
    3. The value of the generated image's output from the discriminator will be real (1) as its task is to fool the discriminator.
    4. The loss of a generator network is the binary cross-entropy of the prediction from the input image and the actual value (which is 1 for all the generated images)—this ensures that the generator network weights are fine-tuned:
        - Note that the discriminator network weights are frozen in this step
        - Freezing the discriminator ensures that the generator network learns from the feedback provided by the discriminator
    5. Repeat these steps multiple times until you generate realistic images.

How to do it...

In the *Adversarial attack to fool a neural network section*, we discussed our strategy of how to generate an image that looks very similar to the original images. In this section, we will implement the process of generating a digit's image from the MNIST dataset (the code file is available as `Vanilla_and_DC_GAN.ipynb` in GitHub):

1. Import the relevant packages:

    ```
    import numpy as np
    from keras.datasets import mnist
    from keras.layers import Input, Dense, Reshape, Flatten, Dropout
    from keras.layers import BatchNormalization
    from keras.layers.advanced_activations import LeakyReLU
    from keras.models import Sequential
    from keras.optimizers import Adam
    import matplotlib.pyplot as plt
    %matplotlib inline
    plt.switch_backend('agg')
    from keras.models import Sequential
    from keras.layers import Dense
    from keras.layers import Reshape
    from keras.layers.core import Activation
    from keras.layers.normalization import BatchNormalization
    from keras.layers.convolutional import UpSampling2D
    from keras.layers.convolutional import Conv2D, MaxPooling2D
    from keras.layers.core import Flatten
    from keras.optimizers import SGD
    from keras.datasets import mnist
    import numpy as np
    from PIL import Image
    import argparse
    import math
    ```

2. Define the parameters:

    ```
    shape = (28, 28, 1)
    epochs = 400
    batch = 32
    save_interval = 100
    ```

Image Generation

3. Define the generator and discriminator networks:

```
def generator():
    model = Sequential()
    model.add(Dense(256, input_shape=(100,)))
    model.add(LeakyReLU(alpha=0.2))
    model.add(BatchNormalization(momentum=0.8))
    model.add(Dense(512))
    model.add(LeakyReLU(alpha=0.2))
    model.add(BatchNormalization(momentum=0.8))
    model.add(Dense(1024))
    model.add(LeakyReLU(alpha=0.2))
    model.add(BatchNormalization(momentum=0.8))
    model.add(Dense(28 * 28 * 1, activation='tanh'))
    model.add(Reshape(shape))
    return model
```

For the generator, we are building a model that takes a noise vector that is 100 dimensions in shape and will be converting it into an image that is 28 x 28 x 1 in shape. Note that we used `LeakyReLU` activation in the model. A summary of the generator network is as follows:

```
Layer (type)                    Output Shape              Param #
=================================================================
dense_1 (Dense)                 (None, 256)               25856

leaky_re_lu_1 (LeakyReLU)       (None, 256)               0

batch_normalization_1 (Batch    (None, 256)               1024

dense_2 (Dense)                 (None, 512)               131584

leaky_re_lu_2 (LeakyReLU)       (None, 512)               0

batch_normalization_2 (Batch    (None, 512)               2048

dense_3 (Dense)                 (None, 1024)              525312

leaky_re_lu_3 (LeakyReLU)       (None, 1024)              0

batch_normalization_3 (Batch    (None, 1024)              4096

dense_4 (Dense)                 (None, 784)               803600

reshape_1 (Reshape)             (None, 28, 28, 1)         0
=================================================================
Total params: 1,493,520
Trainable params: 1,489,936
Non-trainable params: 3,584
```

In the following code, we are building a discriminator model where we take an input image that is 28 x 28 x 1 in shape and produce an output that is either 1 or 0, which indicates whether the input image is an original image or a fake image:

```
def discriminator():
    model = Sequential()
    model.add(Flatten(input_shape=shape))
    model.add(Dense((28 * 28 * 1), input_shape=shape))
    model.add(LeakyReLU(alpha=0.2))
    model.add(Dense(int((28 * 28 * 1) / 2)))
    model.add(LeakyReLU(alpha=0.2))
    model.add(Dense(1, activation='sigmoid'))
    return model
```

A summary of the discriminator network is as follows:

```
Layer (type)                    Output Shape              Param #
=================================================================
flatten_1 (Flatten)             (None, 784)               0
_____
dense_5 (Dense)                 (None, 784)               615440
_____
leaky_re_lu_4 (LeakyReLU)       (None, 784)               0
_____
dense_6 (Dense)                 (None, 392)               307720
_____
leaky_re_lu_5 (LeakyReLU)       (None, 392)               0
_____
dense_7 (Dense)                 (None, 1)                 393
=================================================================
Total params: 923,553
Trainable params: 923,553
Non-trainable params: 0
```

Compile the generator and discriminator models:

```
Generator = generator()
Generator.compile(loss='binary_crossentropy',
optimizer=Adam(lr=0.0002, beta_1=0.5, decay=8e-8))

Discriminator = discriminator()
Discriminator.compile(loss='binary_crossentropy',
optimizer=Adam(lr=0.0002, beta_1=0.5,
decay=8e-8),metrics=['accuracy'])
```

Image Generation

4. Define the stacked generator discriminator model that helps to optimize weights for the generator while freezing weights for the discriminator network. The stacked generator discriminator takes the random noise that we pass to the model as input and converts that noise into an image that is 28 x 28 in shape using the generator network. Furthermore, it determines whether the 28 x 28 image is a real or fake image:

```
def stacked_generator_discriminator(D, G):
    D.trainable = False
    model = Sequential()
    model.add(G)
    model.add(D)
    return model

stacked_generator_discriminator =
stacked_generator_discriminator(Discriminator, Generator)
stacked_generator_discriminator.compile(loss='binary_crossentropy',
optimizer=Adam(lr=0.0002, beta_1=0.5, decay=8e-8))
```

5. Define a function to plot the generated images:

```
def plot_images(samples=16, step=0):
    noise = np.random.normal(0, 1, (samples, 100))
    images = Generator.predict(noise)
    plt.figure(figsize=(10, 10))
    for i in range(images.shape[0]):
        plt.subplot(4, 4, i + 1)
        image = images[i, :, :, :]
        image = np.reshape(image, [28, 28])
        plt.imshow(image, cmap='gray')
        plt.axis('off')
    plt.tight_layout()
    plt.show()
```

6. Provide the input images:

```
(X_train, _), (_, _) = mnist.load_data()
X_train = (X_train.astype(np.float32) - 127.5) / 127.5
X_train = np.expand_dims(X_train, axis=3)
```

We are discarding the y_train dataset, as we do not need the output labels, since our model generates new images based on the given set of images, that is X_train.

7. Optimize the images by running them over multiple epochs:

In the following code, we are obtaining the real images (`legit_images`) and generating the fake image (`synthetic_images`) data, which we will try to convert into a realistic image by modifying noise data (`gen_noise`) as the input, as follows:

```
for cnt in range(4000):
    random_index = np.random.randint(0, len(X_train) - batch / 2)
    legit_images = X_train[random_index: random_index + batch // 2].reshape(batch // 2, 28, 28, 1)
    gen_noise = np.random.normal(-1, 1, (batch // 2, 100))/2
    synthetic_images = Generator.predict(gen_noise)
```

In the following code, we are training the discriminator (using the `train_on_batch` method), where the real images are expected to have a value of 1 and the fake images are expected to have a value of zero in the output:

```
x_combined_batch = np.concatenate((legit_images, synthetic_images))
y_combined_batch = np.concatenate((np.ones((batch // 2, 1)), np.zeros((batch // 2, 1))))
d_loss = Discriminator.train_on_batch(x_combined_batch, y_combined_batch)
```

In the following code, we are preparing a new set of data where `noise` is the input and `y_mislabeled` is the output to train the generator (note that the output is the exact opposite of what the output was when we were training the discriminator):

```
noise = np.random.normal(-1, 1, (batch, 100))/2
y_mislabled = np.ones((batch, 1))
```

In the following code, we are training the stacked combination of the generator and discriminator, where the discriminator weights are frozen while the generator's weights get updated to minimize the loss value. The generator's task is to generate images that can trick the discriminator to output a value of 1:

```
g_loss = stacked_generator_discriminator.train_on_batch(noise, y_mislabled)
```

In the following code, we are looking at the output of generator loss and discriminator loss across various epochs:

```
logger.info('epoch: {}, [Discriminator: {}], [Generator: {}]'.format(cnt, d_loss[0], g_loss))
    if cnt % 100 == 0:
        plot_images(step=cnt)
```

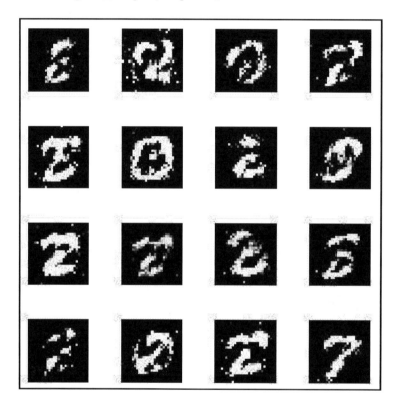

The variation of discriminator and generator loss of increasing epochs is as follows:

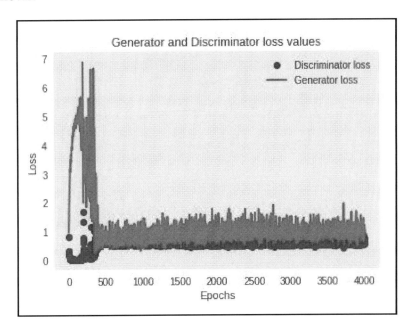

Note that the preceding output has a lot of scope for improvement in terms of how realistic the generated images look.

There's more...

The output that we saw here is also a function of the model's architecture. For example, vary the activation function in various layers of model to tanh and see how the resulting output looks to get an idea of what the resulting generated images look like.

Generating images using a Deep Convolutional GAN

In the previous section, we looked at generating digits using a vanilla generator and a discriminator network. However, we can have a scenario where the network can learn the features in an image much better by using the convolution architectures, as the filters in a CNN learn specific details within an image. **Deep Convolutional Generative Adversarial Networks (DCGANs)** take advantage of this phenomenon to come up with new images.

How to do it...

While the intuition of how a DCGAN works is very similar to that of a GAN (which we worked with in the previous recipe), the major difference is in the architecture of the generator and discriminator of the DCGAN, which looks as follows (The code file is available as `Vanilla_and_DC_GAN.ipynb` in GitHub):

```
def generator():
    model = Sequential()
    model.add(Dense(input_dim=100, output_dim=1024))
    model.add(Activation('tanh'))
    model.add(Dense(128*7*7))
    model.add(BatchNormalization())
    model.add(Activation('tanh'))
    model.add(Reshape((7, 7, 128), input_shape=(128*7*7,)))
    model.add(UpSampling2D(size=(2, 2)))
    model.add(Conv2D(64, (5, 5), padding='same'))
    model.add(Activation('tanh'))
    model.add(UpSampling2D(size=(2, 2)))
    model.add(Conv2D(1, (5, 5), padding='same'))
    model.add(Activation('tanh'))
    return model


def discriminator():
    model = Sequential()
    model.add(Conv2D(64, (5, 5),padding='same',input_shape=(28, 28, 1)))
    model.add(Activation('tanh'))
    model.add(MaxPooling2D(pool_size=(2, 2)))
    model.add(Conv2D(128, (5, 5)))
    model.add(Activation('tanh'))
    model.add(MaxPooling2D(pool_size=(2, 2)))
    model.add(Flatten())
    model.add(Dense(1024))
```

```
model.add(Activation('tanh'))
model.add(Dense(1))
model.add(Activation('sigmoid'))
return model
```

Note that, in the DCGAN, we performed multiple convolution and pooling operations on the input data.

If we rerun the exact same steps that we performed in the Vanilla GAN (the *Generative Adversarial Network to generate images* recipe), but this time using the models defined with a convolution and pooling architecture (and thus DCGAN), we get the following generated image:

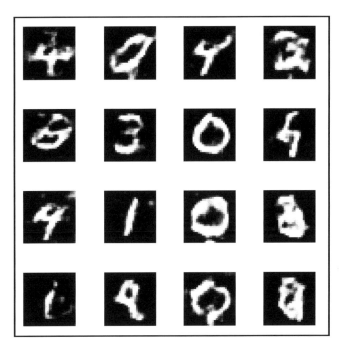

Image Generation

The variation of generator and discriminator loss values over increasing epochs is as follows:

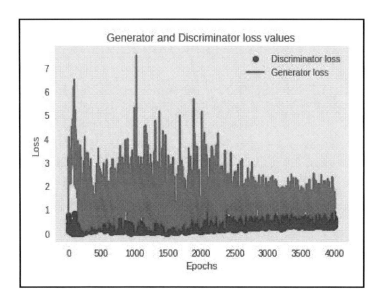

We can see that, while everything else remains the same and only the model architecture has changed, the resulting images through DCGAN are a lot more realistic than the results of a Vanilla GAN.

Face generation using a Deep Convolutional GAN

So far, we have seen how to generate new images. In this section, we will learn how to generate a new set of faces from an existing dataset of faces.

Getting ready

The approach we will be adopting for this exercise will be very similar to what we adopted in the *Generating images using a Deep Convolutional GAN* recipe:

1. Collect a dataset that contains multiple face images.
2. Generate random images at the start.

3. Train a discriminator by showing it a combination of faces and random images, where the discriminator is expected to differentiate between an actual face image and a generated face image.
4. Once the discriminator model is trained, freeze it and adjust the random images in such a way that the discriminator now assigns a higher probability of belonging to the original face images to the adjusted random images.
5. Repeat the preceding two steps through multiple iterations until the generator does not get trained any further.

How to do it...

Face generation is implemented in code as follows (the code file is available as `Face_generation.ipynb` in GitHub):

1. Download the dataset. The recommended dataset to be downloaded and the associated code is provided in GitHub. A sample of images is as follows:

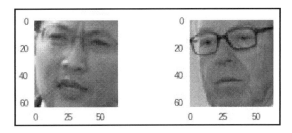

2. Define the model architecture:

```
def generator():
    model = Sequential()
    model.add(Dense(input_dim=100, output_dim=1024))
    model.add(Activation('tanh'))
    model.add(Dense(128*7*7))
    model.add(BatchNormalization())
    model.add(Activation('tanh'))
    model.add(Reshape((7, 7, 128), input_shape=(128*7*7,)))
    model.add(UpSampling2D(size=(2, 2)))
    model.add(Conv2D(64, (5, 5), padding='same'))
    model.add(Activation('tanh'))
    model.add(UpSampling2D(size=(2, 2)))
    model.add(Conv2D(1, (5, 5), padding='same'))
    model.add(Activation('tanh'))
    return model
```

Image Generation

Note that the preceding code is the same as the generator we built in the *Deep convolutional generative adversarial networks* recipe:

```
def discriminator():
    model = Sequential()
    model.add(Conv2D(64, (5, 5),padding='same',input_shape=(28, 28, 1)))
    model.add(Activation('tanh'))
    model.add(MaxPooling2D(pool_size=(2, 2)))
    model.add(Conv2D(128, (5, 5)))
    model.add(Activation('tanh'))
    model.add(MaxPooling2D(pool_size=(2, 2)))
    model.add(Flatten())
    model.add(Dense(1024))
    model.add(Activation('tanh'))
    model.add(Dense(1))
    model.add(Activation('sigmoid'))
    return model
```

Note that the preceding architecture is the same as the one we built in the *Generating images using Deep Convolutional GAN* section:

```
def stacked_generator_discriminator(D, G):
    D.trainable = False
    model = Sequential()
    model.add(G)
    model.add(D)
    return model
```

3. Define the utility functions to load, preprocess, and de-process the image and also to plot the images:

```
def plot_images(samples=16, step=0):
    noise = np.random.normal(0, 1, (samples, 100))
    images = deprocess(Generator.predict(noise))
    plt.figure(figsize=(5, 5))
    for i in range(images.shape[0]):
        plt.subplot(4, 4, i + 1)
        image = images[i, :, :, :]
        image = np.reshape(image, [56, 56,3])
        plt.imshow(image, cmap='gray')
        plt.axis('off')
    plt.tight_layout()
    plt.show()
```

Note that we are resizing our images to a smaller shape so that the the number of parameters that need to be tweaked through the model is minimal:

```
def preprocess(x):
    return (x/255)*2-1

def deprocess(x):
    return np.uint8((x+1)/2*255)
```

4. Import the dataset and preprocess it:

```
from skimage import io
import os
import glob
root_dir = '/content/lfwcrop_color/'
all_img_paths = glob.glob(os.path.join(root_dir, '*/*.ppm'))
```

In the following code, we are creating the input dataset and converting it into an array:

```
import numpy as np
X_train = []
for i in range(len(all_img_paths)):
    img = cv2.imread(all_img_paths[i])
    X_train.append(preprocess(img))
len(X_train)
X_train = np.array(X_train)
```

5. Compile the generator, discriminator, and stacked generator discriminator models:

```
Generator = generator()
Generator.compile(loss='binary_crossentropy',
optimizer=Adam(lr=0.0002, beta_1=0.5, decay=8e-8))

Discriminator = discriminator()
Discriminator.compile(loss='binary_crossentropy',
optimizer=Adam(lr=0.0002, beta_1=0.5,
decay=8e-8),metrics=['accuracy'])

stacked_generator_discriminator =
stacked_generator_discriminator(Discriminator, Generator)
stacked_generator_discriminator.compile(loss='binary_crossentropy',
optimizer=Adam(lr=0.0002, beta_1=0.5, decay=8e-8))
```

Image Generation

6. Run the model over multiple epochs in a manner that is very similar to what we employed in the *Deep Convolutional Generative Adversarial Networks* recipe:

```
%matplotlib inline
$pip install logger
from logger import logger
for cnt in range(10000):
    random_index = np.random.randint(0, len(X_train) - batch / 2)
    legit_images = X_train[random_index: random_index + batch // 2].reshape(batch // 2, 56, 56, 3)
    gen_noise = np.random.normal(0, 1, (batch // 2, 100))
    syntetic_images = Generator.predict(gen_noise)
    x_combined_batch = np.concatenate((legit_images, syntetic_images))
    y_combined_batch = np.concatenate((np.ones((batch // 2, 1)), np.zeros((batch // 2, 1))))
    d_loss = Discriminator.train_on_batch(x_combined_batch, y_combined_batch)
    noise = np.random.normal(0, 1, (batch*2, 100))
    y_mislabled = np.ones((batch*2, 1))
    g_loss = stacked_generator_discriminator.train_on_batch(noise, y_mislabled)
    logger.info('epoch: {}, [Discriminator: {}], [Generator: {}]'.format(cnt, d_loss[0], g_loss))
    if cnt % 100 == 0:
        plot_images(step=cnt)
```

The preceding code generates images that look as follows:

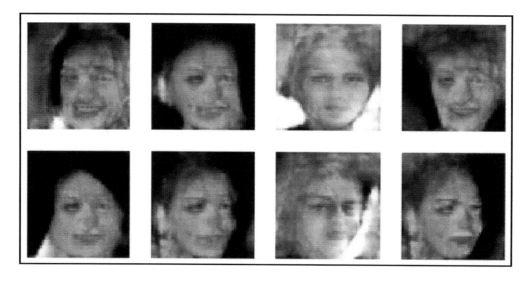

Note that, while these images look very blurry, the picture is an original one that is not present in the original dataset. There is a lot of scope for improvement in this output by varying the model architecture and having deeper layers.

The variation of discriminator and generator loss values over increasing epochs looks as follows:

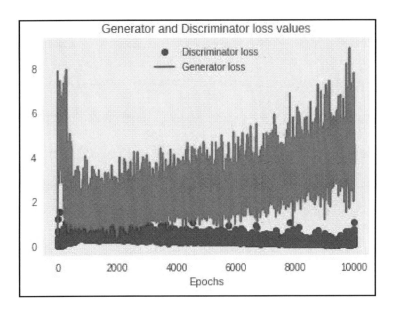

Note that, from the preceding diagram, we might want to train the model for a fewer number of epochs so that the generator loss is not very high.

Face transition from one to another

Now that we are in a position to generate faces, let's go ahead and perform some vector arithmetic on top of the generated images.

For this exercise, we will perform the transition of face generation from one face to another.

Getting ready

We'll continue from the image generation model that we built in the *Face generation using a Deep Convolutional GAN* section.

Image Generation

Let's say we want to see the transition of one generated face image into another generated face image. This process is enabled by slowly varying the vector from the first vector (the vector of the first generated image) to the second vector (the vector of the second generated image). You can essentially think of each of the latent (vector) dimensions as representing a certain aspect about the image.

The strategy that we'll adopt is as follows:

1. Generate two images
2. Translate the first generated image in to the second generated image in 10 steps
3. Assigning a weight of 1 to the first generated image and a weight of 0 to the second generated image in the first step
4. In the second step, assign a weight of 0.9 to the first generated image and a weight of 0.1 to the second generated image
5. Repeat the preceding steps until we assign a weight of 0 to the first generated image and a weight of 1 to the second generated image

How to do it...

We'll code up the strategy that we laid out in the *Getting ready* section, as follows (The code file is available as `Face_generation.ipynb` in GitHub):

1. Generate the first image from random noise (note that we'll continue from step 6 in *Face generation using a Deep Convolutional GAN* section):

   ```
   gen_noise = np.random.normal(0, 1, (1, 100))
   syntetic_images = Generator.predict(gen_noise)
   plt.imshow(deprocess(syntetic_images)[0])
   plt.axis('off')
   ```

   The generated image looks as follows:

2. Generate the second image from random noise:

```
gen_noise2 = np.random.normal(0, 1, (1, 100))
syntetic_images = Generator.predict(gen_noise2)
plt.imshow(deprocess(syntetic_images)[0])
plt.axis('off')
plt.show()
```

The following is the output of the preceding code snippet:

3. Generate the visualization of obtaining the second image from the first image:

```
plt.figure(figsize=(10, 8))
for i in range(10):
  gen_noise3 = gen_noise + (gen_noise2 - gen_noise)*(i+1)/10
  syntetic_images = Generator.predict(gen_noise3)
  plt.subplot(1, 10, i+1)
  plt.imshow(deprocess(syntetic_images)[0])
  plt.axis('off')
```

We will get the following output:

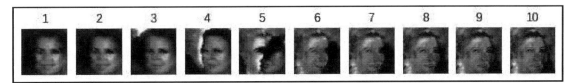

Note that, in the preceding output, we have slowly transformed the first image into the second image.

Performing vector arithmetic on generated images

Now that we understand that the latent vector representations play a key part in changing the outcome of the generated image, let's further build our intuition with images that have a certain face alignment.

Getting ready

The strategy that we'll adopt to perform vector arithmetic on a generated image is as follows:

1. Generate three images that are based on the random noise of 100 vector values
2. Ensure that two of the three images have generated faces that look to the left, and that one looks to the right
3. Calculate a new vector that is the sum of images that are aligned in the same direction, which is further subtracted from the image that is aligned in the opposite direction
4. Generate the image from the resulting vector obtained in the previous step

How to do it...

We'll code up the strategy that we listed out as follows (The code file is available as `Face_generation.ipynb` in GitHub). Note that we'll continue from step 6 in *Face generation using a Deep Convolutional GAN* section):

1. Generate three vectors (ensure that two images are aligned in one direction and that the other is aligned in the opposite direction by varying the generated noise):

```
gen_noise = np.random.normal(0, 1, (1, 100))
gen_noise2 = np.random.normal(0, 1, (1, 100))
gen_noise3 = np.random.normal(0, 1, (1, 100))
syntetic_images = Generator.predict(gen_noise4)
plt.imshow(deprocess(syntetic_images)[0])
plt.axis('off')
plt.show()
```

2. Plot the generated images:

   ```
   plt.subplot(131)
   syntetic_images = Generator.predict(gen_noise)
   plt.imshow(deprocess(syntetic_images)[0])
   plt.axis('off')
   plt.title('Image 1')
   plt.subplot(132)
   syntetic_images = Generator.predict(gen_noise2)
   plt.imshow(deprocess(syntetic_images)[0])
   plt.axis('off')
   plt.title('Image 2')
   plt.subplot(133)
   syntetic_images = Generator.predict(gen_noise3)
   plt.imshow(deprocess(syntetic_images)[0])
   plt.axis('off')
   plt.title('Image 3')
   ```

   The three generated images are as follows:

   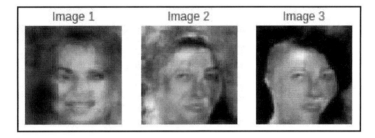

   We can see that images 2 and 3 have the face looking to the right, while image 1 has the face looking straight ahead.

3. Perform a vector arithmetic of the vector representations of each of these images to see the outcome:

   ```
   gen_noise4 = gen_noise + gen_noise2 - gen_noise3
   syntetic_images = Generator.predict(gen_noise4)
   plt.imshow(deprocess(syntetic_images)[0])
   plt.axis('off')
   plt.show()
   ```

The preceding code generates a face, as follows:

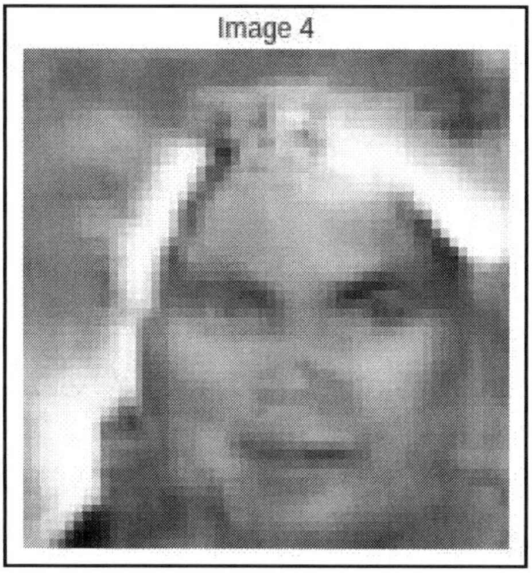

Image 4

The preceding arithmetic shows that the vector arithmetic (vector of image 1 + image 2 - image 3) generated an image has the face looking straight ahead and thus strengthening our intuition of the workings of latent vector representations.

There's more...

We have merely touched on the basics of GAN; there are a variety of GAN-based techniques that are currently becoming popular. We will discuss the applications of a few of them:

- **pix2pix**: Imagine a scenario where you doodle (sketch) the structure of an object and the object shapes up in a variety of forms. pix2pix is an algorithm that helps in enabling this.
- **Cycle GAN**: Imagine a scenario where you want an object to look like a completely different object (for example, you want a horse object to look like a zebra and vice versa). You also want to ensure that every other aspect of the image remains the same, except the change in the object. Cycle GAN comes in handy in such a scenario.
- **BigGAN** is a recent development that comes up with extremely realistic-looking generated images.

9
Encoding Inputs

In this chapter, we will be covering the following recipes:

- Need for encoding
- Encoding an image
- Encoding for recommender systems

Introduction

A typical image is comprised thousands of pixels; text is also comprised thousands of unique words, and the number of distinct customers of a company could be in the millions. Given this, all three—user, text, and images—would have to be represented as a vector in thousands of dimensional planes. The drawback of representing a vector in such a high dimensional space is that we will not able to calculate the similarity of vectors efficiently.

Representing an image, text, or user in a lower dimension helps us in grouping entities that are very similar. Encoding is a way to perform unsupervised learning to represent an input in a lower dimension with minimal loss of information while retaining the information about images that are similar.

In this chapter, we will be learning about the following:

- Encoding an image to a much a lower dimension
    - Vanilla autoencoder
    - Multilayer autoencoder
    - Convolutional autoencoder
- Visualizing encodings
- Encoding users and items in recommender systems
- Calculating the similarity between encoded entities

Need for encoding

Encoding is typically used where the number of dimensions in a vector is huge. Encoding helps turn a large vector into a vector that has far fewer dimensions without losing much information from the original vector. In the following sections, let's explore the need for encoding images, text, and recommender systems.

Need for encoding in text analysis

To understand the need for encoding in text analysis, let's consider the following scenario. Let's go through the following two sentences:

Input sentences
I like playing Chess
I enjoy playing Chess

In traditional text analysis, the preceding two sentences are one-hot encoded, as follows:

	I	like	playing	Chess	enjoy
I	1	0	0	0	0
like	0	1	0	0	0
playing	0	0	1	0	0
Chess	0	0	0	1	0
enjoy	0	0	0	0	1

Note that there are five unique words in the two sentences.

The preceding one-hot encoded versions of the words result in an encoded version of sentences as follows:

	I	like	playing	Chess	enjoy
I like playing Chess	1	1	1	1	0
I enjoy playing Chess	1	0	1	1	1

In the preceding scenario, we can see that the Euclidian distance between the two sentences is greater than zero, as the encodings of **like** and **enjoy** are different. However, intuitively, we know that the words enjoy and like are very similar to each other. Further, the distance between (**I, Chess**) is the same as (**like, enjoy**).

Note that, given that there are five unique words across the two sentences, we represent each word in a five-dimensional space. In an encoded version, we represent a word in a lower dimension (let's say, three-dimensions) in such a way that words that are similar will have less distance between them when compared to words that are not similar.

Need for encoding in image analysis

To understand the need for encoding in image analysis, let's consider the scenario where we group images; however, the labels of images are not present. For further clarification, let's consider the following images of the same label in the MNIST dataset:

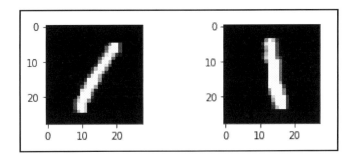

Intuitively, we know that both the preceding images correspond to the same label. However, when we take the Euclidian distance between the preceding two images, the distance is greater than zero, as different pixels are highlighted in the preceding two images.

You should notice the following issue in storing the information of an image:

While the image comprises a total of 28 x 28 = 784 pixels, the majority of the columns are black and thus no information is composed in them, resulting in them occupying more space while storing information than is needed.

Using autoencoders, we represent the preceding two images in a lower dimension in such a way that the distance between the two encoded versions is now much smaller and at the same time ensuring that the encoded version does not lose much information from the original image.

Need for encoding in recommender systems

To understand the need for encoding in recommender systems, let's consider the scenario of movie recommendations for customers. Similar to text analysis, if we were to one-hot encode each movie/customer, we would end up with multiple thousand-dimensional vectors for each movie (as there are thousands of movies). Encoding users in a much lower dimension based on the viewing habits of customers, which results in grouping movies based on the similarity of movies, could help us map movies that a user is more likely to watch.

A similar concept can also be applied to e-commerce recommendation engines, as well as recommending products to a customer in a supermarket.

Encoding an image

Image encoding can be performed in multiple ways. In the following sections, we will contrast the performance of vanilla autoencoders, multilayer autoencoders, and convolutional autoencoders. The term auto-encoding refers to encoding in such a way that the original input is recreated with a far fewer number of dimensions in an image.

An autoencoder takes an image as input and encodes the input image into a lower dimension in such a way that we can reconstruct the original image by using only the encoded version of the input image. Essentially, you can think of the encoded version of similar images as having similar encoded values.

Getting ready

Before we define our strategy, let's get a feel for how autoencoders work:

1. We'll define a toy dataset that has one vector with 11 values
2. We'll represent the 11 values in a lower dimension (two-dimensions):
    - The information present in input data is preserved as much as possible while lowering the dimensions
    - The vector in low dimensional space is called an **embedding/encoded vector**, **bottleneck feature/vector**, or a **compressed representation**

- The 11 values are converted into two values by performing a matrix multiplication of input values with a random weight matrix that is 11 x 2 in dimensions
- The lower dimension vector represents bottleneck features. Bottleneck features are features that are required to reconstruct the original image

2. We'll reconstruct the lower dimension bottleneck feature vector to obtain the output vector:
   - The two-dimension feature vector is multiplied by a matrix that is 2 x 11 in shape to obtain an output that is 1 x 11 in shape. Matrix multiplication of 1 x 2 with 2 x 11 vectors gives an output that is 1 x 11 in shape.
3. We'll calculate the sum of squared difference between the input vector and the output vector
4. We vary the randomly initialized weight vectors to minimize the sum of squared difference between the input and output vectors
5. The resulting encoded vector would be a lower dimensional vector that represents an 11-dimensional vector in two-dimensional space

While leveraging neural networks, you can consider the encoded vector as a hidden layer that connects the input and output layer.

Additionally, for the neural network, the input and output layer values are exactly the same and the hidden layer has a lower dimension than the input layer.

In this recipe, we'll learn about multiple autoencoders:

- Vanilla autoencoder
- Multilayer autoencoder
- Convolutional autoencoder

How to do it...

In the following sections, we will implement multiple variations of autoencoders in Python (the code file is available as `Auto_encoder.ipynb` in GitHub).

Vanilla autoencoder

A vanilla autoencoder looks as follows:

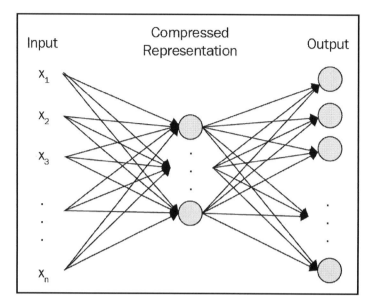

As displayed in the preceding diagram, a Vanilla autoencoder reconstructs the input with a minimal number of hidden layers and hidden units in its network.

To understand how a vanilla autoencoder works, let's go through the following recipe, where we reconstruct MNIST images using a lower-dimensional encoded version of the original image (the code file is available as Auto_encoder.ipynb in GitHub):

1. Import the relevant packages:

```
import tensorflow as tf
import keras
import numpy as np
from keras.datasets import mnist
from keras.models import Sequential
from keras.layers import Dense
from keras.layers import Dropout
from keras.layers import Flatten
from keras.layers.convolutional import Conv2D
from keras.layers.convolutional import MaxPooling2D
from keras.utils import np_utils
```

2. Import the dataset:

   ```
   (X_train, y_train), (X_test, y_test) =
   keras.datasets.mnist.load_data()
   ```

3. Reshape and scale the dataset:

   ```
   X_train =
   X_train.reshape(X_train.shape[0],X_train.shape[1]*X_train.shape[2])
   X_test =
   X_test.reshape(X_test.shape[0],X_test.shape[1]*X_test.shape[2])
   X_train = X_train/255
   X_test = X_test/255
   ```

4. Construct the network architecture:

   ```
   model = Sequential()
   model.add(Dense(32, input_dim=784, activation='relu'))
   model.add(Dense(784, activation='relu'))
   model.summary()
   ```

   A summary of model is as follows:

   ```
   Layer (type)                 Output Shape              Param #
   =================================================================
   dense_1 (Dense)              (None, 32)                25120
   _____
   dense_2 (Dense)              (None, 784)               25872
   =================================================================
   Total params: 50,992
   Trainable params: 50,992
   Non-trainable params: 0
   ```

   In the preceding code, we are representing a 784-dimensional input in a 32-dimensional encoded version.

5. Compile and fit the model:

   ```
   model.compile(loss='mean_squared_error',
   optimizer='adam',metrics=['accuracy'])
   model.fit(X_train, X_train, validation_data=(X_test,
   X_test),epochs=10, batch_size=1024, verbose=1)
   ```

   Note that we are using the mean squared error loss function, as the pixel values are continuous. Additionally, the input and output arrays are just the same—X_train.

Encoding Inputs

6. Print a reconstruction of the first four input images:

```
import matplotlib.pyplot as plt
%matplotlib inline
plt.subplot(221)
plt.imshow(model.predict(X_test[0,:].reshape(1,784)).reshape(28,28)
, cmap=plt.get_cmap('gray'))
plt.axis('off')
plt.subplot(222)
plt.imshow(model.predict(X_test[1,:].reshape(1,784)).reshape(28,28)
, cmap=plt.get_cmap('gray'))
plt.axis('off')
plt.subplot(223)
plt.imshow(model.predict(X_test[2,:].reshape(1,784)).reshape(28,28)
, cmap=plt.get_cmap('gray'))
plt.axis('off')
plt.subplot(224)
plt.imshow(model.predict(X_test[3,:].reshape(1,784)).reshape(28,28)
, cmap=plt.get_cmap('gray'))
plt.axis('off')
plt.show()
```

The reconstructured MNIST digits are as follows:

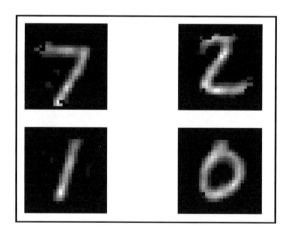

To understand how well the autoencoder worked, let's compare the preceding predictions with the original input images:

The original MNIST digits are as follows:

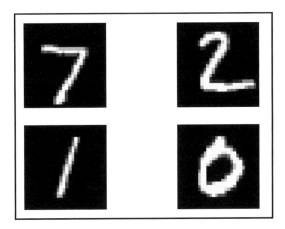

From the preceding images, we can see that the reconstructed images are blurred when compared to the original input image.

To get around the issue of blurring, let's build multilayer autoencoders that are deep (thereby resulting in more parameters) and thus potentially a better representation of the original image.

Multilayer autoencoder

A multilayer autoencoder looks as follows, where there are more number of hidden layers connecting the input layer to output layer:

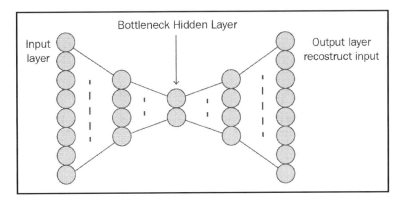

Encoding Inputs

Essentially, a multilayer autoencoder reconstructs the input with more hidden layers in its network.

To build a multilayer autoencoder, we will repeat the same steps that we had in the previous section, up until *step 3*. However, *step 4*, where the network architecture is defined, will be modified to include multilayers, as follows:

```
model = Sequential()
model.add(Dense(100, input_dim=784, activation='relu'))
model.add(Dense(32,activation='relu'))
model.add(Dense(100,activation='relu'))
model.add(Dense(784, activation='relu'))
model.summary()
```

A summary of model is as follows:

Layer (type)	Output Shape	Param #
dense_18 (Dense)	(None, 100)	78500
dense_19 (Dense)	(None, 32)	3232
dense_20 (Dense)	(None, 100)	3300
dense_21 (Dense)	(None, 784)	79184

Total params: 164,216
Trainable params: 164,216
Non-trainable params: 0

In the preceding network, our first hidden layer has 100 units, the second hidden layer (which is the embedded version of the image) is 32-dimensional, and the third hidden layer is 100-dimensional in shape.

Once the network architecture is defined, we compile and run it, as follows:

```
model.compile(loss='mean_squared_error', optimizer='adam')
model.fit(X_train, X_train, validation_data=(X_test, X_test),epochs=25, batch_size=1024, verbose=1)
```

The predictions of the preceding model are as follows:

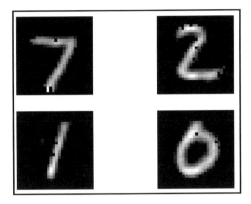

Note that the preceding predictions are still a little blurred compared to the original images.

Convolutional autoencoder

So far, we have explored vanilla and multilayer autoencoders. In this section, we will see how convolutional autoencoders work in reconstructing the original images from a lower-dimensional vector.

Convolutional autoencoders look as follows:

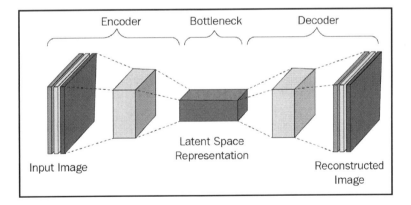

Essentially, a convolutional autoencoder reconstructs the input with more hidden layers in its network where the hidden layers consist of convolution, pooling, and upsampling the downsampled image.

Encoding Inputs

Similar to a multilayer autoencoder, a convolutional autoencoder differs from other types of autoencoder in its model architecture. In the following code, we will define the model architecture for the convolutional autoencoder while every other step remains similar to the vanilla autoencoder up until *step 3*.

The only differences between the `X_train` and `X_test` shapes are defined as follows:

```
(X_train, y_train), (X_test, y_test) = keras.datasets.mnist.load_data()

X_train =
X_train.reshape(X_train.shape[0],X_train.shape[1],X_train.shape[2],1)
X_test = X_test.reshape(X_test.shape[0],X_test.shape[1],X_test.shape[2],1)
X_train = X_train/255
X_test = X_test/255
```

Note that, in the preceding step, we are reshaping the image so that it can be passed to a `conv2D` method:

1. Define the model architecture:

   ```
   model = Sequential()
   model.add(Conv2D(32, (3,3), input_shape=(28, 28,1),
   activation='relu',padding='same',name='conv1'))
   model.add(MaxPooling2D(pool_size=(2, 2),name='pool1'))
   model.add(Conv2D(16, (3,3),
   activation='relu',padding='same',name='conv2'))
   model.add(MaxPooling2D(pool_size=(2, 2),name='pool2'))
   model.add(Conv2D(8, (3,3),
   activation='relu',padding='same',name='conv3'))
   model.add(MaxPooling2D(pool_size=(2, 2),name='pool3'))
   model.add(Conv2D(32, (3,3),
   activation='relu',padding='same',name='conv4'))
   model.add(MaxPooling2D(pool_size=(2, 2),name='pool4'))
   model.add(Flatten(name='flatten'))
   model.add(Reshape((1,1,32)))
   model.add(Conv2DTranspose(8, kernel_size = (3,3), activation='relu'))
   model.add(Conv2DTranspose(16, kernel_size = (5,5), activation='relu'))
   model.add(Conv2DTranspose(32, kernel_size = (8,8), activation='relu'))
   model.add(Conv2DTranspose(32, kernel_size = (15,15),
   activation='relu'))
   model.add(Conv2D(1, (3, 3), activation='relu',padding='same'))
   model.summary()
   ```

In the preceding code, we have defined a convolutional architecture where we reshaped the input image so that it has a 32-dimensional embedded version in the middle of its architecture and finally upsample it so that we are able to reconstruct it.

A summary of the model is as follows:

Layer (type)	Output Shape	Param #
conv1 (Conv2D)	(None, 28, 28, 32)	320
pool1 (MaxPooling2D)	(None, 14, 14, 32)	0
conv2 (Conv2D)	(None, 14, 14, 16)	4624
pool2 (MaxPooling2D)	(None, 7, 7, 16)	0
conv3 (Conv2D)	(None, 7, 7, 8)	1160
pool3 (MaxPooling2D)	(None, 3, 3, 8)	0
conv4 (Conv2D)	(None, 3, 3, 32)	2336
pool4 (MaxPooling2D)	(None, 1, 1, 32)	0
flatten (Flatten)	(None, 32)	0
reshape_2 (Reshape)	(None, 1, 1, 32)	0
conv2d_transpose_5 (Conv2DTr	(None, 3, 3, 8)	2312
conv2d_transpose_6 (Conv2DTr	(None, 7, 7, 16)	3216
conv2d_transpose_7 (Conv2DTr	(None, 14, 14, 32)	32800
conv2d_transpose_8 (Conv2DTr	(None, 28, 28, 32)	230432
conv2d_2 (Conv2D)	(None, 28, 28, 1)	289

Total params: 277,489
Trainable params: 277,489
Non-trainable params: 0

2. Compile and fit the model

```
from keras.optimizers import Adam
adam = Adam(lr=0.001)
model.compile(loss='mean_squared_error', optimizer='adam')
model.fit(X_train, X_train, validation_data=(X_test, X_test),epochs=10,
batch_size=1024, verbose=1)
```

Once we make predictions on the first four test data points, the reconstructed images look as follows:

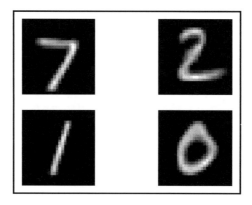

Note that the reconstruction is now slightly better than the previous two reconstructions (using Vanilla and multilayer autoencoders) of the test images.

Grouping similar images

In the previous sections, we represented each image in a much lower dimension with the intuition that images that are similar will have similar embeddings and images that are not similar will have dissimilar embeddings. However, we have not yet looked at the similarity measure or examined embeddings in detail.

In this section, we will try and plot embeddings in a 2D space. We can reduce the 32-dimensional vector to a two-dimensional space by using a technique called **t-SNE**. (More about t-SNE can be found here: http://www.jmlr.org/papers/v9/vandermaaten08a.html.)

This way, our feeling that similar images will have similar embeddings can be proved, as similar images should be clustered together in the two-dimensional plane.

In the following code, we will represent embeddings of all the test images in a two-dimensional plane:

1. Extract the 32-dimensional vector of each of the 10,000 images in the test:

    ```
    from keras.models import Model
    layer_name = 'flatten'
    intermediate_layer_model = Model(inputs=model.input,outputs=model.get_layer(layer_name).output)
    intermediate_output = intermediate_layer_model.predict(X_test)
    ```

2. Perform t-SNE to generate a two-dimensional vector:

    ```
    from sklearn.manifold import TSNE
    tsne_model = TSNE(n_components=2, verbose=1, random_state=0)
    tsne_img_label = tsne_model.fit_transform(intermediate_output)
    tsne_df = pd.DataFrame(tsne_img_label, columns=['x', 'y'])
    tsne_df['image_label'] = y_test
    ```

3. Plot the visualization of the t-SNE dimensions for the test image embeddings:

    ```
    from ggplot import *
    chart = ggplot(tsne_df, aes(x='x', y='y', color='factor(image_label)'))+ geom_point(size=70,alpha=0.5)
    chart
    ```

A visualization of embeddings in two dimensional space is as follows:

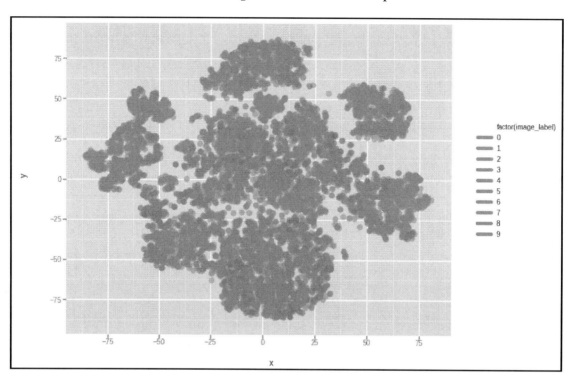

Note that, in the preceding chart, we see that, more often than not, clusters are formed among images that correspond to the same label.

Encoding for recommender systems

So far, in the previous sections, we have encoded an image. In this section, we will encode users and movies in a movie-related dataset. The reason for this is that there could be millions of users as customers and thousands of movies in a catalog. Thus, we are not in a position to one-hot encode such data straight away. Encoding comes in handy in such a scenario. One of the most popular techniques that's used in encoding for recommender systems is matrix factorization. In the next section, we'll understand how it works and generate embeddings for users and movies.

Getting ready

The thinking behind encoding users and movies is as follows:

If two users are similar in terms of liking certain movies, the vectors that represent the two users should be similar. In the same manner, if two movies are similar (potentially, they belong to the same genre or have the same cast), they should have similar vectors.

The strategy that we'll adopt to encode movies, so that we recommend a new set of movies based on the historical set of movies watched by a user, is as follows:

1. Import the dataset that contains information of the users and the rating they gave to different movies that they watched
2. Assign IDs to both users and movies
3. Convert users and movies into 32-dimensional vectors
4. Use the functional API in Keras to perform the dot product of the 32-dimensional vectors of movies and users:
    - If there are 100,000 users and 1,000 movies, the movie matrix will be 1,000 x 32 dimensions and the user matrix will be 100,000 x 32 dimensions
    - The dot product of the two will be 100,000 x 1,000 in dimension
5. Flatten the output and pass it through a dense layer, before connecting to the output layer, which has a linear activation and has output values ranging from 1 to 5
6. Fit the model
7. Extract the embedding weights of movies
8. Extract the embedding weights of users
9. Movies that are similar to a given movie of interest can be found by calculating the pairwise similarity of the movie of interest with every other movie in the dataset

Encoding Inputs

How to do it...

In the following code, we will come up with with a vector for a user and a movie in a typical recommender system (The code file is available as `Recommender_systems.ipynb` in GitHub):

1. Import the dataset. The recommended dataset is available in code in GitHub.

   ```
   import numpy as np
   import pandas as pd
   from keras.layers import Input, Embedding, Dense, Dropout, merge, Flatten, dot
   from keras.models import Model
   from keras.optimizers import Adam
   ratings = pd.read_csv('...') # Path to the user-movie-ratings file
   ```

User	Movies	rating	timestamp
1	100	5	1394496000
2	101	3	1395546000
3	100	5	1445578000

2. Convert the user and movies into a categorical variable. In the following code, we create two new variables—`User2` and `Movies2`—which are categorical:

   ```
   ratings['User2']=ratings['User'].astype('category')
   ratings['Movies2']=ratings['Movies'].astype('category')
   ```

3. Assign a unique ID to each user and movie:

   ```
   users = ratings.User.unique()
   movies = ratings.Movies.unique()
   userid2idx = {o:i for i,o in enumerate(users)}
   moviesid2idx = {o:i for i,o in enumerate(movies)}
   idx2userid = {i:o for i,o in enumerate(users)}
   idx2moviesid = {i:o for i,o in enumerate(movies)}
   ```

4. Add the unique IDs as new columns to our original table:

```
ratings['Movies2'] = ratings.Movies.apply(lambda x: moviesid2idx[x])
ratings['User2'] = ratings.User.apply(lambda x: userid2idx[x])
```

5. Define embeddings for each user ID and unique ID:

```
n_users = ratings.User.nunique()
n_movies = ratings.Movies.nunique()
```

In the preceding code, we are extracting the total number of unique users and unique movies in the dataset:

```
def embedding_input(name,n_in,n_out):
    inp = Input(shape=(1,),dtype='int64',name=name)
    return inp, Embedding(n_in,n_out,input_length=1)(inp)
```

In the preceding code, we are defining a function that takes an ID as input and converts it into an embedding vector that is n_out in dimensions for the total of n_in values:

```
n_factors = 100
user_in, u = embedding_input('user_in', n_users, n_factors)
article_in, a = embedding_input('article_in', n_movies, n_factors)
```

In the preceding code, we are extracting 100 dimensions for each unique user and also for each unique movie.

6. Define the model:

```
x = dot([u,a], axes=1)
x=Flatten()(x)
x = Dense(500, activation='relu')(x)
x = Dense(1)(x)
model = Model([user_in,article_in],x)
adam = Adam(lr=0.01)
model.compile(adam,loss='mse')
model.summary()
```

Encoding Inputs

A summary of model is as follows:

```
Layer (type)                 Output Shape         Param #     Connected to
====================================================================================================
user_in (InputLayer)         (None, 1)            0
_____
article_in (InputLayer)      (None, 1)            0
_____
embedding_1 (Embedding)      (None, 1, 100)       94300       user_in[0][0]
_____
embedding_2 (Embedding)      (None, 1, 100)       168200      article_in[0][0]
_____
dot_4 (Dot)                  (None, 100, 100)     0           embedding_1[0][0]
                                                              embedding_2[0][0]
_____
flatten_4 (Flatten)          (None, 10000)        0           dot_4[0][0]
_____
dense_7 (Dense)              (None, 500)          5000500     flatten_4[0][0]
_____
dense_8 (Dense)              (None, 1)            501         dense_7[0][0]
====================================================================================================
Total params: 5,263,501
Trainable params: 5,263,501
Non-trainable params: 0
```

7. Fit the model:

    ```
    model.fit([ratings.User2,ratings.Movies2], ratings.rating,
    epochs=50,batch_size=128)
    ```

8. Extract the vectors of each user or movie:

    ```
    # Extracting user vectors
    model.get_weights()[0]

    # Extracting movie vectors
    model.get_weights()[1]
    ```

As we thought earlier, movies that are similar should have similar vectors.

Typically, while identifying the similarity between embeddings, we use a measure named cosine similarity (there's more information on how cosine similarity is calculated in the next chapter).

For a randomly selected movie that is located in the 574th position, cosine similarity is calculated as follows:

```
from sklearn.metrics.pairwise import cosine_similarity
np.argmax(cosine_similarity(model.get_weights()[1][574].reshape(1,-1),model.get_weights()[1][:574].reshape(574,100)))
```

From the preceding code, we can calculate the ID that is most similar to the movie located in the 574th location of the categorical movie column.

Once we look into the movie ID list, we should see that the most similar movies to the given movie, indeed happen to be similar, intuitively.

10
Text Analysis Using Word Vectors

In the previous chapter, we learned about encoding an image or encoding users or movies for recommender systems, where the items that are similar have similar vectors. In this chapter, we will be discussing how to encode text data.

You will be learning about the following topics:

- Building a word vector from scratch in Python
- Building a word vector using skip-gram and CBOW models
- Performing vector arithmetic using pre-trained word vectors
- Creating a document vector
- Building word vectors using fastText
- Building word vectors using GloVe
- Building sentiment classification using word vectors

Introduction

In the traditional approach of solving text-related problems, we would one-hot encode the word. However, if the dataset has thousands of unique words, the resulting one-hot-encoded vector would have thousands of dimensions, which is likely to result in computation issues. Additionally, similar words will not have similar vectors in this scenario. Word2Vec is an approach that helps us to achieve similar vectors for similar words.

To understand how Word2Vec is useful, let's explore the following problem.

Let's say we have two input sentences:

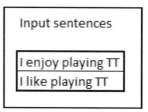

Intuitively, we know that **enjoy** and **like** are similar words. However, in traditional text mining, when we one-hot encode the words, our output looks as follows:

Unique words		One hot encoding				
I	I	1	0	0	0	0
enjoy	enjoy	0	1	0	0	0
playing	playing	0	0	1	0	0
TT	TT	0	0	0	1	0
like	like	0	0	0	0	1

Notice that one-hot encoding results in each word being assigned a column. The major issue with one-hot encoding such as this is that the Euclidean distance between **I** and **enjoy** is the same as the Euclidean distance between **enjoy** and **like**.

However, intuitively, we know that the distance between **enjoy** and **like** should be lower than the distance between **I** and **enjoy**, as **enjoy** and **like** are similar to each other.

Building a word vector from scratch in Python

The principle based on which we'll build a word vector is *related words will have similar words surrounding them*.

For example: the words *queen* and *princess* will have similar words (related to a *kingdom*) around them more frequently. In a way, the context (surrounding words) of these words would be similar.

Getting ready

Our dataset (of two sentences) looks as follows when we take the surrounding words as input and the remaining (middle) word as output:

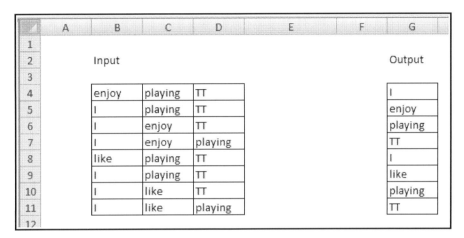

Notice that we are using the middle word as output and the remaining words as input. A vectorized form of this input and output looks as follows (recall the way in which we converted a sentence into a vector in the *Need for encoding in text analysis* section in `Chapter 9, Encoding Input`):

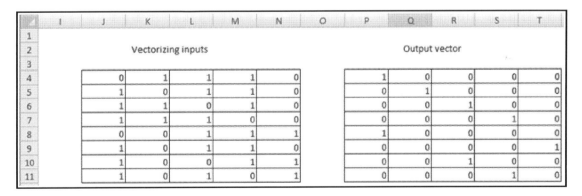

Notice that the vectorized form of input in the first row is *{0, 1, 1, 1, 0}*, as the input word index is *{1, 2, 3}*, and the output is *{1, 0, 0, 0, 0}* as the output word's index is *{1}*.

In such a scenario, our hidden layer has three neurons associated with it. Our neural network would look as follows:

Text Analysis Using Word Vectors

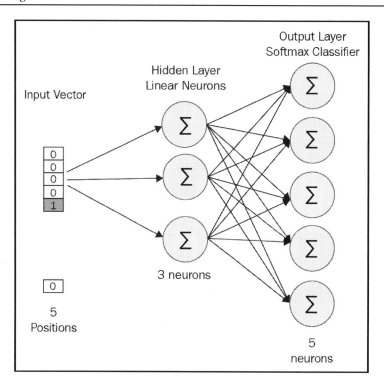

The dimensions of each layer are as follows:

Layer	Shape of weights	Commentary
Input layer	1 x 5	Each row is multiplied by five weights.
Hidden layer	5 x 3	There are five input weights each to the three neurons in the hidden layer.
Output of hidden layer	1 x 3	This is the matrix multiplication of the input and the hidden layer.
Weights from hidden to output	3 x 5	Three output hidden units are mapped to five output columns (as there are five unique words).
Output layer	1 x 5	This is the matrix multiplication between the output of the hidden layer and the weights from the hidden to the output layer.

Note that we would not be applying activation on top of the hidden layer while building a word vector.

The output layer's values are not restricted to a specific range. Hence, we pass them through the softmax function so that we arrive at the probability of words. Furthermore, we minimize the cross-entropy loss to arrive at the optimal weight values across the network. Now, the word vector of a given word is the hidden-layer unit values when the input is the one-hot encoded version of the word (not the input sentence).

How to do it...

Now that we know how word vectors are generated, let's code up the process of generating word vectors (the code file is available as `Word_vector_generation.ipynb` in GitHub):

1. Define the sentences of interest:

   ```
   docs = ["I enjoy playing TT", "I like playing TT"]
   ```

   From the preceding, we should expect the word vectors of `enjoy` and `like` to be similar, as the words around `enjoy` and `like` are exactly the same.

2. Let's now create the one-hot encoded version of each sentence:

   ```
   from sklearn.feature_extraction.text import CountVectorizer
   vectorizer = CountVectorizer(min_df=0, token_pattern=r"\b\w+\b")
   vectorizer.fit(docs)
   ```

   Note that vectorizer defines the parameters that convert a document into a vector format. Additionally, we pass in more parameters so that words such as `I` do not get filtered out in the `CountVectorizer`.

   Furthermore, we will fit our documents to the defined vectorizer.

3. Transform the documents into a vector format:

   ```
   vector = vectorizer.transform(docs)
   ```

Text Analysis Using Word Vectors

4. Validate the transformations performed:

```
print(vectorizer.vocabulary_)
print(vector.shape)
print(vector.toarray())
```

```
{'i': 1, 'enjoy': 0, 'playing': 3, 'tt': 4, 'like': 2}
(2, 5)
[[1 1 0 1 1]
 [0 1 1 1 1]]
```

Note that `vocabulary_` returns the index of various words, and that converting the `toarray` vector returns the one-hot encoded version of sentences.

5. Create the input and the output dataset:

```
x = []
y = []
for i in range(len(docs)):
    for j in range(len(docs[i].split())):
        t_x = []
        t_y = []
        for k in range(4):
            if(j==k):
                t_y.append(docs[i].split()[k])
                continue
            else:
                t_x.append(docs[i].split()[k])
        x.append(t_x)
        y.append(t_y)

x2 = []
y2 = []
for i in range(len(x)):
    x2.append(' '.join(x[i]))
    y2.append(' '.join(y[i]))
```

From the preceding code, we have created the input and output datasets. Here is the input dataset:

[326]

```
['enjoy playing TT',
 'I playing TT',
 'I enjoy TT',
 'I enjoy playing',
 'like playing TT',
 'I playing TT',
 'I like TT',
 'I like playing']
```

And here is the output dataset:

```
['I', 'enjoy', 'playing', 'TT', 'I', 'like', 'playing', 'TT']
```

6. Transform the preceding input and output words into vectors:

   ```
   vector_x = vectorizer.transform(x2)
   vector_x.toarray()
   vector_y = vectorizer.transform(y2)
   vector_y.toarray()
   ```

   Here is the input array:

   ```
   array([[1, 0, 0, 1, 1],
          [0, 1, 0, 1, 1],
          [1, 1, 0, 0, 1],
          [1, 1, 0, 1, 0],
          [0, 0, 1, 1, 1],
          [0, 1, 0, 1, 1],
          [0, 1, 1, 0, 1],
          [0, 1, 1, 1, 0]])
   ```

   Here is the output array:

   ```
   array([[0, 1, 0, 0, 0],
          [1, 0, 0, 0, 0],
          [0, 0, 0, 1, 0],
          [0, 0, 0, 0, 1],
          [0, 1, 0, 0, 0],
          [0, 0, 1, 0, 0],
          [0, 0, 0, 1, 0],
          [0, 0, 0, 0, 1]])
   ```

Text Analysis Using Word Vectors

7. Define the neural network model that maps the input and output vector with a hidden layer that has three units:

```
model = Sequential()
model.add(Dense(3, activation='linear', input_shape=(5,)))
model.add(Dense(5,activation='sigmoid'))
```

8. Compile and fit the model:

```
model.compile(loss='binary_crossentropy',optimizer='adam')

model.fit(vector_x, vector_y, epochs=1000, batch_size=4,verbose=1)
```

9. Extract the word vectors by fetching the intermediate layer values where the inputs are the vectors of each individual word (not a sentence):

```
from keras.models import Model
layer_name = 'dense_5'
intermediate_layer_model =
Model(inputs=model.input,outputs=model.get_layer(layer_name).output
)
```

In the preceding code, we are extracting the output from the layer we are interested in: a layer named `dense_5` in the model we initialized.

In the code below, we are extracting the output of intermediate layer when we pass the one-hot-encoded version of the word as input:

```
for i in range(len(vectorizer.vocabulary_)):
    word = list(vectorizer.vocabulary_.keys())[i]
    word_vec =
vectorizer.transform([list(vectorizer.vocabulary_.keys())[i]]).toarray()
    print(word, intermediate_layer_model.predict(word_vec))
```

The word vectors of individual words are as follows:

```
i          [[ 1.6032135   1.3119363  -1.7557099]]
enjoy      [[-1.4379208  -0.94042814 -2.4946306 ]]
playing         [[ 0.77564436 -2.887907   -0.4725666 ]]
tt         [[-2.0346394   0.82441056  0.67760855]]
like       [[-1.4300524  -0.94189996 -2.6602516 ]]
```

Note that the words `enjoy` and `like` are more correlated to each other than others are and hence a better representation of word vectors.

TIP: The name could be different for the model you run, as we did not specify the layer name in our model build. Also, the layer name changes for every new run of model initialization when we do not explicitly specify the model name in the layer.

Measuring the similarity between word vectors

The similarity between word vectors could be measured using multiple metrics—here are two of the more common ones:

- Cosine similarity
- Eucledian distance

The cosine similarity between two different vectors, A and B, is calculated as follows:

$$similarity = cos(\theta) = \frac{A.B}{\|A\|_2\|B\|_2} = \frac{\sum_{i=1}^{n} A_i B_i}{\sqrt{\sum_{i=1}^{n} A_i^2}\sqrt{\sum_{i=1}^{n} B_i^2}}$$

In the example in previous section, the cosine similarity between *enjoy* and *like* is calculated as follows:

enjoy = (-1.43, -0.94, -2.49)

like = (-1.43, -0.94, -2.66)

Here is the similarity between the *enjoy* and *like* vectors:

(-1.43*-1.43 + -0.94*-0.94 +-2.49*-2.66)/ sqrt((-1.43)² + (-0.94)² + (-2.49)²)* sqrt((-1.43)^2 + (-0.94)^2 + (-2.66)^2) = 0.99

The Eucledian distance between two different vectors, A and B, is calculated as follows:

distance = sqrt(A-B)^2

= sqrt((-1.43 - (-1.43))^2 + (-0.94 - (-0.94))^2 + (-2.49 - (-2.66))^2)

= 0.03

Building a word vector using the skip-gram and CBOW models

In the previous recipe, we built a word vector. In this recipe, we'll build skip-gram and CBOW models using the `gensim` library.

Getting ready

The method that we have adopted to build a word vector in this recipe is called a **continuous bag of words** (**CBOW**) model. The reason it is called as CBOW is explained as follows:

Let's use this sentence as an example: *I enjoy playing TT*.

Here's how the CBOW model handles this sentence:

1. Fix a window of certain size—let's say 1.
    - By specifying the window size, we are specifying the number of words that will be considered to the right as well as to the left of the given word.
2. Given the window size, the input and output vectors would look as follows:

Input words	Output word
{I, playing}	{enjoy}
{enjoy, TT}	{playing}

Another approach to building a word vector is the skip-gram model, where the preceding step is reversed, as follows:

Input words	Output word
{enjoy}	{I, playing}
{playing}	{enjoy, TT}

The approach to arrive at the hidden layer values of a word remains the same as we discussed in previous section regardless of whether it is a skip-gram model or a CBOW model.

How to do it

Now that we understand the backend of how a word vector gets built, let's build word vectors using the skip-gram and CBOW models. To build the model, we will be using the airline sentiment dataset, where tweet texts are given and the sentiments corresponding to the tweets are provided. To generate word vectors, we will be using the gensim package, as follows (the code file is available as word2vec.ipynb in GitHub):

1. Install the gensim package:

    ```
    $pip install gensim
    ```

2. Import the relevant packages:

    ```
    import gensim
    import pandas as pd
    ```

3. Read the airline tweets sentiment dataset, which contains comments (text) related to airlines and their corresponding sentiment. The dataset can be obtained from https://d1p17r2m4rzlbo.cloudfront.net/wp-content/uploads/2016/03/Airline-Sentiment-2-w-AA.csv:

    ```
    data=pd.read_csv('https://www.dropbox.com/s/8yq0edd4q908xqw/airline_sentiment.csv')
    data.head()
    ```

    A sample of the dataset looks as follows:

	airline_sentiment	text
0	1	@VirginAmerica plus you've added commercials t...
1	0	@VirginAmerica it's really aggressive to blast...
2	0	@VirginAmerica and it's a really big bad thing...
3	0	@VirginAmerica seriously would pay $30 a fligh...
4	1	@VirginAmerica yes, nearly every time I fly VX...

4. Preprocess the preceding text to do the following:
   - Normalize every word to lower case.
   - Remove punctuation and retain only numbers and alphabets.
   - Remove stop words:

   ```
   import re
   import nltk
   from nltk.corpus import stopwords
   nltk.download('stopwords')
   stop = set(stopwords.words('english'))
   def preprocess(text):
       text=text.lower()
       text=re.sub('[^0-9a-zA-Z]+',' ',text)
       words = text.split()
       words2 = [i for i in words if i not in stop]
       words3=' '.join(words2)
       return(words3)
   data['text'] = data['text'].apply(preprocess)
   ```

5. Split sentences into a list of tokens so that they can then be passed to `gensim`. The output of the first sentence should look as follows:

   ```
   data['text'][0].split()
   ```

   The above code splits the sentence by space and thus looks as follows:

   ```
   ['virginamerica', 'plus', 'added', 'commercials', 'experience', 'tacky']
   ```

   We will loop through all the text we have and append it in a list, as follows:

   ```
   list_words=[]
   for i in range(len(data)):
       list_words.append(data['text'][i].split())
   ```

   Let's inspect the first three lists within the list of lists:

   ```
   list_words[:3]
   ```

The list of lists of the first three sentences is as follows:

```
[['virginamerica', 'plus', 'added', 'commercials', 'experience', 'tacky'],
 ['virginamerica',
  'really',
  'aggressive',
  'blast',
  'obnoxious',
  'entertainment',
  'guests',
  'faces',
  'amp',
  'little',
  'recourse'],
 ['virginamerica', 'really', 'big', 'bad', 'thing']]
```

6. Build the `Word2Vec` model:

   ```
   from gensim.models import Word2Vec
   ```

   Define the vector size, context window size to look into, and the minimum count of a word for it to be eligible to have a word vector, as follows:

   ```
   model = Word2Vec(size=100,window=5,min_count=30, sg=0, alpha = 0.025)
   ```

   In the preceding code, `size` represents the size (dimension) of word vectors, `window` represents the context size of words that would be considered, `min_count` specifies the minimum frequency based on which a word is considered, `sg` represents whether skip-gram would be used (when `sg=1`) or CBOW (when `sg = 0`) would be used, and alpha represents the learning rate of the model.

   Once the model is defined, we will pass our list of lists to build a vocabulary, as follows:

   ```
   model.build_vocab(list_words)
   ```

   Once the vocabulary is built, the final words that would be left after filtering out the words that occur fewer than 30 times in the whole corpus can be found as follows:

   ```
   model.wv.vocab.keys()
   ```

7. Train the model by specifying the total number of examples (lists) that need to be considered and the number of epochs to be run, as follows:

```
model.train(list_words, total_examples=model.corpus_count, epochs=100)
```

In the preceding code, `list_words` (the list of words) is the input, `total_examples` represents the total number of lists to be considered, and epochs is the number of epochs to be run.

Alternatively, you can also train the model by specifying the `iter` parameter in the `Word2Vec` method, as follows:

```
model = Word2Vec(list_words,size=100,window=5,min_count=30, iter = 100)
```

8. Extract the word vectors of a given word (`month`), as follows:

```
model['month']
```

The word vector corresponding to the word "month" is as follows:

```
array([ 0.3419442 , -0.660853  , -0.8875737 , -0.11866002,  3.848598  ,
       -1.859917  ,  1.2849951 ,  1.5322515 , -0.42655924,  0.74873245,
        0.7576644 ,  0.53542703,  1.6549652 ,  1.4168224 ,  1.4571517 ,
       -1.1921175 , -0.83038306, -1.6139846 ,  0.5910155 ,  3.1234474 ,
        1.9208    , -1.0543962 , -0.7666846 , -1.590045  , -0.1548474 ,
        1.1117342 , -0.4835291 , -1.7931118 , -0.22642556, -2.1773818 ,
        0.38367364, -2.0263271 , -2.9695885 , -0.3920376 , -0.8466245 ,
        0.43550012,  1.7326713 ,  2.0108004 , -0.5395172 , -0.04537094,
        0.76008844,  0.74664325,  0.4459887 ,  1.1571167 ,  2.0812125 ,
       -0.7367794 , -0.72291315, -1.3603346 , -0.13599452,  2.689772  ,
       -2.524463  ,  0.5480051 ,  1.689171  ,  0.044644  , -0.27298477,
        1.5061239 , -1.0514534 , -0.02589583,  1.5114399 ,  0.4221726 ,
       -0.9640717 , -1.3412739 , -0.19521172, -1.8486487 ,  0.04619067,
       -0.8271076 , -0.7997853 , -1.3049688 ,  2.0880153 , -0.9300234 ,
        1.1623387 , -0.09183449, -1.8364261 , -0.5820482 ,  1.1316198 ,
       -0.3580541 ,  1.2225895 , -0.85193574, -1.0722245 , -0.7914595 ,
       -1.0597026 ,  0.48279345,  0.7167691 ,  1.4192754 ,  1.9140383 ,
       -1.6390625 , -2.2567384 ,  0.3889435 ,  2.1803992 ,  1.7071763 ,
        0.54344946, -0.50497335,  0.30110064, -0.12276804, -0.34828255,
       -1.041366  , -0.6226012 ,  2.1155527 , -0.7881018 , -0.902104  ]
```

The similarity between two words can be calculated as follows:

```
model.similarity('month','year')
0.48
```

The words that are most similar to a given word is calculated as follows:

```
model.most_similar('month')
```

The most similar words of the word `month` are as follows:

```
[('year', 0.4818694591522217),
 ('week', 0.4710841774940491),
 ('months', 0.35927000641822815),
 ('weeks', 0.35357385873794556),
 ('leg', 0.33413201570510864),
 ('days', 0.3019614517688751),
 ('miles', 0.289564490318298934),
 ('lt', 0.2536947727203369),
 ('pm', 0.25144699215888977),
 ('traveling', 0.2485567033290863)]
```

Note that, while these similarities look low and some of the most similar words do not look intuitive, it will be more realistic once we train on a huge dataset than the 11,000-tweet dataset that we have.

In the preceding scenario, let's see the output of most similar words to the word "month", when we run the model for a few number of epochs:

```
model = Word2Vec(size=100,window=5,min_count=30, sg=0)
model.build_vocab(list_words)
model.train(list_words, total_examples=model.corpus_count,
epochs=5)
model.most_similar('month')
```

The most similar words to the word "month" are as follows:

```
[('traveling', 0.9996585249900818),
 ('im', 0.9996532201766968),
 ('kids', 0.9996105432510376),
 ('happened', 0.9995968341827393),
 ('plus', 0.9995967745780945),
 ('computer', 0.999592661857605),
 ('list', 0.9995923638343811),
 ('support', 0.99958676099777722),
 ('something', 0.9995864629745483),
 ('extremely', 0.9995763301849365)]
```

We can see that if we have few epochs, the most similar words to the word `month` are not intuitive while the results are intuitive when there are many epochs, particularly as the weights are not fully optimized for few epochs.

 The same operations can be replicated for skip-gram by replacing the value of the `sg` parameter with `1`.

Performing vector arithmetic using pre-trained word vectors

In the previous section, one of the limitations that we saw is that the number of sentences is too small for us to build a model that is robust (we saw that the correlation of month and year is around 0.4 in the previous section, which is relatively low, as they belong to the same type of words).

To overcome this scenario, we will use the word vectors trained by Google. The pre-trained word vectors from Google include word vectors for a vocabulary of 3,000,000 words and phrases that were trained on words from Google News dataset.

How to do it...

1. Download the pre-trained word vectors from Google News (the code file is available as `word2vec.ipynb` in GitHub):

   ```
   $wget
   https://s3.amazonaws.com/dl4j-distribution/GoogleNews-vectors-negat
   ive300.bin.gz
   ```

   Unzip the downloaded file:

   ```
   $gunzip '/content/GoogleNews-vectors-negative300.bin.gz'
   ```

   This command unzips the `bin` file, which is the saved version of the model.

2. Load the model:

   ```
   from gensim.models import KeyedVectors
   filename = '/content/GoogleNews-vectors-negative300.bin'
   model = KeyedVectors.load_word2vec_format(filename, binary=True)
   ```

3. Load the most similar words to the given word, month:

   ```
   model.most_similar('month')
   ```

   The words that are most similar to month are as follows:

   ```
   [(u'week', 0.8365199565887451),
    (u'year', 0.7653313875198364),
    (u'months', 0.681006133556366),
    (u'weeks', 0.65276038646698),
    (u'August', 0.6166313290596008),
    (u'February', 0.6136031746864319),
    (u'October', 0.6114892363548279),
    (u'January', 0.6091349124908447),
    (u'day', 0.600459098815918),
    (u'September', 0.5990685224533081)]
   ```

4. We will perform vector arithmetic; that is, we will try to answer the following analogy: woman is to man as what is to king? Check out the following code:

   ```
   result = model.most_similar(positive=['woman', 'king'],
   negative=['man'], topn=1)
   print(result)
   ```

   The output of above arithmetic is as follows:

   ```
   [(u'queen', 0.7118192911148071)]
   ```

In this scenario, the word vector of woman is subtracted from the word vector of man and added to the word vector of king – resulting in a vector that is closest to the word queen.

Creating a document vector

To understand the reason for having a document vector, let's go through the following intuition.

The word *bank* is used in the context of finance and also in the context of a river. How do we identify whether the word *bank* in the given sentence or document is related to the topic of a river or the topic of finance?

This problem could be solved by adding a document vector, which works in a similar way to word-vector generation but with the addition of a one-hot encoded version of the paragraph ID, as follows:

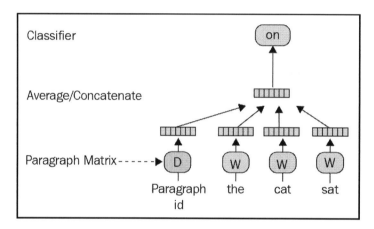

In the preceding scenario, the paragraph ID encompasses the delta that is not captured by just the words. For example, in the sentence *on the bank of river* where *on the bank of* is the input and *river* is the output, the words *on*, *the*, and *of* do not contribute to the prediction as they are frequently-occurring words, while the word *bank* confuses the output prediction to be either river or America. The document ID of this particular document/sentence will help to identify whether the document is related to the topic of rivers or to the topic of finance. This model is called the **Distributed Memory Model of Paragraph Vectors (PV-DM)**.

For example, if the number of documents is 100, the one-hot encoded version of the paragraph ID will be 100-dimensional. Similarly, if the number of unique words that meet the minimum frequency of a word is 1,000, the one-hot encoded version of the words is 1,000 in size. When the hidden-layer size (which is the word vector size) is 300, the total number of parameters would be 100 * 300 + 1,000 * 300 = 330,000

The document vector would be the value of the hidden layer when the one-hot encoded versions of all input words are 0 (that is, the effect of the words is neutralized and only the effect of the document/paragraph ID is considered).

Similar to the way in which input and output switch between the skip-gram and CBOW models, even for a document vector, the output and input can be switched as follows:

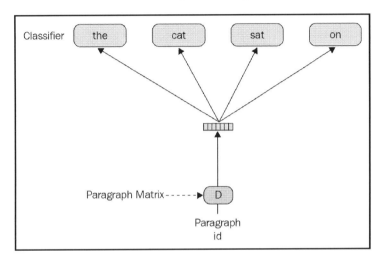

This representation of the model is called a **paragraph vector with a distributed bag of words** (**PVDBOW**).

Getting ready

The strategy that we'll adopt to build a document vector is as follows:

- Preprocess the input sentences to remove punctuation as well as lowercasing for all words, and remove the stop words (words that occur very frequently and do not add context to sentence, for example, *and* and *the*)
- Tag each sentence with its sentence ID.
    - We are assigning an ID for each sentence.
- Use the Doc2Vec method to extract vectors for document IDs as well as words.
    - Train the Doc2Vec method over a high number of epochs, so that the model is trained.

Text Analysis Using Word Vectors

How to do it...

Now that we have the intuition of how a document vector gets generated and a strategy in place to build a document vector, let's generate the document vectors of the airline tweets dataset (the code file is available as `word2vec.ipynb` in GitHub):

1. Import the relevant packages:

```
from gensim.models.doc2vec import Doc2Vec, TaggedDocument
from nltk.tokenize import word_tokenize
```

2. Preprocess the tweets' text:

```
import re
import nltk
from nltk.corpus import stopwords
nltk.download('stopwords')
stop = set(stopwords.words('english'))
def preprocess(text):
    text=text.lower()
    text=re.sub('[^0-9a-zA-Z]+',' ',text)
    words = text.split()
    words2 = [i for i in words if i not in stop]
    words3=' '.join(words2)
    return(words3)
data['text'] = data['text'].apply(preprocess)
```

3. Create a dictionary of tagged documents where the document ID is generated along with the text (tweet):

```
import nltk
nltk.download('punkt')
tagged_data = [TaggedDocument(words=word_tokenize(_d.lower()),
tags=[str(i)]) for i, _d in enumerate(data['text'])]
```

The tagged document data looks as follows:

```
[TaggedDocument(words=['virginamerica', 'plus', 'added', 'commercials', 'experience', 'tacky'], tags=['0']),
TaggedDocument(words=['virginamerica', 'really', 'aggressive', 'blast', 'obnoxious', 'entertainment', 'guests', 'faces', 'amp', 'little', 'recourse'], tags=['1']),
TaggedDocument(words=['virginamerica', 'really', 'big', 'bad', 'thing'], tags=['2']),
```

In the preceding code, we are extracting a list of all the constituent words in a sentence (document).

4. Initialize a model with parameters, as follows:

```
max_epochs = 100
vec_size = 300
alpha = 0.025
model = Doc2Vec(size=vec_size,
                alpha=alpha,
                min_alpha=0.00025,
                min_count=30,
                dm =1)
```

In the preceding code snippet, `size` represents the vector size of the document, `alpha` represents the learning rate, `min_count` represents the minimum frequency for a word to be considered, and `dm = 1` represents the PV-DM

Build a vocabulary:

```
model.build_vocab(tagged_data)
```

6. Train the model for a high number of epochs on the tagged data:

```
model.train(tagged_data,epochs=100,total_examples=model.corpus_count)
```

7. The training process would generate vectors for words as well as for the document/paragraph ID.

Word vectors can be fetched similarly to how we fetched them in the previous section, as follows:

```
model['wife']
```

Document vectors can be fetched as follows:

```
model.docvecs[0]
```

The preceding code snippet generates snippets for the document vectors for the first document.

8. Extract the most similar document to a given document ID:

```
similar_doc = model.docvecs.most_similar('457')
print(similar_doc)
```

```
[('827', 0.9669191837310791), ('5076', 0.951378583908081), ('2394', 0.9232662916183472)]
```

Text Analysis Using Word Vectors

In the preceding code snippet, we are extracting the document ID that is most similar to the document ID number 457, which is 827.

Let's look into the text of documents 457 and 827:

```
data['text'][457]
```

```
'united thanks just sent'
```

```
data['text'][827]
```

```
'united sent thanks'
```

If we inspect the vocabulary of the model, we would see that apart from the word `just`, all the other words occur between the two sentences—hence it is obvious that document ID `457` is most similar to document ID `827`.

Building word vectors using fastText

fastText is a library created by the Facebook Research Team for the efficient learning of word representations and sentence classification.

fastText differs from word2vec in the sense that word2vec treats every single word as the smallest unit whose vector representation is to be found, but fastText assumes a word to be formed by a n-grams of character; for example, sunny is composed of *[sun, sunn, sunny],[sunny, unny, nny]*, and so on, where we see a subset of the original word of size *n*, where *n* could range from *1* to the length of the original word.

Another reason for the use of fastText would be that the words do not meet the minimum frequency cut-off in the skip-gram or CBOW models. For example, the word *appended* would not be very different than *append*. However, if *append* occurs frequently, and in the new sentence we have the word *appended* instead of *append*, we are not in a position to have a vector for *appended*. The n-gram consideration of fastText comes in handy in such a scenario.

Practically, fastText uses skip-gram/CBOW models, however, it augments the input dataset so that the unseen words are also taken into consideration.

Getting ready

The strategy that we'll adopt to extract word vectors using fastText is as follows:

1. Use the fastText method in the gensim library
2. Preprocess the input data
3. Break each input sentence into a list of lists
4. Build a vocabulary on top of the input list of lists
5. Train the model with the preceding input data over multiple epochs
6. Calculate the similarity between words

How to do it...

In the following code, let's look at how to generate word vectors using fastText (the code file is available as `word2vec.ipynb` in GitHub):

1. Import the relevant packages:

    ```
    from gensim.models.fasttext import FastText
    ```

2. Preprocess and prepare the dataset into a list of lists, just like we did for the word2vec models:

    ```
    import re
    import nltk
    from nltk.corpus import stopwords
    nltk.download('stopwords')
    stop = set(stopwords.words('english'))
    def preprocess(text):
        text=text.lower()
        text=re.sub('[^0-9a-zA-Z]+',' ',text)
        words = text.split()
        words2 = [i for i in words if i not in stop]
        words3=' '.join(words2)
        return(words3)
    data['text'] = data['text'].apply(preprocess)
    ```

    In the preceding code, we are preprocessing the input text. Next, let's convert the input text into a list of lists:

    ```
    list_words=[]
    for i in range(len(data)):
        list_words.append(data['text'][i].split())
    ```

Text Analysis Using Word Vectors

3. Define the model (specify the number of vectors per word) and build a vocabulary:

   ```
   ft_model = FastText(size=100)
   ft_model.build_vocab(list_words)
   ```

4. Train the model:

   ```
   ft_model.train(list_words,
   total_examples=ft_model.corpus_count,epochs=100)
   ```

5. Check the word vectors of a word that is not present in the vocabulary of the model. For example, the word `first` is present in the vocabulary; however, the word `firstli` is not present in the vocabulary. In such a scenario, check the similarity between the word vectors for `first` and `firstli`:

   ```
   ft_model.similarity('first','firstli')
   ```

The output of the preceding code snippet is 0.97, which indicates a very high correlation between the two words.

Thus, we can see that fastText word vectors help us to generate word vectors for words that are not present in the vocabulary.

The preceding method could also be leveraged to correct the spelling mistakes, if any, within our corpus of data, as the incorrectly-spelled words are likely to occur rarely, and the most similar word with the highest frequency is more likely to be the correctly-spelled version of the misspelled word.

Spelling corrections can be performed using vector arithmetic, as follows:

```
result = ft_model.most_similar(positive=['exprience', 'prmise'],
negative=['experience'], topn=1)
print(result)
```

Note that in the preceding code, the positive words have a spelling mistake, while the negative word does not. The output of the code is `promise`. So this potentially corrects our spelling mistake.

Additionally, it can also be performed as follows:

```
ft_model.most_similar('exprience', topn=1)
```

[('experience', 0.9027844071388245)]

However, note that this does not work when there are multiple spelling mistakes.

Building word vectors using GloVe

Similar to the way word2vec generates word vectors, **GloVe** (short for **Global Vectors for Word Representation**), also generates word vectors but using a different method. In this section, we will explore how GloVe works and then get into the implementation details of GloVe.

Getting ready

GloVe aims to achieve two goals:

- Creating word vectors that capture meaning in vector space
- Taking advantage of global count statistics instead of only local information

GloVe learns word vectors by looking at the cooccurrence matrix of words and optimizing for a loss function. The working details of the GloVe algorithm can be understood from the following example:

Let's consider a scenario where there are two sentences, as follows:

Sentences
This is test
This is also a

Let's try to build a word-cooccurrence matrix. There is a total of five unique words within our toy dataset of sentences, and from there the word-cooccurrence matrix looks as follows:

	this	is	test	also	a
this	0	2	1	1	1
is	0	0	1	1	1
test	0	0	0	0	0
also	0	0	0	0	1
a	0	0	0	0	0

Text Analysis Using Word Vectors

In the preceding table, the words *this* and *is* occur together in the two rows of the dataset and hence have a cooccurrence value of 2. Similarly, the words *this* and *test* occur together only once in the dataset and hence have a cooccurrence value of 1.

However, in the preceding matrix, we have not taken the distance between the two words into consideration. The intuition for considering the distance between the two words is that the farther the cooccurring words are from each other, the less relevant they might be for the cooccurrence.

We will introduce a new metric—*offset*, which penalizes for having a high distance between the given word and the cooccurring word. For example, *test* occurs at a distance of 2 from *this* in the first sentence, so we will divide the cooccurrence number by a value of 2.

The transformed cooccurrence matrix now looks as follows:

	this	is	test	also	a
this	0	2	0.5	0.5	0.33
is	0	0	1	1	0.5
test	0	0	0	0	0
also	0	0	0	0	1
a	0	0	0	0	0

Now that we have built the matrix, let's bring in one additional parameter: the *context* of the words to be considered. For example, if the window size is 2, the cooccurrence value corresponding to the words *this* and *a* would be a value of 0 as the distance between the two words is greater than 2. The transformed cooccurrence matrix when the context window size is 2 looks as follows:

	this	is	test	also	a
this	0	2	0.5	0.5	0
is	0	0	1	1	0.5
test	0	0	0	0	0
also	0	0	0	0	1
a	0	0	0	0	0

Now that we have arrived at a modified cooccurrence matrix, we randomly initialize the word vectors of each word with a dimension of 2 in this instance. The randomly-initialized weights and bias values of each word, where each word has a vector size of 3, look as follows:

Word	Weights 1	Weights 2	Weights 3	Bias
this	-0.64	0.82	-0.08	0.16
is	-0.89	-0.31	0.79	-0.34
test	-0.01	0.14	0.82	-0.35
also	-0.1	-0.67	0.89	0.26
a	-0.1	-0.84	0.35	0.36

Given that the preceding weights and biases are randomly initialized, we modify the weights to optimize the loss function. In order to do that, let's define the loss function of interest, as follows:

$$J = \sum_{i,j=1}^{V} f(X_{ij})(w_i^T \bar{w}_j + b_i + \bar{b}_j - \log X_{ij})^2$$

In the preceding equation, w_i represents the word vector of the ith word, and w_j represents the word vector of jth word; b_i and b_j are the biases that correspond to the ith and j^{th} words, respectively. X_{ij} represents the values in the final cooccurrence value that we defined earlier.

For example, the value of X_{ij} where i is the word *this* and j is the word *also* is 0.5

When the value of X_{ij} is 0, the value of $f(x_{ij})$ is 0; otherwise, it is as follows:

$$f(x) = \begin{cases} (x/x_{max})^\alpha & if \ x < x_{max} \\ 1 & otherwise. \end{cases}$$

In the preceding equation, alpha is empirically found to be 0.75, x_{max} is 100, and x is the value of x_{ij}.

Text Analysis Using Word Vectors

Now that the equation is defined, let's apply that to our matrix, as follows:

	E	F	G	H	I	J	K	L	M	N
1										
2	Word	this	is	test	also	a	Weights			bias
3	this	0	2	0.5	0.5	0	0.0574	-0.1704	-0.0123	-0.284
4	is	0	0	1	1	0.5	0.2076	-0.1984	-0.0494	0.109
5	test	0	0	0	0	0	0.0261	0.0927	-0.1035	-0.190
6	also	0	0	0	0	1	-0.2130	0.0088	0.04839	-0.059
7	a	0	0	0	0	0	-0.2810	0.1941	-0.0807	-0.223
8										
9										
10	The weightage function	loss value	Weighted loss value							
11	=(G3/100)^(0.75)	=(SUMPRODUCT(K3:M3,K4:M4)+N3+N4-LOG(G3))^2	=F11^2*E11							
12	=(H3/100)^0.75	=(SUMPRODUCT(K3:M3,K5:M5)+N3+N5-LOG(H3))^2	=F12^2*E12							
13	=(I3/100)^0.75	=(SUMPRODUCT(K3:M3,K6:M6)+N3+N6-LOG(I3))^2	=F13^2*E13							
14	=(H4/100)^0.75	=(SUMPRODUCT(K4:M4,K5:M5)+N4+N5-LOG(H4))^2	=F14^2*E14							
15	=(I4/100)^0.75	=(SUMPRODUCT(K4:M4,K6:M6)+N4+N6-LOG(I4))^2	=F15^2*E15							
16	=(J4/100)^0.75	=(SUMPRODUCT(K4:M4,K7:M7)+N4+N7-LOG(J4))^2	=F16^2*E16							
17	=(J6/100)^0.75	=(SUMPRODUCT(K6:M6,K7:M7)+N6+N7-LOG(J6))^2	=F17^2*E17							
18		Overall weighted loss value	=SUM(G11:G17)							

The first table represents the word-cooccurrence matrix and the randomly-initialized weights and biases.

The second table represents the loss-value calculation, where we calculate the overall weighted loss value.

We optimize the weights and biases until the overall weighted loss value is the least.

How to do it...

Now that we know how word vectors are generated using GloVe, let's implement the same in Python (the code file is available as word2vec.ipynb in GitHub):

1. Install GloVe:

    ```
    $pip install glove_python
    ```

2. Import the relevant packages:

    ```
    from glove import Corpus, Glove
    ```

3. Preprocess the dataset the way we preprocessed in word2vec, skip-gram, and CBOW algorithms, as follows:

    ```
    import re
    import nltk
    from nltk.corpus import stopwords
    ```

```
import pandas as pd
nltk.download('stopwords')
stop = set(stopwords.words('english'))
data =
pd.read_csv('https://www.dropbox.com/s/8yq0edd4q908xqw/airline_sent
iment.csv?dl=1')
def preprocess(text):
    text=text.lower()
    text=re.sub('[^0-9a-zA-Z]+',' ',text)
    words = text.split()
    words2 = [i for i in words if i not in stop]
    words3=' '.join(words2)
    return(words3)
data['text'] = data['text'].apply(preprocess)
list_words=[]
for i in range(len(data)):
    list_words.append(data['text'][i].split())
```

4. Create a corpus and fit it with a vocabulary:

   ```
   corpus.fit(list_words, window=5)
   ```

   The dictionary of the corpus can be found as follows:

   ```
   corpus.dictionary
   ```

   The unique words and their corresponding word IDs are obtained as follows:

   ```
   {'xaizw2isml': 4425,
    'twetpxuppn': 11367,
    'cussed': 10939,
    'h44uj63cjg': 6394,
    'vn3jjia53o': 6795,
    'yellow': 9424,
    'four': 350,
    'jparkermastin': 6641,
    'hsv': 11104,
   ```

   The preceding screenshot represents the key values of the words and their corresponding index.

Text Analysis Using Word Vectors

The following code snippet gives us the cooccurrence matrix:

```
corpus.matrix.todense()
```

```
matrix([[0. , 1. , 0.75, ..., 0. , 0. , 0. ],
        [0. , 0. , 1. , ..., 0. , 0. , 0. ],
        [0. , 0. , 0. , ..., 0. , 0. , 0. ],
        ...,
        [0. , 0. , 0. , ..., 0. , 0. , 0. ],
        [0. , 0. , 0. , ..., 0. , 0. , 0. ],
        [0. , 0. , 0. , ..., 0. , 0. , 0. ]])
```

5. Let's define the model parameters, that is, the number of dimensions of a vector, the learning rate, and the number of epochs to be run, as follows:

```
glove = Glove(no_components=100, learning_rate=0.025)
glove.fit(corpus.matrix, epochs=30, no_threads=4, verbose=True)
```

6. Once the model is fit, the weights and biases of word vectors can be found as follows:

```
glove.word_biases.tolist()
glove.word_vectors.tolist()
```

7. The word vector for a given word can be determined as follows:

```
glove.word_vectors[glove.dictionary['united']]
```

8. The most similar words for a given word can be determined as follows:

```
glove.most_similar('united')
```

The output of most similar words to "united" is as follows:

```
[('usairways', 0.9319100099683549),
 ('southwestair', 0.9165424743315992),
 ('americanair', 0.9123728213792929),
 ('jetblue', 0.900383830727353)]
```

Note that the words that are the most similar to the word `united` are the words that belong to other airlines.

[350]

Building sentiment classification using word vectors

In the previous sections, we learned how to generate word vectors using multiple models. In this section, we will learn how to build a sentiment classifier for a given sentence. We will continue using the airline sentiment tweet dataset for this exercise.

How to do it...

Generate word vectors like the way we extracted in previous recipes (the code file is available as `word2vec.ipynb` in GitHub):

1. Import the packages and download the dataset:

    ```
    import re
    import nltk
    from nltk.corpus import stopwords
    import pandas as pd
    nltk.download('stopwords')
    stop = set(stopwords.words('english'))
    data=pd.read_csv('https://www.dropbox.com/s/8yq0edd4q908xqw/airline_sentiment.csv?dl=1')
    ```

2. Preprocess the input text:

    ```
    def preprocess(text):
     text=text.lower()
     text=re.sub('[^0-9a-zA-Z]+',' ',text)
     words = text.split()
     words2 = [i for i in words if i not in stop]
     words3=' '.join(words2)
     return(words3)
    data['text'] = data['text'].apply(preprocess)
    ```

3. Extract a list of lists across all the sentences in the dataset:

    ```
    t=[]
    for i in range(len(data)):
     t.append(data['text'][i].split())
    ```

4. Build a CBOW model, where the context window `size` is 5 and the vector length is 100:

   ```
   from gensim.models import Word2Vec
   model = Word2Vec(size=100,window=5,min_count=30, sg=0)
   ```

5. Specify the vocabulary to model and then train it:

   ```
   model.build_vocab(t)
   model.train(t, total_examples=model.corpus_count, epochs=100)
   ```

6. Extract the average vector of a given tweet:

   ```
   import numpy as np
   features= []
   for i in range(len(t)):
       t2 = t[i]
       z = np.zeros((1,100))
       k=0
       for j in range(len(t2)):
           try:
               z = z+model[t2[j]]
               k= k+1
           except KeyError:
               continue
       features.append(z/k)
   ```

   We are taking the average of the word vectors for all the words present in the input sentence. Additionally, there will be certain words that are not in the vocabulary (words that occur less frequently) and would result in an error if we try to extract their vectors. We've deployed `try` and `catch` errors for this specific scenario.

7. Preprocess features to convert them into an array, split the dataset, into train and test datasets and reshape the datasets so that they can be passed to model:

   ```
   features = np.array(features)

   from sklearn.cross_validation import train_test_split
   X_train, X_test, y_train, y_test = train_test_split(features,
   data['airline_sentiment'], test_size=0.30,random_state=10)
   X_train = X_train.reshape(X_train.shape[0],100)
   X_test = X_test.reshape(X_test.shape[0],100)
   ```

8. Compile and build the neural network to predict the sentiment of a tweet:

   ```
   from keras.layers import Dense, Activation
   from keras.models import Sequential
   from keras.utils import to_categorical
   from keras.layers.embeddings import Embedding
   model = Sequential()
   model.add(Dense(1000,input_dim = 100,activation='relu'))
   model.add(Dense(1))
   model.add(Activation('sigmoid'))
   model.compile(loss='binary_crossentropy', optimizer='adam', metrics=['accuracy'])
   model.summary()
   ```

The summary of model defined above is as follows:

```
Layer (type)                 Output Shape              Param #
=================================================================
dense_20 (Dense)             (None, 1000)              101000
_____
dense_21 (Dense)             (None, 1)                 1001
_____
activation_10 (Activation)   (None, 1)                 0
=================================================================
Total params: 102,001
Trainable params: 102,001
Non-trainable params: 0
```

In the preceding model, we have a 1,000-dimensional hidden layer that connects the 100 inputted average word vector values to the output, which has a value of 1 (1 or 0 for a positive or negative sentiment, respectively):

```
model.fit(X_train, y_train, batch_size=128, nb_epoch=5,
validation_data=(X_test, y_test),verbose = 1)
```

We can see that the accuracy of our model is ~90% in predicting the sentiment of a tweet.

9. Plot the confusion matrix of predictions:

```
pred = model.predict(X_test)
pred2 = np.where(pred>0.5,1,0)
from sklearn.metrics import confusion_matrix
confusion_matrix(y_test, pred2)
```

The output of confusion matrix is as follows:

```
array([[2644,  125],
       [ 209,  485]])
```

From the above, we see that in 2,644 sentences, we predicted them to be positive and they are actually positive. 125 sentences were predicted to be negative and happened to be positive. 209 sentences were predicted to be positive and happened to be negative and finally, 485 sentences were predicted negative and were actually negative.

There's more...

While we implemented the sentiment classification using the CBOW model and an average of all the word vectors that are present in the tweets, the other ways we could have proceeded are as follows:

- Use the skip-gram model.
- Use the doc2vec model to build a model using document vectors.
- Use the fastText-model-based word vectors.
- Use the GloVe-based word vectors.
- Use pre-trained models' word vector values.

While these methods work in a similar fashion, one of the limitations of the preceding model is that it does not take word order into consideration. There are more sophisticated algorithms that solve the problem of word order, which will be discussed in the next chapter.

11
Building a Recurrent Neural Network

In the previous chapter, we looked at multiple ways of representing text as a vector and then performed sentiment classification on top of those representations.

One of the drawbacks of this approach is that we did not take the order of words into consideration—for example, the sentence *A is faster than B* would have the same representation as *B is faster than A*, as the words in both sentences are exactly the same, while the order of words is different.

Recurrent neural networks (**RNNs**) come in handy in scenarios when the word order needs to be preserved. In this chapter, you will learn about the following topics:

- Building RNN and LSTM from scratch in Python
- Implementing RNN for sentiment classification
- Implementing LSTM for sentiment classification
- Implementing stacked LSTM for sentiment classification

Introduction

RNN can be architected in multiple ways. Some of the possible ways are as follows:

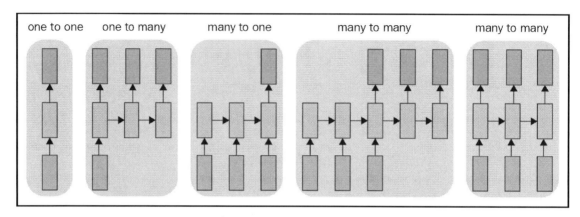

The box in the bottom is the input, followed by the hidden layer (as the middle box), and the box on top is the output layer. The one-to-one architecture is the typical neural network with a hidden layer between the input and the output layer. The examples of different architectures are as follows:

Architecture	Example
One-to-many	Input is image and output is caption of image
Many-to-one	Input is a movie's review (multiple words in input) and output is sentiment associated with the review
Many-to-many	Machine translation of a sentence in one language to a sentence in another language

Intuition of RNN architecture

RNN is useful when we want to predict the next event given a sequence of events.

An example of that could be to predict the word that comes after *This is an* _____.

Let's say, in reality, the sentence is *This is an example*.

Traditional text-mining techniques would solve the problem in the following way:

1. Encode each word while having an additional index for potential new words:

   ```
   This: {1,0,0,0}
   is:   {0,1,0,0}
   an:   {0,0,1,0}
   ```

2. Encode the phrase `This is an`:

   `This is an: {1,1,1,0}`

3. Create the training dataset:

   ```
   Input  --> {1,1,1,0}
   Output --> {0,0,0,1}
   ```

4. Build a model with input and output

One of the major drawbacks of the model is that the input representation does not change in the input sentence; it is either `this is an`, or `an is this`, or `this an is`.

However, intuitively, we know that each of the preceding sentences is different and cannot be represented by the same structure mathematically. This calls for having a different architecture, which looks as follows:

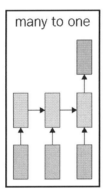

In the preceding architecture, each of the individual words from the sentence enter into individual box among the input boxes. However the structure of the sentence will be preserved, for example `this` enters the first box, `is` enters second box and `an` enters the third box.

The output box at the top will be the output that is `example`.

Interpreting an RNN

You can think of RNN as a mechanism to hold memory—where the memory is contained within the hidden layer. It can be visualized as follows:

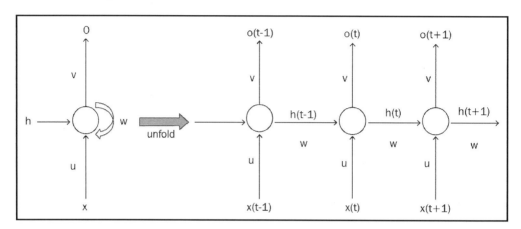

The network on the right is an unrolled version of the network on the left. The network on the right takes one input in each time step and extracts the output at each time step. However, if we are interested in the output in the fourth time step, we'll provide input in the previous three time steps and the output of the third time step is the predicted value for fourth time step.

Note that, while predicting the output of third time step, we are incorporating values from the first three time steps through the hidden layer, which is connecting the values across time steps.

Let's explore the preceding diagram:

- The **U** weight represents the weights that connect the input layer to the hidden layer
- The **W** weight represents the hidden-layer-to-hidden-layer connection
- The **V** weight represents the hidden-layer-to-output-layer connection

Why store memory?

There is a need to store memory, as in the preceding example or even in text-generation in general, the next word does not necessarily depend only on the preceding word, but the context of the words preceding the word to predict.

Given that we are looking at the preceding words, there should be a way to keep them in memory, so that we can predict the next word more accurately.

Moreover, we should also have the memory in order; that is, more often than not, the recent words are more useful in predicting the next word than the words that are far away from the word to predict.

Building an RNN from scratch in Python

In this recipe, we will build an RNN from scratch using a toy example, so that you gain a solid intuition of how RNN helps in solving the problem of taking the order of events (words) into consideration.

Getting ready

Note that a typical NN has an input layer, followed by an activation in the hidden layer, and then a softmax activation at the output layer.

RNN follows a similar structure, with modifications done in such a way that the hidden layers of the previous time steps are considered in the current time step.

We'll build the working details of RNN with a simplistic example before implementing it on more practical use cases.

Let's consider an example text that looks as follows: `This is an example`.

The task at hand is to predict the third word given a sequence of two words.

So, the dataset translates as follows:

Input	Output
this, is	an
is, an	example

Given an input of `this is`, we are expected to predict `example` as the output.

Building a Recurrent Neural Network

The strategy that we'll adopt to build an RNN is as follows:

1. One-hot encode the words
2. Identify the maximum length of input:
    - Pad the rest of input to the maximum length so that all the inputs are of the same length
3. Convert the words in the input into a one-hot-encoded version
4. Convert the words in the output into a one-hot-encoded version
5. Process the input and the output data, then fit the RNN model

How to do it...

The strategy discussed above is coded as follows (the code file is available as `Building_a_Recurrent_Neural_Network_from_scratch-in_Python.ipynb` in GitHub):

1. Let's define the input and output in code, as follows:

    ```
    #define documents
    docs = ['this, is','is an']
    # define class labels
    labels = ['an','example']
    ```

2. Let's preprocess our dataset so that it can be passed to an RNN:

    ```
    from collections import Counter
    counts = Counter()
    for i,review in enumerate(docs+labels):
        counts.update(review.split())
    words = sorted(counts, key=counts.get, reverse=True)
    vocab_size=len(words)
    word_to_int = {word: i for i, word in enumerate(words, 1)}
    ```

    In the preceding step, we are identifying all the unique words and their corresponding frequency (counts) in a given dataset, and we are assigning an ID number to each word. The output of `word_to_int` in the preceding code looks as follows:

    ```
    print(word_to_int)
    # {'an': 2, 'example': 4, 'is': 1, 'this': 3}
    ```

3. Modify the input and output words with their corresponding IDs, as follows:

```
encoded_docs = []
for doc in docs:
      encoded_docs.append([word_to_int[word] for word in doc.split()])
encoded_labels = []
for label in labels:
      encoded_labels.append([word_to_int[word] for word in label.split()])
print('encoded_docs: ',encoded_docs)
print('encoded_labels: ',encoded_labels)
# encoded_docs: [[3, 1], [1, 2]]
# encoded_labels: [[2], [4]]
```

In the preceding code, we are appending the ID of each word of an input sentence into a list, thus making the input (`encoded_docs`) a list of lists.

Similarly, we are appending the ID of each word of the output into a list.

4. One additional factor to take care of while encoding the input is the input length. In cases of sentiment analysis, the input text length can vary from one review to another. However, the neural network expects the input size to be fixed. To get around this problem, we perform padding on top of the input. Padding ensures that all inputs are encoded to have a similar length. While the lengths of both examples in our case is 2, in practice, we are very likely to face the scenario of differing lengths between input. In code, we perform padding as follows:

```
# pad documents to a max length of 2 words
max_length = 2
padded_docs = pad_sequences(encoded_docs, maxlen=max_length, padding='pre')
```

In the preceding code, we are passing `encoded_docs` to the `pad_sequences` function, which ensures that all the input data points have the same length—which is equal to the `maxlen` parameter. Additionally, for those parameters that are shorter than `maxlen`, it pads those data points with a value of 0 to achieve a total length of `maxlen` and the zero padding is done `pre`—that is, to the left of the original encoded sentence.

Now that the input dataset is created, let's preprocess the output dataset so that it can be passed to the model-training step.

5. The typical processing for outputs is to make them into dummy values, that is, make a one-hot-encoded version of the output labels, which is done as follows:

```
one_hot_encoded_labels = to_categorical(encoded_labels,
num_classes=5)
print(one_hot_encoded_labels)
# [[0. 0. 1. 0. 0.] [0. 0. 0. 0. 1.]]
```

Note that, given the output values (`encoded_labels`) are {2, 4}, the output vectors have a value of 1 at the second and fourth positions, respectively.

6. Let's build the model:
    1. An RNN expects the input to be (`batch_size`, `time_steps`, and `features_per_timestep`) in shape. Hence, we first reshape the `padded_docs` input into the following format:

        ```
        padded_docs = padded_docs.reshape(2,2,1)
        ```

        Note that ideally we would have created a word embedding for each word (ID in this specific case). However, given that the intent of this recipe is only to understand the working details of RNN, we will exclude the embedding of IDs and assume that each input is not an ID but a value. Having said that, we will learn how to perform ID-embedding in the next recipe.

    2. Define the model—where we are specifying that we will initialize an RNN by using the `SimpleRNN` method:

        ```
        # define the model
        embed_length=1
        max_length=2
        model = Sequential()
        model.add(SimpleRNN(1,activation='tanh',
        return_sequences=False,recurrent_initializer='Zeros',input_
        shape=(max_length,embed_length),unroll=True))
        ```

        In the preceding step, we explicitly specified the `recurrent_initializer` to be zero so that we understand the working details of RNN more easily. In practice, we would not be initializing the recurrent initializer to 0.

The `return_sequences` parameter specifies whether we want to obtain the hidden layer values at each time step. A false value for `return_sequences` specifies that we want the hidden layer output only at the final timestep.

Typically, in a many-to-one task, where there are many inputs (one input in each time step) and outputs, `return_sequences` will be false, resulting in the output being obtained only in the final time step. An example of this could be the stock price on the next day, given a sequence of historical five-day stock prices.

However, in cases where we try to obtain hidden-layer values in each time step, `return_sequences` will be set to `True`. An example of this could be machine translation, where there are many inputs and many outputs.

3. Connect the RNN output to five nodes of the output layer:

```
model.add(Dense(5, activation='softmax'))
```

We have performed a `Dense(5)`, as there are five possible classes of output (the output of each example has 5 values, where each value corresponds to the probability of it belonging to word ID 0 to word ID 4).

4. Compile and summarize the model:

```
# compile the model
model.compile(optimizer='adam',
loss='categorical_crossentropy', metrics=['acc'])
# summarize the model
print(model.summary())
```

A summary of model is as follows:

```
Layer (type)                 Output Shape              Param #
=================================================================
simple_rnn_3 (SimpleRNN)     (None, 1)                 3
_____
dense_3 (Dense)              (None, 5)                 10
=================================================================
Total params: 13
Trainable params: 13
Non-trainable params: 0
_____
None
```

Now that we have defined the model, before we fit the input and output, let's understand the reason why there are certain number of parameters in each layer.

The simple RNN part of the model has an output shape of `(None, 1)`. The `None` in the output shape represents the `batch_size`. None is a way of specifying that the `batch_size` could be any number. Given that we have specified that there shall be one unit of hidden that is to be outputted from simple RNN, the number of columns is one.

Now that we understand the output shape of `simpleRNN`, let's understand why the number of parameters is three in the `simpleRNN` layer. Note that the hidden-layer value is outputted at the final time step. Given that the input has a value of one in each time step (one feature per time step) and the output is also of one value, the input is essentially multiplied by a weight that is of a single value. Had the output (hidden-layer value) been 40 units of hidden-layer values, the input should have been multiplied by 40 units to get the output (more on this in the *Implementing RNN for sentiment classification* recipe). Apart from the one weight connecting the input to the hidden-layer value, there is a bias term that accompanies the weight. The other 1 parameter comes from the connection of the previous time step's hidden layer value to the current time step's hidden layer, resulting in a total of three parameters.

There are 10 parameters from the hidden layer to the final output as there are five possible classes resulting in five weights and five biases connecting the hidden-layer value (which is of one unit)—a total of 10 parameters.

5. Fit the model to predict the output from the input:

```
model.fit(padded_docs,np.array(one_hot_encoded_labels),epochs=500)
```

7. Extract prediction on the first input data point

```
model.predict(padded_docs[0].reshape(1,2,1))
```

The extracted output is as follows:

```
array([[0.3684635, 0.33566403, 0.61344165, 0.378485, 0.4069949 ]], dtype=float32)
```

Validating the output

Now that the model is fit, let's gain an understanding of how an RNN works by working backward—that is, extract the weights of model, feed forward the input through the weights to match the predicted value using NumPy (the code file is available as Building_a_Recurrent_Neural_Network_from_scratch_in_Python.ipynb in GitHub).

1. Inspect the weights:

```
model.weights
[<tf.Variable 'simple_rnn_2/kernel:0' shape=(1, 1) dtype=float32_ref>,
 <tf.Variable 'simple_rnn_2/recurrent_kernel:0' shape=(1, 1) dtype=float32_ref>,
 <tf.Variable 'simple_rnn_2/bias:0' shape=(1,) dtype=float32_ref>,
 <tf.Variable 'dense_2/kernel:0' shape=(1, 5) dtype=float32_ref>,
 <tf.Variable 'dense_2/bias:0' shape=(5,) dtype=float32_ref>]
```

The preceding gives us an intuition of the order in which weights are presented in the output.

In the preceding example, `kernel` represents the weights and `recurrent` represents the connection of the hidden layer from one step to another.

Note that a `simpleRNN` has weights that connect the input to the hidden layer and also weights that connect the previous time step's hidden layer to the current time step's hidden layer.

Building a Recurrent Neural Network

The kernel and bias in the `dense_2` layer represent the layer that connects the hidden layer value to the final output:

1. Extract weights:

   ```
   model.get_weights()
   ```

   The preceding line of code gives us the computed values of each of the weights.

2. Pass the input through the first time step—the input is as follows:

   ```
   padded_docs[0]
   #array([3, 1], dtype=int32)
   ```

   In the preceding code, the first time step has a value of 3 and the second time step has a value of 1. We'll initialize the value at first time step as follows:

   ```
   input_t0 = 3
   ```

   1. The value at the first time step is multiplied by the weight connecting the input to the hidden layer, then the bias value is added:

      ```
      input_t0_kernel_bias = input_t0*model.get_weights()[0] + model.get_weights()[2]
      ```

   2. The hidden layer value at this time step is calculated by passing the preceding output through the `tanh` activation (as that is the activation we specified when we defined the model):

      ```
      hidden_layer0_value = np.tanh(input_t0_kernel_bias)
      ```

4. Calculate the hidden-layer value at time step 2; where the input has a value of 1 (note the value of `padded_docs[0]` is [3, 1]):

   ```
   input_t1 = 1
   ```

   1. The output value when the input at the second time step is passed through the weight and bias is as follows:

      ```
      input_t1_kernel_bias = input_t1*model.get_weights()[0] + model.get_weights()[2]
      ```

   Note that the weights that multiply the input remain the same, regardless of the time step being considered.

2. The calculation for the hidden-layer at various time steps is performed as follows:

$$h^{(t)} = \phi_h(z_h^{(t)}) = \phi_h(W_{xh}x^{(t)} + W_{hh}h^{(t-1)} + b_h)$$

Where Φ is an activation that is performed (In general, `tanh` activation is used).

The calculation from the input layer to the hidden-layer constitutes two components:

- Matrix multiplication of the input layer value and kernel weights
- Matrix multiplication of the hidden layer of the previous time step and recurrent weights

The final calculation of the hidden-layer value at a given time step would be the summation of the preceding two matrix multiplications. Pass the result through a tanh activation function:

```
input_t1_recurrent = hidden_layer0_value*model.get_weights()[1]
```

The total value before passing through the `tanh` activation is as follows:

```
total_input_t1 = input_t1_kernel_bias + input_t1_recurrent
```

The output of the hidden-layer value is calculated by passing the preceding output through the `tanh` activation, as follows:

```
output_t1 = np.tanh(total_input_t1)
```

5. Pass the hidden layer output from the final time step through the dense layer, which connects the hidden layer to the output layer:

```
final_output = output_t1*model.get_weights()[3] +
model.get_weights()[4]
```

Note that the fourth and fifth output of the `model.get_weights()` method correspond to the connection from the hidden layer to the output layer.

6. Pass the preceding output through the softmax activation (as defined in the model) to obtain the final output:

```
np.exp(final_output)/np.sum(np.exp(final_output))
# array([[0.3684635, 0.33566403, 0.61344165, 0.378485,
0.40699497]], dtype=float32)
```

You should notice that the output we obtained through the forward pass of input through the network is the same as what the `model.predict` function gave as output.

Implementing RNN for sentiment classification

To understand how RNN is implemented in Keras, let's implement the airline-tweet sentiment classification exercise that we performed in the `Chapter 10`, *Text Analysis Using Word Vectors* chapter.

How to do it...

The task would be performed as follows (the code file is available as `RNN_and_LSTM_sentiment_classification.ipynb` in GitHub):

1. Import the relevant packages and dataset:

    ```
    from keras.layers import Dense, Activation
    from keras.layers.recurrent import SimpleRNN
    from keras.models import Sequential
    from keras.utils import to_categorical
    from keras.layers.embeddings import Embedding
    from sklearn.cross_validation import train_test_split
    import numpy as np
    import nltk
    from nltk.corpus import stopwords
    import re
    import pandas as pd
    data=pd.read_csv('https://www.dropbox.com/s/8yq0edd4q908xqw/airline
    _sentiment.csv')
    data.head()
    ```

2. Preprocess the text to remove punctuation, normalize all words to lowercase, and remove the stopwords, as follows:

    ```
    import nltk
    nltk.download('stopwords')
    stop = nltk.corpus.stopwords.words('english')
    def preprocess(text):
        text=text.lower()
        text=re.sub('[^0-9a-zA-Z]+',' ',text)
        words = text.split()
    ```

```
        words2=[w for w in words if (w not in stop)]
        #words3=[ps.stem(w) for w in words]
        words4=' '.join(words2)
        return(words4)
data['text'] = data['text'].apply(preprocess)
```

3. Extract the word-to-integer mapping of all the words that constitute the dataset:

```
from collections import Counter
counts = Counter()
for i,review in enumerate(t['text']):
    counts.update(review.split())
words = sorted(counts, key=counts.get, reverse=True)
```

In the preceding step, we are extracting the frequency of all the words in the dataset. A sample of extracted words are as follows:

```
['united',
 'flight',
 'usairways',
 'americanair',
 'southwestair',
 'jetblue',
 'get',
 'cancelled',
 'thanks',
 'service']
```

```
nb_chars = len(words)
word_to_int = {word: i for i, word in enumerate(words, 1)}
int_to_word = {i: word for i, word in enumerate(words, 1)}
```

In the preceding code, we are looping through all the words and are assigning an index for each word. A sample of integer to word dictionary is as follows:

```
{1: 'united',
 2: 'flight',
 3: 'usairways',
 4: 'americanair',
 5: 'southwestair',
 6: 'jetblue',
```

4. Map each word in a given sentence to the corresponding word associated with it:

   ```
   mapped_reviews = []
   for review in data['text']:
       mapped_reviews.append([word_to_int[word] for word in review.split()])
   ```

   In the preceding step, we are converting a text review into a list of lists where each list constitutes the ID of words contained in a sentence. A sample of original and mapped review is as follows:

   ```
   ('Original text:', 'virginamerica plus added commercials experience tacky')
   ('Mapped text:', [44, 459, 1198, 2482, 100, 9958])
   ```

5. Extract the maximum length of a sentence and normalize all sentences to the same length by padding them. In the following code, we are looping through all the reviews and storing the length corresponding to each review. Additionally, we are also calculating the maximum length of a review (tweet text):

   ```
   length_sent = []
   for i in range(len(mapped_reviews)):
       length_sent.append(len(mapped_reviews[i]))
   sequence_length = max(length_sent)
   ```

   We should note that different tweets have different lengths. However, RNN expects the number of time steps for each input to be the same. In the code below, we are padding a mapped review with a value of 0, if the length of the review is less than the maximum length of all reviews in dataset. This way, all inputs will have the same length.

   ```
   from keras.preprocessing.sequence import pad_sequences
   X = pad_sequences(maxlen=sequence_length, sequences=mapped_reviews, padding="post", value=0)
   ```

6. Prepare the training and test datasets:

   ```
   y=data['airline_sentiment'].values
   X_train, X_test, y_train, y_test = train_test_split(X, y, test_size=0.30, random_state=42)
   y_train2 = to_categorical(y_train)
   y_test2 = to_categorical(y_test)
   ```

   In the preceding step, we are splitting the original data into the train and test datasets, and are converting the dependent variable into a one-hot-encoded variable.

7. Build the RNN architecture and compile the model:

   ```
   embedding_vecor_length=32
   max_review_length=26
   model = Sequential()
   model.add(Embedding(input_dim=12533, output_dim=32, input_length = 26))
   ```

   Note that embedding takes the total number of distinct words as input, and creates a vector for each word, where `output_dim` represents the number of dimensions in which the word is to be represented. `input_length` represents the number of words in each sentence:

   ```
   model.add(SimpleRNN(40, return_sequences=False))
   ```

   Note that, in the RNN layer, if we want to extract the output of each time step, we say the `return_sequences` parameter is `True`. However, in the use case that we are solving now, we extract the output only after reading through all the input words and thus `return_sequences = False`:

   ```
   model.add(Dense(2, activation='softmax'))
   model.compile(loss='categorical_crossentropy', optimizer='adam', metrics=['accuracy'])
   print(model.summary())
   ```

   The summary of model is as follows:

   ```
   Layer (type)                 Output Shape              Param #
   =================================================================
   embedding_16 (Embedding)     (None, 26, 32)            401056
   _____
   simple_rnn_12 (SimpleRNN)    (None, 40)                2920
   _____
   dense_11 (Dense)             (None, 2)                 82
   =================================================================
   Total params: 404,058
   Trainable params: 404,058
   Non-trainable params: 0
   ```

Let's understand why there are `401056` parameters to be estimated in the embedding layer. There are a total of 12, 532 unique words, and if we consider that there is no word with an index of 0, it results in a total of 12,533 possible words where each is represented in 32 dimensions and hence (12,533 x 32 = 401,056) parameters to be estimated.

Now, let's try to understand why there are 2,920 parameters in the `simpleRNN` layer.

There is a set of weights that connect the input to the 40 units of RNN. Given that there are 32 inputs at each time step (where the same set of weights is repeated for each time step), a total of 32 x 40 weights is used to connect the input to the hidden layer. This gives an output that is of 1 x 40 in dimension for each input.

Additionally, for the summation between the $X * W_{xh}$ and $h_{(t-1)} * W_{hh}$ to happen (where X is is the input values, W_{xh} is the weights-connecting input layer to the hidden layer, W_{hh} is the weights-connecting the previous time step's hidden layer to the current time step's hidden layer, and $h_{(t-1)}$ is the hidden layer of previous time step)—given that the output of the $X\ W_{xh}$ input is 1 x 40—the output of $h_{(t-1)}\ X\ W_{hh}$ should also be 1 x 40 in size. Thus, the W_{hh} matrix will be 40 x 40 in dimension, as the dimensions of $h_{(t-1)}$ are 1 x 40.

Along with weights, we would also have 40 bias terms associated with each of the 40 output and thus a total of (32 x 40 + 40 x 40 + 40 = 2,920) weights.

There are a total of 82 weights in the final layer, as the 40 units of the final time step are connected to the two possible output, resulting 40 x 2 weights and 2 biases, and thus a total of 82 units.

8. Fit the model:

   ```
   model.fit(X_train, y_train2, validation_data=(X_test, y_test2),
   epochs=10, batch_size=32)
   ```

   The plot of accuracy and loss values in training, test dataset are as follows:

Chapter 11

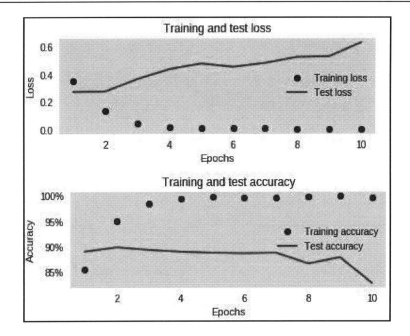

The output of the preceding model is also ~89%, and does not offer any significant improvement over the word-vector-based network that we built in *Text analysis using word vectors* chapter.

However, it is expected to have better accuracy as the number of data points increases.

There's more...

A traditional RNN that takes multiple time steps into account for giving predictions can be visualized as follows:

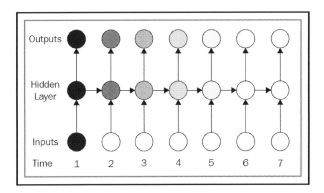

Notice that, as time step increases, the impact of input at a much earlier layer would be lower. An intuition of that can be seen here (for a moment, let's ignore the bias terms):

$$h_5 = WX_5 + Uh_4 = WX5 + UWX_4 + U^2WX_3 + U^3WX_2 + U^4WX_1$$

You can see that, as the time step increases, the value of hidden layer is highly dependent on X_1 if $U>1$, or much less dependent on X_1 if $U<1$.

The dependency on U matrix can also result in vanishing gradient when the value of U is very small and can result in exploding gradient when the value of U is very high.

The above phenomenon results in an issue when there is a long-term dependency in predicting the next word. To solve this problem, we'll use the **Long Short Term Memory (LSTM)** architecture in the next recipe.

Building a LSTM Network from scratch in Python

In the previous section on issues with traditional RNN, we learned about how RNN does not help when there is a long-term dependency. For example, imagine the input sentence is as follows:

I live in India. I speak ____.

The blank space in the preceding statement could be filled by looking at the key word, *India*, which is three time steps prior to the word we are trying to predict.

In a similar manner, if the key word is far away from the word to predict, vanishing/exploding gradient problems need to be solved.

Getting ready

In this recipe, we'll learn how LSTM helps in overcoming the long-term dependency drawback of the RNN architecture and also build a toy example so that we understand the various components of LSTM.

LSTM looks as follows:

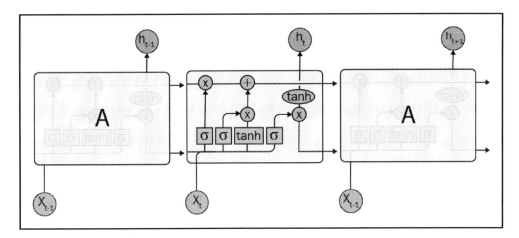

You can see that while the input, **X**, and the output of the hidden layer, (**h**), remain the same, there are different activations that happen in the hidden layer (sigmoid activation in certain cases and tanh activation in others).

Let's closely examine the various activations that happen in one of the time steps:

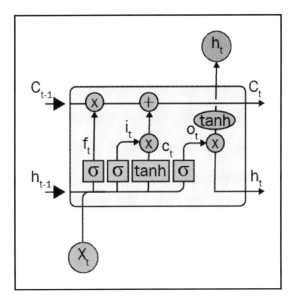

Building a Recurrent Neural Network

In the preceding diagram, **X** and **h** represent the input layer and the hidden layer.

The longterm memory is stored in cell state **C**.

The content that needs to be forgotten is obtained using the forget gate:

$$f_t = \sigma(W_{xf}x^{(t)} + W_{hf}h^{(t-1)} + b_f)$$

Sigmoid activation enables the network to selectively identify the content that needs to be forgotten.

The updated cell state after we determine the content that needs to be forgotten is as follows:

$$c_t = (c_{t-1} \otimes f)$$

Note that $\otimes$ represents element-to-element multiplication.

For example, if the input input sequence of the sentence is *I live in India. I speak ___, the* blank space can be filled based on the input word *India*. After filling in the blank, we do not necessarily need the specific information of the name of the country.

We update the cell state based on what needs to be forgotten at the current time step.

In the next step, we will be adding additional information to the cell state based on the input provided in the current time step. Additionally, the magnitude of the update (either positive or negative) is obtained through the tanh activation.

The input can be specified as follows:

$$i_t = \sigma(W_{xi}x^{(t)} + W_{hi}h^{(t-1)} + bi)$$

The modulation (magnitude of the input update) can be specified as follows:

$$g_t = \tanh(W_{xg}x^{(t)} + W_{hg}h^{(t-1)} + bg)$$

The cell state—where we are forgetting certain things in a time step and also adding additional information in the same time step—gets updated as follows:

$$C^{(t)} = (C^{(t-1)} \odot f_t) \oplus (i_t \odot g_t)$$

In the final gate, we need to specify what part of the combination of input (combination of current time step input and previous time step's hidden layer value) and the cell state needs to be outputted to the next hidden layer:

$$o_t = \sigma(W_{xo}x^{(t)} + W_{ho}h^{(t-1)} + b_o)$$

The final hidden layer is represented as follows:

$$h^{(t)} = o_t \odot tanh(c^{(t)})$$

This way, we are in a position to leverage the various gates in LSTM to selectively identify the information that needs to be stored in memory and thus overcome the limitation of RNN.

How to do it...

To gain a practical intuition of how this theory works, let's look at the same example we worked out in understanding RNN but this time using LSTM.

Note that the data preprocessing steps are common between the two examples. Hence, we will reuse the preprocessing part (*step 1* to *step 4* in the *Building an RNN from scratch in Python* recipe) and directly head over to the model-building part (the code file is available as LSTM_working_details.ipynb in GitHub):

1. Define the model:

```
embed_length=1
max_length=2
model = Sequential()
model.add(LSTM(1,activation='tanh',return_sequences=False,
recurrent_initializer='Zeros',recurrent_activation='sigmoid',
input_shape=(max_length,embed_length),unroll=True))
```

Note that, in the preceding code, we initialized the recurrent initializer and recurrent activation to certain values only to make this example simpler; the purpose is only to help you understand what is happening in the backend.

```
model.add(Dense(5, activation='softmax'))

# compile the model
model.compile(optimizer='adam', loss='binary_crossentropy',
metrics=['acc'])
# summarize the model
print(model.summary())
```

A summary of the model is as follows:

```
Layer (type)                 Output Shape              Param #
=================================================================
lstm_19 (LSTM)               (None, 1)                 12
_____
dense_18 (Dense)             (None, 5)                 10
=================================================================
Total params: 22
Trainable params: 22
Non-trainable params: 0
_____
```

The number of parameters is 12 in the LSTM layer as there are four gates (forget, input, cell, and output), which results in four weights and four biases connecting the input to the hidden layer. Additionally, the recurrent layer contains weight values that correspond to the four gates, which gives us a total of 12 parameters.

The dense layer has a total of 10 parameters as there are five possible classes as output, and thus five weights and five biases that correspond to each connection from the hidden layer to the output layer.

2. Let's fit the model:

```
model.fit(padded_docs.reshape(2,2,1),np.array(one_hot_encoded_label
s),epochs=500)
```

3. The order of weights of this model are as follows:

```
model.weights[<tf.Variable 'lstm_19/kernel:0' shape=(1, 4) dtype=float32_ref>,
 <tf.Variable 'lstm_19/recurrent_kernel:0' shape=(1, 4) dtype=float32_ref>,
 <tf.Variable 'lstm_19/bias:0' shape=(4,) dtype=float32_ref>,
 <tf.Variable 'dense_18/kernel:0' shape=(1, 5) dtype=float32_ref>,
 <tf.Variable 'dense_18/bias:0' shape=(5,) dtype=float32_ref>]
```

The weights can be obtained as follows:

```
model.get_weights()
```

From the preceding code (`model.weights`), we can see that the order of weights in the LSTM layer is as follows:

- Weights of the input (kernel)
- Weights corresponding to the hidden layer (`recurrent_kernel`)
- Bias in the LSTM layer

Similarly, in the dense layer (the layer that connects the hidden layer to the output), the order of weights is as follows:

- Weight to be multiplied with the hidden layer
- Bias

Here is the order in which the weights and biases appear (not provided in the preceding output, but available in the GitHub repository of Keras) in the LSTM layer:

- Input gate
- Forget gate
- Modulation gate (cell gate)
- Output gate

3. Calculate the predictions for the input.

We are using raw-encoded input values (1,2,3) without converting them into embedding values—only to see how the calculation works. In practice, we would be converting the input into embedding values.

4. Reshape the input for the predict method, so that it is as per the data format expected by LSTM (batch size, number of time steps, features per time step):

```
model.predict(padded_docs[0].reshape(1,2,1))
# array([[0.05610514, 0.11013522, 0.38451442, 0.0529648,
0.39628044]], dtype=float32)
```

The output of predict method is provided in commented line in the code above.

Validating the output

Now that we have a predicted probability from the model, let's run the input through the forward pass of weights using NumPy to obtain the same output as we just did.

This is done so that we validate our understanding of how LSTM works under the hood. The steps that we take to validate the output of model we built are as follows:

1. Update the forget gate in time step 1. This step looks at the input and then provides an estimate of how much of the cell state (memory) known so far is to be forgotten (note the usage of the sigmoid function):

```
input_t0 = 3
cell_state0 = 0
forget0 = input_t0*model.get_weights()[0][0][1] +
model.get_weights()[2][1]
forget1 = 1/(1+np.exp(-(forget0)))
```

2. Update the cell state based on the updated forget gate. The output of the previous step is being used here to direct the amount of values to be forgotten from the cell state (memory):

```
cell_state1 = forget1 * cell_state0
```

3. Update the input gate value in time step 1. This step gives an estimate of how much new information is to be injected into the cell state based on the current input:

```
input_t0_1 = input_t0*model.get_weights()[0][0][0] +
model.get_weights()[2][0]
input_t0_2 = 1/(1+np.exp(-(input_t0_1)))
```

4. Update the cell state based on the updated input value. This is the step where the output from the previous step is being used to dictate the amount of information update that is to happen to cell state (memory):

```
input_t0_cell1 = input_t0*model.get_weights()[0][0][2]
+model.get_weights()[2][2]
input_t0_cell2 = np.tanh(input_t0_cell1)
```

The preceding tanh activation helps to determine whether the update from the input will add to or subtract from the cell state (memory). This provides an additional lever, as, if certain information is already conveyed in the current time step and is not useful in future time steps, we are better off wiping it off from the cell state so that this extra information (which might not be helpful in the next step) is wiped from memory:

```
input_t0_cell3 = input_t0_cell2*input_t0_2
input_t0_cell4 = input_t0_cell3 + cell_state1
```

5. Update the output gate. This step provides an estimate of how much information will be conveyed in the current time step (note the usage of the sigmoid function in this regard):

```
output_t0_1 = input_t0*model.get_weights()[0][0][3] +
model.get_weights()[2][3]
output_t0_2 = 1/(1+np.exp(-output_t0_1))
```

6. Calculate the hidden layer value at time step 1. Note that the final hidden-layer value at a time step is a combination of how much memory and output in the current time step is used to convey for a single time step:

```
hidden_layer_1 = np.tanh(input_t0_cell4)*output_t0_2
```

We are done calculating the hidden layer value output from the first time step. In the next steps, we will pass the updated cell state value from time step 1 and the output of the hidden layer value from time step 1 as inputs to time step 2.

7. Pass the input value at time step 2 and the cell state value going into time step 2:

```
input_t1 = 1
cell_state1 = input_t0_cell4
```

8. Update the forget gate value:

```
forget21 = hidden_layer_1*model.get_weights()[1][0][1] +
model.get_weights()[2][1] + input_t1*model.get_weights()[0][0][1]
forget_22 = 1/(1+np.exp(-(forget21)))
```

Building a Recurrent Neural Network

9. Update the cell state value in time step 2:

```
cell_state2 = cell_state1 * forget_22
input_t1_1 = input_t1*model.get_weights()[0][0][0] +
model.get_weights()[2][0] +
hidden_layer_1*model.get_weights()[1][0][0]
input_t1_2 = 1/(1+np.exp(-(input_t1_1)))
input_t1_cell1 = input_t1*model.get_weights()[0][0][2] +
model.get_weights()[2][2]+
hidden_layer_1*model.get_weights()[1][0][2]
input_t1_cell2 = np.tanh(input_t1_cell1)
input_t1_cell3 = input_t1_cell2*input_t1_2
input_t1_cell4 = input_t1_cell3 + cell_state2
```

10. Update the hidden layer output value based on the combination of updated cell state and the magnitude of output that is to be made:

```
output_t1_1 = input_t1*model.get_weights()[0][0][3] +
model.get_weights()[2][3]+
hidden_layer_1*model.get_weights()[1][0][3]
output_t1_2 = 1/(1+np.exp(-output_t1_1))
hidden_layer_2 = np.tanh(input_t1_cell4)*output_t1_2
```

11. Pass the hidden layer output through the dense layer:

```
final_output = hidden_layer_2 * model.get_weights()[3][0]
+model.get_weights()[4]
```

12. Run softmax on top of the output we just obtained:

```
np.exp(final_output)/np.sum(np.exp(final_output))

# array([0.05610514, 0.11013523, 0.3845144, 0.05296481,
0.39628044],dtype=float32)
```

You should notice that the output obtained here is exactly the same as what we obtained from the `model.predict` method.

With this exercise, we are in a better position to appreciate the working details of LSTM.

Implementing LSTM for sentiment classification

In *Implementing RNN for sentiment classification* recipe, we implemented sentiment classification using RNN. In this recipe, we will look at implementing it using LSTM.

How to do it...

The steps we'll adopt are as follows (the code file is available as `RNN_and_LSTM_sentiment_classification.ipynb` in GitHub):

1. Define the model. The only change from the code we saw in *Implementing RNN for sentiment classification* recipe will be the change from `simpleRNN` to LSTM in the model architecture part (we will be reusing the code from *step 1* to *step 6* in the *Implementing RNN for sentiment classification* recipe):

   ```
   embedding_vecor_length=32
   max_review_length=26
   model = Sequential()
   model.add(Embedding(input_dim=12533, output_dim=32, input_length = 26))
   ```

   The input for the embedding layer is the total number of unique IDs present in the dataset and the expected dimension to which each word needs to be converted (`output_dim`).

   Additionally, we'll also specify the maximum length of input, so that the LSTM layer in the next step has the required information—batch size, number of time steps (`input_length`), and the number of features per time (step (`output_dim`)):

   ```
   model.add(LSTM(40, return_sequences=False))
   model.add(Dense(2, activation='softmax'))
   model.compile(loss='categorical_crossentropy', optimizer='adam', metrics=['accuracy'])
   print(model.summary())
   ```

A summary of the model is as follows:

```
Layer (type)                 Output Shape              Param #
=================================================================
embedding_20 (Embedding)     (None, 26, 32)            401056
_____
lstm_1 (LSTM)                (None, 40)                11680
_____
dense_14 (Dense)             (None, 2)                 82
=================================================================
Total params: 412,818
Trainable params: 412,818
Non-trainable params: 0
```

While the parameters in the first and last layer are the same as what saw in the *Implementing RNN for sentiment classification* recipe, the LSTM layer has a different number of parameters.

Let's understand how 11,680 parameters are obtained in the LSTM layer:

```
W = model.layers[1].get_weights()[0]
U = model.layers[1].get_weights()[1]
b = model.layers[1].get_weights()[2]
print(W.shape,U.shape,b.shape)
```

The output will look like the following:

```
((32, 160), (40, 160), (160,))
```

Note that the total of the preceding weights has *(32*160) + (40*160) + 160 = 11,680* parameters.

W represents the weights that connect the input to each of the four cells (i, f, c, o), U represents the hidden-layer-to-hidden-layer connection, and b represents the bias in each gate.

Individual weights of the input, forget, cell state, and output gates can be obtained as follows:

```
units = 40
W_i = W[:, :units]
W_f = W[:, units: units * 2]
W_c = W[:, units * 2: units * 3]
W_o = W[:, units * 3:]
```

```
U_i = U[:, :units]
U_f = U[:, units: units * 2]
U_c = U[:, units * 2: units * 3]
U_o = U[:, units * 3:]

b_i = b[:units]
b_f = b[units: units * 2]
b_c = b[units * 2: units * 3]
b_o = b[units * 3:]
```

2. Fit the model as follows:

```
model.fit(X_train, y_train2, validation_data=(X_test, y_test2),
epochs=50, batch_size=32)
```

The variation of loss and accuracy over increasing epochs in training and test datasets are as follows:

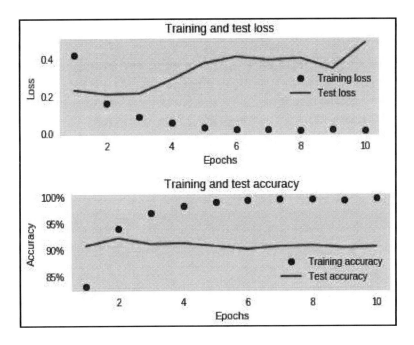

The prediction accuracy is 91% when using the LSTM layer, which is slightly better than the prediction accuracy when we are using the simpleRNN layer. Potentially, we can further improve upon the result by fine-tuning the number of LSTM units.

Implementing stacked LSTM for sentiment classification

In the previous recipe, we implemented sentiment classification using LSTM in Keras. In this recipe, we will look at implementing the same thing but stack multiple LSTMs. Stacking multiple LSTMs is likely to capture more variation in the data and thus potentially a better accuracy.

How to do it...

Stacked LSTM is implemented as follows (the code file is available as `RNN_and_LSTM_sentiment_classification.ipynb` in GitHub):

1. The only change in the code we saw earlier will be to change the `return_sequences` parameter to true. This ensures that the first LSTM returns a sequence of output (as many output as the number of LSTM units), which can then be passed to another LSTM as an input on top of the original LSTM in the model architecture part (more details on the `return_sequences` parameter can be found in the *Sequence to Sequence learning* chapter):

```
embedding_vecor_length=32
max_review_length=26
model = Sequential()
model.add(Embedding(input_dim=12533, output_dim=32, input_length = 26))
model.add(LSTM(40, return_sequences=True))
model.add(LSTM(40, return_sequences=False))
model.add(Dense(2, activation='softmax'))
model.compile(loss='categorical_crossentropy', optimizer='adam', metrics=['accuracy'])
print(model.summary())
```

A summary of model architecture is as follows:

```
Layer (type)                 Output Shape              Param #
=================================================================
embedding_21 (Embedding)     (None, 26, 32)            401056
_____
lstm_2 (LSTM)                (None, 26, 40)            11680
_____
lstm_3 (LSTM)                (None, 40)                12960
_____
dense_15 (Dense)             (None, 2)                 82
=================================================================
Total params: 425,778
Trainable params: 425,778
Non-trainable params: 0
```

Note that, in the preceding architecture, there is an additional LSTM that is stacked on top of another LSTM. The output at each time step of the first LSTM is 40 values and thus an output shape of (None, 26, 40), where None represents the batch_size, 26 represents the number of time steps, and 40 represents the number of LSTM units considered.

Now that there are 40 input values, the number of parameters in the second LSTM is considered in the same fashion as in the previous recipe, as follows:

```
W = model.layers[2].get_weights()[0]
U = model.layers[2].get_weights()[1]
b = model.layers[2].get_weights()[2]
print(W.shape,U.shape,b.shape)
```

The following are the values we get by executing preceding code:

```
((40, 160), (40, 160), (160,))
```

This results in a total of 12,960 parameters, as seen in the output.

W is 40 x 160 in shape, as it has 40 inputs that are mapped to 40 output and also 4 different gates to be controlled, and hence a total of 40 x 40 x 4 weights.

2. Implement the model, as follows:

```
model.fit(X_train, y_train2, validation_data=(X_test, y_test2),
epochs=50, batch_size=32)
```

The variation of loss and accuracy over increasing epochs in training and test datasets are as follows:

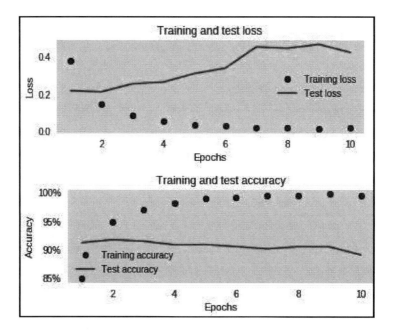

This results in an accuracy of 91%, as we saw with a single LSTM layer; however, with more data, stacked LSTM is likely to capture more variation in the data than the vanilla LSTM.

There's more...

Gated Recurrent Unit (GRU) is another architecture we can use and has accuracy that is similar to that of LSTM. For more information about GRU, visit `https://arxiv.org/abs/1412.3555`.

12
Applications of a Many-to-One Architecture RNN

In the previous chapter, we learned about the workings of RNN and LSTM. We also learned about sentiment classification, which is a classic many-to-one application, as many words in the input correspond to one output (positive or negative sentiment).

In this chapter, we will further our understanding of the many-to-one architecture RNN by going through the following recipes:

- Generating text
- Movie recommendations
- Topic-modeling using embeddings
- Forecasting the value of a stock's price

Generating text

In the sentiment-classification recipes that we performed in Chapter 11, *Building a Recurrent Neural Network*, we were trying to predict a discrete event (sentiment classification). This falls under the many-to-one architecture. In this recipe, we will learn how to implement a many-to-many architecture, where the output would be the next possible 50 words of a given sequence of 10 words.

Getting ready

The strategy that we'll adopt to generate text is as follows:

1. Import project Gutenberg's *Alice's Adventures in Wonderland* dataset, which can be downloaded from https://www.gutenberg.org/files/11/11-0.txt.

2. Preprocess the text data so that we bring every word to the same case, and remove punctuation.
3. Assign an ID to each unique word and then convert the dataset into a sequence of word IDs.
4. Loop through the total dataset, 10 words at a time. Consider the 10 words as input and the subsequent 11th word as output.
5. Build and train a model, by performing embedding on top of the input word IDs and then connecting the embeddings to an LSTM, which is connected to the output layer through a hidden layer. The value in the output layer is the one-hot-encoded version of the output.
6. Make a prediction for the subsequent word by taking a random location of word and consider the historical words prior to the location of the random word chosen.
7. Move the window of the input words by one from the seed word's location that we chose earlier and the tenth time step word shall be the word that we predicted in the previous step.
8. Continue this process to keep generating text.

How to do it...

Typical to the need for RNN, we will look at a given sequence of 10 words to predict the next possible word. For this exercise, we will take the Alice dataset to generate words, as follows (the code file is available as `RNN_text_generation.ipynb` in GitHub):

1. Import the relevant packages and dataset:

```
from keras.models import Sequential
from keras.layers import Dense,Activation
from keras.layers.recurrent import SimpleRNN
from keras.layers import LSTM
import numpy as np
fin=open('alice.txt',encoding='utf-8-sig')
lines=[]
for line in fin:
    line = line.strip().lower()
    if(len(line)==0):
        continue
    lines.append(line)
fin.close()
text = " ".join(lines)
```

A sample of the input text looks as follows:

```
'her sister on the bank, and of having nothing to'
```

2. Normalize the text to remove punctuations and convert it to lowercase:

```
import re
text = text.lower()
text = re.sub('[^0-9a-zA-Z]+',' ',text)
```

3. Assign the unique words to an index so that they can be referenced when constructing the training and test datasets:

```
from collections import Counter
counts = Counter()
counts.update(text.split())
words = sorted(counts, key=counts.get, reverse=True)
nb_words = len(text.split())
word2index = {word: i for i, word in enumerate(words)}
index2word = {i: word for i, word in enumerate(words)}
```

4. Construct the input set of words that leads to an output word. Note that we are considering a sequence of 10 words and trying to predict the 11th word:

```
SEQLEN = 10
STEP = 1
input_words = []
label_words = []
text2=text.split()
for i in range(0,nb_words-SEQLEN,STEP):
    x=text2[i:(i+SEQLEN)]
    y=text2[i+SEQLEN]
    input_words.append(x)
    label_words.append(y)
```

A sample of the `input_words` and `label_words` lists is as follows:

```
input words list:
 ['alice', 'was', 'beginning', 'to', 'get', 'very', 'tired', 'of', 'sitting', 'by']
label(output) words list:
 her
```

Note that `input_words` is a list of lists and the `output_words` list is not.

Applications of a Many-to-One Architecture RNN

5. Construct the vectors of the input and the output datasets:

```
total_words = len(set(words))
X = np.zeros((len(input_words), SEQLEN, total_words),
dtype=np.bool)
y = np.zeros((len(input_words), total_words), dtype=np.bool)
```

We are creating empty arrays in the preceding step, which will be populated in the following code:

```
# Create encoded vectors for the input and output values
for i, input_word in enumerate(input_words):
    for j, word in enumerate(input_word):
        X[i, j, word2index[word]] = 1
    y[i,word2index[label_words[i]]]=1
```

In the preceding code, the first `for` loop is used to loop through all the words in the input sequence of words (`10` words in input), and the second `for` loop is used to loop through an individual word in the chosen sequence of input words. Additionally, given that the output is a list, we do not need to update it using the second `for` loop (as there is no sequence of IDs). The output shapes of X and y are as follows:

```
Shape of X:  (30407, 10, 3028)
Shape of y:  (30407, 3028)
```

6. Define the architecture of the model:

```
HIDDEN_SIZE = 128
BATCH_SIZE = 32
NUM_ITERATIONS = 100
NUM_EPOCHS_PER_ITERATION = 1
NUM_PREDS_PER_EPOCH = 100

model = Sequential()
model.add(LSTM(HIDDEN_SIZE,return_sequences=False,input_shape=(SEQL
EN,total_words)))
model.add(Dense(total_words, activation='softmax'))
model.compile(optimizer='adam', loss='categorical_crossentropy')
model.summary()
```

A summary of the model is as follows:

```
Layer (type)                 Output Shape              Param #
=================================================================
lstm_2 (LSTM)                (None, 128)               1616384
_____
dense_2 (Dense)              (None, 3028)              390612
=================================================================
Total params: 2,006,996
Trainable params: 2,006,996
Non-trainable params: 0
```

7. Fit the model. Look at how the output varies over an increasing number of epochs. Generate a random set of sequences of 10 words and try to predict the next possible word. We are in a position to observe how our predictions are getting better over an increasing number of epochs:

```
for iteration in range(50):
    print("=" * 50)
    print("Iteration #: %d" % (iteration))
    model.fit(X, y, batch_size=BATCH_SIZE,
epochs=NUM_EPOCHS_PER_ITERATION, validation_split = 0.1)
    test_idx = np.random.randint(int(len(input_words)*0.1)) * (-1)
    test_words = input_words[test_idx]
    print("Generating from seed: %s" % (test_words))
    for i in range(NUM_PREDS_PER_EPOCH):
        Xtest = np.zeros((1, SEQLEN, total_words))
        for i, ch in enumerate(test_words):
            Xtest[0, i, word2index[ch]] = 1
        pred = model.predict(Xtest, verbose=0)[0]
        ypred = index2word[np.argmax(pred)]
        print(ypred,end=' ')
        test_words = test_words[1:] + [ypred]
```

In the preceding code, we are fitting our model on input and output arrays for one epoch. Furthermore, we are choosing a random seed word (test_idx – which is a random number that is among the last 10% of the input array (as validation_split is 0.1) and are collecting the input words at a random location. We are converting the input sequence of IDs into a one-hot-encoded version (thus obtaining an array that is 1 x 10 x total_words in shape).

Applications of a Many-to-One Architecture RNN

Finally, we make a prediction on the array we just created and obtain the word that has the highest probability. Let's look at the output in the first epoch and contrast that with output in the 25th epoch:

```
Iteration #: 0
Train on 27366 samples, validate on 3041 samples
Epoch 1/1
27366/27366 [==============================] - 33s 1ms/step - loss: 6.2146 - val_loss: 8.2937
Generating from seed: ['not', 'met', 'the', 'solicitation', 'requirements', 'we', 'know', 'of', 'no', 'prohibition']
the the the the the the the the the the the the the the the the the the the the
```

Note that the output is always `the` in the first epoch. However, it becomes more reasonable as follows at the end of 50 epochs:

```
Iteration #: 49
Train on 27366 samples, validate on 3041 samples
Epoch 1/1
27366/27366 [==============================] - 35s 1ms/step - loss: 0.0066 - val_loss: 14.0219
Generating from seed: ['by', 'all', 'the', 'terms', 'of', 'this', 'agreement', 'you', 'must', 'cease']
like all all they they re from him at the march hare said the queen the words rabbit dropped the dormouse
```

The `Generating from seed` line is the collection of predictions.

Note that while the training loss decreased over increasing epochs, the validation loss has become worse by the end of 50 epochs. This will improve as we train on more text and/or further fine-tune our model.

Additionally, this model could further be improved by using a bidirectional LSTM, which we will discuss in *Sequence to Sequence learning* chapter. The output of having a bidirectional LSTM is as follows:

```
Iteration #: 48
Train on 27366 samples, validate on 3041 samples
Epoch 1/1
27366/27366 [==============================] - 58s 2ms/step - loss: 0.0422 - val_loss: 13.5398
Generating from seed: ['to', 'meet', 'and', 'keep', 'up', 'with', 'these', 'requirements', 'we', 'do']
with some time you were the hatter said was in a low voice which only taught us said the duchess and are
```

Movie recommendations

Recommendation systems play a major role in the discovery process for a user. Think of an e-commerce catalog that has thousands of distinct products. Additionally, variants of a product also exist. In such cases, educating the user about the products or events (in case certain products are on sale) becomes the key to increasing sales.

Getting ready

In this recipe, we will be learning about building a recommendation system for a database of ratings given by users to movies. The objective of the exercise is to maximize the relevance of a movie to a user. While defining the objective, we should also consider that a movie that is recommended might still be relevant, but might not be watched by the user immediately. At the same time, we should also ensure that all the recommendations are not about the same genre. This is especially applicable in the case of recommendations given out in a retail setting, where we do not want to be recommending the variants of the same product across all the recommendations we are providing.

Let's formalize our objective and constraints:

- **Objective**: Maximize the relevance of recommendations to a user
- **Constraint**: Increase the diversity of a recommendation and offer a maximum of 12 recommendations to the user

The definition of relevance can vary from use case to use case and is generally guided by the business principles. In this recipe, let's define relevance narrowly; that is, if the user buys any product that is in the top 12 recommended items for the given user, it is a success.

With this, let's go ahead and define the steps that we will adopt to build the model:

1. Import the data.
2. Recommend a movie that a user would rate highly—hence, let us train our model based on movies that a user liked in the history. The insight that a user disliked certain movies will be useful into further improving our recommendations. However, let's keep this simple for now.
3. Keep only the users who have watched more than five movies.
4. Assign IDs to unique users and movies.

5. Given that a user's preference might change over time, we need to consider the history of a user where different events in history have different weightages associated with them. Given that is a time series analysis problem now, we will leverage RNN to solve this problem.
6. Preprocess the data so that it can then passed to an LSTM:
   - The input will be the historical five movies watched by a user
   - The output is the sixth movie watched by a user
7. Build a model that does the following:
   1. Creates embeddings for the input movies
   2. Passes the embeddings through an LSTM layer
   3. Passes the LSTM output through a dense layer
   4. Apply softmax in final layer to come up with a list of movies to recommend

How to do it...

Now that we have gone through the strategy of various steps to perform, let's code it up (the code file is available as `Chapter_12_Recommender_systems.ipynb` in GitHub):

1. Import the data. We'll be working on a dataset that has the list of users, the ratings provided for different movies by a user, and the corresponding time stamp of when the user has provided the ratings:

   ```
   import numpy as np
   import pandas as pd
   ratings = pd.read_csv('..') # Path to the file containing required fields
   ```

   A sample of the dataset looks as follows:

User	Movies	rating	timestamp
1	100	5	1394496000
2	101	3	1395546000
3	100	5	1445578000

2. Filter out the data points where the user did not like the movie or the users where the user did not have enough history. In the following code, we are excluding the movies that users provided low ratings for:

```
ratings = ratings[ratings['rating']>3]
ratings = ratings.sort_values(by='timestamp')
ratings.reset_index(inplace=True)
ratings = ratings.drop(['index'],axis=1)
```

In the following code, we are keeping only those users who have more than 5 ratings (a rating value greater than 3) provided in the history:

```
user_movie_count
=ratings.groupby('User').agg({'Movies':'nunique'}).reset_index()
user_movie_count.columns = ['User','Movie_count']
ratings2 = ratings.merge(user_movie_count,on='User',how='inner')
movie_count = ratings2[ratings2['Movie_count']>5]
movie_count = movie_count.sort_values('timestamp')
movie_count.reset_index(inplace=True)
movie_count = movie_count.drop(['index'],axis=1)
```

3. Assign IDs to unique users and Movies so that we use them subsequently:

```
ratings = movie_count
users = ratings.User.unique()
articles = ratings.Movies.unique()
userid2idx = {o:i for i,o in enumerate(users)}
articlesid2idx = {o:i for i,o in enumerate(articles)}
idx2userid = {i:o for i,o in enumerate(users)}
idx2articlesid = {i:o for i,o in enumerate(articles)}

ratings['Movies2'] = ratings.Movies.apply(lambda x:
articlesid2idx[x])
ratings['User2'] = ratings.User.apply(lambda x: userid2idx[x])
```

4. Preprocess the data so that the input is the last five movies and the output is the sixth movie watched:

```
user_list = movie_count['User2'].unique()
historical5_watched = []
movie_to_predict = []
for i in range(len(user_list)):
    total_user_movies =
movie_count[movie_count['User2']==user_list[i]].copy()
    total_user_movies.reset_index(inplace=True)
    total_user_movies = total_user_movies.drop(['index'],axis=1)
    for j in range(total_user_movies.shape[0]-6):
historical5_watched.append(total_user_movies.loc[j:(j+4),'Movies2']
```

[397]

```
        .tolist())
    movie_to_predict.append(total_user_movies.loc[(j+5),'Movies2'].toli
    st())
```

5. Preprocess the `historical5_watched` and the `movie_to_predict` variables so that they can be passed to the model, and then create the train and test datasets:

```
movie_to_predict2 = to_categorical(y, num_classes = max(y)+1)
trainX = np.array(historical5_watched[:40000])
testX = np.array(historical5_watched[40000:])
trainY = np.array(movie_to_predict2[:40000])
testY = np.array(movie_to_predict2[40000:])
```

6. Build the model:

```
src_vocab = ratings['Movies2'].nunique()
n_units = 32
src_timesteps = 5
tar_vocab = len(set(y))

from keras.models import Sequential, Model
from keras.layers import Embedding
from keras.layers import LSTM, RepeatVector, TimeDistributed,
Dense, Bidirectional

model = Sequential()
model.add(Embedding(src_vocab, n_units,
input_length=src_timesteps))
model.add((LSTM(100)))
model.add(Dense(1000,activation='relu'))
model.add(Dense(max(y)+1,activation='softmax'))
model.summary()
```

Note that, in the final layer, we are adding 1 to the possible activations, as there is no movie with an ID of 0, and the final movie would have been left out had we just set the value to `max(y)`.

A summary of the model is as follows:

```
Layer (type)                 Output Shape              Param #
=================================================================
embedding_1 (Embedding)      (None, 5, 32)             46304
_____
lstm_1 (LSTM)                (None, 100)               53200
_____
dense_1 (Dense)              (None, 1000)              101000
_____
dense_2 (Dense)              (None, 1447)              1448447
=================================================================
Total params: 1,648,951
Trainable params: 1,648,951
Non-trainable params: 0
```

7. Fit the model:

   ```
   model.fit(trainX, trainY, epochs=5, batch_size=32,
   validation_data=(testX, testY), verbose = 1)
   ```

8. Make predictions on the test data:

   ```
   pred = model.predict(testX)
   ```

9. Understand the number of data points (users) where the movie watched next after the historical five movies is among the top 12 recommendations:

   ```
   count = 0
   for i in range(testX.shape[0]):
       rank = 
   np.argmax(np.argsort(pred[i])[::-1]==np.argmax(testY[i]))
       if rank<12:
           count+=1
   count/testX.shape[0]
   # 0.104
   ```

We should notice that in 10.4% of the total cases, we have the movie recommended being watched by the user as the immediate next movie.

Taking user history into consideration

One of the considerations when sending out the top 12 recommendations that we missed in the previous iteration is that *if a user has already watched a movie, they are less likely to watch the same movie again* (note that this hypothesis does not hold true in a retail setting, where there are a considerable amount of re-orders).

Let's go ahead and apply this logic in making our top 12 predictions.

First, we'll store all the (not just the most recent five) movies that were watched by a user prior to watching the movie that we are trying to predict:

```
historically_watched = []
for i in range(len(user_list)):
    total_user_movies = movie_count[movie_count['User2']==user_list[i]].copy()
    total_user_movies.reset_index(inplace=True)
    total_user_movies = total_user_movies.drop(['index'],axis=1)
    for j in range(total_user_movies.shape[0]-6):
        historically_watched.append(total_user_movies.loc[0:(j+4),'Movies2'].tolist())
```

In the preceding code, we are filtering all the movies watched by a user.

If a user has already watched a movie, we will overwrite the probability to a value of zero for that user-movie combination:

```
for j in range(pred.shape[0]):
  for i in range(pred.shape[1]):
     pred[j][i]= np.where(i in historically_watched[j], 0 , pred[j][i])
```

In the following code, we are calculating the percent of the total scenario in test data where the user watched a movie among the top 12 recommended movies:

```
count = 0
for i in range(testX.shape[0]):
  rank = np.argmax(np.argsort(pred[i])[::-1]==np.argmax(testY[i]))
  if rank<12:
    count+=1
count/testX.shape[0]
#12.6
```

The preceding results in the recommendations being valid for 12.6% of total users now, up from 10.4% relevance in the previous iteration.

Topic-modeling, using embeddings

In the previous recipe, we learned about generating predictions for movies that a user is likely to watch. One of the limitations of the previous way of generating predictions is that the variety of movie recommendations would be limited if we did not perform further processing on top of the movie predictions.

A variety of recommendations is important; if there were no variety, only certain types of products would be discovered by users.

In this recipe, we will group movies based on their similarity and identify the common themes of the movies. Additionally, we will also look into how we can increase the variety of recommendations that can be provided to a user. Having said that, it is highly likely that this strategy will work less in the specific case of movie recommendations, as the variety would be much lower when compared to a retail/e-commerce setting, where the number of categories and substitutes of a product are much higher when compared to movies.

Getting ready

The strategy that we will adopt to group movies based on similarity is as follows:

1. Extract the embedding value of each movie from the model that we built in the Movie recommendations recipe
    - We can also create embeddings for each movie using gensim
    - All the movies watched by a user can be thought of as words in a sentence
    - Create a list of lists of word IDs that form a sentence
    - Pass the list of lists through the `Word2Vec` method of gensim to extract the word vectors (movie ID vectors)
2. Pass the embedded values (vectors) of movies through a k-means clustering process to extract a certain number of clusters
3. Identify the optimal number of clusters
4. Identify the high probability to buy products (among the products that were not bought in history) in each cluster and re-rank the products based on their probability
5. Recommend the top *n* products

In this process, one of the variables is the number of clusters to be formed. The greater the number of clusters, the fewer the products in each cluster, and, at the same time, the greater the similarity between each product within a cluster. Essentially, there is a trade-off between the number of points in a group and the similarity of data points within the same cluster.

We can come up with a measure of the similarity of points within a group by calculating the sum of the squared distances of all points with respect to their cluster centers. The number of clusters beyond which the inertia metric does not decrease considerably is the optimal number of clusters.

How to do it...

Now that we have formed a strategy of fetching a variety of products within our recommendation, let's code it up (We'll continue from step 3 of *Movie recommendations* recipe). The code file is available as `Chapter_12_Recommender_systems.ipynb` in GitHub.

1. Extract the embedding values of each movie using `Word2Vec`.
   1. Create a list of lists of various movies watched by all users:

      ```
      user_list = movie_count['User2'].unique()
      user_movies = []
      for i in range(len(user_list)):
          total_user_movies = movie_count[movie_count['User2']==user_list[i]].copy()
          total_user_movies.reset_index(inplace=True)
          total_user_movies = total_user_movies.drop(['index'],axis=1)
          total_user_movies['Movies3'] = total_user_movies['Movies2'].astype(str)
          user_movies.append(total_user_movies['Movies3'].tolist())
      ```

      In the preceding code, we are filtering all the movies watched by a user and creating a list of movies watched by all users.

2. Extract the word vectors of each movie:

   ```
   from gensim.models import Word2Vec
   w2v_model = Word2Vec(user_movies,size=100,window=5,min_count=5, iter = 500)
   ```

4. Extract the `TSNE` values of the movies to have a visual representation of the word embeddings of the movies that we extracted in previous step:

   ```
   from sklearn.manifold import TSNE
   tsne_model = TSNE(n_components=2, verbose=1, random_state=0)
   tsne_img_label = tsne_model.fit_transform(w2v_model.wv.syn0)
   tsne_df = pd.DataFrame(tsne_img_label, columns=['x', 'y'])
   tsne_df['image_label'] = list(w2v_model.wv.vocab.keys())

   from ggplot import *
   chart = ggplot(tsne_df, aes(x='x', y='y'))+geom_point(size=70,alpha=0.5)
   chart
   ```

A visualization of embeddings in 2-Dimensional space is as follows:

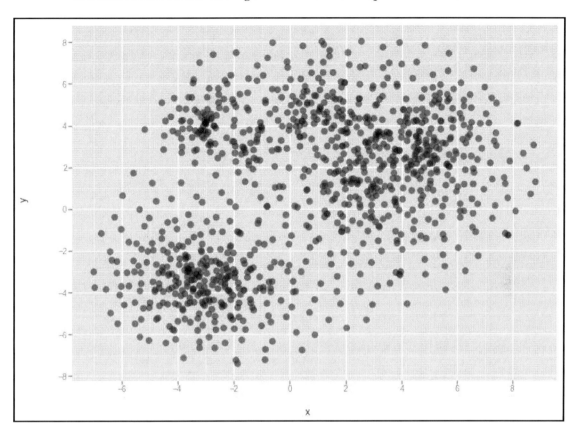

From the preceding output, we can see that there are clusters of movies that are grouped together (the regions that are thick).

5. Store the movie ID and movie index values in a dataframe:

```
idx2movie = pd.DataFrame([idx2moviesid.keys(),
idx2moviesid.values()]).T
idx2movie.columns = ['image_label','movieId']
```

6. Merge the `tsne_df` and `idx2movie` datasets so that we have all the values in a single dataframe:

   ```
   tsne_df['image_label'] = tsne_df['image_label'].astype(int)
   tsne_df2 = pd.merge(tsne_df, idx2movie, on='image_label',
   how='right')
   ```

7. Import the `movies` dataset:

   ```
   movies = pd.read_csv('...') # Path to movies dataset
   ```

8. Merge the TSNE dataset with the movies data, and drop the unwanted columns:

   ```
   tsne_df3 = pd.merge(tsne_df2, movies, left_on='movieId', right_on =
   0, how='inner')
   tsne_df4 = tsne_df3.drop([2,3,4],axis=1)
   tsne_df4.rename(columns={1:'movie_name'}, inplace=True)
   ```

9. Exclude the rows that have an NaN value (we have null values for certain movies, as certain movies occur less frequently, resulting in `Word2Vec` not giving the word vector for rarely occurring words (due to the `min_count` parameter):

   ```
   tsne_df5 = tsne_df4.loc[~np.isnan(tsne_df4['x']),]
   ```

10. Identify the optimal number of clusters by understanding the variation of inertia (total sum of squared distance of all points from their respective cluster centers):

    ```
    X = tsne_df5.loc[:,['x','y']]
    inertia = []
    for i in range(10):
        km = KMeans((i+1)*10)
        km.fit(X)
        inertia.append(km.inertia_)

    import matplotlib.pyplot as plt
    %matplotlib inline
    plt.plot((np.arange(10)+1)*10,inertia)
    plt.title('Variation of inertia over different number of clusters')
    plt.xlabel('Number of clusters')
    plt.ylabel('Inertia')
    ```

The variation of inertia for different number of clusters is as follows:

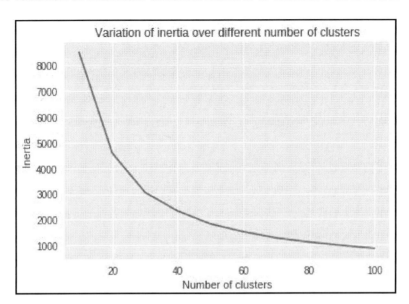

From the preceding curve, we can see that the decrease is inertia not as high as the number of clusters passes 40. Hence, we shall have 40 as the optimal number of clusters of movies within our dataset.

11. Validate the cluster results by manually checking for some of the movies that fall in the same cluster, if it makes sense for the movies to be in the same cluster:

    ```
    km = KMeans(40)
    km.fit(X)
    tsne_df5['clusterlabel'] = km.labels
    tsne_df5[tsne_df5['cluster_label']==0].head()
    ```

    Once you execute the code, you will notice that movies located in cluster_label: 0 are primarily Romance and Comedy movies.

12. Remove the movies that have already been watched by the user:

    ```
    for j in range(pred.shape[0]):
        for i in range(pred.shape[1]):
            pred[j][i]= np.where(i in historically_watched[j], 0 ,
    pred[j][i])
    ```

13. For each user, map the probability of a movie and the cluster number that a movie belongs to so that we extract the movie that has the highest probability within a cluster for a given user. Then recommend the top 12 movies from the resulting top movies within different clusters:

```
movie_cluster_id = tsne_df5[['image_label','cluster_label']]
count = 0
for j in range(pred.shape[0]):
    t = movie_cluster_id.copy()
    t['pred']=pred[j,list(movie_cluster_id['image_label'])]
    t2= t.sort_values(by='pred',ascending=False).groupby('cluster_label').first().reset_index()
    t3 = t2.sort_values(by='pred',ascending=False).reset_index()
    final_top_preds = t3.loc[:11]['image_label'].values
    if (np.argmax(testY[j]) in final_top_preds):
        count+=1
```

The preceding results in 13.6% of all users watching a movie that is recommended to them.

While the preceding results are only slightly better than the result of 12.6% without having any variety in recommendations, having a variety in recommendations is more likely to be better when we consider not just the next purchase but all future purchases by a user.

There's more...

While we have looked into generating predictions for a user and also into increasing the variety of predictions that are served to a user, we can further improve the results by considering the following:

- Incorporating the information about the movies the user did not like
- Incorporating the user's demographic information
- Incorporating the details related to the movie, for example the release year and the cast

Forecasting the value of a stock's price

There is a variety of technical analysis that experts perform to come up with buy-and-sell recommendations on stocks. The majority of the technical analysis relies on historical patterns with an assumption that history repeats as long as we normalize for certain events.

Given that what we have been performing so far has also been about making decisions by considering history, let's go ahead and apply the skills we've learned so far to predict the price of a stock.

However, be extremely careful when relying on algorithmic analysis in applications such as stock-price prediction to make a buy-or-sell decision. The big difference between the other recipes and this one is that, while the decisions made in other recipes are reversible (for example: you can revoke it if a generated text does not look appropriate) or cost money (a bad recommendation means the customer won't buy the product again), the decisions made in stock-price prediction are irreversible. Once the money is lost, it is not coming back.

With this in mind, let's go ahead and apply the techniques we've learned so far to predict the price of a stock.

Getting ready

To predict the price of a stock, let's apply two strategies:

- Predict the stock price solely based on the last five days' stock prices
- Predict the stock price based on a combination of the last five days' stock prices and the latest news about the company of interest

For the first analysis, we can prepare the dataset in a way that is very similar to the way we prepared the dataset for LSTM; the second analysis will require a different way of preparing the dataset, as it involves both numeric and text data.

The way in which we will process data for the two approaches discussed above is as follows:

- **Last five days' stock prices only**:
    1. Order the dataset from the oldest to the newest date
    2. Take the first 5 stock prices as input and the sixth stock price as output
    3. Slide it across so that in the next data point, the second to sixth data points are the input and the seventh data point is the output, and so on until we reach the final data point:
        1. Each of the five data points are the input to the five time steps in an LSTM
        2. The sixth data point is the output
    4. Given that we are predicting a continuous number, the loss function this time will be the *mean squared error* value

- **Last five days' stock prices plus news headlines, data about the company**: For this analysis, there are two types of data preprocessing. While the data preprocessing for the last five days' stock prices remains the same, the data pre-preparation step for the news headlines, data is the additional step that is to be performed in this analysis. Let's look into how we can incorporate both of them into our model:
    1. Given that these are two data types, let's have two different models:
        - One model that takes historical five-day stock-price data.
        - Another model that modifies the output of the last five days' stock-price model by either increasing or decreasing the output.
        - The second model is a result of the news headlines, dataset. The hypothesis is that positive headlines are likely to increase the stock price value and that negative headlines will reduce the stock value.
    2. To keep the problem simple, assume that only the most recent headline prior to the day of the prediction of the stock's value will have an impact on the outcome of the stock value on the day of prediction
    3. Given that we have two different models, use the functional API so that we combine the effects of both factors

How to do it...

We'll break our approach of solving this into three sections (The code file is available as `Chapter_12_stock_price_prediction.ipynb` in GitHub):

- Predict a stock price based on the last five days' stock prices only
    - The pitfall of the random train-and-test split
- Assign a higher weight to more recent stock price values
- Combine the last five days' stock price with text data of news article headlines

The last five days' stock prices only

In this recipe, we will predict a stock price based on its last 5 data points only. In the next recipe, we will predict the stock price based on news and historical data:

1. Import the relevant packages and dataset:

   ```
   import pandas as pd
   data2 = pd.read_csv('/content/stock_data.csv')
   ```

2. Prepare the dataset where the input is the last five days' stock-price values and the output is the stock-price value on the sixth day:

   ```
   x= []
   y = []
   for i in range(data2.shape[0]-5):
       x.append(data2.loc[i:(i+4)]['Close'].values)
       y.append(data2.loc[i+5]['Close'])

   import numpy as np
   x = np.array(x)
   y = np.array(y)
   ```

3. Reshape the dataset so that it is of the `batch_size, time_steps, features_per_time_step` form:

   ```
   x = x.reshape(x.shape[0],x.shape[1],1)
   ```

4. Create the train-and-test datasets:

   ```
   from sklearn.model_selection import train_test_split
   X_train, X_test, y_train, y_test = train_test_split(x, y, test_size=0.30,random_state=10)
   ```

5. Build the model:

   ```
   model = Sequential()
   model.add(Dense(100, input_shape = (5,1), activation = 'relu'))
   model.add((LSTM(100)))
   model.add(Dense(1000,activation='relu'))
   model.add(Dense(1,activation='linear'))
   model.summary()
   ```

A summary of the model is as follows:

```
Layer (type)                 Output Shape              Param #
=================================================================
dense_1 (Dense)              (None, 5, 100)            200
_____
lstm_1 (LSTM)                (None, 100)               80400
_____
dense_2 (Dense)              (None, 1000)              101000
_____
dense_3 (Dense)              (None, 1)                 1001
=================================================================
Total params: 182,601
Trainable params: 182,601
Non-trainable params: 0
```

6. Compile the model so that we define the `loss` function and adjust the learning-rate value:

   ```
   from keras.optimizers import Adam
   adam = Adam(lr=0.0001)
   model.compile(optimizer=adam, loss='mean_squared_error')
   ```

7. Fit the model:

   ```
   model.fit(X_train, y_train, epochs=400, batch_size=64,
   validation_data=(X_test, y_test), verbose = 1)
   ```

The preceding results in a mean squared error value of $641 (An average of ~$25 per prediction) on the test dataset. The plot of the predicted versus actual stock price is as follows:

```
pred = model.predict(X_test)

import matplotlib.pyplot as plt
%matplotlib inline
plt.figure(figsize=(20,10))
plt.plot(y_test,'r')
plt.plot(pred,'--')

plt.title('Variation of actual and predicted stock price')
plt.ylabel('Stock price')
```

The variation of the predicted and the actual price is as follows:

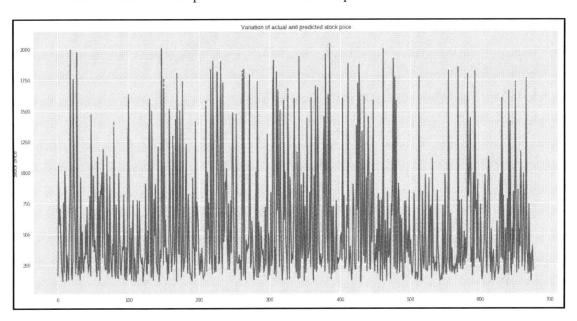

The pitfalls

Now that we have predictions that are fairly accurate, and in fact, good predictions, let's dive deep to understand the reason for such good predictions.

In our training dataset, we have data points from a long time ago as well as the data points that are very recent. This is a form of leakage, as, at the time of model building, we do not have future stock prices. Due to the way we construct data, we could have the data from December 20 in our training dataset, while December 19 could be in the test dataset.

Let's rebuild our model with the training-and-test datasets demarcated by their corresponding dates:

```
X_train = x[:2100,:,:]
y_train = y[:2100]
X_test = x[2100:,:,:]
y_test = y[2100:]
```

Applications of a Many-to-One Architecture RNN

The output of the model that we built in the *last 5 days' stock prices only* section on the new test dataset is as follows (with a test dataset loss of ~57,000):

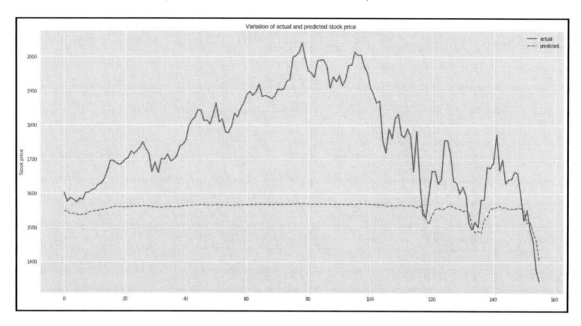

Note that the resulting actual versus predicted stock-price graph now is much worse when compared to the previous iteration. However, the graph generated in this section is a more realistic scenario data than the graph obtained in *last 5 days' stock prices only* section.

Now that we have obtained the preceding graph, let's try to understand the reason the graph might have looked as it did by examining the plot of the variation of stock-price data over time, which is as follows:

```
plt.plot(data2['Close'])
```

A plot of the variation of the stock-price over time is as follows:

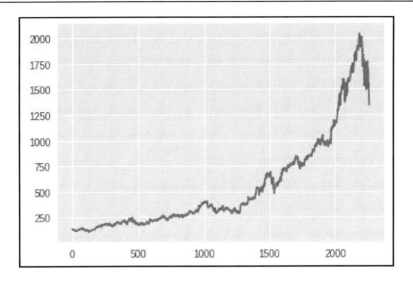

Note that the price of stock increased slowly at the start and accelerated in the middle while decelerating at the end.

The model did not work out well for the following reasons:

- Equal weight is given to errors for predictions made much earlier in the history as well as more recent ones
- We didn't factor for the trend in deceleration

Assigning different weights to different time periods

We learned that we will be assigning higher weight for the most recent time period and a lower weight for historical time periods.

We can come up with training `weights` as follows:

```
weights = np.arange(X_train.shape[0]).reshape((X_train.shape[0]),1)/2100
```

The preceding code assigns a weight of 0 to the most historical data point and a weight of 1 to the most recent data point. All the intermediate data points will have a weight value between 0 and 1.

Now that we have defined `weights`, let's define our custom loss function, which applies the previously-initialized losses while calculating the squared error loss:

```
import numpy as np
from keras.layers import Dense, Input
from keras import Model
import keras.backend as K
from functools import partial

def custom_loss(y_true, y_pred, weights):
    return K.square(K.abs(y_true - y_pred) * weights)
cl = partial(custom_loss, weights=weights_tensor)
```

Now that we have initialized `weights` and also defined the custom loss function, let's supply the input layer and the weight values to the model using the functional API (we are using a functional API as we are passing multiple input while training the model):

```
input_layer = Input(shape=(5,1))
weights_tensor = Input(shape=(1,))

i1 = Dense(100, activation='relu')(input_layer)
i2 = LSTM(100)(i1)
i3 = Dense(1000, activation='relu')(i2)
out = Dense(1, activation='linear')(i3)
model = Model([input_layer, weights_tensor], out)
```

Now that we have defined the model, which has the same parameters as in the *last 5 days' stock prices only* section, but there is an additional input, which is the weights tensor. Let's compile our model:

```
from keras.optimizers import Adam
adam = Adam(lr=0.0001)
model = Model([input_layer, weights_tensor], out)
model.compile(adam, cl)
```

Now that we have compiled our model, let's fit it:

```
model.fit(x=[X_train, weights], y=y_train, epochs=300,batch_size = 32,
validation_data = ([X_test, test_weights], y_test))
```

The model returns a squared error loss of 40,000 on the test dataset, as opposed to the loss of 57,000 from the *The pitfalls* section. Let's plot the values of predicted versus actual stock prices on the test dataset:

Chapter 12

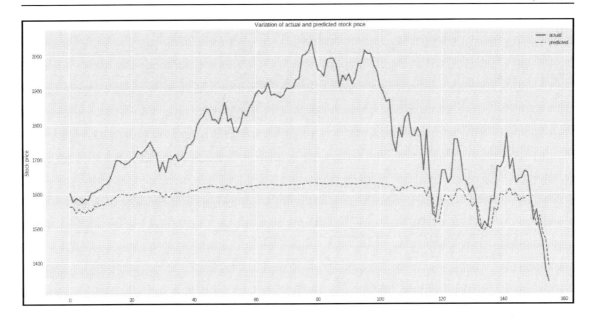

We now notice that there is a correlation between the predicted and the actual stock price in the most recent history (right-most part of the chart), while the spike in the middle of graph is not being accounted for in the predictions.

In the next recipe, let's see whether the news headlines can incorporate the spike in middle.

The last five days' stock prices plus news data

In the following code, we will incorporate text data about the headlines generated by the company of interest (which is fetched from the open source API provided by the Guardian's website) along with the last five days' stock price data. Then we'll couple the custom loss function, which takes the recency of an event into account:

1. Import the headlines data from the Guardian website from here: https://open-platform.theguardian.com/ (note that you would have to apply for your own access key to be able to download the dataset from the website). Download the title and the corresponding date when the title appeared, and then preprocess the date so that it is converted into a date format:

```
from bs4 import BeautifulSoup
from bs4 import BeautifulSoup
import urllib, json

dates = []
```

Applications of a Many-to-One Architecture RNN

```
titles = []
for i in range(100):
 try:
        url =
'https://content.guardianapis.com/search?from-date=2010-01-01&secti
on=business&page-          size=200&order-
by=newest&page='+str(i+1)+'&q=amazon&api-key=0d7'
        response = urllib.request.urlopen(url)
        encoding = response.info().get_content_charset('utf8')
        data = json.loads(response.read().decode(encoding))
        print(i)
        for j in range(len(data['response']['results'])):
dates.append(data['response']['results'][j]['webPublicationDate'])
titles.append(data['response']['results'][j]['webTitle'])
 except:
        break


import pandas as pd
data = pd.DataFrame(dates, titles)
data = data.reset_index()
data.columns = ['title','date']
data['date']=data['date'].str[:10]
data['date']=pd.to_datetime(data['date'], format = '%Y-%m-%d')
data = data.sort_values(by='date')
data_final = data.groupby('date').first().reset_index()
```

2. Join the historical price dataset and the article title dataset by `Date`:

   ```
   data2['Date'] = pd.to_datetime(data2['Date'],format='%Y-%m-%d')
   data3 = pd.merge(data2,data_final, left_on = 'Date', right_on =
   'date', how='left')
   ```

3. Preprocess the text data to remove the stop-words and punctuation, and then encode the text input just as we did in the sentiment-classification exercise in `Chapter 11`, *Building a Recurrent Neural Network*:

   ```
   import nltk
   import re
   nltk.download('stopwords')
   stop = nltk.corpus.stopwords.words('english')
   def preprocess(text):
       text = str(text)
       text=text.lower()
       text=re.sub('[^0-9a-zA-Z]+',' ',text)
       words = text.split()
       words2=[w for w in words if (w not in stop)]
       words3=' '.join(words2)
   ```

```
        return(words3)
data3['title'] = data3['title'].apply(preprocess)
data3['title']=np.where(data3['title'].isnull(),'-','-
'+data3['title'])
docs = data3['title'].values
from collections import Counter
counts = Counter()
for i,review in enumerate(docs):
    counts.update(review.split())
words = sorted(counts, key=counts.get, reverse=True)
vocab_size=len(words)
word_to_int = {word: i for i, word in enumerate(words, 1)}
encoded_docs = []
for doc in docs:
    encoded_docs.append([word_to_int[word] for word in
doc.split()])
max_length = 20
from keras.preprocessing.sequence import pad_sequences
padded_docs = pad_sequences(encoded_docs,
maxlen=max_length,padding='pre')
```

4. Take the last five days' stock prices and the most recent title (prior to the date of the stock-price prediction) as input. Let's preprocess our data to get the input and the output values and then prepare the training and test datasets:

   In the following code, x1 corresponds to the historical stock prices and x2 corresponds to the article title on the date of the stock prediction:

   ```
   x1 = []
   x2 = []
   y = []
   for i in range(data3.shape[0]-5):
       x1.append(data3.loc[i:(i+4)]['Close'].values)
       x2.append(padded_docs[i+5])
       y.append(data3.loc[i+5]['Close'])
   
   x1 = np.array(x1)
   x2 = np.array(x2)
   y = np.array(y)
   x1 = x1.reshape(x1.shape[0],x1.shape[1],1)
   X1_train = x1[:2100,:,:]
   X2_train = x2[:2100,:]
   y_train = y[:2100]
   
   X1_test = x1[2100:,:,:]
   X2_test = x2[2100:,:]
   y_test = y[2100:]
   ```

5. Given that we are passing multiple variables as input (historical stock prices, encoded text data, and weight values), we will be using functional API to build the model:

```
input1 = Input(shape=(20,))
model = Embedding(input_dim=vocab_size+1, output_dim=32, input_length=20)(input1)
model = (LSTM(units=100))(model)
model = (Dense(1, activation='tanh'))(model)

input2 = Input(shape=(5,1))
model2 = Dense(100, activation='relu')(input2)
model2 = LSTM(units=100)(model2)
model2 = (Dense(1000, activation="relu"))(model2)
model2 = (Dense(1, activation="linear"))(model2)

from keras.layers import multiply
conc = multiply([model, model2])
conc2 = (Dense(1000, activation="relu"))(conc)
out = (Dense(1, activation="linear"))(conc2)
```

Note that we have multiplied the output values of the stock-price model and the text-data model, as the text data is expected to adjust to the output of the historical stock-price model:

```
model = Model([input1, input2, weights_tensor], out)
```

The architecture of the preceding model is as follows:

Chapter 12

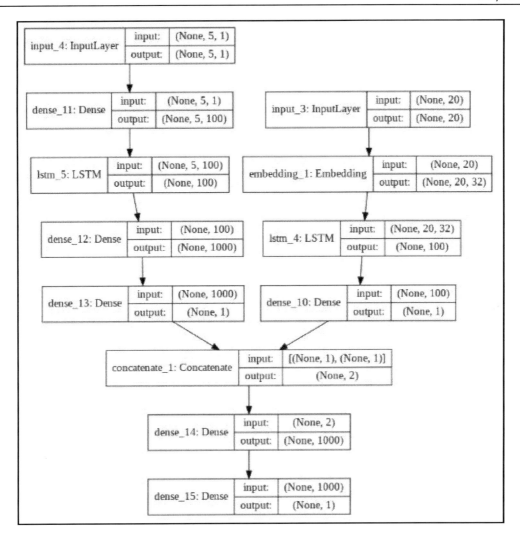

6. Define the loss function and compile the model:

```
def custom_loss(y_true, y_pred, weights):
  return K.square(K.abs(y_true - y_pred) * weights)
cl = partial(custom_loss, weights=weights_tensor)

model = Model([input1, input2, weights_tensor], out)
model.compile(adam, cl)
```

7. Fit the model:

```
model.fit(x=[X2_train, X1_train, weights], y=y_train,
epochs=300,batch_size = 32, validation_data = ([X2_test, X1_test,
test_weights], y_test))
```

8. Plot the actual versus predicted values of stock prices in the test dataset:

```
pred = model.predict([X2_test, X1_test, test_weights])

import matplotlib.pyplot as plt
%matplotlib inline
plt.figure(figsize=(20,10))
plt.plot(y_test,'r',label='actual')
plt.plot(pred,'--', label = 'predicted')
plt.title('Variation of actual and predicted stock price')
plt.ylabel('Stock price')
plt.legend()
```

The variation of actual and predicted stock price is as follows:

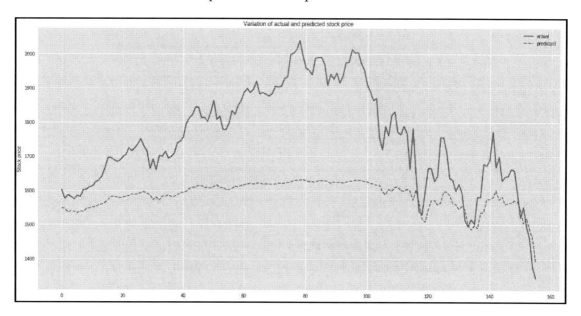

Note that, in this iteration, the middle portion has a slightly better slope when compared to the no-text data version and also has a slightly lower squared error at 35,000 when compared to the 40,000 value of the previous iteration.

There's more...

As mentioned at the start of this recipe, be extremely careful when predicting the values of a stock price, as there are a variety of factors that can affect the movement of stock prices, and all of them need to be taken into consideration when making a prediction.

Additionally, you should also notice that while the actual and predicted values seem correlated, there is a small delay in the predicted values line when compared to the actual values line. This delay can considerably change the optimal strategy from a buy decision to a sell decision. Hence, there should be a greater weight for the rows where the movement of a stock price is significant from the previous date—further complicating our loss function.

We could also potentially incorporate more sources of information, such as additional news headlines and seasonality (for example: certain stocks typically fare well during the holiday season) and other macroeconomic factors, when making the predictions.

Finally, we could have scaled the dataset so that the input to the neural network is not a huge number.

13
Sequence-to-Sequence Learning

In the previous chapters, we learned about RNN applications, where there are multiple inputs (one each in each time step) and a single output. However, there are a few more applications where there are multiple inputs, and also multiple time steps—machine translation for example, where there are multiple input words in a source sentence and multiple output words in the target sentence. Given the multiple inputs and multiple outputs, this becomes a multi-output RNN-based application—essentially, a sequence to sequence learning task. This calls for building our model architecture differently to what we have built so far, which we will learn about in this chapter. In this chapter, we are going to learn about the following:

- Returning sequences from a network
- How bidirectional LSTM helps in named entity extraction
- Extract intent and entities to build a chatbot
- Functioning of an encoder decoder network architecture
- Translating a sentence form English to French using encoder decoder architecture
- Improving the translations by using an attention mechanism

Introduction

In the previous chapters, we learned that the LSTM, or even the RNN, returns results from the last time step (hidden state values from the last time step are passed on to the next layer). Imagine a scenario where the output is five dimensions in size where the five dimensions are the five outputs (not softmax values for five classes). To further explain this idea, let's say we are predicting, not just the stock price on the next date, but the stock prices for the next five days. Or, we want to predict not just the next word, but a sequence of the next five words for a given combination of input sequence.

This situation calls for a different approach in building the network. In the following section, we will look into multiple scenarios of building a network to extract the outputs in different time steps.

Scenario 1: Named entity extraction

In named entity extraction, we are trying to assign a label for each word that is present in a sentence—whether it is related to a person or place or not. Hence, it becomes a problem of one-to-one mapping between the input word and the output classes of it being a name or not. While it is a one-to-one mapping between input and output, there are cases where surrounding words play a role in deciding whether the considered input(s) is a named entity or not. For example, the word *new* in itself might not be a named entity. However, if *new* is accompanied by *york*, then we know that it is a named entity. Thus, it is a problem where the input time steps play a role in determining whether a word is a named entity or not, even though in a majority of the cases, there might exist a one-to-one mapping between inputs and outputs.

Additionally, this is a sequence returning problem as we are assigning the output sequence of the named entity or not based on the input sequence of words. Given that, this is a problem where there is a one-to-one connection between inputs, and also the inputs in surrounding time steps playing a key role in determining the output. The traditional LSTM we have learned about so far would work, as long as we are ensuring that words in both directions of the time step influence the output. Thus, a bidirectional LSTM comes in handy in solving such problems.

The architecture of a bidirectional LSTM looks as follows:

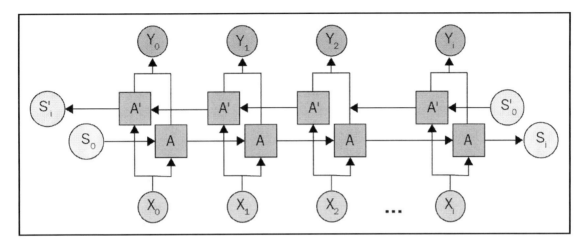

Note that, in the preceding diagram, we have modified the traditional LSTM by having the inputs connecting to each other in the opposite direction too, and thus, ensuring that information flows from both directions. We will learn more about how bidirectional LSTM works and how it is to be applied in a later section.

Scenario 2: Text summarization

A text summarization task would require a different architecture to what we discussed previously as we would typically be in a position to generate a summary from text only after finishing reading the whole of the input sentence (input text/review in this case).

This calls for encoding all the input into a vector, and then generating output based on the encoded vector of input. Additionally, given that there are multiple outputs (multiple words) for a given sequence of words in a text, it becomes a multi output generation problem, and thus, another scenario that can leverage the multi-input multi-output power of an RNN.

Sequence-to-Sequence Learning

Let's look at how we can potentially architect the model to arrive at a solution:

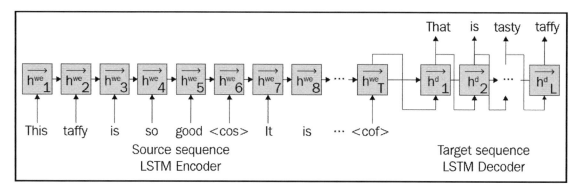

Note that, in the preceding architecture, we encode all the input text into the vector that is produced at the ending word of the input sequence, and that encoded vector is passed as an input to the decoder sequence. More information on how to build this network will be provided in a later section of this chapter.

Scenario 3: Machine translation

In the previous scenario, we encoded the input into a vector, and hopefully, the vector also incorporates the word order. But, what if we explicitly provide a mechanism through a network where the network is able to assign a different weightage of an input word located at a given position, depending on the position of the word we are decoding? For example, if the source and target words are aligned similarly, that is, both languages have similar word order, then the word that comes at the start of source language has very little impact on the last word of target language, but has a very high impact in deciding the first word in the target language.

Attention mechanism looks as follows:

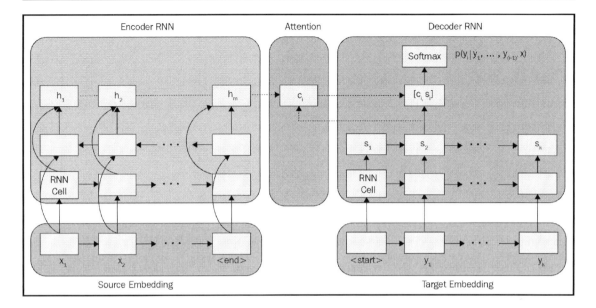

Note that the attention vector (in the middle) is influenced by both the input encoded vector and the hidden state of output values. More on how the attention mechanism can be leveraged will be discussed in a .

With this intuition of the reasons for different encoder decoder architectures, let's dive into understanding more about generating sequences of outputs in Keras.

Returning sequences of outputs from a network

As we discussed in the previous section, there are multiple ways of architecting a network to generate sequences of outputs. In this section, we will learn about the encoder decoder way of generating outputs, and also about the one-to-one mapping of inputs to outputs network on a toy dataset so that we have a strong understanding of how this works.

Let's define a sequence of inputs and a corresponding sequence of outputs, as follows (the code file is available as `Return_state_and_sequences_working_details.ipynb` in GitHub):

```
input_data = np.array([[1,2],[3,4]])
output_data = np.array([[3,4],[5,6]])
```

Sequence-to-Sequence Learning

We can see that there are two time steps in an input and that there is a corresponding output to the input.

If we were to solve this problem in a traditional way, we would define the model architecture as in the following code. Note that we are using a functional API as in the later scenario, we will be extracting multiple outputs, along with inspecting intermediate layers:

```
# define model
inputs1 = Input(shape=(2,1))
lstm1 = LSTM(1, activation = 'tanh',
return_sequences=False,recurrent_initializer='Zeros',recurrent_activation='sigmoid')(inputs1)
out= Dense(2, activation='linear')(lstm1)
model = Model(inputs=inputs1, outputs=out)
model.summary()
```

```
Layer (type)                 Output Shape              Param #
=================================================================
input_9 (InputLayer)         (None, 2, 1)              0
_____
lstm_9 (LSTM)                (None, 1)                 12
_____
dense_8 (Dense)              (None, 2)                 4
=================================================================
Total params: 16
Trainable params: 16
Non-trainable params: 0
```

Note that, in the preceding scenario, the LSTM is fed data that is of the shape (`batch_size`, time steps, features per time step). Given that the LSTM is not returning a sequence of outputs, the output of the LSTM is one value at the hidden layer (as the number of units in the LSTM is one).

Given that the output is two dimensional, we shall add a dense layer that takes the hidden layer output and extracts 2 values from it.

Let's go ahead and fit the model, as follows:

```
model.compile(optimizer='adam',loss='mean_squared_error')
model.fit(input_data.reshape(2,2,1), output_data,epochs=1000)

print(model.predict(input_data[0].reshape(1,2,1)))
# [[2.079641 1.8290598]]
```

Now that we have the output, let's go ahead and validate the results as we did in previous chapter (note that, this is exactly the same code as what we had in the previous chapter—and the explanations of it are provided in the *Building an LSTM from scratch in Python* section of `Chapter 11`, *Building a Recurrent Neural Network*):

```
input_t0 = 1
cell_state0 = 0
forget0 = input_t0*model.get_weights()[0][0][1] + model.get_weights()[2][1]
forget1 = 1/(1+np.exp(-(forget0)))
cell_state1 = forget1 * cell_state0
input_t0_1 = input_t0*model.get_weights()[0][0][0] +
model.get_weights()[2][0]
input_t0_2 = 1/(1+np.exp(-(input_t0_1)))
input_t0_cell1 = input_t0*model.get_weights()[0][0][2] +
model.get_weights()[2][2]
input_t0_cell2 = np.tanh(input_t0_cell1)
input_t0_cell3 = input_t0_cell2*input_t0_2
input_t0_cell4 = input_t0_cell3 + cell_state1
output_t0_1 = input_t0*model.get_weights()[0][0][3] +
model.get_weights()[2][3]
output_t0_2 = 1/(1+np.exp(-output_t0_1))
hidden_layer_1 = np.tanh(input_t0_cell4)*output_t0_2

input_t1 = 2
cell_state1 = input_t0_cell4
forget21 = hidden_layer_1*model.get_weights()[1][0][1] +
model.get_weights()[2][1] + input_t1*model.get_weights()[0][0][1]
forget_22 = 1/(1+np.exp(-(forget21)))
cell_state2 = cell_state1 * forget_22
input_t1_1 = input_t1*model.get_weights()[0][0][0] +
model.get_weights()[2][0] + hidden_layer_1*model.get_weights()[1][0][0]
input_t1_2 = 1/(1+np.exp(-(input_t1_1)))
input_t1_cell1 = input_t1*model.get_weights()[0][0][2] +
model.get_weights()[2][2]+ hidden_layer_1*model.get_weights()[1][0][2]
input_t1_cell2 = np.tanh(input_t1_cell1)
input_t1_cell3 = input_t1_cell2*input_t1_2
input_t1_cell4 = input_t1_cell3 + cell_state2
output_t1_1 = input_t1*model.get_weights()[0][0][3] +
model.get_weights()[2][3]+ hidden_layer_1*model.get_weights()[1][0][3]
output_t1_2 = 1/(1+np.exp(-output_t1_1))
hidden_layer_2 = np.tanh(input_t1_cell4)*output_t1_2
final_output = hidden_layer_2 * model.get_weights()[3][0] +
model.get_weights()[4]
```

Sequence-to-Sequence Learning

The output of `final_output` is as follows:

```
[[2.079 1.829]]
```

You should note that the preceding `final_output` that is generated is exactly the same as what we saw in the `model.predict` output.

One of the drawbacks of generating output this way is that, in cases where the output of time *step 1* is definitely not dependent on time *step 2*, we are making it hard for the model to come up with a way of segregating the influence of time *step 2* value on time *step 1* as we are taking the hidden layer output from time *step 2* (which is a combination of input value at time *step 1* and time *step 2*).

We can get around this problem by extracting hidden layer values from each time step and then passing it to the dense layer.

Returning sequences of hidden layer values at each time step

In the following code, we will understand how returning sequences of hidden layer values at each time step works:

```
# define model
inputs1 = Input(shape=(2,1))
lstm1 = LSTM(1, activation = 'tanh',
return_sequences=False,recurrent_initializer='Zeros',recurrent_activation='sigmoid')(inputs1)
out= Dense(1, activation='linear')(lstm1)
model = Model(inputs=inputs1, outputs=out)
model.summary()
```

Notice that the two changes in code that we have done are as follows:

- Changing the value of the `return_sequences` parameter to `True`
- The dense layer, giving a value of 1 as output:

```
Layer (type)                 Output Shape              Param #
=================================================================
input_2 (InputLayer)         (None, 2, 1)              0
_____
lstm_2 (LSTM)                (None, 2, 1)              12
_____
dense_2 (Dense)              (None, 2, 1)              2
=================================================================
Total params: 14
Trainable params: 14
Non-trainable params: 0
```

Notice that, because we have extracted the output of the hidden layer value at each time step (where the hidden layer has one unit), the output shape of LSTM is (batch size, time steps, 1).

Additionally, because there is one dense layer connecting the LSTM output to the final output for each of the time steps, the output shape remains the same.

Let's go ahead and fit the model, as follows:

```
model.compile(optimizer='adam',loss='mean_squared_error')
model.fit(input_data.reshape(2,2,1),
output_data.reshape(2,2,1),epochs=1000)
```

The predicted values are as follows:

```
print(model.predict(input_data[0].reshape(1,2,1)))
```

The preceding execution will give the following output:

```
[[[1.7584195] [2.2500749]]]
```

Similar to the previous section, we shall validate our results by performing a forward pass of input through weights and then match our predicted values.

We shall extract the output of the first time step as follows:

```
input_t0 = 1
cell_state0 = 0
forget0 = input_t0*model.get_weights()[0][0][1] + model.get_weights()[2][1]
forget1 = 1/(1+np.exp(-(forget0)))
cell_state1 = forget1 * cell_state0
input_t0_1 = input_t0*model.get_weights()[0][0][0] +
model.get_weights()[2][0]
input_t0_2 = 1/(1+np.exp(-(input_t0_1)))
```

Sequence-to-Sequence Learning

```
input_t0_cell1 = input_t0*model.get_weights()[0][0][2] +
model.get_weights()[2][2]
input_t0_cell2 = np.tanh(input_t0_cell1)
input_t0_cell3 = input_t0_cell2*input_t0_2
input_t0_cell4 = input_t0_cell3 + cell_state1
output_t0_1 = input_t0*model.get_weights()[0][0][3] +
model.get_weights()[2][3]
output_t0_2 = 1/(1+np.exp(-output_t0_1))
hidden_layer_1 = np.tanh(input_t0_cell4)*output_t0_2
final_output_1 = hidden_layer_1 * model.get_weights()[3][0] +
model.get_weights()[4]
final_output_1
# 1.7584
```

You should notice that the `final_output_1` value matches with the predicted value at the first time step. Similarly, let's go ahead and validate predictions on second time step:

```
input_t1 = 2
cell_state1 = input_t0_cell4
forget21 = hidden_layer_1*model.get_weights()[1][0][1] +
model.get_weights()[2][1] + input_t1*model.get_weights()[0][0][1]
forget_22 = 1/(1+np.exp(-(forget21)))
cell_state2 = cell_state1 * forget_22
input_t1_1 = input_t1*model.get_weights()[0][0][0] +
model.get_weights()[2][0] + hidden_layer_1*model.get_weights()[1][0][0]
input_t1_2 = 1/(1+np.exp(-(input_t1_1)))
input_t1_cell1 = input_t1*model.get_weights()[0][0][2] +
model.get_weights()[2][2]+ hidden_layer_1*model.get_weights()[1][0][2]
input_t1_cell2 = np.tanh(input_t1_cell1)
input_t1_cell3 = input_t1_cell2*input_t1_2
input_t1_cell4 = input_t1_cell3 + cell_state2
output_t1_1 = input_t1*model.get_weights()[0][0][3] +
model.get_weights()[2][3]+ hidden_layer_1*model.get_weights()[1][0][3]
output_t1_2 = 1/(1+np.exp(-output_t1_1))
hidden_layer_2 = np.tanh(input_t1_cell4)*output_t1_2
final_output_2 = hidden_layer_2 * model.get_weights()[3][0] +
model.get_weights()[4]
final_output_2
# 2.250
```

You should notice that this returns the exact same value as the `model.predict` value of second time step.

Now that we understand the return_sequences parameter in our network, let us go ahead and learn about another parameter called return_state. We know that the two outputs of a network are hidden layer values (which is the also output of LSTM in the final time step when return_sequences is False and output of LSTM in each time step when return_sequences is True) and cell state values.

The return_state helps in extracting the cell state value of a network.

Extracting the cell state is useful when the input text is encoded into a vector and we pass, not only the encoded vector, but also the final cell state of the input encoder to the decoder network (more on this in the *Encoder decoder architecture for machine translation* section).

In the following section, let's understand how return_state works. Note that it is only for us to understand how the cell states are generated at each time step, as in practice, we would use the output of this step (hidden layer value and cell state value) as an input to the decoder:

```
inputs1 = Input(shape=(2,1))
lstm1,state_h,state_c = LSTM(1, activation = 'tanh', return_sequences=True,
return_state = True,
recurrent_initializer='Zeros',recurrent_activation='sigmoid')(inputs1)
model = Model(inputs=inputs1, outputs=[lstm1, state_h, state_c])
```

In the preceding code, we set the return_state parameter to True as well. Notice the output of the LSTM now:

- lstm1: Hidden layer at each time step (as return_sequences is True in the preceding scenario)
- state_h: Hidden layer value at the final time step
- state_c: Cell state value at the final time step

Let's go ahead and predict values, as follows:

```
print(model.predict(input_data[0].reshape(1,2,1)))
```

We will get the following values:

```
[array([[[-0.256911 ], [-0.6683883]]], dtype=float32),
array([[-0.6683883]], dtype=float32), array([[-0.96862674]],
dtype=float32)]
```

You should see that there are three arrays of outputs, as we discussed previously: hidden layer value sequences, final hidden layer value, and the cell state value in the order.

Sequence-to-Sequence Learning

Let's validate the numbers, as we arrived at previously:

```
input_t0 = 1
cell_state0 = 0
forget0 = input_t0*model.get_weights()[0][0][1] + model.get_weights()[2][1]
forget1 = 1/(1+np.exp(-(forget0)))
cell_state1 = forget1 * cell_state0
input_t0_1 = input_t0*model.get_weights()[0][0][0] +
model.get_weights()[2][0]
input_t0_2 = 1/(1+np.exp(-(input_t0_1)))
input_t0_cell1 = input_t0*model.get_weights()[0][0][2] +
model.get_weights()[2][2]
input_t0_cell2 = np.tanh(input_t0_cell1)
input_t0_cell3 = input_t0_cell2*input_t0_2
input_t0_cell4 = input_t0_cell3 + cell_state1
output_t0_1 = input_t0*model.get_weights()[0][0][3] +
model.get_weights()[2][3]
output_t0_2 = 1/(1+np.exp(-output_t0_1))
hidden_layer_1 = np.tanh(input_t0_cell4)*output_t0_2
print(hidden_layer_1)
```

The value of `hidden_layer_1` in the preceding calculation is -0.2569, which is what we obtained from the `model.predict` method:

```
input_t1 = 2
cell_state1 = input_t0_cell4
forget21 = hidden_layer_1*model.get_weights()[1][0][1] +
model.get_weights()[2][1] + input_t1*model.get_weights()[0][0][1]
forget_22 = 1/(1+np.exp(-(forget21)))
cell_state2 = cell_state1 * forget_22
input_t1_1 = input_t1*model.get_weights()[0][0][0] +
model.get_weights()[2][0] + hidden_layer_1*model.get_weights()[1][0][0]
input_t1_2 = 1/(1+np.exp(-(input_t1_1)))
input_t1_cell1 = input_t1*model.get_weights()[0][0][2] +
model.get_weights()[2][2]+ hidden_layer_1*model.get_weights()[1][0][2]
input_t1_cell2 = np.tanh(input_t1_cell1)
input_t1_cell3 = input_t1_cell2*input_t1_2
input_t1_cell4 = input_t1_cell3 + cell_state2
output_t1_1 = input_t1*model.get_weights()[0][0][3] +
model.get_weights()[2][3]+ hidden_layer_1*model.get_weights()[1][0][3]
output_t1_2 = 1/(1+np.exp(-output_t1_1))
hidden_layer_2 = np.tanh(input_t1_cell4)*output_t1_2
print(hidden_layer_2, input_t1_cell4)
```

The values of `hidden_layer_2` and `input_t1_cell4` are -0.6683 and -0.9686, respectively.

You will notice that the outputs are exactly the same as what we have seen in the predict function.

In the case of a bidirectional network, where we are incorporating the hidden layer values as we calculate them from both sides, we code it as follows:

```
inputs1 = Input(shape=(2,1))
lstm1,state_fh,state_fc,state_bh,state_bc = Bidirectional(LSTM(1,
activation = 'tanh', return_sequences=True, return_state = True,
recurrent_initializer='Zeros',recurrent_activation='sigmoid'))(inputs1)
model = Model(inputs=inputs1, outputs=[lstm1,
state_fh,state_fc,state_bh,state_bc])
model.summary()
```

Note that, in a bidirectional LSTM, there are two outputs for the final hidden state, one when the input time steps are considered from left to right, and another when the input time steps are considered from right to left. In a similar manner, we have two possible cell state values.

Typically, we would concatenate the resulting hidden states to a single vector, and also the cell states into another concatenated single vector.

For brevity, we are not validating the outputs of bidirectional LSTM in this book. However, you can check the validations in the accompanying Jupyter Notebook of this chapter.

Building a chatbot

A chatbot is helpful in a scenario where the bot automates some of the more common queries. This is very useful in a practical scenario, especially in cases where you would have to just look up the result from a database or query an API to obtain the result that the query is about.

Given this, there are potentially two ways that you can design a chatbot, as follows:

- Convert the unstructured user query into a structured format:
  - Query from the database based on the converted structure
- Generate responses based on the input text

For this exercise, we will be adopting the first approach, as it is more likely to give predictions that can be tweaked further before presenting them to the user. Additionally, we will also understand the reason why we might not want to generate responses based on input text after we go through the machine translation and text summarization case studies.

Converting a user query into a structured format involves the following two steps:

1. Assign entities to each word in a query
2. Understand the intent of query

Named entity recognition is one of the applications that has multiple use cases across industries. For example, where does the user want to travel to? Which product is a user considering to purchase? And so on. From these examples, it might occur that named entity recognition is a simple lookup from a dictionary of existing city names or product names. However, think of a scenario where a user says *I want to travel from Boston to Seattle*. In this case, while the machine understands that both *Boston* and *Seattle* are city names, we are not in a position to resolve which is the *from* city and which is the *to* city.

While we can add some heuristics like a name that has a *to* before it is the *to city* and the other is the *from city*, it is not scalable as we replicate this process across multiple such examples. Neural networks come in handy in that scenario, where there is a less dependency on us to hand-tune the features. We shall let the machine take care of the feature engineering part to give us the output.

Getting ready

With the preceding intuition, let's go ahead and define our approach in solving this problem for a dataset that has user queries related to airlines.

Objective: Extract the various entities from a query and also the intent of the query.

Approach:

- We shall find a dataset that has the labels of query and the entity that each word within the query belongs to:
    - If we do not have a labeled dataset, we shall manually annotate the entities within a query for a reasonable number of examples, so that we can train our model
- Given that the surrounding words can have an impact on the given word's classification into one or the other class, let's use the RNN-based technique to solve this problem
- Additionally, given that the surrounding word could be either on the left or the right side of given word, we shall use a bidirectional RNN to solve the problem

- Preprocess the input dataset so that it could be fed into the multiple time steps of an RNN
- One-hot-encode the output dataset so that we can optimize the model
- Build the model that returns the entities that each word within a query belongs to
- Similarly, build another model that extracts the intent of a query

How to do it...

Let's code up the approach we defined previously, as follows (the code file is available as Intent_and_entity_extraction.ipynb in GitHub):

1. Import the datasets, as shown in the following code:

```
!wget https://www.dropbox.com/s/qpw1wnmho8v0gi4/atis.zip
!unzip atis.zip
```

Load the training dataset:

```
import numpy as np
import pandas as pd
import pickle
DATA_DIR="/content"
def load_ds(fname='atis.train.pkl'):
    with open(fname, 'rb') as stream:
    ds,dicts = pickle.load(stream)
    print('Done loading: ', fname)
    print('      samples: {:4d}'.format(len(ds['query'])))
    print('   vocab_size: {:4d}'.format(len(dicts['token_ids'])))
    print('   slot count: {:4d}'.format(len(dicts['slot_ids'])))
    print(' intent count: {:4d}'.format(len(dicts['intent_ids'])))
    return ds,dicts

import os
train_ds, dicts = load_ds(os.path.join(DATA_DIR,'atis.train.pkl'))
test_ds, dicts = load_ds(os.path.join(DATA_DIR,'atis.test.pkl'))
```

Sequence-to-Sequence Learning

The preceding code gives the following output:

```
Done loading:  /content/atis.train.pkl
     samples:  4978
  vocab_size:  943
  slot count:  129
intent count:  26
Done loading:  /content/atis.test.pkl
     samples:  893
  vocab_size:  943
  slot count:  129
intent count:  26
```

Note that the samples in the attached dataset is the user query, slot is the entity a word belongs to, and intent is the overall intent of the query.

2. Apply IDs to each of the words in query, slot, and intent:

```
t2i, s2i, in2i = map(dicts.get, ['token_ids',
'slot_ids','intent_ids'])
i2t, i2s, i2in = map(lambda d: {d[k]:k for k in d.keys()},
[t2i,s2i,in2i])
query, slots, intent = map(train_ds.get, ['query', 'slot_labels',
'intent_labels'])
```

A sample of IDs for token (words in vocabulary), slots (entity of a word), and intent is as follows:

Token	Entity	Intent
'air': 195,	'B-aircraft_code': 0,	'abbreviation': 0,
'aircraft': 196,	'B-airline_code': 1,	'aircraft': 1,
'airfare': 197,	'B-airline_name': 2,	'aircraft+flight+flight_no': 2,
'airfares': 198,	'B-airport_code': 3,	'airfare': 3,
'airline': 199,	'B-airport_name': 4,	'airfare+flight': 4,

Finally, the query, slots, and intent are converted into ID values, as follows (where we report the output of the first query, intent, and slots):

```
query[0]

array([178, 479, 902, 851, 431, 444, 266, 240,
       351, 240,  27, 482, 827, 606, 179])

slots[0]

array([128, 128, 128, 128, 128, 128,  48, 128,
        78, 128,  14, 128, 128,  12, 128])

intent[0]

array([14])
```

A sample of query, intent, and entities corresponding to the words in query is as follows:

```
for j in range(len(query[i])):
    print('{:>33} {:>40}'.format(i2t[query[i][j]],
                                 i2s[slots[i][j]]))
```

```
0:         flight: BOS i want to fly from boston at 838 am and arrive in denver at 1110 in the morning EOS
intent: flight
                              BOS                                        0
                                i                                        0
                             want                                        0
                               to                                        0
                              fly                                        0
                             from                                        0
                           boston                        B-fromloc.city_name
                               at                                        0
                              838                         B-depart_time.time
                               am                         I-depart_time.time
                              and                                        0
                           arrive                                        0
                               in                                        0
                           denver                          B-toloc.city_name
                               at                                        0
                             1110                         B-arrive_time.time
                               in                                        0
                              the                                        0
                          morning                B-arrive_time.period_of_day
                              EOS                                        0
```

Sequence-to-Sequence Learning

Query is the statement at the top in the preceding screenshot. Slots represent the type of object each word belongs to. Note that O represents an object, and every other entity name is self-descriptive. Additionally, there are a total of 23 possible classes of intents that describe the query at an overall level.

In the following code, we are converting the total data into a list of lists where each list corresponds to one query in the dataset:

```
i2t2 = []
i2s2 = []
c_intent=[]
for i in range(4978):
    a_query = []
    b_slot = []
    c_intent.append(i2in[intent[i][0]])
    for j in range(len(query[i])):
        a_query.append(i2t[query[i][j]])
        b_slot.append(i2s[slots[i][j]])
    i2t2.append(a_query)
    i2s2.append(b_slot)
i2t2 = np.array(i2t2)
i2s2 = np.array(i2s2)
i2in2 = np.array(c_intent)
```

A sample of tokens, intent, and query are as follows:

```
print(i2t2[0])
print(i2s2[0])
print(i2in2[0])

['BOS', 'i', 'want', 'to', 'fly', 'from', 'boston', 'at', '
['O', 'O', 'O', 'O', 'O', 'O', 'B-fromloc.city_name', 'O',
flight
```

3. Create the indexed inputs and outputs:

```
final_sentences = []
final_targets = []
final_docs = []
for i in range(len(i2t2)):
    tokens = ''
    entities = ''
    intent = ''
    for j in range(len(i2t2[i])):
        tokens= tokens + i2t2[i][j] + ' '
        entities = entities + i2s2[i][j] +' '
```

```
        intent = i2in2[i]
        final_sentences.append(tokens)
        final_targets.append(entities)
        final_docs.append(intent)
```

The preceding code gives us a list of final queries and targets as follows:

```
print('tokens: ',i2t2[0])
print('slots: ',i2s2[0])
print('intent: ',i2in2[0])

tokens: ['BOS', 'i', 'want', 'to', 'fly', 'from', 'boston',
slots:  ['O', 'O', 'O', 'O', 'O', 'O', 'B-fromloc.city_name',
intent: flight
```

Now, we are converting each **input** sentence into a corresponding list of IDs of constituent words:

```
from collections import Counter
counts = Counter()
for i,sentence in enumerate(final_sentences):
    counts.update(sentence.split())
sentence_words = sorted(counts, key=counts.get, reverse=True)
chars = sentence_words
nb_chars = len(chars)
sentence_word_to_int = {word: i for i, word in
enumerate(sentence_words, 1)}
sentence_int_to_word = {i: word for i, word in
enumerate(sentence_words, 1)}
mapped_reviews = []
for review in final_sentences:
    mapped_reviews.append([sentence_word_to_int[word] for word in
review.split()])
```

In the following code, we are converting each **output** word into its constituent word IDs:

```
from collections import Counter
counts = Counter()
for i,sentence in enumerate(final_targets):
    counts.update(sentence.split())
target_words = sorted(counts, key=counts.get, reverse=True)
chars = target_words
nb_chars = len(target_words)

target_word_to_int = {word: i for i, word in
```

Sequence-to-Sequence Learning

```
enumerate(target_words, 1)}
target_int_to_word = {i: word for i, word in
enumerate(target_words, 1)}
mapped_targets = []
for review in final_targets:
    mapped_targets.append([target_word_to_int[word] for word in
review.split()])
```

4. Pad the input and one-hot-encode the output:

   ```
   from keras.preprocessing.sequence import pad_sequences
   y = pad_sequences(maxlen=124, sequences=mapped_targets,
   padding="post", value=0)
   from keras.utils import to_categorical
   y2 = [to_categorical(i, num_classes=124) for i in y]
   y3 = np.array(y2)
   ```

   In the following code, we are deciding the maximum length of the query before padding the input:

   ```
   length_sent = []
   for i in range(len(mapped_reviews)):
       a = mapped_reviews[i]
       b = len(a)
       length_sent.append(b)
   np.max(length_sent)
   ```

   In the preceding code, we are deciding the maximum length of the query before padding the input—which happens to be `48`.

   In the following code, we are padding the input and output with a max length of `50`, as there is no input query that is beyond `48` words in length (which is the `max(length_sent)`):

   ```
   from keras.preprocessing.sequence import pad_sequences
   X = pad_sequences(maxlen=50, sequences=mapped_reviews,
   padding="post", value=0)
   Y = pad_sequences(maxlen=50, sequences=mapped_targets,
   padding="post", value=0)
   ```

   In the following code, we are converting the output into a one-hot-encoded version:

   ```
   from keras.utils import to_categorical
   y2 = [to_categorical(i, num_classes=124) for i in Y]
   y2 = np.array(y2)
   ```

We have a total of 124 classes, as there are a total 123 unique classes and the word index starts with 1.

5. Build, train, and test the dataset, as well as the model:

```
from sklearn.model_selection import train_test_split
X_train, X_test, y_train, y_test = train_test_split(X,y2,
test_size=0.30,random_state=10)
```

In the preceding code, we are splitting the dataset into train and test datasets:

```
input = Input(shape=(50,))
model = Embedding(input_dim=891, output_dim=32,
input_length=50)(input)
model = Dropout(0.1)(model)
model = Bidirectional(LSTM(units=100, return_sequences=True,
recurrent_dropout=0.1))(model)
out = (Dense(124, activation="softmax"))(model)

model = Model(input, out)
model.summary()
```

A summary of the model is as follows:

```
Layer (type)                 Output Shape              Param #
=================================================================
input_1 (InputLayer)         (None, 50)                0
_____
embedding_1 (Embedding)      (None, 50, 32)            28512
_____
dropout_1 (Dropout)          (None, 50, 32)            0
_____
bidirectional_1 (Bidirection (None, 50, 200)           106400
_____
time_distributed_1 (TimeDist (None, 50, 124)           24924
=================================================================
Total params: 159,836
Trainable params: 159,836
Non-trainable params: 0
```

Note that, in the preceding code, we have a bidirectional LSTM, and hence, the hidden layer has 200 units (as the LSTM layer has 100 units).

6. Compile and fit the model, as shown follows:

```
model.compile(optimizer="adam", loss="categorical_crossentropy",
metrics=["accuracy"])
model.fit(X_train,y_train, batch_size=32, epochs=5, validation_data
= (X_test,y_test), verbose=1)
```

The preceding code results in a model that is 95% accurate in identifying the right entity for a given word within a query:

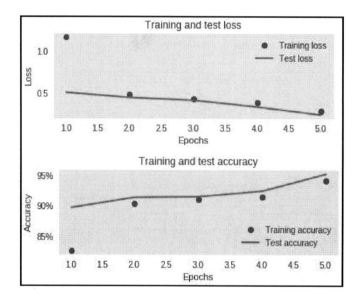

From the preceding output, we can see that our accuracy in assigning the right entity to each word is >95%.

Intent extraction

Now that we have built a model that has a good accuracy in predicting the entities within a query, let's go ahead and find the intent of the query.

We will be reusing most of the variables that we initialized in the previous model:

1. Convert the intent of each query into an ID:

```
from collections import Counter
counts = Counter()
for i,sentence in enumerate(final_docs):
    counts.update(sentence.split())
```

```
intent_words = sorted(counts, key=counts.get, reverse=True)
chars = intent_words
nb_chars = len(intent_words)
intent_word_to_int = {word: i for i, word in
enumerate(intent_words, 1)}
intent_int_to_word = {i: word for i, word in
enumerate(intent_words, 1)}
mapped_docs = []
for review in final_docs:
    mapped_docs.append([intent_word_to_int[word] for word in
review.split()])
```

2. Extract the one-hot-encoded version of the intents:

```
from keras.utils import to_categorical
doc2 = [to_categorical(i[0], num_classes=23) for i in mapped_docs]
doc3 = np.array(doc2)
```

3. Build the model, as shown in the following code:

```
from sklearn.model_selection import train_test_split
X_train, X_test, y_train, y_test = train_test_split(X,doc3,
test_size=0.30,random_state=10)

input = Input(shape=(50,))
model2 = Embedding(input_dim=891, output_dim=32,
input_length=50)(input)
model2 = Dropout(0.1)(model2)
model2 = Bidirectional(LSTM(units=100))(model2)
out = (Dense(23, activation="softmax"))(model2)
model2 = Model(input, out)

model2.compile(optimizer="adam", loss="categorical_crossentropy",
metrics=["accuracy"])

model2.fit(X_train,y_train, batch_size=32, epochs=5,
validation_data = (X_test,y_test), verbose=1)
```

Sequence-to-Sequence Learning

The preceding code results in a model that has an accuracy of 90% in identifying the right intent of a query in the validation dataset:

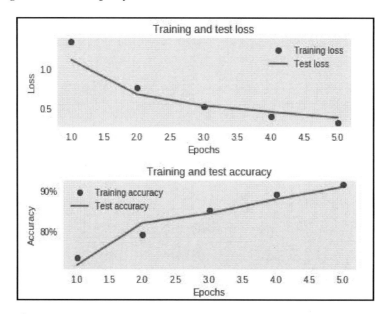

Putting it all together

In the previous section, we built two models, where the first model predicts the entities in a query and the second model extracts the intent of queries.

In this section, we will define a function that takes a query and converts it into a structured format:

1. Preprocess the new input text so that it can be passed to the model:

```
def preprocessing(text):
    text2 = text.split()
    a=[]
    for i in range(len(text2)):
        a.append(sentence_word_to_int[text2[i]])
    return a
```

2. Pre-process the input text to convert it into a list of word IDs:

```
text = "BOS i would fly from boston to dallas EOS"

indexed_text = preprocessing(text)
padded_text=np.zeros(50)
padded_text[:len(indexed_text)]=indexed_text
padded_text=padded_text.reshape(1,50)
```

The preceding results in processed input text as follows:

```
[[ 1., 14., 41., 40.,  4., 11.,  3., 23.,  2.,  0.,  0.,  0.,  0.,
    0.,  0.,  0.,  0.,  0.,  0.,  0.,  0.,  0.,  0.,  0.,  0.,  0.,
    0.,  0.,  0.,  0.,  0.,  0.,  0.,  0.,  0.,  0.,  0.,  0.,  0.,
    0.,  0.,  0.,  0.,  0.,  0.,  0.,  0.,  0.,  0.,  0.]])
```

Now, we'll predict the intent of the preceding list:

```
pred_index_intent = np.argmax(model2.predict(c),axis=1)
entity_int_to_word[pred_index_intent[0]]
```

The preceding code results in the intent of the query being about a flight, as follows:

```
intent_int_to_word[pred_index_intent[0]]

'flight'
```

3. Extract the entities related to words in a query:

```
pred_entities = np.argmax(model.predict(padded_text),axis=2)

for i in range(len(pred_entities[0])):
    if pred_entities[0][i]>1:
        print('word: ',text.split()[i], 'entity: ',target_int_to_word[pred_entities[0][i]])
```

```
word:  boston entity:  B-fromloc.city_name
word:  dallas entity:  B-toloc.city_name
```

[447]

From the preceding code, we can see that the model has correctly classified a word into the right entity.

Now that we have the entities and intent identified, we can have a pre-defined SQL query (or API) whose parameters are filled by the extracted entities, and each intent could potentially have a different API/SQL query to extract information for the user.

Machine translation

So far, we have seen a scenario where the input and output are mapped one-to-one. In this section, we will look into ways in which we can construct architectures that result in mapping all input data into a vector, and then decoding it into the output vector.

We will be translating an input text in English into text in French in this case study.

Getting ready

The architecture that we will be defining to perform machine translation is as follows:

- Take a labeled dataset where the input sentence and the corresponding translation in French is available
- Tokenize and extract words that are frequent in each of the English and French texts:
    - To identify the frequent words, we will count the frequency of each word
    - The words that constitute the top 80% of total cumulative frequency of all words are considered the frequent words
- For all the words that are not among the frequent words, replace them with an unknown (unk) symbol
- Assign an ID to each word
- Build an encoder LSTM that fetches the vector of the input text
- Pass the encoded vector through dense layer so that we extract the probabilities of decoded text at each time step
- Fit a model to minimize the loss at the output

How to do it...

There could be multiple model architectures that can help in translating the input text. We will go through a few of them in the following sections (the code file is available as Machine_translation.ipynb in GitHub).

Preprocessing the data

To pass the input and output data to our model, we would have to preprocess the datasets as follows:

1. Import the relevant packages and dataset:

```
import pandas as pd
import numpy as np
import string
from string import digits
import matplotlib.pyplot as plt
%matplotlib inline
import re
from sklearn.model_selection import train_test_split
from keras.models import Model
from keras.layers import Input, LSTM, Dense
import numpy as np
```

$ wget https://www.dropbox.com/s/2vag8w6yov9c1qz/english%20to%20french.txt

```
lines= pd.read_table('english to french.txt', names=['eng', 'fr'])
```

2. Given that there are more than 140,000 sentences in the dataset, let's consider only the first 50,000 sentence-translation pairs to build the model:

```
lines = lines[0:50000]
```

3. Convert the input and output text into lower case and also remove the punctuation:

```
lines.eng=lines.eng.apply(lambda x: x.lower())
lines.fr=lines.fr.apply(lambda x: x.lower())
exclude = set(string.punctuation)
lines.eng=lines.eng.apply(lambda x: ''.join(ch for ch in x if ch not in exclude))
lines.fr=lines.fr.apply(lambda x: ''.join(ch for ch in x if ch not in exclude))
```

4. Add start and end tokens to the output sentences (French sentences). We add these so that the start and end tokens are helpful in the encoder decoder architecture. The reason why this will be helpful will be provided in the *Encoder decoder architecture for machine translation* section:

   ```
   lines.fr = lines.fr.apply(lambda x : 'start '+ x + ' end')
   ```

   A sample of the data looks as follows:

   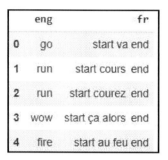

5. Identify the frequent words. We define a word as frequent if it is among the words that have a frequency that constitutes 80% of the total frequency of all words:

   ```
   # fit a tokenizer
   from keras.preprocessing.text import Tokenizer
   import json
   from collections import OrderedDict
   def create_tokenizer(lines):
       tokenizer = Tokenizer()
       tokenizer.fit_on_texts(lines)
       return tokenizer

   eng_tokenizer = create_tokenizer(lines.eng)
   output_dict = json.loads(json.dumps(eng_tokenizer.word_counts))
   df =pd.DataFrame([output_dict.keys(), output_dict.values()]).T
   df.columns = ['word','count']
   df = df.sort_values(by='count',ascending = False)
   df['cum_count']=df['count'].cumsum()
   df['cum_perc'] = df['cum_count']/df['cum_count'].max()
   final_eng_words = df[df['cum_perc']<0.8]['word'].values
   ```

The preceding code, extracts the number of English words that cumulatively constitute 80% of total English words in input:

```
fr_tokenizer = create_tokenizer(lines.fr)
output_dict = json.loads(json.dumps(fr_tokenizer.word_counts))
df =pd.DataFrame([output_dict.keys(), output_dict.values()]).T
df.columns = ['word','count']
df = df.sort_values(by='count',ascending = False)
df['cum_count']=df['count'].cumsum()
df['cum_perc'] = df['cum_count']/df['cum_count'].max()
final_fr_words = df[df['cum_perc']<0.8]['word'].values
```

The preceding code, extracts the number of French words that cumulatively constitute 80% of total French words in output.

6. Filter out the less frequent words. If a word is not among the frequent words, we shall replace it with an unknown word—unk:

```
def filter_eng_words(x):
    t = []
    x = x.split()
    for i in range(len(x)):
        if x[i] in final_eng_words:
            t.append(x[i])
        else:
            t.append('unk')
    x3 = ''
    for i in range(len(t)):
        x3 = x3+t[i]+' '
    return x3
```

The preceding code takes a sentence as input, extracts the unique words, and if a word does not exist among the more frequent English words (`final_eng_words`), then it shall be replaced by `unk`:

```
def filter_fr_words(x):
    t = []
    x = x.split()
    for i in range(len(x)):
        if x[i] in final_fr_words:
            t.append(x[i])
        else:
            t.append('unk')
    x3 = ''
    for i in range(len(t)):
        x3 = x3+t[i]+' '
    return x3
```

The preceding code takes a sentence as input, extracts the unique words, and if a word does not exist among the more frequent French words (`final_fr_words`), then it shall be replaced by `unk`.

For example, on a random sentence with frequent words and also infrequent words, the output looks as follows:

```
filter_eng_words('he is extremely good')
```

```
'he is unk good '
```

```
lines['fr']=lines['fr'].apply(filter_fr_words)
lines['eng']=lines['eng'].apply(filter_eng_words)
```

In the preceding code, we are replacing all the English and French sentences based on the functions we defined previously.

7. Assign ID to each word across both English (input) and French (output) sentences:
   1. Store the list of all unique words in data (English and French sentences):

```
all_eng_words=set()
for eng in lines.eng:
    for word in eng.split():
        if word not in all_eng_words:
            all_eng_words.add(word)

all_french_words=set()
for fr in lines.fr:
    for word in fr.split():
        if word not in all_french_words:
            all_french_words.add(word)

input_words = sorted(list(all_eng_words))
target_words = sorted(list(all_french_words))
num_encoder_tokens = len(all_eng_words)
num_decoder_tokens = len(all_french_words)
```

   2. Create a dictionary of input words and their corresponding index:

```
input_token_index = dict( [(word, i+1) for i, word in enumerate(input_words)])
target_token_index = dict( [(word, i+1) for i, word in enumerate(target_words)])
```

8. Extract the maximum length of input and target sentences so that all of the sentences can have the same size:

```
length_list=[]
for l in lines.fr:
    length_list.append(len(l.split(' ')))
fr_max_length = np.max(length_list)

length_list=[]
for l in lines.eng:
    length_list.append(len(l.split(' ')))
eng_max_length = np.max(length_list)
```

Now that we have preprocessed the datasets, let's try out multiple architectures on the dataset to compare their performance.

Traditional many to many architecture

In this architecture, we will embed each input word into a 128 dimensional vector, resulting in an output vector of shape (batch_size, 128, 17). We want to do this because, in this version, we want to test out the scenario where the input data has 17 time steps and the output dataset also has 17 time steps.

We shall connect each input time step to the output time step through an LSTM, and then perform a softmax on top of the predictions:

1. Create input and output datasets. Note that we have decoder_input_data and decoder_target_data. For now, let us create decoder_input_data as the word ID corresponding to the target sentence words.
   The decoder_target_data is the one-hot-encoded version of the target data for all words after the start token:

```
encoder_input_data = np.zeros((len(lines.eng), fr_max_length),dtype='float32')
decoder_input_data = np.zeros((len(lines.fr), fr_max_length),dtype='float32')
decoder_target_data = np.zeros((len(lines.fr), fr_max_length, num_decoder_tokens+1),dtype='float32')
```

Note that we are adding a +1 to num_decodder_tokens, as there is no word corresponding to index 0 in the dictionary we created in *step 7b* of the previous section:

```
for i, (input_text, target_text) in enumerate(zip(lines.eng,
lines.fr)):
    for t, word in enumerate(input_text.split()):
        encoder_input_data[i, t] = input_token_index[word]
    for t, word in enumerate(target_text.split()):
 # decoder_target_data is ahead of decoder_input_data by one
timestep
        decoder_input_data[i, t] = target_token_index[word]
        if t>0:
 # decoder_target_data will be ahead by one timestep
 # and will not include the start character.
            decoder_target_data[i, t - 1,
target_token_index[word]] = 1.
        if t== len(target_text.split())-1:
            decoder_target_data[i, t:, 89] = 1
```

In the preceding code, we are looping through the input text and target text to replace a sentence that is in English or French to its corresponding word IDs in English and French.

Furthermore, we are one-hot-encoding the target data in the decoder so that we can pass it to the model. Additionally, given that all sentences have the same length now, we are replacing the values of the target data with one at the 89th index (as `89` belongs to the end index) after the sentence length is exceeded in the `for` loop:

```
for i in range(decoder_input_data.shape[0]):
    for j in range(decoder_input_data.shape[1]):
        if(decoder_input_data[i][j]==0):
            decoder_input_data[i][j] = 89
```

In the preceding code, we are replacing the value of zero in the decoder input data with 89 (as 89 is the ending token and zero does not have any word associated with it in the word indices that we created).

Note that the shapes of the three datasets that we created are as follows:

```
print(decoder_input_data.shape,encoder_input_data.shape,decoder_tar
get_data.shape)
```

The following is the output of the preceding code:

```
(50000, 17) (50000, 17) (50000, 17, 359)
```

Chapter 13

2. Build and fit the model, as follows:

```
model = Sequential()
model.add(Embedding(len(input_words)+1, 128,
input_length=fr_max_length, mask_zero=True))
model.add((Bidirectional(LSTM(256, return_sequences = True))))
model.add((LSTM(256, return_sequences=True)))
model.add((Dense(len(target_token_index)+1, activation='softmax')))
```

```
Layer (type)                 Output Shape              Param #
=================================================================
embedding_8 (Embedding)      (None, 17, 128)           49408
_____
bidirectional_6 (Bidirection (None, 17, 512)           788480
_____
lstm_14 (LSTM)               (None, 17, 256)           787456
_____
dense_8 (Dense)              (None, 17, 359)           92263
=================================================================
Total params: 1,717,607
Trainable params: 1,717,607
Non-trainable params: 0
```

```
model.compile(optimizer='adam',
loss='categorical_crossentropy',metrics=['acc'])

model.fit(encoder_input_data, decoder_target_data,
 batch_size=32, epochs=5, validation_split=0.05)
```

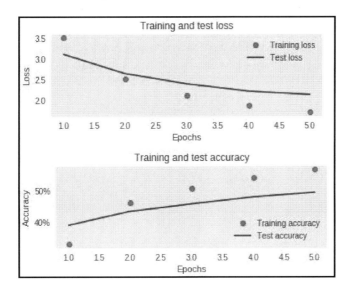

[455]

Sequence-to-Sequence Learning

Note that the accuracy number coming from the model could be misleading as it counts the end token in its accuracy measure as well.

3. Calculate the number of words that were correctly translated:

```
count = 0
correct_count = 0
pred = model2.predict(encoder_input_data[47500:])
for i in range(2500):
  t = np.argmax(pred[i], axis=1)
  act = np.argmax(decoder_target_data[47500],axis=1)
  correct_count += np.sum((act==t) & (act!=89))
  count += np.sum(act!=89)
correct_count/count
# 0.19
```

In the preceding code, we are making a prediction on test data (which is the last 5% of total dataset as the validation split is 5%).

From the preceding code, we can see that ~19% of the total words were correctly translated.

Many to hidden to many architecture

One of the drawbacks of the previous architecture was that we had to artificially increase the number of time steps in input to 17, even though we knew that the input has a maximum of eight time steps where there was some input.

In this architecture, let's go ahead and build a model that extracts hidden state value at the last time step of input. Furthermore, it replicates the hidden state value 17 times (as there are 17 time steps in the output). It passes the replicated hidden time steps through a Dense layer to finally extract the probable classes in output. Let's code the logic as follows:

1. Redo the creation of input and output datasets so that we have eight time steps in the input and 17 in the output. This is different from the previous iteration as the input had 17 time steps in that versus eight in the current version:

```
encoder_input_data = np.zeros(
    (len(lines.eng), eng_max_length),
    dtype='float32')
decoder_input_data = np.zeros(
    (len(lines.fr), fr_max_length),
    dtype='float32')
decoder_target_data = np.zeros(
    (len(lines.fr), fr_max_length, num_decoder_tokens+1),
    dtype='float32')
```

```
for i, (input_text, target_text) in enumerate(zip(lines.eng,
lines.fr)):
    for t, word in enumerate(input_text.split()):
        encoder_input_data[i, t] = input_token_index[word]
    for t, word in enumerate(target_text.split()):
        # decoder_target_data is ahead of decoder_input_data by one
timestep
        decoder_input_data[i, t] = target_token_index[word]
        if t>0:
            # decoder_target_data will be ahead by one timestep
            # and will not include the start character.
            decoder_target_data[i, t - 1, target_token_index[word]] =
1.
        if t== len(target_text.split())-1:
            decoder_target_data[i, t:, 89] = 1
for i in range(decoder_input_data.shape[0]):
    for j in range(decoder_input_data.shape[1]):
        if(decoder_input_data[i][j]==0):
            decoder_input_data[i][j] = 89
```

2. Build the model. Note that the `RepeatVector` layer replicates the output of the bidirectional layer's output 17 times:

```
model2 = Sequential()
model2.add(Embedding(len(input_words)+1, 128,
input_length=eng_max_length, mask_zero=True))
model2.add((Bidirectional(LSTM(256))))
model2.add(RepeatVector(fr_max_length))
model2.add((LSTM(256, return_sequences=True)))
model2.add((Dense(len(target_token_index)+1,
activation='softmax')))
```

A summary of model is as follows:

```
Layer (type)                    Output Shape        Param #
=================================================================
embedding_9 (Embedding)         (None, 8, 128)      49408
_____
bidirectional_7 (Bidirection    (None, 512)         788480
_____
repeat_vector_2 (RepeatVecto    (None, 17, 512)     0
_____
lstm_16 (LSTM)                  (None, 17, 256)     787456
_____
time_distributed_2 (TimeDist    (None, 17, 359)     92263
=================================================================
Total params: 1,717,607
Trainable params: 1,717,607
Non-trainable params: 0
```

Sequence-to-Sequence Learning

3. Compile and fit the model:

```
model2.compile(optimizer='adam',
loss='categorical_crossentropy',metrics=['acc'])
model2.fit(encoder_input_data, decoder_target_data,
 batch_size=128,epochs=5,validation_split=0.05)
```

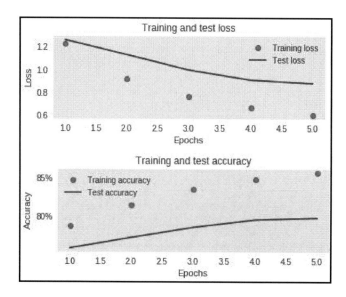

4. Calculate the % of total words that are correctly translated:

```
count = 0
correct_count = 0
pred = model2.predict(encoder_input_data[47500:])
for i in range(2500):
  t = np.argmax(pred[i], axis=1)
  act = np.argmax(decoder_target_data[47500],axis=1)
  correct_count += np.sum((act==t) & (act!=89))
  count += np.sum(act!=89)
correct_count/count
```

The preceding results in an accuracy of 19%, which is almost on par compared to the previous iteration.

The preceding is expected, as we tend to lose considerable amounts of information when all the input time steps' information is stored only in the last hidden layer value.

Additionally, we are not making use of the cell state that contains considerable amounts of information about what needs to be forgotten in which time step.

Encoder decoder architecture for machine translation

There are two potential logical enhancements to the architecture we defined in the previous section:

1. Make use of the information present in the cell state while generating translations
2. Make use of the previously translated words as an input in predicting the next word

The second technique is called **Teacher Forcing**. Essentially, by giving the previous time step's actual value as input while generating the current time step, we are tuning the network faster, and practically more accurately.

Getting ready

The strategy that we'll adopt to build a machine translation system using the encoder decoder architecture is as follows:

- We have two decoder datasets while preparing input and output datasets:
    - The `decoder_input_data` combined with `encoder_input_data` is the input and `decoder_target_data` is the output
    - The `decoder_input_data` starts with the `start` word
- When we are predicting the first word in the decoder, we are using the input set of words, converting them into a vector, which then gets passed through a decoder model that has `start` as input. The expected output is the first word after `start` in output
- We proceed in a similar manner, where the actual first word in the output is the input, while predicting the second word
- We'll calculate the accuracy of model based on this strategy

How to do it...

With this, let us go ahead and build the model on the input and output datasets that we already prepared in the previous section (*step 1* of many to hidden to many architecture of the previous section remains the same). The code file is available as `Machine_translation.ipynb` in GitHub.

1. Build the model, as follows:

   ```
   # We shall convert each word into a 128 sized vector
   embedding_size = 128
   ```

   1. Prepare the encoder model:

   ```
   encoder_inputs = Input(shape=(None,))
   en_x= Embedding(num_encoder_tokens+1, embedding_size)(encoder_inputs)
   encoder = LSTM(256, return_state=True)
   encoder_outputs, state_h, state_c = encoder(en_x)
   # We discard `encoder_outputs` and only keep the states.
   encoder_states = [state_h, state_c]
   ```

   Note that we are using a functional API since we are extracting the intermediate layers of the encoder network and will be passing multiple datasets as input (encoder input data and decoder input data).

   2. Prepare the decoder model:

   ```
   decoder_inputs = Input(shape=(None,))
   dex= Embedding(num_decoder_tokens+1, embedding_size)
   final_dex= dex(decoder_inputs)
   decoder_lstm = LSTM(256, return_sequences=True, return_state=True)
   decoder_outputs, _, _ = decoder_lstm(final_dex,
   initial_state=encoder_states)
   decoder_outputs = Dense(2000,activation='tanh')(decoder_outputs)
   decoder_dense = Dense(num_decoder_tokens+1, activation='softmax')
   decoder_outputs = decoder_dense(decoder_outputs)
   ```

2. Build the model, as follows:

```
model3 = Model([encoder_inputs, decoder_inputs], decoder_outputs)
model3.compile(optimizer='adam', loss='categorical_crossentropy',
metrics=['acc'])
```

```
Layer (type)                 Output Shape              Param #     Connected to
==================================================================================================
input_3 (InputLayer)         (None, None)              0
_____
input_4 (InputLayer)         (None, None)              0
_____
embedding_10 (Embedding)     (None, None, 128)         49408       input_3[0][0]
_____
embedding_11 (Embedding)     (None, None, 128)         45952       input_4[0][0]
_____
lstm_17 (LSTM)               [(None, 256), (None,      394240      embedding_10[0][0]
_____
lstm_18 (LSTM)               [(None, None, 256),       394240      embedding_11[0][0]
                                                                   lstm_17[0][1]
                                                                   lstm_17[0][2]
_____
dense_10 (Dense)             (None, None, 2000)        514000      lstm_18[0][0]
_____
dense_11 (Dense)             (None, None, 359)         718359      dense_10[0][0]
==================================================================================================
Total params: 2,116,199
Trainable params: 2,116,199
Non-trainable params: 0
```

Sequence-to-Sequence Learning

3. Fit the model, as shown in the following code:

```
history3 = model3.fit([encoder_input_data, decoder_input_data],
decoder_target_data,
 batch_size=32,epochs=5,validation_split=0.05)
```

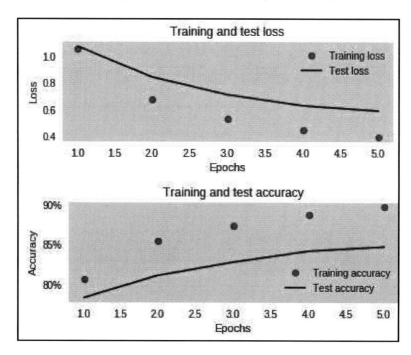

4. Calculate the % of words that are accurately transcribed:

```
act = np.argmax(decoder_target_data, axis=2)
```
```
count = 0
correct_count = 0
pred =
model3.predict([encoder_input_data[47500:],decoder_input_data[47500
:]])
for i in range(2500):
    t = np.argmax(pred[i], axis=1)
    correct_count += np.sum((act[47500+i]==t) & (act[47500+i]!=0))
    count += np.sum(decoder_input_data[47500+i]!=0)
correct_count/count
```

Note that we have correctly translated 44% of the total words in this scenario.

However, note that we should not be using `decoder_input_data` while calculating accuracy on the test dataset, as we do not have access to this during a real-time scenario.

This calls for us to use the predicted word in the previous time step as the decoder input word for the current time step, as follows.

We will re-initialize the `decoder_input_data` as `decoder_input_data_pred`:

```
decoder_input_data_pred =
np.zeros((len(lines.fr),fr_max_length),dtype='float32')

final_pred = []
for i in range(2500):
word = 284
    for j in range(17):
        decoder_input_data_pred[(47500+i), j] = word
        pred = model3.predict([encoder_input_data[(47500+i)].reshape(1,8),decoder_input_data_pred[47500+i].reshape(1,17)])
        t = np.argmax(pred[0][j])
        word = t
        if word==89:
            break
    final_pred.append(list(decoder_input_data_pred[47500+i]))
```

Note that, in the preceding code, the word index 284 corresponds to the start word. We are passing the start word as the first word in the decoder input and predicting the word with the highest probability in the next time step.

Once we predict the second word, we update `decoder_input_word_pred`, predict the third word, and continue until we encounter the stop word.

Now that we have modified our predicted translated words, let us calculate the accuracy of our translation:

```
final_pred2 = np.array(final_pred)

count = 0
correct_count = 0
for i in range(2500):
    correct_count += np.sum((decoder_input_data[47500+i]==final_pred2[i]) & (decoder_input_data[47500+i]!=89))
    count += np.sum(decoder_input_data[47500+i]!=89)
correct_count/count
```

The preceding results in 46% of all words that are correctly translated through this method.

While there is a considerable improvement in the accuracy of translation from the previous methods, we are still not taking the intuition that words that are at the start in the source language are quite likely to be at the start, even in the target language, that is, the word alignment is not taken into consideration. In the next section, we will look into solving the problem of word alignment.

Encoder decoder architecture with attention for machine translation

In the previous section, we learned that we could increase the accuracy of translation by enabling the teacher forcing technique, where the actual word in the previous time step of target was used as an input to the model.

In this section, we will extend this idea further and assign weightage to the input encoder based on how similar the encoder and decoder vectors are at each time step. This way, we are enabling that certain words have a higher weightage in the encoder's hidden vector, depending on the time step of the decoder.

How to do it...

With this, let's look at how we can build the encoder decoder architecture, along with the attention mechanism. The code file is available as `Machine_translation.ipynb` in GitHub.

1. Build the encoder, as shown in the following code:

```
encoder_inputs = Input(shape=(eng_max_length,))
en_x= Embedding(num_encoder_tokens+1, embedding_size)(encoder_inputs)
en_x = Dropout(0.1)(en_x)
encoder = LSTM(256, return_sequences=True, unroll=True)(en_x)
encoder_last = encoder[:,-1,:]
```

2. Build the decoder, as follows:

```
decoder_inputs = Input(shape=(fr_max_length,))
dex= Embedding(num_decoder_tokens+1, embedding_size)
decoder= dex(decoder_inputs)
decoder = Dropout(0.1)(decoder)
decoder = LSTM(256, return_sequences=True, unroll=True)(decoder, initial_state=[encoder_last, encoder_last])
```

Note that, in the preceding code, we have not finalized the decoder architecture. We have only extracted the hidden layer values at the decoder.

3. Build the attention mechanism. The attention mechanism will be based on how similar the encoder hidden vector and the decoder hidden vector are at each time step. Based on this similarity (softmax performed to give a weight value that sums up to one across all possible input time steps), we assign weightage to the encoder vector, as follows.

Passing the encoder decoder vectors through an activation and dense layer so that we achieve further non-linearity before taking the dot product (a measure of similarity—cosine similarity) between the vectors:

```
t = Dense(5000, activation='tanh')(decoder)
t2 = Dense(5000, activation='tanh')(encoder)
attention = dot([t, t2], axes=[2, 2])
```

Identify the weightage that is to be given to the input time steps:

```
attention = Dense(eng_max_length, activation='tanh')(attention)
attention = Activation('softmax')(attention)
```

Calculate the weighted encoder vector, as follows:

```
context = dot([attention, encoder], axes = [2,1])
```

4. Combine the decoder and weighted encoder vector:

```
decoder_combined_context = concatenate([context, decoder])
```

5. Connect the combination of decoder and weighted encoded vector to output layer:

```
output_dict_size = num_decoder_tokens+1
decoder_combined_context=Dense(2000,
activation='tanh')(decoder_combined_context)
output=(Dense(output_dict_size,
activation="softmax"))(decoder_combined_context)
```

6. Compile and fit the model, shown in the following code:

```
model4 = Model(inputs=[encoder_inputs, decoder_inputs],
outputs=[output])
model4.compile(optimizer='adam',
loss='categorical_crossentropy',metrics = ['accuracy'])
```

Sequence-to-Sequence Learning

A plot of architecture is as follows:

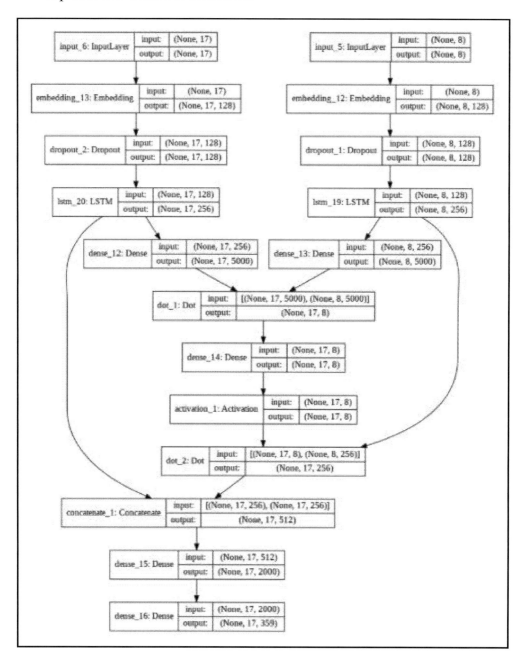

```
model4.fit([encoder_input_data, decoder_input_data],
decoder_target_data,
 batch_size=32,epochs=5,validation_split=0.05)
```

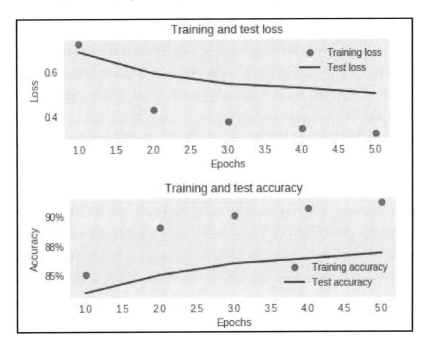

Once you fit the model, you will notice that the validation loss in this model is slightly better than the previous iteration.

7. Calculate the accuracy of translation in a similar way to what we did in the previous section:

```
decoder_input_data_pred=np.zeros((len(lines.fr), fr_max_length),
dtype='float32')

final_pred_att = []
for i in range(2500):
    word = 284
    for j in range(17):
        decoder_input_data_pred[(47500+i), j] = word
        pred = model4.predict([encoder_input_data[(47500+i)].reshape(1,8),decoder_input_data_pred[47500+i].reshape(1,17)])
        t = np.argmax(pred[0][j])
        word = t
        if word==89:
            break
```

Sequence-to-Sequence Learning

```
        final_pred_att.append(list(decoder_input_data_pred[47500+i]))

final_pred2_att = np.array(final_pred_att)
count = 0
correct_count = 0
for i in range(2500):
    correct_count += np.sum((decoder_input_data[47500+i]==final_pred2_att[i]) & (decoder_input_data[47500+i]!=89))
    count += np.sum(decoder_input_data[47500+i]!=89)
correct_count/count
```

The preceding code results in 52% of total words that are correctly translated, which is an improvement from the previous iteration.

8. Now that we have built a translation system that has a reasonable accuracy, let us inspect a few translations in the test dataset (the test dataset is the last 5% of the total dataset as we specified the `validation_split` to be 5%), as follows:

```
k = -1500
t = model4.predict([encoder_input_data[k].reshape(1,encoder_input_data.shape[1]),decoder_input_data[k].reshape(1,decoder_input_data.shape[1])]).reshape(decoder_input_data.shape[1], num_decoder_tokens+1)
```

Extract the predicted translations in terms of words:

```
t2 = np.argmax(t,axis=1)
for i in range(len(t2)):
    if int(t2[i])!=0:
        print(list(target_token_index.keys())[int(t2[i]-1)])
```

The output of the preceding code after converting English sentence to French is as follows:

```
je unk manger pas manger end end
```

Extract the actual translations in terms of words:

```
t2 = decoder_input_data[k]
for i in range(len(t2)):
    if int(t2[i])!=89:
        print(list(target_token_index.keys())[int(t2[i]-1)])
```

The output of the preceding code is as follows:

```
je unk ne pas manger ça end
```

We see that the predicted translation is fairly close to the original translation. In a similar manner, let us explore a few more translations on the validation dataset:

Original translation	Predicted translation
jétais tellement occupée la unk unk end	jétais tellement occupé pour plus unk end
je ne fais que ce unk me dit end	je viens fais que ce unk me fait end
jai unk de faire la unk end	je unk de unk la unk end

From the preceding table, we can see that there is a decent translation, however there are a few areas of potential improvement:

- Accounting for word similarities:
    - Words like *je* and *j'ai* are fairly similar, and so they should not be penalized heavily, even though it is decreasing the accuracy metric
- Reducing the number of unk words:
    - We have reduced the number of unk words to reduce the dimensionality of our dataset
    - We can potentially work on high dimensional data when we collect a larger corpus and work on a machine with industrial scale configuration

14
End-to-End Learning

In the previous chapters, we have learnt about analyzing sequential data (text) using the **Recurrent Neural Network (RNN)**, and also about analyzing image data using the **Convolutional Neural Network (CNN)**.

In this chapter, we will be learning about using the CNN + RNN combination to solve the following case studies:

- Handwritten-text recognition
- Generating caption from image

Additionally, we will also be learning about a new loss function called **Connectionist Temporal Classification (CTC)** loss while solving the handwritten-text-recognition problem.

Finally, we will be learning about beam search to come up with plausible alternatives to the generated text, while solving the caption generating from image problem.

Introduction

Consider a scenario where we are transcribing the image of a handwritten text. In this case, we would be dealing with image data and also sequential data (as the content in the image needs to be transcribed sequentially).

In traditional analysis, we would have hand-crafted the solution—for example: we might have slid a window across the image (where the window is of the average size of a character) so that the window would detect each character, and then output characters that it detects, with high confidence.

However, in this scenario, the size of the window or the number of windows we shall slide is hand crafted by us—which becomes a feature-engineering (feature generation) problem.

End-to-End Learning

A more end-to-end approach shall be extracting the features obtained by passing the image through a CNN and then passing these features as inputs to various time steps of an RNN, so that we extract the output at various time steps.

Thus, we will be using a combination of CNN and RNN, and by approaching the problem this way, we do not have to build a hand-crafted feature at all and let the model figure the optimal parameters of CNN and RNN.

Connectionist temporal classification (CTC)

One of the limitations to perform supervised learning on top of handwritten text recognition or in speech transcription is that, using a traditional approach, we would have to provide the label of which part of the image contain a certain character (in the case of hand-writing recognition) or which subsegment of the audio contains a certain phoneme (multiple phonemes combine to form a word utterance).

However, providing the ground truth for each character in image, or each phoneme in speech transcription, is prohibitively costly when building the dataset, where there are thousands of words or hundreds of hours of speech to transcribe.

CTC comes in handy to address the issue of not knowing the mapping of different parts of images to different characters. In this section, we will learn about how CTC loss functions.

Decoding CTC

Let's say, we are transcribing an image that contains the text **ab**. The example can look like any of the following (with varying space between the characters **a** and **b**) and the output label (ground truth) is just the same **ab**:

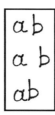

In the next step, we shall divide these examples into multiple time steps, as follows (where each box represents a time step):

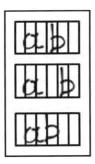

In the preceding example, we have a total of six time steps (each cell represents a time step).

We shall be predicting the output from each time step where the output of a time step is the softmax across the vocabulary.

Given that we are performing softmax, let's say the output of each time step for the first picture of **ab** is as follows:

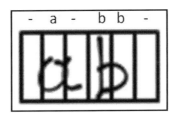

Note that, the - in the preceding picture represents a blank space. Additionally, the output in the fourth and fifth time steps can be **b** if the features of the image are passed through a bidirectional LSTM (or GRU)—as the information in the next time step can also influence the output in a previous time step while performing a bidirectional analysis.

In the final step, we shall be squashing all the softmax outputs that have the same value in consecutive time steps.

The preceding results in our final output being: **-a-b-** for this example.

If, in case the ground truth is **abb**, we shall expect a - in between the two **b**s so that the consecutive **b**s do not get squashed into one.

Calculating the CTC loss value

For the problem we were solving in the previous section, let's consider we have the following scenario, where the probability of having the character in a given time step is provided in the circle of the following diagram (note that, the probabilities add up to one in each time step from **t0** to **t5**):

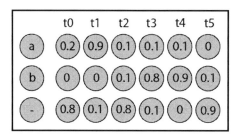

However, to keep the calculation simple for us to understand, let's consider the scenario where the ground truth is **a** and not **ab** and also that the output has only three time steps and not six. The modified output across the three time steps looks as follows:

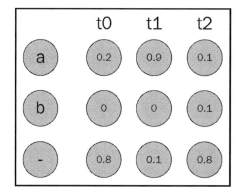

We can obtain the ground truth of **a** if the softmax in each time step is any of the following scenarios:

Output in each time step	Prob of character in time step 1	Prob of character in time step 2	Prob of character in time step 3	Probability of combination	Final probability
- - a	0.8	0.1	0.1	0.8 x 0.1 x 0.1	0.008
- a a	0.8	0.9	0.1	0.8 x 0.9 x 0.1	0.072
a a a	0.2	0.9	0.1	0.2 x 0.9 x 0.1	0.018
- a -	0.8	0.9	0.8	0.8 x 0.9 x 0.8	0.576

- a a	0.8	0.9	0.1	0.8 x 0.9 x 0.1	0.072
a - -	0.2	0.1	0.8	0.2 x 0.1 x 0.8	0.016
a a -	0.2	0.9	0.8	0.2 x 0.9 x 0.8	0.144
Overall probability					0.906

From the preceding results, we see that the overall probability of obtaining the ground truth **a** is 0.906.

CTC loss is the negative logarithm of the overall probability = $-log(0.906) = 0.04$.

Note that, as the combination of characters with the highest probability in each time step indicate the ground truth of **a**, the CTC loss is close to zero.

Handwritten-text recognition

In this case study, we will be working toward transcribing the handwritten images so that we extract the text that is present in the pictures.

A sample of the handwriting looks as follows:

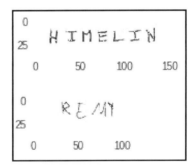

Note that in the preceding diagram, the handwritten characters have varied length, the images are of different dimensions, the separation between the characters is varied, and the images are of different quality.

In this section, we will be learning about using CNN, RNN, and the CTC loss function together to transcribe the handwritten examples.

Getting ready

The strategy we will adopt to transcribe the handwritten examples is as follows:

- Download images that contain images of handwritten text:
    - Multiple datasets containing handwritten text images are provided in the code file associated with this case study in GitHub
    - Ensure that, along with the images, you have also taken the ground truth corresponding to the images
- Resize all images to be of the same size, let's say 32 x 128 in size
- While resizing, we should also ensure that the aspect ratio of the picture is not distorted:
    - This is to ensure that images cannot look very blurred because the original image was changed to 32 x 128 in size
- We'll resize the images without distorting the aspect ratio, and then superimpose each of them on a different blank 32 x 128 image
- Invert the colors of the images so that the background is in black and the handwritten content is in white
- Scale the images so that their value is between zero and one
- Pre-process the output (ground truth):
    - Extract all the unique characters in output
    - Assign an index for each character
    - Find the maximum length of output, and then ensure that the number of time steps for which we are predicting the content of time step is more than the maximum length of output
    - Ensure the same length of output for all outputs by padding the ground truths
- Pass the processed picture through a CNN so that we extract features that are of 32 x 256 in shape
- Pass the extracted features from CNN through GRU unit that is bidirectional so that we encapsulate the information that is present in adjacent time steps
- Each of the 256 features in 32 time steps is an input for the respective time step

- Pass the output through a dense layer that has as many output values as the total number of unique characters in ground truth (the padded value (- in the example given in the introduction to the CTC loss section) shall also be one of the unique characters—where the padded value - represents either the space between characters, or the padding in the blank portion of the picture
- Extract the softmax and its corresponding output character at each of the 32 time steps

How to do it...

The preceding algorithm in code is performed as follows (the code file is available as Handwritten_text_recognition.ipynb in GitHub):

1. Download and import the dataset. This dataset will contain the images of handwritten text and their corresponding ground truth (transcription).
2. Build a function that resizes pictures without distorting the aspect ratio and pad the rest of pictures so that all of them have the same shape:

```
def extract_img(img):
    target = np.ones((32,128))*255
    new_shape1 = 32/img.shape[0]
    new_shape2 = 128/img.shape[1]
    final_shape = min(new_shape1, new_shape2)
    new_x = int(img.shape[0]*final_shape)
    new_y = int(img.shape[1]*final_shape)
    img2 = cv2.resize(img, (new_y,new_x ))
    target[:new_x,:new_y] = img2[:,:,0]
    target[new_x:,new_y:]=255
    return 255-target
```

In the preceding code, we are creating a blank picture (named target). In the next step, we have reshaped the picture to maintain its aspect ratio.

Finally, we have overwritten the rescaled picture on top of the blank one we created, and have returned the picture where the background is in black (255-target).

End-to-End Learning

3. Read the pictures and store them in a list, as shown in the following code:

```
filepath = '/content/words.txt'
f = open(filepath)
import cv2
count = 0
x = []
y = []
x_new = []
chars = set()
for line in f:
    if not line or line[0]=='#':
        continue
    try:
        lineSplit = line.strip().split(' ')
        fileNameSplit = lineSplit[0].split('-')
        img_path = '/content/'+fileNameSplit[0]+'/'+fileNameSplit[0] + '-' + fileNameSplit[1]+'/'+lineSplit[0]+'.png'
        img_word = lineSplit[-1]
        img = cv2.imread(img_path)
        img2 = extract_img(img)
        x_new.append(img2)
        x.append(img)
        y.append(img_word)
        count+=1
    except:
        continue
```

In the preceding code, we are extracting each picture and also are modifying it per the function that we defined. The input and modified examples for different scenario:

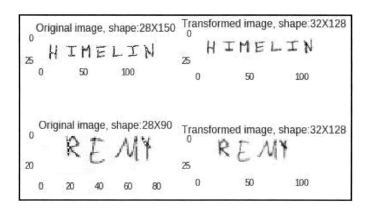

4. Extract the unique characters in output, shown as follows:

```
import itertools
list2d = y
charList = list(set(list(itertools.chain(*list2d))))
```

5. Create the output ground truth, as demonstrated in the following code:

```
num_images = 50000

import numpy as np
y2 = []
input_lengths = np.ones((num_images,1))*32
label_lengths = np.zeros((num_images,1))
for i in range(num_images):
    val = list(map(lambda x: charList.index(x), y[i]))
    while len(val)<32:
        val.append(79)
    y2.append(val)
    label_lengths[i] = len(y[i])
    input_lengths[i] = 32
```

In the preceding code, we are storing the index of each character in an output into a list. Additionally, if the output is less than 32 characters in size, we pad it with 79, which represents the blank value.

Finally, we are also storing the label length (in the ground truth) and also the input length (which is always 32 in size).

6. Convert the input and output into NumPy arrays, as follows:

```
x = np.asarray(x_new[:num_images])
y2 = np.asarray(y2)
x= x.reshape(x.shape[0], x.shape[1], x.shape[2],1)
```

7. Define the objective, as shown here:

```
outputs = {'ctc': np.zeros([32])}
```

We are initializing 32 zeros, as the batch size will be 32. For each value in batch size, we expect the loss value to be zero.

End-to-End Learning

8. Define the CTC loss function as follows:

```
def ctc_loss(args):
    y_pred, labels, input_length, label_length = args
    return K.ctc_batch_cost(labels, y_pred, input_length, label_length)
```

The preceding function takes the predicted values, ground truth (labels) and input, label lengths as input and calculates the CTC loss value.

9. Define the model, demonstrated as follows:

```
input_data = Input(name='the_input', shape = (32, 128,1), dtype='float32')

inner = Conv2D(32, (3,3), padding='same')(input_data)
inner = Activation('relu')(inner)
inner = MaxPooling2D(pool_size=(2,2),name='max1')(inner)
inner = Conv2D(64, (3,3), padding='same')(inner)
inner = Activation('relu')(inner)
inner = MaxPooling2D(pool_size=(2,2),name='max2')(inner)
inner = Conv2D(128, (3,3), padding='same')(input_data)
inner = Activation('relu')(inner)
inner = MaxPooling2D(pool_size=(2,2),name='max3')(inner)
inner = Conv2D(128, (3,3), padding='same')(inner)
inner = Activation('relu')(inner)
inner = MaxPooling2D(pool_size=(2,2),name='max4')(inner)
inner = Conv2D(256, (3,3), padding='same')(inner)
inner = Activation('relu')(inner)
inner = MaxPooling2D(pool_size=(4,2),name='max5')(inner)
inner = Reshape(target_shape = ((32,256)), name='reshape')(inner)
```

In the preceding code, we are building the CNN that converts a picture with 32 x 128 shape into a picture of 32 x 256 in shape:

```
gru_1 = GRU(256, return_sequences = True, name = 'gru_1')(inner)
gru_2 = GRU(256, return_sequences = True, go_backwards = True, name = 'gru_2')(inner)
mix_1 = add([gru_1, gru_2])
gru_3 = GRU(256, return_sequences = True, name = 'gru_3')(inner)
gru_4 = GRU(256, return_sequences = True, go_backwards = True, name = 'gru_4')(inner)
```

The architecture of model till the layers defined previously are as follows:

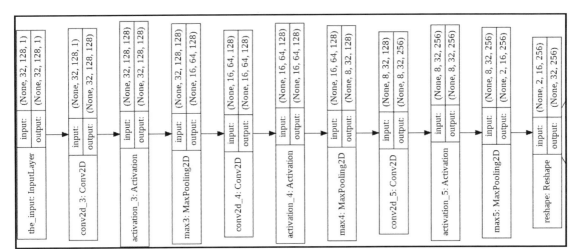

In the preceding code, we are passing the features obtained from CNN into a GRU. The architecture defined previously continues from the preceding graph shown is as follows:

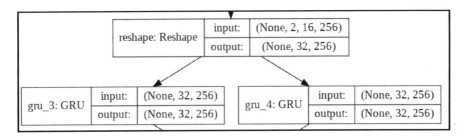

In the following code, we are concatenating the output of two GRUs so that we take both bidirectional GRU and normal GRU-generated features into account:

```
merged = concatenate([gru_3, gru_4])
```

The architecture after adding the preceding layer is as follows:

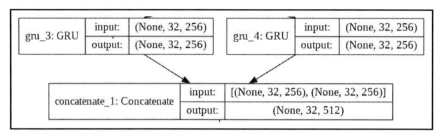

In the following code, we are passing the features of GRU output through a dense layer and applying softmax to get one of the possible 80 values as output:

```
dense = TimeDistributed(Dense(80))(merged)
y_pred = TimeDistributed(Activation('softmax',
name='softmax'))(dense)
```

The architecture of the model continues as follows:

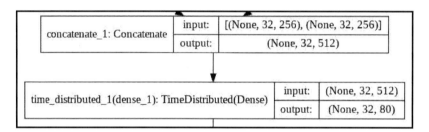

10. Initialize the variables that are required for the CTC loss:

```
from keras.optimizers import Adam
Optimizer = Adam()
labels = Input(name = 'the_labels', shape=[32], dtype='float32')
input_length = Input(name='input_length', shape=[1],dtype='int64')
label_length = Input(name='label_length',shape=[1],dtype='int64')
output = Lambda(ctc_loss, output_shape=(1,),name='ctc')([y_pred,
labels, input_length, label_length])
```

In the preceding code, we are mentioning that `y_pred` (predicted character values), actual labels, input length, and the label length are the inputs to the CTC loss function.

11. Build and compile the model as follows:

    ```
    model = Model(inputs = [input_data, labels, input_length,
    label_length], outputs= output)
    model.compile(loss={'ctc': lambda y_true, y_pred: y_pred},
    optimizer = Optimizer)
    ```

    Note that there are multiple inputs that we are passing to our model. The CTC calculation is as follows:

    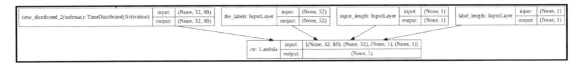

12. Create the following vectors of inputs and outputs:

    ```
    x2 = 1-np.array(x_new[:num_images])/255
    x2 = x2.reshape(x2.shape[0],x2.shape[1],x2.shape[2],1)
    y2 = np.array(y2[:num_images])
    input_lengths = input_lengths[:num_images]
    label_lengths = label_lengths[:num_images]
    ```

13. Fit the model on multiple batches of pictures, demonstrated in the following code:

    ```
    import random

    for i in range(100):
        samp=random.sample(range(x2.shape[0]-100),32)
        x3=[x2[i] for i in samp]
        x3 = np.array(x3)
        y3 = [y2[i] for i in samp]
        y3 = np.array(y3)
        input_lengths2 = [input_lengths[i] for i in samp]
        label_lengths2 = [label_lengths[i] for i in samp]
        input_lengths2 = np.array(input_lengths2)
        label_lengths2 = np.array(label_lengths2)
        inputs = {
        'the_input': x3,
        'the_labels': y3,
        'input_length': input_lengths2,
        'label_length': label_lengths2,
        }
        outputs = {'ctc': np.zeros([32])}
        model.fit(inputs, outputs,batch_size = 32, epochs=1, verbose
    =2)
    ```

End-to-End Learning

In the preceding code, we are sampling 32 pictures at a time, converting them into an array, and fitting the model to ensure that the CTC loss is zero.

Note that, we are excluding the last 100 pictures (in x2) from passing as input to model, so that we can test our model's accuracy on that data.

Furthermore, we are looping through the total dataset multiple times, as fetching all pictures into RAM and converting them into an array is very likely to crash the system, due to the huge memory requirement.

The training loss over increasing epochs is as follows:

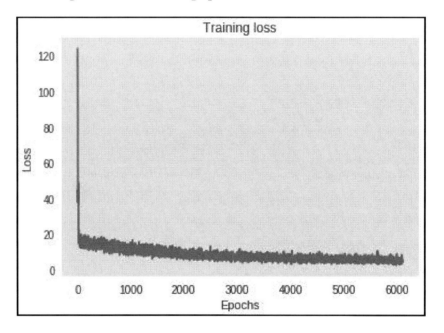

14. Predict the output at each time for a test picture, using the following code:

```
model2 = Model(inputs = input_data, outputs = y_pred)
pred = model2.predict(x2[-5].reshape(1,32,128,1))

pred2 = np.argmax(pred[0,:],axis=1)
out = ""
for i in pred2:
  if(i==79):
    continue
  else:
    out += charList[i]
plt.imshow(x2[k].reshape(32,128))
```

```
plt.title('Predicted word: '+out)
plt.grid('off')
```

In the preceding code, we are discarding the output if the predicted character at a time step is the character of 79.

A test examples and its corresponding predictions (in title) are as follows:

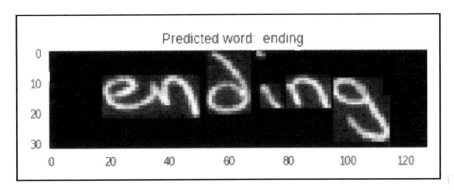

Image caption generation

In the previous case study, we learned about using CNN, RNN, and CTC loss together to transcribe the handwritten digits.

In this case study, we will learn about integrating CNN and RNN architectures to generate captions for a given picture.

Here is a sample of the picture:

- A girl in red dress with Christmas tree in background
- A girl is showing the Christmas tree
- A girl is playing in the park
- A girl is celebrating Christmas

Getting ready

In this section, let's list the strategy that we shall adopt to transcribe pictures:

- We'll be working toward generating captions from pictures by working on a dataset that has images as well as the captions associated with the images. Links of datasets that have images and their corresponding captions are provided in the corresponding notebook in GitHub.
- We'll extract the VGG16 features of each picture.
- We will also preprocess the captions text:
    - Convert all words to lower case
    - Remove punctuation
    - Add start and end tokens to each caption
- Keep only the pictures that are of a dog or a girl (we are performing this analysis only so that we train our model faster, as it takes ~5 hours to run this model, even on a GPU).
- Assign an index to each unique word in the vocabulary of captions.
- Pad all captions (where each word is represented by an index value) so that all captions are now of the same size.
- To predict the first word, the model shall take the combination of the VGG16 features and the embedding of the start token.
- Similarly, to predict the second word, the model will take the combination of the VGG16 features and the embedding combination of start token and the first word.
- In a similar manner, we proceed to fetch all the predicted words.
- We continue with the preceding steps until we predict the end token.

How to do it...

We'll code up the strategy that we have defined previously, as follows (the code file is available as `Image_captioning.ipynb` in GitHub):

1. Download and import a dataset that contains images and their corresponding captions. The recommended datasets are provided in GitHub

2. Import the relevant packages, as follows:

```
import glob
from PIL import Image
import numpy as np
import matplotlib.pyplot as plt
%matplotlib inline
import pickle
from tqdm import tqdm
import pandas as pd
from keras.preprocessing import sequence
from keras.models import Sequential
from keras.layers import LSTM, Embedding, TimeDistributed, Dense, RepeatVector, merge, Activation, Flatten
from keras.optimizers import Adam, RMSprop
from keras.layers.wrappers import Bidirectional
from keras.applications.inception_v3 import InceptionV3
from keras.preprocessing import image
import nltk
```

3. Load the caption dataset, shown in the following code:

```
caption_file = '...'
captions = open(caption_file, 'r').read().strip().split('\n')
d = {}
for i, row in enumerate(captions):
    row = row.split('\t')
    row[0] = row[0][:len(row[0])-2]
    if row[0] in d:
        d[row[0]].append(row[1])
    else:
        d[row[0]] = [row[1]]
total_images = list(d.keys())
```

4. Load the pictures and store the VGG16 features:

```
image_path = '...'
from keras.applications.vgg16 import VGG16
vgg16=VGG16(include_top=False, weights='imagenet', input_shape=(224,224,3))

import cv2
x = []
y = []
x2 = []
tot_images = ''
for i in range(len(d.keys())):
    for j in range(len(d[total_images[i]])):
```

```
            img_path = image_path+total_images[i]
            img = cv2.imread(img_path)
            try:
                img2 = cv2.resize(img, (224, 224))/255
                img3 = vgg16.predict(img2.reshape(1,224,224,3))
                x.append(img3)
                y.append(d[total_images[i]][j])
                tot_images = tot_images + ' '+total_images[i]
            except:
                continue
```

5. Convert the VGG16 features into NumPy arrays:

```
x = np.array(x)
x = x.reshape(x.shape[0],7,7,512)
```

6. Build a function that removes the punctuation in captions, and also converts all words to lowercase:

```
def preprocess(text):
    text=text.lower()
    text=re.sub('[^0-9a-zA-Z]+',' ',text)
    words = text.split()
    words2 = words
    words4=' '.join(words2)
    return(words4)
```

In the following code, we preprocess all the captions and also append the start and end tokens:

```
caps = []
for key, val in d.items():
    if(key in img_path2):
        for i in val:
            i = preprocess(i)
            caps.append('<start> ' + i + ' <end>')
```

7. Append only the pictures that are of a child or a dog:

```
caps2 = []
x2 = []
img_path3 = []
for i in range(len(caps)):
    if (('girl') in caps[i]):
        caps2.append(caps[i])
        x2.append(x[i])
        img_path2.append(img_path[i])
    elif 'dog' in caps[i]:
```

[489]

End-to-End Learning

```
            caps2.append(caps[i])
            x2.append(x[i])
            img_path2.append(img_path[i])
        else:
            continue
```

8. Extract all the unique words in captions, as follows:

```
words = [i.split() for i in caps2]
unique = []
for i in words:
    unique.extend(i)
unique = list(set(unique))
vocab_size = len(unique)
```

9. Assign indexes to words in the vocabulary, demonstrated in the following code:

```
word2idx = {val:(index+1) for index, val in enumerate(unique)}
idx2word = {(index+1):val for index, val in enumerate(unique)}
```

10. Identify the maximum length of a caption so that we pad all captions to be of the same length:

```
max_len = 0
for c in caps:
    c = c.split()
    if len(c) > max_len:
        max_len = len(c)
```

11. Pad all the captions to be of the same length, as follows:

```
n = np.zeros(vocab_size+1)
y = []
y2 = []
for k in range(len(caps2)):
    t= [word2idx[i] for i in caps2[k].split()]
    y.append(len(t))
    while(len(t)<max_len):
        t.append(word2idx['<end>'])
    y2.append(t)
```

12. Build the model that takes pictures as input and creates features from it:

```
from keras.layers import Input
embedding_size = 300
inp = Input(shape=(7,7,512))
inp1 = Conv2D(512, (3,3), activation='relu')(inp)
inp11 = MaxPooling2D(pool_size=(2, 2))(inp1)
```

```
inp2 = Flatten()(inp11)
img_emb = Dense(embedding_size, activation='relu')(inp2)
img_emb2 = RepeatVector(max_len)(img_emb)
```

13. Build a model that takes captions as input and creates features from it:

    ```
    inp2 = Input(shape=(max_len,))
    cap_emb = Embedding((vocab_size+1), embedding_size,
    input_length=max_len)(inp2)
    cap_emb2 = LSTM(256, return_sequences=True)(cap_emb)
    cap_emb3 = TimeDistributed(Dense(300))(cap_emb2)
    ```

14. Concatenate the two models and come up with a softmax of probabilities across all the possible output words:

    ```
    final1 = concatenate([img_emb2, cap_emb3])
    final2 = Bidirectional(LSTM(256, return_sequences=False))(final1)
    final3 = Dense(vocab_size+1)(final2)
    final4 = Activation('softmax')(final3)

    final_model = Model([inp, inp2], final4)
    ```

15. Compile the model, as follows:

    ```
    from keras.optimizers import Adam
    adam = Adam(lr = 0.0001)
    final_model.compile(loss='categorical_crossentropy', optimizer = adam, metrics=['accuracy'])
    ```

16. Fit the model, shown in the following code:

    ```
    for i in range(500):
        x3 = []
        x3_sent = []
        y3 = []
        shortlist_y = random.sample(range(len(y)-100),32)
        for j in range(len(shortlist_y)):
            for k in range(y[shortlist_y[j]]-1):
                n = np.zeros(vocab_size+1)
                x3.append(x2[shortlist_y[j]])
                pad_sent = pad_sequences([y2[shortlist_y[j]][:(k+1)]],
    maxlen=max_len, padding='post')
                x3_sent.append(pad_sent)
                n[y2[shortlist_y[j]][(k+1)]] = 1
                y3.append(n)
        x3 = np.array(x3)
        x3_sent =np.array(x3_sent)
        x3_sent = x3_sent.reshape(x3_sent.shape[0],
    ```

```
                x3_sent.shape[2])
                y3 = np.array(y3)
                final_model.fit([x3/12, x3_sent], y3, batch_size = 32,
epochs = 3, verbose = 1)
```

In the preceding code, we are looping through all the pictures, 32 at a time. Additionally, we are creating the input dataset in such a way that the first *n* number of output words in a caption are input along with the VGG16 features of a picture, and the corresponding output is the $n+1^{th}$ word of the caption.

Furthermore, we are dividing the VGG16 features (x3) by 12, as we need to scale the input values between zero and one.

17. The output caption of a sample picture can be obtained as follows:

```
l=-25
im_path = image_path+ img_path3[l]
img1 = cv2.imread(im_path)
plt.imshow(img1)
```

The output is decoded as follows:

```
p = np.zeros(max_len)
p[0] = word2idx['<start>']
for i in range(max_len-1):
    pred= final_model.predict([x33[1].reshape(1,7,7,512)/12,
p.reshape(1,max_len)])
    pred2 = np.argmax(pred)
    print(idx2word[pred2])
    p[i+1] = pred2
    if(idx2word[pred2]=='<end>'):
        break
```

The output of the preceding code is as follows:

```
a
black
dog
is
jumping
in
the
air
<end>
```

Note that the generated caption correctly detected that the dog is black and is also jumping.

Generating captions, using beam search

In the previous section on caption generation, we have decoded based on the word that has the highest probability in a given time step. In this section, we'll improve upon the predicted captions by using beam search.

Getting ready

Beam search works as follows:

- Extract the probability of various words in first time step (where VGG16 features of the picture and the start token are the input)
- Instead of providing the most probable word as the output, we'll consider the top three probable words
- We'll proceed to the next time step, where we extract the top three characters in this time step
- We'll loop through the top three predictions in first time step, as an input to the prediction of second time step, and extract the top three predictions for each of the possible top three predictions in input:
    - Let's say that a, b, and c are the top three predictions in time-step one
    - We'll use a as input along with VGG16 features to predict the top three probable characters in time-step two, and similarly for b and c
    - We have a total of nine combinations of outputs between the first time- step and the second time-step
    - Along with the combination, we'll also store the confidence of each prediction across all nine combinations:
        - For example: if the probability of a in time-step one is 0.4 and the probability of x in time step two is 0.5, then the probability of combination is 0.4 x 0.5 = 0.2
    - We'll keep the top three combinations and discard the rest of the combinations
- We'll repeat the preceding step of shortlisting the top three combinations until we reach the end of the sentence

The value of three is the beam length across which we are searching for the combination.

How to do it...

In this section, we'll code up the beam-search strategy that we discussed previously (the code file is available as Image_captioning.ipynb in GitHub):

1. Define a function that takes the VGG16 features of the picture as input, along with the sequence of words and their corresponding confidences from the previous time steps and return the top three predictions in the current time step:

```
beamsize = 3
def get_top3(img, string_with_conf):
    tokens, confidence = string_with_conf
    p = np.zeros((1, max_len))
    p[0, :len(tokens)] = np.array(tokens)
    pred = final_model.predict([img.reshape(1,7,7,512)/12, p])
    best_pred = list(np.argsort(pred)[0][-beamsize:])
    best_confs = list(pred[0,best_pred])
    top_best = [(tokens + list([best_pred[i]]),
confidence*best_confs[i]) for i in range(beamsize)]
    return top_best
```

In the preceding step, we are separating the word IDs and their corresponding confidences provided in the string_with_conf parameter. Furthermore, we are storing the sequence of tokens in an array and using that to make a prediction.

In the next step, we are extracting the top three predictions in the next time step and storing it in best_pred.

Additionally, along with the best prediction of word IDs, we are also storing the confidence associated with each top three prediction in the current time step.

Finally, we are returning the three predictions of the second time step.

2. Loop through the range of the maximum possible length of sentence and extract the top three possible combinations of words across all time steps:

```
start_token = word2idx['<start>']
best_strings = [([start_token], 1)]
for i in range(max_len):
    new_best_strings = []
    for string in best_strings:
        strings = get_top3(x33[1], string)
        new_best_strings.extend(strings)
        best_strings = sorted(new_best_strings, key=lambda x:
x[1], reverse=True)[:beamsize]
```

3. Loop through the preceding `best_strings` obtained to print the output:

```
for i in range(3):
    string = best_strings[i][0]
    print('============')
    for j in string:
        print(idx2word[j])
        if(idx2word[j]=='<end>'):
            break
```

The output sentences for the same picture that we tested in the previous section are as follows:

<start>	<start>	<start>
a	a	a
black	black	black
dog	dog	dog
is	is	is
playing	jumping	playing
in	in	in
the	the	the
grass	grass	grass
<end>	<end>	<end>

Note that, in this specific case, the first and second sentences differed when it came to the words `jumping` and `playing`, and the third sentence happened to be the same as the first, as the probability of combination was much higher.

15
Audio Analysis

In the previous chapters, we learned about dealing with sequential text data. Audio can also be considered sequential data, with varying amplitudes over time. In this chapter, we will be learning about the following:

- Classifying a song by genre
- Music generation using deep learning
- Transcribing audio into text

Classifying a song by genre

In this case study, we will be classifying a song into one of 10 possible genres. Imagine a scenario where we are tasked to automatically classify the genre of a song without manually listening to it. This way, we can potentially minimize operational overload as far as possible.

Getting ready

The strategy we'll adopt is as follows:

1. Download a dataset of various audio recordings and the genre they fit into.
2. Visualize and contrast a spectrogram of the audio signal for various genres.
3. Perform CNN operations on top of a spectrogram:
    - Note that we will be performing a CNN 1D operation on a spectrogram, as the concept of translation does not apply in the case of audio recordings

4. Extract features from the CNN after multiple convolution and pooling operations.
5. Flatten the output and pass it through a dense layer that has 10 possible classes in an output layer.
6. Minimize categorical cross-entropy to classify the audio recording to one of the 10 possible classes.

Once we classify the audio, we'll plot the embeddings of each audio input so that similar audio recordings are grouped together. This way, we will be in a position to identify the genre of a new song without listening to it, thus automatically classifying the audio input into a genre.

How to do it...

The strategy discussed above is coded as follows (the code file is available as Genre_classification.ipynb in GitHub):

1. Download the dataset and import the relevant packages:

   ```
   import sys, re, numpy as np, pandas as pd, music21, IPython,
   pickle, librosa, librosa.dsiplay, os
   from glob import glob
   from tqdm import tqdm
   from keras.utils import np_utils
   ```

2. Loop through the audio files to extract the `mel spectrogram` input features of the input audio, and store the output genre for the audio input:

   ```
   song_specs=[]
   genres = []
   for genre in os.listdir('...'): # Path to genres folder
     song_folder = '...' # Path to songs folder
     for song in os.listdir(song_folder):
       if song.endswith('.au'):
         signal, sr = librosa.load(os.path.join(song_folder, song), sr=16000)
         melspec = librosa.feature.melspectrogram(signal, sr=sr).T[:1280,]
         song_specs.append(melspec)
         genres.append(genre)
         print(song)
     print('Done with:', genre)
   ```

In the preceding code, we are loading the audio file and extracting its features. Additionally, we are extracting the `melspectrogram` features of the signal. Finally, we are storing the `mel` features as the input array and the genre as the output array.

3. Visualize the spectrogram:

```
plt.subplot(121)
librosa.display.specshow(librosa.power_to_db(song_specs[302].T),
 y_axis='mel',
 x_axis='time',)
plt.title('Classical audio spectrogram')
plt.subplot(122)
librosa.display.specshow(librosa.power_to_db(song_specs[402].T),
 y_axis='mel',
 x_axis='time',)
plt.title('Rock audio spectrogram')
```

The following is the output of the preceding code:

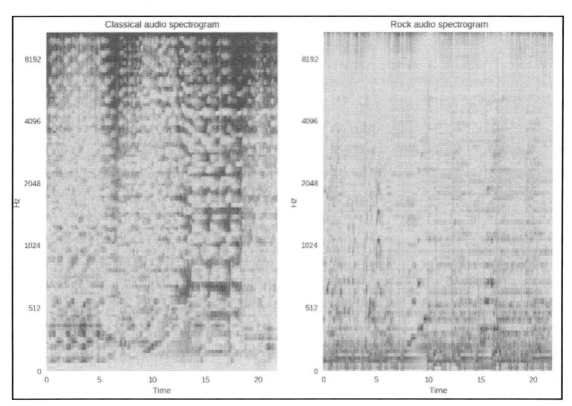

You can see that there is a distinct difference between the classical audio spectrogram and the rock audio spectrogram.

4. Define the input and output arrays:

```
song_specs = np.array(song_specs)

song_specs2 = []
for i in range(len(song_specs)):
    tmp = song_specs[i]
    song_specs2.append(tmp[:900][:])
song_specs2 = np.array(song_specs2)
```

Convert the output classes into one-hot encoded versions:

```
genre_one_hot = pd.get_dummies(genres)
```

5. Create train-and-test datasets:

```
x_train, x_test, y_train, y_test = train_test_split(song_specs2, np.array(genre_one_hot),test_size=0.1,random_state = 42)
```

6. Build and compile the method:

```
input_shape = (1280, 128)
inputs = Input(input_shape)
x = inputs
levels = 64
for level in range(7):
    x = Conv1D(levels, 3, activation='relu')(x)
    x = BatchNormalization()(x)
    x = MaxPooling1D(pool_size=2, strides=2)(x)
    levels *= 2
x = GlobalMaxPooling1D()(x)
for fc in range(2):
    x = Dense(256, activation='relu')(x)
    x = Dropout(0.5)(x)
labels = Dense(10, activation='softmax')(x)
```

Note that the `Conv1D` method in the preceding code works in a manner very similar to that of `Conv2D`; however, it is a one-dimensional filter in `Conv1D` and a two-dimensional one in `Conv2D`:

```
model = Model(inputs=[inputs], outputs=[labels])
adam = keras.optimizers.Adam(lr=0.0001)
model.compile(loss='categorical_crossentropy',optimizer=adam,metrics=['accuracy'])
```

7. Fit the model:

    ```
    history = model.fit(x_train,
    y_train,batch_size=128,epochs=100,verbose=1,validation_data=(x_test
    , y_test))
    ```

    From the preceding code, we can see that the model classifies with an accuracy of ~60% on the test dataset.

8. Extract the output from the pre-final layer of the model:

    ```
    from keras.models import Model
    layer_name = 'dense_14'
    intermediate_layer_model =
    Model(inputs=model.input,outputs=model.get_layer(layer_name).output
    )
    intermediate_output = intermediate_layer_model.predict(song_specs2)
    ```

    The preceding code produces output at the pre-final layer.

9. Reduce the dimensions of the embeddings to 2, using t-SNE so that we can now plot our work on a chart:

    ```
    from sklearn.manifold import TSNE
    tsne_model = TSNE(n_components=2, verbose=1, random_state=0)
    tsne_img_label = tsne_model.fit_transform(intermediate_output)
    tsne_df = pd.DataFrame(tsne_img_label, columns=['x', 'y'])
    tsne_df['image_label'] = genres
    ```

10. Plot the t-SNE output:

    ```
    from ggplot import *
    chart = ggplot(tsne_df, aes(x='x', y='y', color='genres'))+
    geom_point(size=70,alpha=0.5)
    chart
    ```

Audio Analysis

The following is the chart for the preceding code:

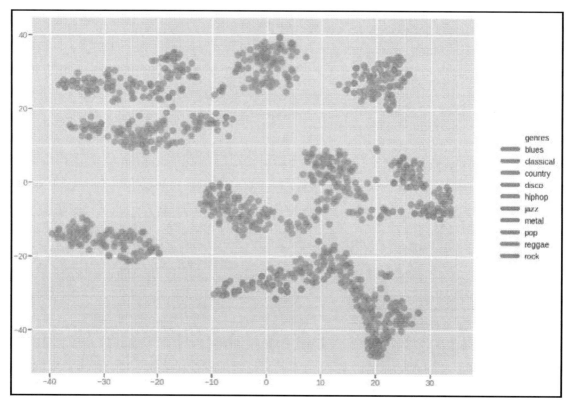

From the preceding diagram, we can see that audio recordings for similar genres are located together. This way, we are now in a position to classify a new song into one of the possible genres automatically, without manual inspection. However, if the probability of an audio belonging to a certain genre is not very high, it will potentially go to a manual review so that misclassifications are uncommon.

Generating music using deep learning

In the previous chapter, we learned about generating text by going through a novel. In this section, we will learn about generating audio from a sequence of audio notes.

Getting ready

A MIDI file typically contains information about the notes and chords of the audio file, whereas the note object contains information about the pitch, octave, and offset of the notes. The chord object contains a set of notes that are played at the same time.

The strategy that we'll adopt to build a music generator is as follows:

- Extract the notes present in audio file
- Assign a unique ID for each note.
- Take a sequence of 100 historical notes, and the 101st note shall be the output.
- Fit an LSTM model.

How to do it...

The strategy discussed above is coded as follows (the code file is available as Music_generation.ipynb in GitHub) along with the recommended audio file:

1. Import the relevant packages and dataset:

    ```
    !pip install mido music21
    import mido, glob, os
    from mido import MidiFile, MidiTrack, Message
    import numpy as np
    from music21 import converter, instrument, note, chord
    from keras.utils import np_utils
    from keras.layers import Input, LSTM, Dropout, Dense, Activation
    from keras.models import Model

    fname = '/content/nintendo.mid'
    ```

2. Read the content of the file:

    ```
    midi = converter.parse(fname)
    ```

    The preceding code reads a stream of scores.

3. Define a function that reads the stream of scores and extracts the notes from it (along with silence, if present in the audio file):

    ```
    def parse_with_silence(midi=midi):
        notes = []
        notes_to_parse = None
        parts = instrument.partitionByInstrument(midi)
    ```

Audio Analysis

```
        if parts: # file has instrument parts
            notes_to_parse = parts.parts[0].recurse()
        else: # file has notes in a flat structure
            notes_to_parse = midi.flat.notes
        for ix, element in enumerate(notes_to_parse):
            if isinstance(element, note.Note):
                _note = str(element.pitch)
                notes.append(_note)
            elif isinstance(element, chord.Chord):
                _note = '.'.join(str(n) for n in element.normalOrder)
                notes.append(_note)
            elif isinstance(element, note.Rest):
                _note = '#'+str(element.seconds)
                notes.append(_note)
    return notes
```

In the preceding code, we are obtaining the notes by looping through the elements and, depending on whether the element is a note, a chord, or a rest (which indicates silence), we extract the corresponding notes, append them, and return the appended list.

4. Extract the notes from the input audio file's stream:

```
notes = parse_with_silence()
```

A sample note output is as follows:

```
['#2.0', '#9.5', '#1.75', 'E-5', 'F5', 'E-3', 'G5', '#0.125', 'E-4', '3.7']
```

Note that the values starting with a # indicate silence (the duration is the same as the number adjacent to #).

5. Create the input and output dataset by creating a dictionary of the note's ID and its corresponding name:

```
# get all unique values in notes
pitchnames = sorted(set(item for item in notes))
# create a dictionary to map pitches to integers
note_to_int = dict((note, number) for number, note in enumerate(pitchnames))
network_input = []
network_output = []
```

1. Create a sequence of input and output arrays:

```
sequence_length = 100
for i in range(0, len(notes) - sequence_length, 1):
    sequence_in = notes[i:i + sequence_length]
    sequence_out = notes[i + sequence_length]
    network_input.append([note_to_int[char] for char in sequence_in])
    network_output.append(note_to_int[sequence_out])
```

In the preceding step, we are taking a sequence of 100 notes as input and extracting the output at the 101st time step.

Additionally, we are also converting the note into its corresponding ID:

```
n_patterns = len(network_input)
# reshape the input into a format compatible with LSTM layers
network_input = np.reshape(network_input, (n_patterns, sequence_length, 1))
# normalize input
network_input = network_input / np.max(network_input)
network_output = np_utils.to_categorical(network_output)

N = 9 * len(network_input)//10
print(network_input.shape, network_output.shape)
# (36501, 100, 1) (36501, 50)
```

In the preceding code, we are reshaping the input data so that it can then be fed into an LSTM layer (which requires the `batch_size` shape, time steps, and the number of features per time step).

Additionally, we are normalizing the input, and we are also converting the output into a one-hot encoded set of vectors.

6. Fit the model:

```
model.fit(network_input, network_output, epochs=100, batch_size=32, verbose = 1)
```

The following is the output of the preceding code:

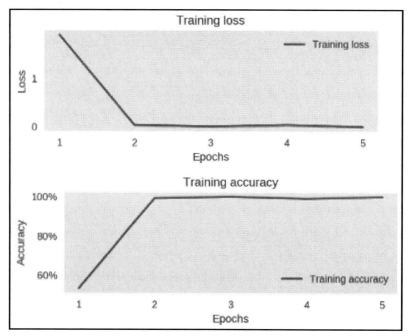

7. Generate predictions:

```
from tqdm import trange
print('generating prediction stream...')
start = np.random.randint(0, len(network_input)-1)
int_to_note = dict((number, note) for number, note in enumerate(pitchnames))
pattern = network_input[start].tolist()
prediction_output = []
```

Note that, in the preceding code, we have chosen a random audio location, from where we'll sample a sequence that will be used as a seed for prediction in future time steps.

Chapter 15

8. Generate predictions by taking a sequence of 100 notes at a time, generating the next prediction, appending it to the input sequence, and generating the next prediction (by taking the latest sequence of the last 100 notes):

```
for note_index in trange(500):
    prediction_input = np.reshape(pattern, (1, len(pattern), 1))
    prediction = model.predict(prediction_input, verbose=0)
    index = np.argmax(prediction)
    result = int_to_note[index]
    prediction_output.append(result)
    pattern.append([index/49])
    pattern = pattern[1:len(pattern)]
```

Note that we are dividing the index (which is the predicted output of the model) by 49, as we did in the same exercise while building the model (divided by `np.max(network_input)`).

The preceding exercise is slightly different than the text generation exercise, where we performed embedding on top of input word IDs, as we are not performing embedding in this scenario. The model is still working without embedding in this scenario, potentially because there are fewer unique values in the input.

9. Create note values based on values generated by the model:

```
offset = 0
output_notes = []

# create note and chord objects based on the values generated by
the model
print('creating notes and chords')
for pattern in prediction_output:
    # pattern is a chord
    if (('.' in pattern) or pattern.isdigit()) and pattern[0]!='#':
        notes_in_chord = pattern.split('.')
        notes = []
        for current_note in notes_in_chord:
            new_note = note.Note(int(current_note))
            new_note.storedInstrument = instrument.Piano()
            notes.append(new_note)
        new_chord = chord.Chord(notes)
        new_chord.offset = offset
        output_notes.append(new_chord)
    # pattern is a note
    elif pattern[0]!='#':
        new_note = note.Note(pattern)
        new_note.offset = offset
```

[507]

Audio Analysis

```
            new_note.storedInstrument = instrument.Piano()
            output_notes.append(new_note)
        # pattern is silence
        else:
            new_note = note.Rest()
            new_note.offset = offset
            new_note.storedInstrument = instrument.Piano()
            new_note.quarterLength = float(pattern[1:])
            output_notes.append(new_note)
        # increase offset each iteration so that notes do not stack
        offset += 0.5
```

Note that, in the preceding code, we are offsetting each note by 0.5 seconds, so that the notes do not stack on top of one another while producing the output.

10. Write the generated predictions into a music stream:

```
from music21 import stream
midi_stream = stream.Stream(output_notes)
midi_stream.write('midi', fp='OP.mid')
```

Now, you should be able to listen to the music that's been generated by your model.

Transcribing audio into text

In `Chapter 14`, *End-to-End Learning*, we learned about transcribing handwritten text images into text. In this section, we will be leveraging a similar end-to-end model to transcribe voices into text.

Getting ready

The strategy that we'll adopt to transcribe voices is as follows:

- Download a dataset that contains the audio file and its corresponding transcriptions (*ground truths*)
- Specify a sampling rate while reading the audio files:
    - If the sampling rate is 16,000, we'll be extracting 16,000 data points per second of audio.

- Extract a Fast Fourier Transformation of the audio array:
    - An FFT ensures that we have only the most important features of a signal.
    - By default, the FFT gives us $n/2$ number of data points, where n is the number of data points in the whole audio recording.
- Sample the FFT features of the audio where we extract 320 data points at a time; that is, we extract 20 milliseconds (320/16000 = 1/50 seconds) of audio data at a time
- Additionally, we will sample 20 milliseconds of data at 10-millisecond intervals.
- For this exercise, we'll be working on an audio recording where the audio duration is, at most, 10 seconds
- We will store the 20 milliseconds of audio data into an array:
    - We have already seen that we sample 20 milliseconds of data for every 10 milliseconds.
    - Thus, for a one-second audio clip, we will have 100 x 320 data points, and for a 10- second audio clip, we'll have 1,000 x 320 = 320,000 data points.
- We will initialize an empty array of 160,000 data points and overwrite the values with the FFT values—as we have already learned that the FFT values are one half of the original number of data points
- For each array of 1,000 x 320 data points, we'll store the corresponding transcriptions
- We'll assign an index for each character and then convert the output into a list of indices
- Additionally, we'll also be storing the input length (which is the predefined number of time steps) and the label lengths (which are the actual number of characters present in the output)
- Furthermore, we will define the CTC loss function that is based on the actual output, the predicted output, the number of time steps (input length), and the label length (the number of characters in the output)
- We'll define the model that is a combination of `conv1D` (as this is audio data) and GRU
- Furthermore, we will ensure that we normalize data using batch normalization so that the gradients do not vanish
- We'll run the model on batches of data, where we randomly sample batches of data and feed them to the model that tries to minimize the CTC loss
- Finally, we will decode the model predictions on a new data point by using the `ctc_decode` method

Audio Analysis

How to do it...

The strategy discussed above is coded as follows (the code file is available as `Voice transcription.ipynb` in GitHub):

1. Download the dataset and import the relevant packages:

    ```
    $wget http://www.openslr.org/resources/12/train-clean-100.tar.gz
    $tar xzvf train-clean-100.tar.gz
    ```

    ```
    import librosa
    import numpy as np
    import pandas as pd
    ```

2. Read all the file names and their corresponding transcriptions and turn them into separate lists:

    ```
    import os, numpy as np
    org_path = '/content/LibriSpeech/train-clean-100/'
    count = 0
    inp = []
    k=0
    audio_name = []
    audio_trans = []
    for dir1 in os.listdir(org_path):
        dir2_path = org_path+dir1+'/'
        for dir2 in os.listdir(dir2_path):
            dir3_path = dir2_path+dir2+'/'

            for audio in os.listdir(dir3_path):
                if audio.endswith('.txt'):
                    k+=1
                    file_path = dir3_path + audio
                    with open(file_path) as f:
                        line = f.readlines()
                        for lines in line:
    audio_name.append(dir3_path+lines.split()[0]+'.flac')
                            words2 = lines.split()[1:]
                            words4=' '.join(words2)
                            audio_trans.append(words4)
    ```

3. Store the length of the transcription into a list so that we can understand the maximum transcription length:

```
import re
len_audio_name=[]
for i in range(len(audio_name)):
    tmp = audio_trans[i]
    len_audio_name.append(len(tmp))
```

4. For this exercise, to be in a position to train a model on a single GPU, we'll perform this exercise on the first 2,000 audio files whose transcriptions are fewer than 100 characters in length:

```
final_audio_name = []
final_audio_trans = []
for i in range(len(audio_name)):
    if(len_audio_name[i]<100):
        final_audio_name.append(audio_name[i])
        final_audio_trans.append(audio_trans[i])
```

In the preceding code, we are storing the audio name and the corresponding audio transcription for only those audio recordings that have a transcription length of fewer than 100 characters.

5. Store the inputs as a 2D array and the corresponding outputs of only those audio files that have a duration of fewer than 10 seconds:

```
inp = []
inp2 = []
op = []
op2 = []
for j in range(len(final_audio_name)):
    t = librosa.core.load(final_audio_name[j],sr=16000, mono=True)
    if(t[0].shape[0]<160000):
        t = np.fft.rfft(t[0])
        t2 = np.zeros(160000)
        t2[:len(t)] = t
        inp = []
        for i in range(t2.shape[0]//160):
            inp.append(t2[(i*160):((i*160)+320)])
        inp2.append(inp)
        op2.append(final_audio_trans[j])
```

Audio Analysis

6. Create an index for each unique character in the data:

    ```
    import itertools
    list2d = op2
    charList = list(set(list(itertools.chain(*list2d))))
    ```

7. Create the input and the label lengths:

    ```
    num_audio = len(op2)
    y2 = []
    input_lengths = np.ones((num_audio,1))*243
    label_lengths = np.zeros((num_audio,1))
    for i in range(num_audio):
        val = list(map(lambda x: charList.index(x), op2[i]))
        while len(val)<243:
            val.append(29)
        y2.append(val)
        label_lengths[i] = len(op2[i])
        input_lengths[i] = 243
    ```

    Note that we are creating an input length that is 243, as the output of the model (which we are going to build in a later step) has 243 time steps.

8. Define the CTC loss function:

    ```
    import keras.backend as K
    def ctc_loss(args):
        y_pred, labels, input_length, label_length = args
        return K.ctc_batch_cost(labels, y_pred, input_length,
    label_length
    ```

9. Define the model:

    ```
    input_data = Input(name='the_input', shape = (999,161),
    dtype='float32')
    inp = BatchNormalization(name="inp")(input_data)
    conv= Conv1D(filters=220, kernel_size = 11,strides = 2,
    padding='valid',activation='relu')(inp)
    conv = BatchNormalization(name="Normal0")(conv)
    conv1= Conv1D(filters=220, kernel_size = 11,strides = 2,
    padding='valid',activation='relu')(conv)
    conv1 = BatchNormalization(name="Normal1")(conv1)
    gru_3 = GRU(512, return_sequences = True, name = 'gru_3')(conv1)
    gru_4 = GRU(512, return_sequences = True, go_backwards = True, name
    = 'gru_4')(conv1)
    merged = concatenate([gru_3, gru_4])
    normalized = BatchNormalization(name="Normal")(merged)
    dense = TimeDistributed(Dense(30))(normalized)
    ```

```
y_pred = TimeDistributed(Activation('softmax',
name='softmax'))(dense)
Model(inputs = input_data, outputs = y_pred).summary()
```

10. Define the input and the output parameters of the CTC loss function:

    ```
    from keras.optimizers import Adam
    Optimizer = Adam(lr = 0.001)
    labels = Input(name = 'the_labels', shape=[243], dtype='float32')
    input_length = Input(name='input_length', shape=[1],dtype='int64')
    label_length = Input(name='label_length',shape=[1],dtype='int64')
    output = Lambda(ctc_loss, output_shape=(1,),name='ctc')([y_pred,
    labels, input_length, label_length])
    ```

11. Build and compile the model:

    ```
    model = Model(inputs = [input_data, labels, input_length,
    label_length], outputs= output)
    model.compile(loss={'ctc': lambda y_true, y_pred: y_pred},
    optimizer = Optimizer, metrics = ['accuracy'])
    ```

    A summary of the model is as follows:

    ```
    Layer (type)                    Output Shape          Param #      Connected to
    ================================================================================
    the_input (InputLayer)          (None, 999, 161)      0
    _____
    inp (BatchNormalization)        (None, 999, 161)      644          the_input[0][0]
    _____
    conv1d_3 (Conv1D)               (None, 495, 220)      389840       inp[0][0]
    _____
    Normal_0 (BatchNormalization)   (None, 495, 220)      880          conv1d_3[0][0]
    _____
    conv1d_4 (Conv1D)               (None, 243, 220)      532620       Normal_0[0][0]
    _____
    Normal_1 (BatchNormalization)   (None, 243, 220)      880          conv1d_4[0][0]
    _____
    gru_3 (GRU)                     (None, 243, 512)      1125888      Normal_1[0][0]
    _____
    gru_4 (GRU)                     (None, 243, 512)      1125888      Normal_1[0][0]
    _____
    concatenate_1 (Concatenate)     (None, 243, 1024)     0            gru_3[0][0]
                                                                       gru_4[0][0]
    _____
    Normal_2 (BatchNormalization)   (None, 243, 1024)     4096         concatenate_1[0][0]
    _____
    time_distributed_1 (TimeDistrib (None, 243, 30)       30750        Normal_2[0][0]
    _____
    time_distributed_2 (TimeDistrib (None, 243, 30)       0            time_distributed_1[0][0]
    ================================================================================
    Total params: 3,211,486
    Trainable params: 3,208,236
    Non-trainable params: 3,250
    _____
    ```

Audio Analysis

12. Fit the model on batches of data that are sampled from the input:

```
for i in range(2500):
    samp=random.sample(range(x2.shape[0]-25),32)
    batch_input=[inp2[i] for i in samp]
    batch_input = np.array(batch_input)
    batch_input = batch_input/np.max(batch_input)
    batch_output = [y2[i] for i in samp]
    batch_output = np.array(batch_output)
    input_lengths2 = [input_lengths[i] for i in samp]
    label_lengths2 = [label_lengths[i] for i in samp]
    input_lengths2 = np.array(input_lengths2)
    label_lengths2 = np.array(label_lengths2)
    inputs = {'the_input': batch_input,
              'the_labels': batch_output,
              'input_length': input_lengths2,
              'label_length': label_lengths2}
    outputs = {'ctc': np.zeros([32])}
    model.fit(inputs, outputs,batch_size = 32, epochs=1, verbose
=1)
```

In the preceding code, we are looping through and extracting batches of data 2,500 times, normalizing the input data, and fitting the model.

Also, we are performing a high number of epochs, as the CTC loss decreases slowly for this particular dataset and model combination.

13. Predict the test audio:

```
model2 = Model(inputs = input_data, outputs = y_pred)

k=-12
pred= model2.predict(np.array(inp2[k]).reshape(1,999,161)/100)
```

In the preceding code, we are specifying a model (model2) that takes the input test array and extracts the model prediction in each of the 243 time steps.

Additionally, we are extracting the prediction for the 12th element from the last of the input array (note that we have excluded the last 25 input data points from being considered while training the model). Furthermore, we have also pre-processed it in the same way that we did before, by passing the input data to the model-training process.

14. Decode the predictions on the new data point:

```
def decoder(pred):
    pred_ints = (K.eval(K.ctc_decode(pred,[243])[0][0])).flatten().tolist()
    out = ""
    for i in range(len(pred_ints)):
        if pred_ints[i]<28:
        out = out+charList[pred_ints[i]]
    print(out)
```

In the preceding code, we were decoding the prediction using the `ctc_decode` method. Alternatively, we could have decoded the prediction in the same way as we extracted the prediction in the handwritten image transcription. Finally, we print out the predictions.

We'll be in a position to decode the predictions by calling the previously defined function:

```
decoder(pred)
```

The output of one of the predictions is as follows:

```
HAT ONTED BYTHO MY POARL OTHE MOUG WESPRN FOURRS S SO LON
```

While the preceding output looks as if it's gibberish, it sounds phonetically similar to the actual audio, which is as follows:

```
I FOUND IT BY THE NINTH PARALLEL OFF THE NORTHWESTERN SHORES OF CEYLON
```

There's more...

Some ways in which we can further improve the accuracy of our transcriptions are as follows:

- Train on more data points
- Incorporate a language model to perform fuzzy matching on the output so that we correct the predicted output

16
Reinforcement Learning

In the previous chapters, we learned about mapping input to a target—where, the input and output values are provided. In this chapter, we will be learning about reinforcement learning, where the objective that we want to achieve and the environment that we operate in are provided, but not any input or output mapping. The way in which reinforcement learning works is that we generate input values (the state in which the agent is) and the corresponding output values (the reward the agent achieves for taking certain actions in a state) by taking random actions at the start and gradually learning from the generated input data (actions in a state) and output values (rewards achieved by taking certain actions).

In this chapter, we will cover the following:

- The optimal action to take in a simulated game with a non-negative reward
- The optimal action to take in a state in a simulated game
- Q-learning to maximize rewards when playing Frozen Lake
- Deep Q-learning to balance a cart pole
- Deep Q-learning to play the Space Invaders game

The optimal action to take in a simulated game with a non-negative reward

In this section, we will understand the way in which we can take the right action for a simulated game. Note that this exercise will primarily help you to grasp how reinforcement learning works.

Getting ready

Let's define the environment we are operating in this simulated setting.

You have three boxes, on which two players are playing a game. Player 1 marks a box with 1 and player 2 marks one with 2. The player who is able to mark two consecutive boxes wins.

The empty board for this game looks as follows:

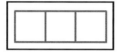

For the problem we just defined, only player 1 has an opportunity to win the game. The possible scenarios in which player 1 wins are either of the following:

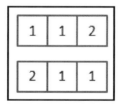

From the problem setting, the intuitive way in which player 1 wins is when player 1 chooses the middle box. This way, irrespective of which box is chosen by player 2, player 1 will win on their subsequent move.

While the first step for player 1 is intuitive for us, in the next section we will learn about how an agent can automatically figure out the optimal first move.

The strategy that we will adopt to solve this problem is as follows:

- We initialize an empty board
- Player 1 chooses a box randomly
- Player 2 chooses a box randomly from the remaining 2 boxes
- Depending on the box player 1 is left with, we update the reward for player 1:
    - If player 1 is able to place 1s in two consecutive boxes, he is a winner and will a reward of 1
    - Otherwise, player 1 will get a reward of 0
- Repeat the preceding exercise 100 times, where the game is played and we store a reward for the given sequence of moves

- Now, we will go ahead and calculate the average reward for the various first moves that were taken
- The box that was chosen in the first move, that has the highest average reward over 100 iterations is the optimal first move for player 1

How to do it...

The strategy defined above is coded as follows (the code file is available as Finding_optimal_policy.ipynb in GitHub):

1. Define the game environment and the function to play the game:

    ```
    def play_game():
        empty_board = [0,0,0]
        move = []
        for step in range(3):
            index_to_choose = [i for i,j in enumerate(empty_board) if j==0]
            samp = random.sample(range(len(index_to_choose)), 1)[0]
            if(step%2==0):
                empty_board[index_to_choose[samp]]=1
                move.append(index_to_choose[samp])
            else:
                empty_board[index_to_choose[samp]]=2
        return(reward(empty_board), move[0])
    ```

    In the preceding code, we are initializing an empty board with zero values and playing a random move named samp. Player 1 takes the first move and then player 2 takes their turn, followed by player 1. We fill up the empty board in this manner.

2. Define a function to calculate the reward at the end of a game:

    ```
    def reward(empty_board):
        reward = 0
        if((empty_board[0]==1 & empty_board[1]==1) | (empty_board[1]==1 & empty_board[2]==1)):
            reward = 1
        else:
            reward = 0
        return reward
    ```

3. Play the game 100 times:

```
rew = []
step = []
for i in range(100):
    r, move = play_game()
    rew.append(r)
    step.append(move)
```

4. Calculate the reward for choosing a certain first move:

```
sub_list = [i for i,j in enumerate(step) if j==1]
final_reward = 0
count = 0
for i in sub_list:
    final_reward += rew[i]
    count+=1
final_reward/count
```

When you repeat the preceding code for multiple options for the first move, you will notice that the average reward is highest when occupying the second square.

The optimal action to take in a state in a simulated game

In the previous scenario, we considered a simplistic case where there is a reward when the objective is achieved. In this scenario, we will complicate game by having negative rewards too. However, the objective remains the same: maximizing the reward in the given problem setting where the environment has both positive and negative rewards.

Getting ready

The environment we are working on is as follows:

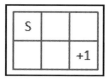

We start at the cell with **S** in it and our objective is to reach the cell where the reward is **+1**. In order to maximize the chances of achieving the reward, we will be using Bellman's equation, which calculates the value of each cell in the preceding grid as follows:

*Value of current cell = reward of moving from the current cell to next cell + discount factor * value of next cell*

Additionally, in the current problem, the reward for moving to any cell other than the cell with a reward of **+1** is *0*.

The discount factor can be thought of as the energy expended moving from one cell to another. Thus, a cell that is far away from the rewarding cell will have a lower value compared to other cells in the current problem setting.

Once we calculate the value of each cell, we move to the cell that has the highest value of all the cells that an agent could move to.

The strategy that we'll adopt to calculate the value of each cell is as follows:

- Initialize an empty board.
- Define the possible actions that an agent could take in a cell.
- Define the state that an agent will be in, for the action the agent takes in the current cell.
- Calculate the value of the current state, which depends on the reward for moving to the next state, as well as the value of the next state.
- Update the cell value of the current state based on the earlier calculation.
- Additionally, store the action taken in the current state to move to the next state.
- Note that, in the initial iterations, the values of cells that are far away from the end goal remain zero, while the values of cells that are adjacent to the end state rise.
- As we iterate the previous steps multiple times, we will be in a position to update the cell values and, thus, in a position to decide the optimal route for the agent to follow.

How to do it...

In this section, we'll code the strategy that we laid out in the previous section (the code file is available as `Finding_optimal_policy.ipynb` in GitHub):

1. Initialize an empty board:

```
empty_board = [[0,0,0]
              ,[0,0,1]]
```

2. Define the actions that can be taken in different states—where D represents moving down, R is right, L is left, and U is moving up:

```
state_actions = {(0,0):('D','R')
                ,(0,1):('D','R','L')
                ,(0,2):('D','L')
                ,(1,0):('U','R')
                ,(1,1):('L','U','R')
                }
```

3. Define the function that extracts the next state given the current state and the action taken in the current state:

```
def get_next_state(curr_state, action):
    i,j = curr_state
    if action=='D':
        i = i+1
    elif action=='U':
        i = i-1
    elif action=='R':
        j = j+1
    elif action=='L':
        j = j-1
    else:
        print('unk')
    return((i,j))
```

4. Initialize the lists where the state, action, and rewards are appended:

```
curr_state = (0,0)
state_action_reward = []
state = []
state_action = []
```

5. Execute 100 actions at most in an episode (an episode is an instance of a game) where random action is taken in a cell (state) and calculate the value of the current state based on the reward for moving to the next state, as well as the value of next state.

   Repeat the above exercise for 100 iterations (episodes/games) and calculate the value of each cell:

   ```
   for m in range(100):
       curr_state = (0,0)
       for k in range(100):
           reward = 0
           action = state_actions[curr_state][random.sample(range(len(state_actions[curr_state])),1)[0]]
           next_state = get_next_state(curr_state, action)
   ```

   In the preceding code, we are taking random actions in a state and then calculating the next state for the action taken in the current state:

   ```
           state.append(curr_state)
           empty_board[curr_state[0]][curr_state[1]] = reward + empty_board[next_state[0]][next_state[1]]*0.9 empty_board[curr_state[0]][curr_state[1]])
   ```

   In the preceding code, we are updating the value of a state:

   ```
           curr_state = next_state
           state_action.append(action)

           if(next_state==(1,2)):
               reward+=1
               break
   ```

   The preceding results in the following final cell state values across all the cells:

   ```
   [0.7290000000000001, 0.81, 0.9]
   [0.81, 0.9, 1]
   ```

Based on the preceding output, the agent can take take either the right action or the down action at the start of the game (where the agent starts from the top-left corner). However, if the agent takes the down action in the first step, it is better off taking the *right* action in the next step, as the cell state value is higher for the state to the right compared to the state that is above the current cell state.

There's more...

Imagine the environment (the cells and their corresponding rewards) looks as follows:

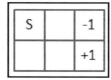

The actions that could be taken at different states areas follows:

```
state_actions = {(0,0):('D','R')
                ,(0,1):('D','R')
                ,(1,0):('R')
                ,(1,1):('R')
                }
```

The cell state values in various cells after iterating through the game multiple times is as follows:

```
[0.7290000000000001, -0.9, -1]
[0.81, 0.9, 1]
```

From the preceding results, we can see that the agent is better off taking an action down from the top-left corner than moving to its right, as the cell state value is higher for the cell state that is below the starting cell.

Q-learning to maximize rewards when playing Frozen Lake

So far, in the previous sections, we have been taking random actions in a given state. Additionally, we have also been defining the environment and calculating the next state, actions, and the reward for a move via code. In this section, we will leverage OpenAI's Gym package to navigate through the Frozen Lake environment.

Getting ready

The Frozen Lake environment looks as follows:

The agent starts from the **S** state and the goal is to reach the **G** state by avoiding the **H** state as far as possible.

In the preceding environment, there are 16 possible states that an agent can be in. Additionally, the agent can take four possible actions (move up, down, right, or left).

We'll define a q-table where there are 16 rows corresponding to the 16 states and four columns corresponding to the four actions that can be taken in each state.

In the previous section, we learned that:

*Value of action taken in a state = reward + discount factor * value of the best possible action taken in the next state*

We'll modify the preceding formula as follows:

Value of action taken in a state = value of action taken in a state + 1*(reward + discount factor* value of the best possible action taken in the next state - value of action taken in a state)

Finally, we'll replace the 1 with the learning rate, so that a value update of an action in a state does not change drastically. This is similar to the effect of having learning rates in neural networks.

Value of action taken in a state = value of action taken in a state + learning rate*(reward + discount factor* value of the best possible action taken in the next state - value of action taken in a state)

From the preceding, we can now update the q-table so that we can identify the optimal action that can be taken in different states.

The strategy that we'll adopt to solve this case study is as follows:

- Register the environment in OpenAI's Gym
- Initialize a zero array q-table shaped as 16 x 4

- Employ an exploration-versus-exploitation approach in choosing an action in a given state:
    - So far, we have merely explored possible overall actions as we randomly chose an action in a given state.
    - In this section, we will explore the initial iterations as we are not sure of the optimal action to take during the initial few episodes of the game.
    - However, as we learn more about the game, we exploit what we have learned in terms of possible actions to take while still taking random actions (with decreasing frequency as the number of episodes increases).
- In a given episode:
    - Choose an action depending on whether we try and explore or exploit
    - Identify the new state and reward, and check whether the game is over by taking the action chosen in the previous step
    - Initialize a learning rate parameter and discount factor
    - Update the value of taking the preceding action in a state in the q-table by using the formula discussed earlier
    - Repeat the preceding steps until the game is over
- Additionally, repeat the preceding steps for 1,000 different games
- Check the q-table to identify the optimal action to take in a given state
- Plot the path of an agent as it takes the actions in a state as per the q-table

How to do it...

In this section, we will code the strategy we discussed earlier (the code file is available as `Frozen_Lake_with_Q_Learning.ipynb` in GitHub):

1. Import the relevant packages:

```
import gym
from gym import envs
from gym.envs.registration import register
```

Gym is a toolkit for developing and comparing reinforcement learning algorithms. It supports teaching agents everything from walking to playing games such as Pong and Pinball.

More about Gym can be found at: https://gym.openai.com/.

2. Register the environment:

```
register(
  id = 'FrozenLakeNotSlippery-v1',
  entry_point = 'gym.envs.toy_text:FrozenLakeEnv',
  kwargs = {'map_name': '4x4', 'is_slippery':False},
  max_episode_steps = 100,
  reward_threshold = 0.8196)
```

3. Create the environment:

```
env = gym.make('FrozenLakeNotSlippery-v1')
```

4. Inspect the created environment:

```
env.render()
```

The preceding step renders (prints) the environment:

```
env.observation_space
```

The preceding code provides the number of state action pairs in the environment. In our case, given that it is a 4 x 4 grid, we have a total of 16 states. Thus, we have a total of 16 observations.

```
env.action_space.n
```

The preceding code defines the number of actions that can be taken in a state in the environment:

```
env.action_space.sample()
```

Reinforcement Learning

The preceding code samples an action from the possible set of actions:

```
env.step(action)
```

The preceding code takes the action and generates the new state and the reward of the action, flags whether the game is done, and provides additional information for the step:

```
env.reset()
```

The preceding code resets the environment so that the agent is back to the starting state.

5. Initialize the q-table:

```
import numpy as np
qtable = np.zeros((16,4))
```

We have initialized it to a shape of (16, 4) as there are 16 states and 4 possible actions in each state.

6. Run multiple iterations of playing a game:

Initialize hyper-parameters:

```
total_episodes=15000
learning_rate=0.8
max_steps=99
gamma=0.95
epsilon=1
max_epsilon=1
min_epsilon=0.01
decay_rate=0.005
```

Play multiple episodes of the game:

```
rewards=[]
for episode in range(total_episodes):
    state=env.reset()
    step=0
    done=False
    total_rewards=0
```

In the code below, we are defining the action to be taken. If eps (which is a random number generated between 0 to 1) is less than 0.5, we explore; otherwise, we exploit (to consider the best action in a q-table)

```
for step in range(max_steps):
    exp_exp_tradeoff=random.uniform(0,1)
    ## Exploitation:
    if exp_exp_tradeoff>epsilon:
        action=np.argmax(qtable[state,:])
    else:
        ## Exploration
        action=env.action_space.sample()
```

In the code below, we are fetching the new state and the reward, and flag whether the game is done by taking the action in the given step:

```
new_state, reward, done, _ = env.step(action)
```

In the code below, we are updating the q-table based on the action taken in a state. Additionally, we are also updating the state with the new state obtained after taking action in the current state:

```
qtable[state,action]=qtable[state,action]+learning_rate*(reward+gamma*np.max(qtable[new_state,:])-qtable[state,action])
    total_rewards+=reward
    state=new_state
```

In the following code, as the game is over, we proceed to a new episode of the game. However, we ensure that the randomness factor (eps), which is used in deciding whether we are going for exploration or exploitation, is updated.

```
    if(done):
        break
epsilon=min_epsilon+(max_epsilon-min_epsilon)*np.exp(decay_rate*episode)
    rewards.append(total_rewards)
```

7. Once we have built the q-table, we now deploy the agent to maneuver in line with the optimal actions suggested by the q-table:

```
env.reset()

for episode in range(1):
    state=env.reset()
    step=0
    done=False
    print("--------------------")
```

```
                print("Episode",episode)
                for step in range(max_steps):
                    env.render()
                    action=np.argmax(qtable[state,:])
                    print(action)
                    new_state,reward,done,info=env.step(action)
                    if done:
                        #env.render()
                        print("Number of Steps",step+1)
                        break
                    state=new_state
```

The preceding gives the optimal path that the agent has to traverse to reach the end goal.

Deep Q-learning to balance a cart pole

In the previous sections, we learned about taking an action based on q-table values. However, arriving at an optimal value is time-consuming, as the agent would have to play multiple times to arrive at the optimal q-table.

In this section, we will learn about using a neural network so that we can arrive at the optimal values faster than what we achieved when we used Q-learning.

Getting ready

For this exercise, we will register the cart-pole environment where the possible actions are to move either right or left so that we balance the pole. Additionally the cart position, cart velocity, pole angle, and pole velocity at the tip is the information we have about the states.

The rules of this game can be found here: https://gym.openai.com/envs/CartPole-v1/.

A pole is attached to a cart by an un-actuated joint, and the cart moves along a frictionless track. The system is controlled by applying a force of +1 or -1 to the cart. The pendulum starts upright, and the goal is to prevent it from falling over. A reward of +1 is provided for every time-step that the pole remains upright. The episode ends when the pole is more than 15 degrees from the vertical, or the cart moves more than 2.4 units from the center.

In order to balance the cart-pole, we'll adopt the same strategy as we adopted in the previous section. However, the difference in deep q-learning is that we'll use a neural network to help us predict the optimal action that the agent needs to take.

The way in which we train the neural network is as follows:

- We'll store the information on state values, the action taken, and the reward achieved:
    - The reward will be 1 if the game does not end (is not over) and 0 otherwise.
- Initially, the model predicts based on randomly initialized weights, where the output layer of the model has two nodes that correspond to the new state's values for the two possible actions.
- The new state value will be based on the action that maximizes the value of new state
- If the game is not over, we update the current state's value with the sum of the reward and the product of the maximum state value of the new state and the discount factor.
- We'll now override the value of the action from the updated current state's value that we obtained previously:
    - If the action taken in the current step is wrong (that is, the game is over) the value of the action in the current state will be 0.
    - Otherwise, the value of the target in the current step is a positive number.
    - This way, we are letting the model figure out the right action to take.
    - Additionally, we can consider this a way to specify that the action is wrong when the reward is zero. However, given that we are not sure whether it is the right action when the reward is 1, we'll just update it for the action we took and leave the new state's value (if we take the other action) untouched.
- We append the state values to the input array, and also the values of taking one or an other action in the current state as the output array.
- We fit the model that minimizes the mean-squared error for the preceding data points.
- Finally, we keep reducing the exploration over an increasing number of episodes.

How to do it...

We'll code the strategy we discussed earlier as follows (the code file is available as `Deep_Q_learning_to_balance_a_cart_pole.ipynb` in GitHub):

1. Create the environment and store the action size and state size in variables:

   ```
   import gym
   env = gym.make('CartPole-v0')
   state_size = env.observation_space.shape[0]
   action_size = env.action_space.n
   ```

   A cart-pole environment looks as follows:

   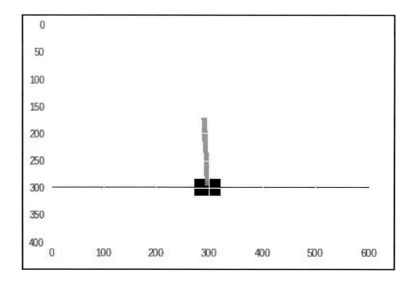

2. Import the relevant packages:

   ```
   import numpy as np
   import random
   from keras.models import Sequential
   from keras.layers import Dense
   from keras.optimizers import Adam
   from collections import deque
   ```

3. Define a model:

   ```
   model=Sequential()
   model.add(Dense(24,input_dim=state_size,activation='relu'))
   model.add(Dense(24,activation='relu'))
   model.add(Dense(2,activation='linear'))
   model.compile(loss='mse',optimizer=Adam(lr=0.01))
   ```

4. Define the lists that need to be appended:

   ```
   memory = deque(maxlen=2000)
   gamma = 0.95 # discount rate
   epsilon = 1.0 # exploration rate
   epsilon_min = 0.01
   epsilon_decay = 0.995
   done = False
   batch_size=32
   ```

5. Define a function that replays the game:

   ```
   def replay(model, batch_size,epsilon):
       epsilon_min = 0.01
       epsilon_decay = 0.995
       minibatch = random.sample(memory, batch_size)
       for state, action, reward, next_state, done in minibatch:
           target = reward
           if not done:
               target = (reward + gamma
   *np.amax(model.predict(next_state)[0]))
           new_action_value = model.predict(state)
           new_action_value[0][action] = target
           model.fit(state,new_action_value, epochs=1, verbose=0)
       if epsilon > epsilon_min:
           epsilon *= epsilon_decay
       return model,epsilon
   ```

In the preceding code, we are defining a function that takes the neural network model, batch size, and epsilon (the parameter that signifies whether we'll explore or exploit). We are fetching a random sample of the size of `batch_size`. Note that you will learn about memory structure (which comprises state, action, reward, and `next_state`) in the next step. If the game is not done, we are updating the reward for taking the action that is taken; otherwise, the target will be 0 (as the reward would be 0 when the game is over).

Additionally, the model predicts the value of taking a certain action (as the model has 2 nodes in the output—where each provides the output of taking one action over the other). The function returns the updated model and the coefficient of exploration/exploitation (epsilon).

6. Play the game over multiple episodes and append the scores obtained by the agent. Additionally, ensure that the actions taken by the agent are dictated by the model based on the epsilon value:

```
episodes=200
maxsteps=200
score_list = []
for e in range(episodes):
    state = env.reset()
    state = np.reshape(state, [1, state_size])
```

In the preceding code, we are playing a total of 200 episodes where we are resetting the environment at the start of the episode. Additionally, we are reshaping the state so that it can be passed to the neural network model:

```
for step in range(maxsteps):
    if np.random.rand()<=epsilon:
        action=env.action_space.sample()
    else:
        action = np.argmax(model.predict(state)[0])
```

In the preceding step, we are taking an action based on the exploration parameter (epsilon), where we take a random action (env.actionspace.sample()) in certain cases, and leverage the model's predictions in other cases:

```
next_state, reward, done, _ = env.step(action)
reward = reward if not done else -10
next_state = np.reshape(next_state, [1, state_size])
memory.append((state, action, reward, next_state, done))
```

In the preceding step, we are performing an action and extracting the next state, the reward, and the information about whether the game is over. Additionally, we are overwriting the reward value with -10 if the game is over (which means the agent made an incorrect move). Further, we are extracting the next state and appending it into the memory. This way, we are creating a dataset for the model to be trained on, where the model takes the current state and reward to calculate the reward for one of the two possible actions:

```
            state = next_state
            if done:
                print("episode: {}/{}, score: {}, exp prob: 
    {:.2}".format(e, episodes, step, epsilon))
                score_list.append(step)
                break
            if len(memory) > batch_size:
                model,epsilon=replay(model, batch_size,epsilon)
```

In the preceding code, if the game is done, we append the score (the number of steps taken during the game); otherwise, we update the model. Additionally, we are updating the model only when memory has as many data points as the predefined batch size.

Plotting the scores over increasing epochs looks as follows:

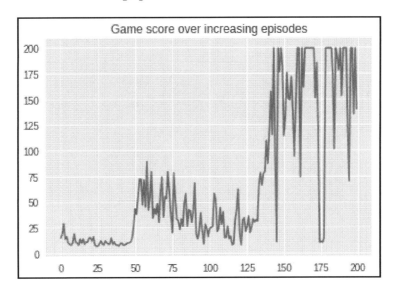

Deep Q-learning to play Space Invaders game

In the previous section, we used Deep Q-learning to play the Cart-Pole game. In this section, we will leverage Deep Q-learning to play Space Invaders, which is a more complex environment than Cart-Pole.

A sample screenshot of the Space Invaders game looks as follows:

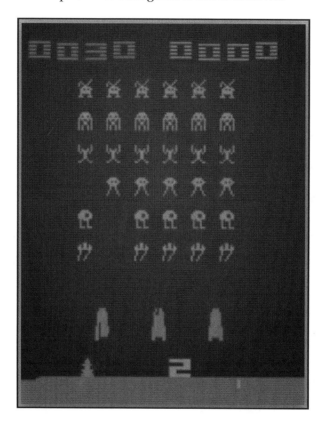

source: https://gym.openai.com/envs/SpaceInvaders-v0/

The objective of this exercise is to maximize the score obtained in a single game.

Getting ready

The strategy that we'll adopt to build an agent that is able to maximize the score is as follows:

- Initialize the environment of the *Space Invaders-Atari2600* game.
- Preprocess the image frame:
    - Remove pixels that do not necessarily impact the action prediction
        - For example, pixels below the location of the player
    - Normalize the input image.
    - Resize the image before passing it to the neural network model
- Stack frames as required by the Gym environment
- Let the agent play the game over multiple episodes:
    - During the initial episodes, we'll have high exploration which decays over increasing episodes.
    - The action that needs to be taken in a state depends on the value of the exploration coefficient.
    - Store the game state and the corresponding reward for the action taken in a state in memory.
    - Update the model depending on the reward that was received in the previous episodes.

How to do it...

The strategy that we discussed earlier is coded as follows:

1. Download the ROM that contains the Space Invaders game and also install the `retro` package:

```
$ wget http://www.atarimania.com/roms/Roms.rar && unrar x Roms.rar && unzip Roms/ROMS.zip
$ pip3 install gym-retro
$ python3 -m retro.import ROMS/
```

2. Create the environment and extract the observation space:

```
env=retro.make(game='SpaceInvaders-Atari2600')
env.observation_space
# Box(210,160,3)
```

Reinforcement Learning

3. Build a function that preprocesses the frame (image/screenshot of the Space Invaders game):

```
def preprocess_frame(frame):
    # Greyscale frame
    gray = rgb2gray(frame)
    # Crop the screen (remove the part below the player)
    # [Up: Down, Left: right]
    cropped_frame = gray[8:-12,4:-12]
    # Normalize Pixel Values
    normalized_frame = cropped_frame/255.0
    # Resize
    preprocessed_frame = transform.resize(normalized_frame, [110,84])
    return preprocessed_frame
```

4. Build a function that stacks frames given a state:

```
stack_size = 4 # We stack 4 frames
# Initialize deque with zero-images one array for each image
stacked_frames = deque([np.zeros((110,84), dtype=np.int) for i in range(stack_size)], maxlen=4)
def stack_frames(stacked_frames, state, is_new_episode):
    # Preprocess frame
    frame = preprocess_frame(state)
    if is_new_episode:
        # Clear our stacked_frames
        stacked_frames = deque([np.zeros((110,84), dtype=np.int) for i in range(stack_size)], maxlen=4)
        # Because we're in a new episode, copy the same frame 4x
        stacked_frames.append(frame)
        stacked_frames.append(frame)
        stacked_frames.append(frame)
        stacked_frames.append(frame)
        # Stack the frames
        stacked_state = np.stack(stacked_frames, axis=2)
    else:
        # Append frame to deque, automatically removes the oldest frame
        stacked_frames.append(frame)
        # Build the stacked state (first dimension specifies different frames)
        stacked_state = np.stack(stacked_frames, axis=2)
    return stacked_state, stacked_frames
```

5. Initialize the model hyperparameters:

   ```
   ### MODEL HYPERPARAMETERS
   state_size = [110, 84, 4] # Our input is a stack of 4 frames hence 110x84x4 (Width, height, channels)
   action_size = env.action_space.n # 8 possible actions
   learning_rate =  0.00025 # Alpha (aka learning rate)

   ### TRAINING HYPERPARAMETERS
   total_episodes = 50 # Total episodes for training
   max_steps = 50000 # Max possible steps in an episode
   batch_size = 32 # Batch size

   # Exploration parameters for epsilon greedy strategy
   explore_start = 1.0 # exploration probability at start
   explore_stop = 0.01 # minimum exploration probability
   decay_rate = 0.00001 # exponential decay rate for exploration prob

   # Q learning hyperparameters
   gamma = 0.9 # Discounting rate

   ### MEMORY HYPERPARAMETERS
   pretrain_length = batch_size # Number of experiences stored in the Memory when initialized for the first time
   memory_size = 1000000 # Number of experiences the Memory can keep

   ### PREPROCESSING HYPERPARAMETERS
   stack_size = 4 # Number of frames stacked

   ### MODIFY THIS TO FALSE IF YOU JUST WANT TO SEE THE TRAINED AGENT
   training = False

   ## TURN THIS TO TRUE IF YOU WANT TO RENDER THE ENVIRONMENT
   episode_render = False
   ```

6. Build a function that samples data from the total memory:

   ```
   memory = deque(maxlen=100000)

   def sample(memory, batch_size):
       buffer_size = len(memory)
       index = np.random.choice(np.arange(buffer_size),
       size = batch_size,
       replace = False)
       return [memory[i] for i in index]
   ```

Reinforcement Learning

7. Build a function that returns the action that the agent needs to take:

```
def predict_action(model,explore_start, explore_stop, decay_rate,
decay_step, state, actions):
    exp_exp_tradeoff = np.random.rand()
    explore_probability = explore_stop + (explore_start -
explore_stop) * np.exp(-decay_rate * decay_step)
    if (explore_probability > exp_exp_tradeoff):
        choice = random.randint(1,len(possible_actions))-1
        action = possible_actions[choice]
    else:
        Qs = model.predict(state.reshape((1, *state.shape)))
        choice = np.argmax(Qs)
        action = possible_actions[choice]
    return action, explore_probability
```

8. Build a function that fine-tunes the model:

```
def replay(agent,batch_size,memory):
    minibatch = sample(memory,batch_size)
    for state, action, reward, next_state, done in minibatch:
        target = reward
        if not done:
            target = reward +
gamma*np.max(agent.predict(next_state.reshape((1,*next_state.shape)
))[0])
        target_f = agent.predict(state.reshape((1,*state.shape)))
        target_f[0][action] = target
        agent.fit(state.reshape((1,*state.shape)), target_f, epochs=1,
verbose=0)
    return agent
```

9. Define the neural network model:

```
def DQNetwork():
    model=Sequential()
    model.add(Convolution2D(32,input_shape=(110,84,4),kernel_size=8,
strides=4, padding='valid',activation='elu'))
    model.add(Convolution2D(64, kernel_size=4, strides=2,
padding='valid',activation='elu'))
    model.add(Convolution2D(128, kernel_size=3, strides=2,
padding='valid',activation='elu'))
    model.add(Flatten())
    model.add(Dense(units=512))
    model.add(Dense(units=3,activation='softmax'))
    model.compile(optimizer=Adam(0.01),loss='mse')
    return model
```

A summary of model is as follows:

```
Layer (type)                 Output Shape              Param #
=================================================================
conv2d_1 (Conv2D)            (None, 26, 20, 32)        8224
_____
conv2d_2 (Conv2D)            (None, 12, 9, 64)         32832
_____
conv2d_3 (Conv2D)            (None, 5, 4, 128)         73856
_____
flatten_1 (Flatten)          (None, 2560)              0
_____
dense_1 (Dense)              (None, 512)               1311232
_____
dense_2 (Dense)              (None, 3)                 1539
=================================================================
Total params: 1,427,683
Trainable params: 1,427,683
Non-trainable params: 0
```

10. Loop through multiple episodes and keep playing the game while updating the model:

    ```
    agent = DQNetwork()
    agent.summary()
    rewards_list=[]
    Episodes=200
    # Iterate the game
    for episode in range(Episodes):
        # reset state in the beginning of each game
        step = 0
        decay_step = 0
        episode_rewards = []
        state = env.reset()
        state, stacked_frames = stack_frames(stacked_frames, state, True)
        while step < max_steps:
            step += 1
            decay_step +=1
            # Predict the action to take and take it
            action, explore_probability = predict_action(agent,explore_start, explore_stop, decay_rate, decay_step, state, possible_actions)
            #Perform the action and get the next_state, reward, and done information
            next_state, reward, done, _ = env.step(action)
    ```

```
            # Add the reward to total reward
            episode_rewards.append(reward)
        if done:
    # The episode ends so no next state
            next_state = np.zeros((110,84), dtype=np.int)
            next_state, stacked_frames = stack_frames(stacked_frames,
    next_state, False)
    # Set step = max_steps to end the episode
            step = max_steps
    # Get the total reward of the episode
            total_reward = np.sum(episode_rewards)
            print('Episode:{}/{} Score:{} Explore
    Prob:{}'.format(episode,Episodes,total_reward,explore_probability))
            rewards_list.append((episode, total_reward))
    # Store transition <st,at,rt+1,st+1> in memory D
            memory.append((state, action, reward, next_state, done))
        else:
    # Stack the frame of the next_state
            next_state, stacked_frames = stack_frames(stacked_frames,
    next_state, False)
    # Add experience to memory
            memory.append((state, action, reward, next_state, done))
    # st+1 is now our current state
            state = next_state
        env.render()
    # train the agent with the experience of the episode
    agent=replay(agent,batch_size,memory)
```

11. Plot the rewards obtained over increasing episodes:

```
score=[]
episode=[]
for e,r in rewards_list:
    episode.append(e)
    score.append(r)
import matplotlib.pyplot as plt
plt.plot(episode,score)
```

Chapter 16

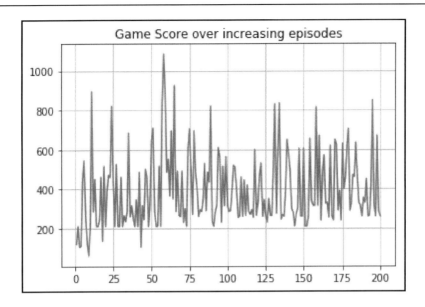

From this, we can see that the model has learned to score over 800 in some episodes.

Other Books You May Enjoy

If you enjoyed this book, you may be interested in these other books by Packt:

Keras 2.x Projects
Giuseppe Ciaburro

ISBN: 9781789536645

- Apply regression methods to your data and understand how the regression algorithm works
- Understand the basic concepts of classification methods and how to implement them in the Keras environment
- Import and organize data for neural network classification analysis
- Learn about the role of rectified linear units in the Keras network architecture
- Implement a recurrent neural network to classify the sentiment of sentences from movie reviews
- Set the embedding layer and the tensor sizes of a network

Other Books You May Enjoy

Keras Reinforcement Learning Projects
Giuseppe Ciaburro

ISBN: 9781789342093

- Practice the Markov decision process in prediction and betting evaluations
- Implement Monte Carlo methods to forecast environment behaviors
- Explore TD learning algorithms to manage warehouse operations
- Construct a Deep Q-Network using Python and Keras to control robot movements
- Apply reinforcement concepts to build a handwritten digit recognition model using an image dataset
- Address a game theory problem using Q-Learning and OpenAI Gym

Leave a review - let other readers know what you think

Please share your thoughts on this book with others by leaving a review on the site that you bought it from. If you purchased the book from Amazon, please leave us an honest review on this book's Amazon page. This is vital so that other potential readers can see and use your unbiased opinion to make purchasing decisions, we can understand what our customers think about our products, and our authors can see your feedback on the title that they have worked with Packt to create. It will only take a few minutes of your time, but is valuable to other potential customers, our authors, and Packt. Thank you!

Index

A

adversarial attack
   images, generating to fool neural network 260, 261, 262, 264, 266
anchor box based algorithm
   used, for detecting person 219, 220, 222, 225, 228, 232
angle
   predicting, for car turning 239, 241, 243, 244
articles
   categorizing, into topics 92, 93, 94, 96
audio
   transcribing, into text 508, 511, 514, 515
autoencoders, Python
   about 303
   convolutional autoencoder 309, 311, 312
   multilayer autoencoder 307, 308
   vanilla autoencoder 304, 305, 307

B

back-propagation
   building, in Python 23, 24, 25, 27, 29
batch normalization
   about 74
   used, for speeding up training process 74, 76
batch size
   impact, on model accuracy 55, 56, 57
beam search
   used, for caption generation 493, 494, 495
bounding box
   dataset, creating 190
   dataset, creating in MacOS 194
   dataset, creating in Ubuntu 194
   dataset, creating in Window 191, 192, 193

C

caption generation
   with beam search 493, 494, 495
cart pole
   balancing, with Deep Q-learning 530, 532, 535
chatbot
   building 435, 436, 438, 440, 443, 447
   intent extraction 444, 446
classes
   weights, assigning for 86, 87, 88
CNN model accuracy
   calculating, with data augmentation 140, 142
   calculating, without data augmentation 137, 139
CNN output
   validating 123, 125
common audio
   classifying 96, 98
compressed representation 303
Connectionist Temporal Classification (CTC)
   about 471, 472
   decoding 472, 473
continuous bag of words (CBOW) model
   about 330
   used, for building word vector 330, 331, 335
convolution 119
convolution, CNN
   filter 115, 116
   padding 117
   strides 117
convolutional autoencoder 309, 311, 312
Convolutional Neural Network (CNN)
   about 109, 471
   accuracy, improving in image translation 125, 126, 128, 129
   building, with Python 114, 120, 121, 122
   convolution 115

convolution function, passing through activation function 117
pooling 118, 119
used, for gender classification 129, 130, 131, 132, 134
used, for gender classification of person in image 143, 144

credit default prediction
about 80, 81, 83, 85
dataset, scaling 86
missing values, imputing 86
outlier values, capping 86

CTC loss value
calculating 474

custom loss function
defining 91

D

data augmentation
used, for improving network accuracy 136, 137

Deep Convolutional Generative Adversarial Networks (DCGAN)
about 286
used, for face generation 288, 289, 290, 292, 293
used, for generating images 286, 287, 288

deep learning
used, for generating music 502, 504, 507

deep neural network
building, to improve network accuracy 57, 58, 60

Deep Q-learning
used, to balance cart pole 530, 532, 535
used, to play Space Invaders game 536, 537, 540, 542

DeepDream algorithm
used, to generate images 266, 267, 268, 270

Distributed Memory Model of Paragraph Vectors (PV-DM) 338

document vector
creating 338, 339, 341, 342

dropout
used, for overcoming overfitting 72

E

embeddings
about 302
used, for topic modeling 400, 401, 402, 403, 405, 406

encoder decoder architecture
for machine translation 459, 461, 463, 464, 465, 468

encoding
for recommender systems 314, 315, 317
in image analysis 301
in recommender systems 302
in text analysis 300
need for 300

F

face generation
with DCGAN 288

face transition 293, 294, 295

fastText
used, for building word vectors 342, 343, 344

feed-forward propagation
in Python 13, 15, 18, 19, 20, 23

G

Gated Recurrent Unit (GRU) 388

gender classification, with CNN
aggressive pooling, on big images 152, 154
big images 145, 148, 149
smaller images 150, 152

gender classification
with CNN 129, 130, 132, 134, 143, 144
with GNN 131
with inception v3 architecture-based model 173, 174, 175, 177
with ResNet 50 architecture-based model 177, 178, 181
with VGG16 architecture-based model 155, 157, 159, 161
with VGG19 architecture-based model 169, 170, 171

Generative Adversarial Network (GAN)
about 260
used, for generating images of digits 277, 278,

280, 281, 284, 285
Global Vectors for Word Representation (GloVe)
  about 345
  used, for building word vectors 345, 346, 348, 349, 350

H

handwritten text recognition 475, 476, 477, 480, 483, 485
house prices
  custom loss function, defining 91
  predicting 89, 90

I

image analysis
  encoding, need for 301
image caption
  generating 485, 487, 488, 492
image embeddings 312, 314
image encoding 302, 303
inception v3 architecture-based model
  used, for gender classification 173, 174, 176, 177
input dataset
  scaling 44, 46, 47, 49
instance segmentation
  with U-net architecture 245, 246, 248, 252
Intersection over Union (IoU)
  calculating, between two images 198, 199, 202

K

Keras
  neural network, building 30
key points of face
  detecting, within images 181, 182, 184, 186

L

learning rate
  varying, to improve network accuracy 60, 62, 64, 65
Long Short Term Memory (LSTM)
  about 374
  implementing, for sentiment classification 383, 384, 385
loss optimizer
  varying, to improve network accuracy 66, 68
LSTM Network, with Python
  output, validating 380, 381, 382
LSTM Network
  building, in Python 374, 376, 377, 379

M

machine translation
  about 448
  data, preprocessing 449, 451, 453
  encoder decoder architecture 459, 462, 463, 464, 465, 468
  many to hidden to many architecture 456, 458
  many to many architecture 453, 456
MacOS
  bounding box, dataset creating 194
many to hidden to many architecture 456, 458
many to many architecture 453, 456
Mel Frequency Cepstral Coefficients (MFCC) 96
model accuracy
  batch size, impact 55, 56, 57
movie recommendations
  about 395, 396, 398, 399
  user history, using in considerations 399, 400
movies
  for recommender systems 319
multilayer autoencoder 307, 308
music
  generating, with deep learning 502, 504, 507

N

network accuracy
  improving, by building deep neural network 57, 58, 60
  improving, by varying learning rate 60, 62, 64, 65
  improving, by varying loss optimizer 66, 68
  improving, with data augmentation 136, 137
network
  sequences of outputs, returning from 427, 429, 431, 434, 435
Neural Network (NN)
  about 110
  applications 12, 13
  architecture 10, 11

building, in Keras 30
intermediate layers, output visualizing 161, 162, 165, 167, 168
problems 112, 114
training 12
neural network, building in Keras
  Keras, installing 31
  model, building 31, 33
neural style transfer 271, 272, 273, 275
non-max suppression
  performing 213, 214, 215, 218

O

object detection
  with region proposal based CNN 202, 203, 204, 207, 211, 213
overfitting
  about 48
  overcoming, dropout used 72
  overcoming, regularization used 70
  scenario 68, 70

P

paragraph vector with a distributed bag of words (PVDBOW) 339
pooling 119
pre-trained word vectors
  used, for performing vector arithmetic 336, 337
Python
  back-propagation, building 23, 24, 25, 27, 29
  feed-forward propagation 13, 15, 18, 19, 20, 23
  LSTM Network, building 374, 376, 377, 379
  recurrent neural networks (RNN), building 359, 360, 361, 362, 364, 365
  used, for building CNN 114, 120, 121, 122
  word vector, building 322, 323, 325, 327, 328

Q

Q-learning
  used, for maximize rewards while playing Frozen Lake 524, 526, 528, 529

R

recommender systems

encoding 314, 315, 317, 319
encoding, need for 302
Recurrent Neural Network (RNN), with Python
  output, validating 365, 367
Recurrent Neural Network (RNN)
  about 355, 471
  architecture 356, 357
  building, in Python 359, 360, 361, 362, 364, 365
  implementing, for sentiment classification 368, 369, 370, 372, 374
  interpreting 358
  store memory 358
region proposal based CNN
  used, for object detection 202, 203, 205, 207, 211, 213
region proposals
  about 194
  generating, in image with selective search 194, 195, 197
regularization
  about 70
  used, for overcoming over-fitting 70
ResNet 50 architecture-based model
  used, for gender classification 177, 178, 181

S

selective search
  use, for generating region proposals in image 194, 195, 197
semantic segmentation of objects
  in image 252, 253, 255, 257
sentiment classification
  building, with word vectors 351, 352, 354
  implementing, for sentiment classification 384, 385
  LSTM, implementing for 383
  RNN, implementing for 368, 369, 370, 372, 374
  stacked LSTM, implementing 386, 387, 388
sequences of outputs
  returning, from network 427, 429, 431, 434, 435
simulated game
  optimal action, taking in state 520, 523, 524
  optimal action, with non-negative reward 517, 519

skip-gram model
  used, for building word vector 330, 331, 335
song
  classifying, by genre 497, 498, 501, 502
Space Invaders game
  playing, with Deep Q-learning 536, 537, 540, 542
stacked LSTM
  implementing, for sentiment classification 386, 387, 388
stochastic gradient descent 24
stock price prediction
  about 99, 100
  accuracy, improving 101, 103, 105, 106
stock's price
  value, forecasting 406, 407, 408, 421

T

t-SNE 312
text analysis
  encoding, need for 300
text
  audio, transcribing to 508, 511, 514, 515
  generating 389, 390, 391, 392, 394
topic modeling
  with embeddings 400, 401, 402, 403, 405, 406
traditional neural networks
  inaccuracy, when images are translated 110, 112
traffic sign identification 233, 235, 238, 239
training impact, vanilla neural network
  when majority of inputs are greater than zero 49, 51, 53, 54
training process
  speeding up, with batch normalization 74, 76

U

U-net architecture
  about 246
  used, for instance segmentation 245, 246, 248, 252
Ubuntu
  bounding box, dataset creating 194

V

valid padding 117
value forecast, stock's price
  different weights, assigning for different time periods 413, 414
  last five days' stock prices only 409, 410, 411
  last five days' stock prices plus news data 415, 418, 420
  pitfalls 411, 412
vanilla autoencoder 304, 305, 307
vanilla neural network
  training 35, 37, 39, 42, 43
vector arithmetic
  performing, on generated images 296, 297, 298
  performing, with pre-trained word vectors 336, 337
VGG16 architecture-based model
  used, for gender classification 155, 157, 159, 161
VGG19 architecture-based model
  used, for gender classification 169, 170, 171

W

weights
  assigning, for classes 86, 87, 88
  defining, by rows 106, 107
Windows
  bounding box, dataset creating 191, 192, 193
word vector
  building, from Python 328
word vectors
  building, from Python 322, 323, 325, 327
  building, with CBOW model 330, 331, 334
  building, with fastText 342, 343, 344
  building, with GloVe 345, 346, 348, 349, 350
  building, with skip-gram model 330, 331, 334
  similarity, measuring between 329
  used, for building sentiment classification 351, 352, 354

Y

You Only Look Once (YOLO) 219